"Dr. Pascale writes with clarity, purpose, and a studied, personal understanding of the human condition. 'The Struggling Class' will be a term new to many, but it is, indeed, the way of life for too many others. The book should be required reading for anyone who wants to understand, in a way that is both supremely accessible and thoroughly researched, how economic, racial, class, caste, geographical, environmental, and other factors converge to create systemic inequalities designed to hold down a diverse stratum of people – from the Native residents on the Standing Rock Nation, where I grew up, to those doing their level best to make life work every day in places like Appalachia, Wind River, and Oakland. It skillfully illustrates key connective tissues that demonstrate how, despite outward differences, we share in the same struggle. In order to reinvent a democracy that works for everyone, we need radical, systemic change that begins to address the financialized, extractive colonial mentality and other, deeply embedded, cultural wrongs. Only in this way can we begin to envision a fairer, healthier future for the next generations."

Chase Iron Eyes, Lakota People's Law Project Co-Director and Lead Counsel

"Is there support for a living wage, free education, and other egalitarian commitments within the low-income population? Yes! In a trenchant analysis, Celine-Marie Pascale shows that egalitarian sensibilities are alive and well among low-income workers, not because they necessarily subscribe to or care about conventional political parties or platforms but because their everyday lives expose a deeply unfair system. A brilliant account of 'hard-knocks egalitarianism.'"

David B. Grusky, Professor of Sociology and Director of the Center on Poverty and Inequality, Stanford University

"This often poignant and moving book presents a vision of America and Americans that is often missing from dominant narratives. One walks away from this book with a better sense of the diversity of average, struggling Americans, as well as what all those people have in common – the struggle. As the author says, 'this is more than a collection of individual troubles; it is the story of a nation in a deep economic and moral crisis.'"

Allison L. Hurst, Associate Professor of Sociology, Oregon State University

"A rare book that combines a humane accounting of lives lived in hardship, attentive to race and gender, with a robust and data-driven critique of the policies that caused their dysfunction – a true bottom-up primer on American poverty with real-world applications for upturning the myths that surround inequality."

Elizabeth Catte, author of *What You Are Getting Wrong About Appalachia*

"This is an impressive book, wide and deep, with diverse people around the country struggling to live. A yarn; no, yarns – economic and much more – always real, face-to-face with the author: what their lives are, sometimes doing themselves no favors, but more often the effects of laws and attitudes both far away and near, government and corporations, and the hate of people. Why it's hard to end poverty. *Living on the Edge* reaches in every direction. Personal, powerful: once you pick it up, you won't put it down."

Peter Edelman, Carmack Waterhouse Professor of Law and Public Policy and Faculty Director of the Center on Poverty and Inequality, Georgetown Law Center

"This thorough and penetrating book offers a convincing argument about why so many families are struggling to make ends meet and who they are as fully rounded people. The writing and narration are superb. I would call this a page turner, which is not my usual experience in reading books on this topic."

Susan Greenbaum, Emerita Professor of Anthropology, University of South Florida

Living on the Edge

Living on the Edge

When Hard Times Become a Way of Life

Celine-Marie Pascale

polity

First published in 2021 by Polity Press

Polity Press
65 Bridge Street
Cambridge CB2 1UR, UK

Polity Press
101 Station Landing
Suite 300
Medford, MA 02155, USA

ISBN-13: 978-1-5095-4823-1
ISBN-13: 978-1-5095-4824-8(pb)

A catalogue record for this book is available from the British Library.

Library of Congress Cataloging-in-Publication Data
Names: Pascale, Celine-Marie, 1956- author.
Title: Living on the edge : when hard times become a way of life / Celine-Marie Pascale.
Description: Cambridge, UK ; Medford, MA : Polity Press, 2021. | Includes bibliographical references. | Summary: "A portrait of struggling America and how it has been left behind"-- Provided by publisher.
Identifiers: LCCN 2021011270 (print) | LCCN 2021011271 (ebook) | ISBN 9781509548231 (hardback) | ISBN 9781509548248 (paperback) | ISBN 9781509548255 (epub)
Subjects: LCSH: Working poor--United States. | Poverty--United States. | Equality--United States. | United States--Economic conditions--2009- | United States--Social conditions--1980-
Classification: LCC HD8072.5 .P38 2021 (print) | LCC HD8072.5 (ebook) | DDC 305.5/620973--dc23
LC record available at https://lccn.loc.gov/2021011270
LC ebook record available at https://lccn.loc.gov/2021011271

Typeset in 10.5 on 12 pt Sabon
by Fakenham Prepress Solutions, Fakenham, Norfolk NR21 8NL
Printed and bound in Great Britain by TJ Books Ltd, Padstow, Cornwall

For further information on Polity, visit our website:
politybooks.com

Contents

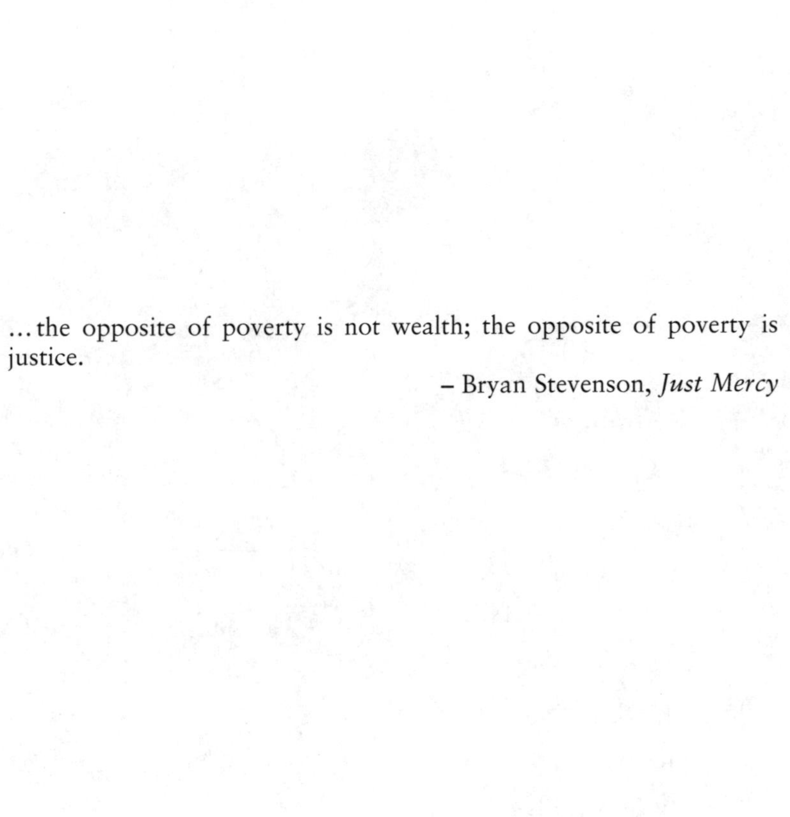

…the opposite of poverty is not wealth; the opposite of poverty is justice.

– Bryan Stevenson, *Just Mercy*

Acknowledgments

Researching and writing *Living on the Edge* was both harder and more rewarding than I ever could have imagined. As many readers will recognize, in challenging times the smallest amount of support has enormous impact, and so it has been for me in the years of writing this book. My efforts have been sustained by the inspiring work of others, small acts of kindness from complete strangers, and the sustenance of colleagues, friends, and family.

My first thanks must go to all of the people in struggling communities who talked with me both casually and in formal interviews. In the interviews people willingly risked a great deal. They trusted me with the details of their lives – often personal details for which they have been shamed. They took such risks because they believed in the importance of the project and they trusted my ability to see the dignity in their struggles, to use their own words in ways they had intended, and to protect their privacy. I am indebted to each of them and I hope this book repays their trust a hundred times over.

The College of Arts & Sciences at American University provided both a research fund and a Mellon Grant to support my research; this was a significant help in getting the project off of the ground. I owe special thanks to my colleague Angie Luvara for inspired and inspiring conversations about Appalachia and the people who live there. Steven Jones helped me to kick-off the project by piloting an interview with me. Riham Amin offered insights as an initial reader on several chapters, as did Chris Guilfry and Allan S. Pollock. Flora Ingenhousz provided invaluable support for the early stages of the project. Throughout the initial framing of the book, Josephine Ross was an invaluable sounding board and a generous reader. I also want to acknowledge the generosity of my colleagues Cynthia Miller-Idriss, Ernesto Castañeda, and Rachel Louise Snyder for their helpful advice. Carlos Barillo, Marie Garcia, and Mike Mullen – thank you for all of the ways large and small that you have supported me and my family through this project and through far more.

Over the years Bandana Purkayastha has threaded through my life as a cherished colleague. Bandana and I first crossed paths at a professional sociology meeting more than twenty years ago. At her invitation I presented a preliminary paper based on research for this book at the Eastern Sociological Society Presidential Panel in 2019. It was there that Bandana introduced me to Jonathan Skerrett, an editor at Polity, with whom she was working. From the start, Jonathan's confidence in this book was matched by his editorial acumen. It was an opportunity of a lifetime to work with Jonathan, his thoughtful suggestions and guidance have shaped every chapter. I owe great thanks to the entire Polity team, from the cover designer Rob Lock, to Rachel Moore for keeping the trains on time, to Tim Clark for spectacular editing, and to John Thompson for his work behind the scenes. Each member of the Polity team brought their areas of expertise to bear on the manuscript to make *Living on the Edge: When Hard Times Become A Way of Life* the best possible version of itself. I owe gratitude as well to the five external reviewers who offered anonymous feedback on the manuscript. Their feedback was equally thoughtful and clarifying.

During the years that I spent researching and writing *Living on the Edge*, my spouse, Mercedes Santos, carried the heaviest burdens of my travel and writing time. Still, she was the one who kept the wheels on the bus and an espresso at easy reach. Her willingness to read everything, regardless of how much sense it made, or how many times she had seen it, was an incredible act of generosity. I am grateful for our many years together and our unending journey of "beginner's mind." There are not enough words. Thank goodness.

Preface

In Oakland, California, twenty-something Angel Perez tells me: "I see people that work two, three jobs just to be able to pay their rent, and sometimes they might not be able to make ends meet to provide food for the family. That's a thing that frustrates me. There's other people that have so much money and so much wealth."

The strain Angel describes is common reality for low-wage workers, many of whom work more than full-time and still can't make ends meet. Most people expect to work hard; they expect they will have to stretch financially from time to time. Yet working full-time is often not enough to pay basic bills, to provide regular access to adequate food, to obtain decent housing, or to cover all of the expenses that come with having children. And this was the case even before the Covid-19 pandemic hit, during a period of low unemployment and strong economic growth. How is this possible? Part of the answer is that four decades of increased productivity have had almost zero impact on the average pay of millions of Americans.[1] The other part of the answer is the proliferation of low-wage work.

The painful truth is that across the United States millions of families work multiple jobs in an effort to make ends meet. They try to pick up extra hours or skip meals to patch through every month on an income that is inadequate and often unreliable. For these families, there are no savings to cover even ordinary expenses – car repairs, a dental problem, or an illness. Faced with economic instability and risk, they often live with poor health, no health insurance, insecure or inadequate housing, and debt. This is not the "other America" that Michael Harrington described in 1962. This is the reality across the United States today. In 2018, national polls showed between 65% and 80% of the US population was living paycheck to paycheck.[2] Before the pandemic of 2020, 43% of households – 50.8 million – were unable to afford a basic monthly budget for housing, food, transportation, child care, health care and a monthly smartphone bill.[3] There are 353 counties in the United States with poverty rates that have been *above* 20% for three consecutive decades.[4] The shocking reality of this level of economic distress is that *it has not happened by accident*. It has not happened in just one part of the country. And it has not happened because of one or two administrations. It is the result of decades of collusion between business and government to maximize corporate profits at the expense of workers.

In 2020 the federal poverty line for a single individual was an annual income of $12,760. As we will see throughout the book, given the costs of living, an income of $12,760 does not mark the *beginning* of poverty for anyone. Much of what we learn about wealth and poverty – about class – is skewed. Not only does the government's unrealistic definition of poverty undercount the numbers of people who are struggling, it also makes their struggle more dire since the federal poverty line is used to determine eligibility for all forms of public support. The economy comes into sharper focus if we account for economic self-sufficiency based on the cost of living, rather than relying on the federal poverty line. This framework helps to explain why so many people are unable to afford a $400 emergency, and why in any given month one-in-five adults are unable to pay their bills in full.[5] The economy is said to be strong when the stock market is doing well, but 84% of the market's value is held by the richest 10% of the population.[6] The nation misses working families every which way it looks.

Just what does the reality of economic struggle look like in the lives of ordinary people? I took a year to travel the country and talk with people who live in economically distressed communities. I listened to people in Appalachia, from southeastern Ohio to the coal fields of Eastern Kentucky and the Cumberland Plateau of Tennessee. I listened to people living on the Standing Rock Sioux Reservation that spans North and South Dakota, and to people living on the Wind River Reservation in Wyoming. I listened to people living in the poor communities of the bustling city of Oakland, California. I listened to anyone who would talk with me. In all, I talked with over a hundred people and conducted in-depth, recorded interviews with twenty-seven.[7] They are Native American, Black, Latinx, and White working women and men who were generous enough to share some very precious time with me.

They appear in *Living on the Edge* with names they created for themselves to protect their privacy. I have taken care to protect them as well by not identifying specific workplaces or the names of towns whose populations are quite small. As I followed the stories of people living in struggling communities, I researched the larger contexts around them. For example, when someone told me they had to take out a medical loan to pay for dental work, I researched the terms of the loans offered by lenders in their area. When someone told me they relied on a dollar store for groceries, I researched dollar stores.

The voices included here complicate dominant national narratives about inequality by making visible not only the lives of ordinary people but also the corporations who profit from their struggles. The book, then, isn't just about particular people or places. It is about how business practices and government policies create, normalize, and entrench economic struggles for many in order to produce extreme wealth for a few. It is not *just* that wages are insufficient, housing is unaffordable, and health care often out of reach – it is that we have a system that cares more for wealth accumulation than for the well-being of its people, for the environment or even for the country itself. *Living on the Edge* looks at government policies and business practices that produce enormous profit for some people by keeping working people submerged in economic quicksand.[8] Ultimately it is a book about power that has been leveraged by government and corporations at the expense of ordinary people.

With that said, the experiences of the individuals featured in this book are both central to and rooted in the places in which they live. For example, some things happen on and around Native American reservations that just don't happen anywhere else. The same can be said of Appalachian communities and the poor neighborhoods of Oakland. But despite these differences, there are also important similarities. From the coal fields of Appalachia, to fracking fields in the Midwest, to lead-contaminated neighborhoods in Oakland, people live in life-threatening conditions of environmental degradation that often leave them without access to clean water. Substance abuse also troubles every community that I visited, and it always falls hardest in the lives and communities that have the least. In different ways, prejudice and violence also figure centrally, often surprisingly, across all narratives.

Across the country people in struggling communities are forced to make impossible choices from among a range of bad options. They might be forced to choose between taking on debt that they can't afford or becoming unemployed. Or between borrowing thousands of dollars to have their teeth fixed or borrowing hundreds of dollars to have them pulled. They ask themselves, do I pay the electric bill or the phone bill? If I buy shoes for my child, can I also buy enough groceries? How do I manage meals among the family when the food is about to run out? A seemingly small trouble, like a broken taillight or a bad case of the flu, can trigger a cascade of events that results in the loss of one's job and subsequently one's housing. No one should have to expect a level of economic struggle like this.

Wage gaps are tethered to wealth gaps. As of this writing in 2020, the richest 0.1% of American households owns almost as much wealth as the bottom 90% of households *combined*; the entire bottom half of America now owns just 1.3 percent of the wealth.[9] As the rich have gotten richer, the poor have been amassing debt.[10] Some people are getting very wealthy precisely because others have been made to endure low wages, high housing costs, underfunded education, systemic sexism and racism, and devastating levels of environmental contamination. As we will see, even the criminal justice system has been leveraged to support corporate profits. And then the pandemic hit.[11]

If there was an initial sentiment that Covid-19 would affect everyone, it soon became clear that the pandemic both highlighted and exacerbated existing inequalities. While the nation's billionaires increased their collective wealth by more than $1 trillion between the onset of the pandemic and the close of 2020, millions of people who had been living paycheck to paycheck suddenly faced unemployment.[12] Even as the Walton family that owns Walmart made over $21 billion in the early *months* of the pandemic, the company continued to pay wages so low that even its full-time workers continued to qualify for food stamps.

Among those who were already living paycheck to paycheck before the pandemic, the ability to stay home and socially isolate has been an inaccessible form of privilege. Low-wage workers who have been declared "essential" are forced to work – often in unsafe conditions and without the benefit of health insurance or sick leave. This is a virus that impacts everyone, but, like all disasters, it doesn't impact everyone equally. For example, we know that people with preexisting health conditions, especially those with respiratory problems, are particularly vulnerable. Poor communities carry the heaviest burdens of pollution, which contributes to these conditions. *Living on the Edge* is about more than individual troubles; it is the story of a nation in a deep economic and moral crisis. Responding to this crisis requires more than a sense of duty to *help* others; it requires a moral obligation to ensure a self-sufficient life is possible for all. To fight inequality is to fight to change the system.

Systemic economic inequality is not the result of individual choices. It is the inevitable consequence of a government overtaken by corporate interests. This is not new. Fortunately, history has shown us over and again that when millions of Americans come to realize just how badly the deck is stacked against them, they will mobilize. In 2017, the coal company Blackjewel abruptly declared bankruptcy and said it was unable to pay what it owed to 1,700 miners in Kentucky, West Virginia, and Virginia. The company might have imagined it would get away with this because there are no longer any unionized coal mines. But in Kentucky, miners and their families occupied railroad tracks in Harlan County to stop trains loaded with $1.4 million worth of coal from leaving.[13] For thirty-eight days, they lived, slept, and ate in a blockade across the train tracks. The coal miners prevailed and Blackjewel eventually agreed to pay $5.7 million in back wages. So much for being broke.

While dramatic stories like that of the Blackjewel miners tend to be the exception, workers demonstrate over and again that they are resilient and determined. *Living on the Edge* is also the story of people who have a vision of the future in which everyone earns a living wage, has access to health care, education, and affordable housing; a world in which everyone enjoys communities free from environmental degradation. These are not the expensive dreams of idealists, or the radical dreams of an un-American few. They are the aspirations of working people who know that the system we have in place is unsustainable for most of the US population.

1

The Lay of the Land

When I began the research for this book, I had expected to hear stories of hard choices. I did indeed hear plenty of these. Many people talked about having hard conversations over the dining-room table about which bills to pay at the end of the month. Across the country I met working people who are forced to make impossible choices from a range of bad options. For example, in many communities it is impossible to hold a job if you don't own a car. Consequently, more than one person faced the choice of either taking out a second loan to cover the payments on their car loan, or losing their job.

I talked with people who have watched their communities succumb to drug addiction and with some who battle addiction themselves. And, I learned there is a surprising amount of money to be made off of the backs of people who struggle to pay their bills – by driving people into poverty and then keeping them trapped there. The lives of the people I talked with unfolded in ways that seem both ordinary and heroic. I hope their stories "true the wheel" of the nation's understanding of poverty: how it is created, lived, and lied about. I want to say from the start that I write this book with skin in the game.

The early part of my life was spent playing in woods, climbing apple trees, and catching salamanders in Southwestern Pennsylvania. Nearly everything we ate, my mother either grew or made from scratch. I was twelve before I learned that applesauce came in a jar and potato chips were sold in bags. I carried sugar and margarine sandwiches with me to school for lunch and reveled in bologna sandwiches, when we could afford them. We lived among farms and fields that were being sold off to real estate developers. The area steadily grew into a very wealthy suburban community. This development and my father's health crisis forced us to move to a run-down, rented house on the edge of a middle-class suburb. As a child playing in dying orchards and new construction sites, I had not recognized that we lived in a segregated community. A few years after moving to the suburb, I understood that our new community was intentionally segregated. This was first made apparent by responses at school to my favorite book, *The Autobiography of Malcolm X*, and by my family's discussion of a rumored local cross burning. My response was a fierce commitment to anti-racism before I had any realistic idea of what that would entail. It turns out that racist perspectives seep into the ordinariness of a child's life – through everything from nursery rhymes to classroom lessons. My commitment to anti-racism has been forged through a lifetime of unlearning.

In our new home six of us shared a bathroom, and "going to the library" was the code we used when planning to take a while in there. I believe I am the only member of my family to actually use a public library. At my new school I met kids whose parents were professionals and took vacations in Europe. Yet my family consistently formed relationships with white people like us, people who lived on the economic margins. For much of my life, just keeping food on the table was an issue for our family. I remember helping my mother steal bags of potatoes from the grocery store. I remember the numbness that would overwhelm me when I found the kitchen cabinets and refrigerator all empty. And I remember that more than once my mother sold her blood to blood banks in order to buy groceries for us. We had informal resources: a butcher who gave my mother baloney butts and soup bones, a relative in a convent who gave us underwear, and other people who passed along clothes. The funny thing is that we told the world, and firmly believed, that we were middle class. We weren't trying to deceive ourselves or others. There simply wasn't a language for our experience that encompassed both the struggle and the dignity.

Things did get better for us – in part because more resources came in and in part because eventually there were fewer mouths to feed. By the time I was in high school, we no longer worried about food. Yet none of us had ever learned to think much about the future. My family's expectations for me were simple: graduate from high school, get married, and have babies. Many of my friends followed that path, some dropped out of high school to get married, or left high school for vocational training, while two became pregnant in senior year. My brothers were expected to graduate from high school (fingers crossed on this one) and get a job through the want ads in the local paper. If that plan failed, joining the military was the only option. The mantra so often attributed to Steve Jobs, "Do what you love; love what you do," has never been an option for everyone. The ability to choose a career because you find it personally rewarding is itself a form of socio-economic privilege.

With the help of someone who was attending college, to whom I will be forever grateful, I hatched what I thought of as an escape plan. It required that I keep my high school grades up while working two part-time jobs. As a result, I am first in my family to go to college. But a college degree isn't necessarily a ticket out of poverty. If a crisis can plunge folks into desperate conditions very quickly, getting out of poverty is much harder. Escaping poverty requires having almost nothing go wrong for about twenty years.[1] As I soon learned, there is no end to the things that can go wrong in twenty years. After graduating from college, sometimes I had a "good job" that didn't pay enough; sometimes I scraped by on temporary work. At various times in my adult life I've stood in food bank lines and received food stamps.[2] I have shared meals with too many good people who will never escape poverty, many of whom survive on commodity foods provided by the USDA. These are also referred to as "canned food products" and I can say from experience that canned meat, cheese, and butter only vaguely resemble food.

Social safety nets, weak as they may be, help many families get to more stable times. Food stamps were once essential to my ability to simply eat twice a day. Today, I buy groceries without keeping a running tab in my head of the cost of each item, and I no longer break into a sweat in the checkout line. I have learned to make a monthly budget, opened a retirement account, and weathered several family medical crises without facing eviction. Against the prevailing odds, I became one of 4.5% of people in the United States who hold a doctorate degree. And rarer yet is that fact that I am a first-generation student who is also a full professor. However, I don't think of my story as one of class mobility so much as a strategic escape – one that comes with tremendous advantages, but which exacts a very high cost. For me, the price of admission into the upper middle class has been alienation in almost limitless forms. I have changed how I speak, the clothes I wear, the food I eat, what I do with my free time – I can't think of any aspect of my life that has been left untouched. Not one. I have rarely been in environments that valued class differences. As kids, we grew up knowing that we were judged as being fundamentally lacking or deficient by wealthier others. We internalized those judgments in different ways, and defended ourselves against them with our own judgments about "people who put on airs" or "who had no common sense." Class migration brings intense pressure to assimilate into the very cultures that judge poorer people. Consequently, even modest assimilation can feel like a profound betrayal of friends and family. On the other side, no amount of assimilation ever seems to bring real belonging.

My personal experience shaped my research for this book – from the questions I asked, to my ability to be a credible partner in the interviews themselves. My training as a sociologist gave me other resources – an understanding of structural issues, an appreciation of the importance of contexts, and the willingness to approach complete strangers. I know from both experience and training that wealth and poverty are structural issues that cannot be explained by personal characteristics – not by ambition or laziness, not by intelligence or ineptitude, not by substance abuse or mental health. I certainly encountered people with unresolved personal issues while on the road, but no more than I encounter among successful professionals. Personal characteristics contribute to one's quality of life, but they do not create systemic poverty in a nation.

The Struggling Class

It's common to hear people use the term "working class" as if it is synonymous with low-wage, unskilled work. But it hasn't always been that way. Well into the 1970s, the term "working class" designated a kind of labor that required various levels of skill and which was physically demanding – so much so that it often placed workers' health and well-being at risk. The blue-collar workers who held those jobs earned a middle-income wage that paid for a mortgage, a family car, often a boat or recreational vehicle, and sometimes a vacation home. Those jobs have largely disappeared. Today's workplace is primarily divided between two kinds of jobs: high-skill, high-wage jobs and low-skill, low-wage jobs.[3] Today the term "working class" is most often used as a euphemism for *poor* people, many of whom work in service sector jobs.

In contrast to working-class jobs, service sector employment is largely characterized by low pay, part-time hours, no benefits and general instability.[4] Some people use terms like "the poor" or "the working poor" to describe people who work full-time yet struggle financially. Honestly, I have never met working people who used these terms to describe *themselves*. My family wasn't alone in calling ourselves middle class, when we couldn't even count on having adequate food. But when I was on the road, I heard something different. When I asked people how they saw themselves in terms of class, some declined to say. They told me they just don't think about class. Many others described themselves as belonging to "the struggling class." Two things about this term are really important to me: First, this isn't a label or an understanding imposed on people from the outside. This is how people talked about *themselves*. Second, the term "the struggling class" addresses economic hardship in ways that I consider to be profound; it encompasses the danger, the dignity and the hope that characterize the lives of people I met. They are not getting ahead, but they have not given up. They struggle. They weigh how long they can go without treating a bad tooth or if they can afford to pay for groceries if they buy shoes for their child. Despite working one or two jobs, they know that a single unexpected event could force them deeper into financial troubles from which they might never emerge. People in the struggling class live paycheck to paycheck, doing the very best they can for themselves, their children, and often their extended families. They live in the hope that one day they will find themselves on a solid economic footing – a hope they hold against all the odds.

The term "the struggling class" seems more accurate than anything I have ever heard used to describe a group of people working hard to keep their heads above water. Belonging to the struggling class isn't a single kind of experience. There are individual differences, of course, but more importantly *class* experience varies by race, gender and region. These differences will become apparent by the kinds of experiences people do or don't encounter. No one featured in this book was asked to speak for anyone but themselves. Yet it is my hope that their voices will help to change how the nation thinks about the struggling class. It is impossible to fully understand the experiences of the struggling class without understanding some of the concepts that are used to identify economic hardship. The concepts may seem a bit technical, but they will help to bring some insight into things that generally don't make sense: a booming economy that leaves most families living paycheck to paycheck, families who can't afford basic living expenses but don't qualify as poor enough for assistance, and the way politicians talk about folks being left behind. The rest of this chapter lays out three key frameworks that are often used when people talk about the economy: work, housing, and poverty.

Framework 1: Work – Unemployment and Underemployment

When we are told good news about unemployment, it can be tempting to personalize poverty: If the economy is good, then there must be something wrong with the people who are struggling to make it. In 2018, unemployment in the US stood at 3.9%.[5] Fifty years ago, this figure would have meant that people were employed in jobs that paid well and that fewer families struggled. In the twenty-first century, however, the unemployment rate means something quite different. The US economy now has both low unemployment and high poverty. Nearly half of US workers are *underemployed* – even though they have jobs, they struggle to make a living.[6] Despite full-time work, indeed despite working two or three jobs, many people have trouble making ends meet each month. Since there is more to the unemployment rate than meets the eye, it's worth taking a moment to wade into the numbers.

When the media and politicians report on unemployment they use what is known as the U-3 rate, developed by the Bureau of Labor Statistics (BLS). The BLS surveys 60,000 randomly selected households regarding the employment status of each person in the household who is sixteen or older and gathers information about the number of people drawing unemployment benefits. To be counted in the unemployment rate, not only do you have to be unemployed, *you must have actively looked for work in the past four weeks*. The survey does not count people who have accepted part-time work but are looking for full-time work, people who are despondent after losing a job and not looking for another one, or people who looked for work and then gave up.

The U-3 rate is used so often that many folks don't know there is another government measure of unemployment known as the U-6 rate. The U-6 rate is based on surveys that identify workers who have been looking for work in the past year as well as those who are considered to be underemployed because they have a part-time job but would like to work full-time. Economists and many other experts consider the U-6 rate to be a more reliable measure of unemployment. It captures a lot of what the U-3 rate misses. As a result, in December 2018, while the media was using the U-3 rate to tout a record low unemployment figure of 3.9%, the U-6 rate was 7.6%.[7]

A devil's advocate might argue that if we always use the U-3 rate then we're comparing apples to apples every year and so downward trends are always good news. The reality is more complicated. Factory layoffs in one state might be balanced by an increase of service jobs in another state, which will make the unemployment rate look stable even as the workers in both states suffer. Job growth in poorly paid sectors of the economy and a general lack of wage growth in other sectors can devastate people's daily lives without disturbing the unemployment numbers. Finally, all unemployment rates go down when unemployed people stop looking for work. Increased hopelessness can produce "good" economic figures. The focus on unemployment provides an overly simplistic picture that completely misses important issues, while the government's narrow definition of underemployment distorts the reality of the economic landscape.

Unlike government officials, many sociologists and economists would call you underemployed if you work full-time but live at or below the poverty line; if you have multiple part-time jobs; or, if you need to work a full-time job and perhaps one or two other part-time jobs to make ends meet. For the most part, underemployed people have taken jobs that don't utilize their skills, experience, or training, because they are desperate to just cover their bills. They might work as many as sixty hours per week at part-time jobs and completely miss opportunities for health insurance, sick time, vacation time, and retirement plans. In the twenty-first-century economy, a growing segment of the US population has been relegated to work that does not provide a basic level of self-sufficiency. They are suffering from structural changes in the economy that have created chronic *underemployment*.

Low-wage work is the primary driver of underemployment and economic struggle. For example, the largest employer in the United States today is Walmart: 2.3 million people work for Walmart. Although it primarily hires part-time workers, even its full-time workers need (and qualify for) federal assistance provided by the Supplemental Nutrition Assistance Program (SNAP).[8] Full-time Walmart employees earn between $20,738 and $21,632 – less than the $25,149 the Walton family earns in dividends in *a single minute*.[9] The Walton family gets $4 million richer every hour. By 2018 they had topped the list of the *world's* richest families with $191 billion.[10]

The fact that Walmart pays its full-time workers an annual wage that places them at or below the federal poverty line is not an accident or an oversight. It is a business plan. A study by Americans for Tax Fairness found that Walmart's low wages across the country cost taxpayers *$13.5 billion* in food assistance provided by SNAP in 2013 alone.[11] By 2015, the business practice of underpaying workers had enabled the Walton family to amass more wealth than 42% of American families *combined*.[12] The second and third largest employers in the nation, Amazon and Kroger are also less than worker friendly. Amazon recently increased its warehouse wage to $15 an hour but still demands unsustainable levels of productivity from workers (more on this in a moment). Meanwhile many of the workers at Kroger, the third largest employer, are paid so little they also are forced to rely on SNAP.[13] Whole Foods, a subsidiary of Amazon, announced in 2018 that it would cut medical benefits for its entire part-time workforce – the annual saving produced by this was about equal to what Jeff Bezos makes in two hours.[14] These are only three examples from a much longer list. But the bad news actually gets worse.

It seems like common sense that if a company pays workers so badly that they need SNAP benefits, or demands levels of worker productivity that consistently result in injury, then cities and states would shun them. Who wants to bring jobs like that to town? Apparently, a lot of highly paid government officials. In 2019, Amazon donated more than $1 million to the campaigns of city council members it judged to be compliant with its agenda.[15] Thanks to deals local governments have negotiated with corporations, taxpayers not only subsidize these companies by providing food assistance to underpaid workers, we also subsidize them when local governments agree to provide them with huge tax breaks, fee waivers, and cash grants. As cities compete against each other to bring in Amazon, successful bids start at $1 billion (Atlanta) and go as high as $7 billion (Newark).[16] Given the company's explicit requests for economic enticements, you might believe that Amazon was a great employer. The question should be great for whom? Politicians point to the number of new jobs the company creates and the increased tax revenue. While Amazon recently raised its wage to $15 an hour, that increase has been offset by injuries to workers caused by a quota system that demands they scan more than 300 items per hour over the course of their ten-hour shifts.[17] Conditions in Amazon warehouses have long been under scrutiny. Like all business, it does promise to generate valuable tax revenue, but that promise is undercut by billions of dollars in tax breaks. Maryland's Montgomery County is reported to have offered Amazon $6.5 billion in tax incentives.[18] This way of doing business is shocking and deserves a book-length analysis on its own. For now, I can only say that this kind of economy makes sense only to the super-rich who benefit from it. To bring these businesses to town, elected officials have to sell out workers – often the very people who voted for them.

When politicians boast of a strong economy and a low unemployment rate, they mask the reality of working people's lives. A more accurate assessment of the quality of life experienced by millions of people needs to focus on self-sufficiency and underemployment. It would seem fairly basic to recognize that any person who has full-time work and does not earn enough to meet baseline living expenses is underemployed. I would also argue that they are underemployed if they don't have the economic stability to cover unexpected expenses like car repairs. How well our families are doing depends not only on what we are earning but also on what we are spending – most especially on housing.

Framework 2: Housing – Fair Market Rent vs Affordable Housing

Across the country, the cost of housing is rising faster than wages. A study of US government data by the United Way Alice Project shows that 43% of all households "can't afford a basic monthly budget for housing, food, transportation, childcare, health care and a monthly smartphone bill."[19] The US Department of Housing and Urban Development (HUD) considers anyone who pays more than 30% of their income on housing to be cost burdened.[20] Yet HUD's own figures show that millions of households spend between 50% and 70% of their income on housing. The widening gap between income and housing costs has created a crisis for families across the nation. Just fifty years ago, it would have been unimaginable that hundreds of thousands – by some counts millions – of people in the US would be unable to afford housing. Yet the rise of tent cities that began in the 1980s has become a living testimony to the pervasive lack of affordable housing. The cost of housing obviously compounds the problem of low wages.

In 1974 HUD developed the concept of Fair Market Rent (FMR) in order to determine standardized payments for their housing voucher program, known as Section 8 Housing, to support extremely low-income families. HUD determines FMR for an area and provides a rent subsidy so that families pay only 30% of their annual income on rent. That's how it works in theory. In 2018, 3 million families were on voucher waitlists.[21] In 2019 only seventeen states had any open waitlists at all. Yet HUD continues to conduct surveys to determine FMR, and since its numbers are widely used by other organizations concerned with rental costs, it is worth understanding what is meant by FMR.

HUD uses regional surveys of rent and designates rents falling in the 40th percentile as FMR. This means that 40% of rents are either at or *less* expensive than the FMR and 60% are *more* expensive.[22] As bad as that might sound, even FMRs tend to be out of reach for many. For example, a survey by the National Low Income Housing Coalition found that on a minimum-wage salary, it is impossible to afford fair market rent for a one-bedroom apartment in all but twenty-two of the nation's 3,000 counties.[23] And there is no relief in sight. In 2019 the White House proposed to slash $8.8 billion from HUD's most important programs and to loosen the caps on rents for landowners enrolled in the federal voucher program.[24]

The government, nonprofits, and businesses also use a term called "affordable housing" to describe housing for which the total cost of rent (or mortgage) plus utilities is no more than 30% of one's pre-tax income. It makes sense that the government thinks in terms of money when considering what counts as affordable housing. That is the easiest calculation for affordability, but it isn't exactly right. It doesn't, for example, take into account things like the quality of the housing, neighborhood schools, public safety, and public transportation. A family might find housing they can afford but that requires a long commute for work. A long commute then increases the length of the workday, the cost of transportation, and the cost of childcare. In addition, living in one community and working in another adds more stressors, like not being able to get to the children's school if there is an emergency. None of these factors fit neatly into the spreadsheets used to calculate affordable housing.

In an effort to provide affordable housing to residents, cities have tried two strategies: rent control and inclusionary housing. Rent control limits how much landlords can increase rent in any given year; yet, as of 2019, only five states[25] had cities with some form of rent control. Rent control legislation varies with respect to evictions. For example, under California's rental laws, owners can evict tenants without cause by providing a written notice. Once a unit is vacated, owners can increase the rent without restriction. Overall, rent control has proven to be of limited use because it applies only to older buildings and often provides a disincentive for owners to maintain the property.

According to the National League of Cities, about 800 cities have mandated "inclusionary housing" or "opportunity housing."[26] While the details vary by city, the general idea is that developers are required to set aside some percentage of new housing for rent at below the open market rent. Cities provide developers with tax credits for these set asides, which are generally 15% of the development.[27] (Just as tax credits vary, so do the required set asides. In some areas developers might be required to set aside as little 5% or as much as 25% of the rental property.)[28] Often inclusionary housing is more expensive than FMR. Price points are based on 40–60% of the area median income and rentals are allocated on a lottery system. For communities, inclusionary housing helps to break down economic segregation and can make good neighborhoods more accessible. However, cities' efforts to find a way to balance local income and local housing costs leave many frustrated. Some developers argue that despite the tax breaks, inclusionary housing laws make it hard for them to recoup their investments. Renters face a lottery system in which hundreds (sometimes thousands) of people apply for a single unit. For many struggling families, in any case, the so-called affordable housing is completely unaffordable.

While government efforts to subsidize rentals (Section 8 housing vouchers, low-income housing tax credit, and public housing) are expensive, the federal government actually spends more on subsidies for homeowners than it does for renters.[29] Housing subsidies for homeowners come in the form of deductions for mortgage interest, real estate tax, and tax exclusions on capital gains from sales and accelerated depreciation (for owners of rental apartments). In 2015, these deductions for homeowners were more than double the combined costs of all federal subsidized rentals. Long story short, families are left to shoulder the burden of rising rents.[30] The US has yet to address the housing crisis that drives families into poverty and too often into homelessness. Throughout my year of travel, I did not meet anyone who paid FMR – everyone paid more for rent and everyone felt the burden of rent in different ways. For some it meant having to live in shared housing, for others it meant being hard pressed to manage monthly bills, and for still others it meant not being able to afford to retire. Yet HUD's calculation of FMR is the only standard measure of market rents available and, as we will see in the next section, it is used for other budget calculations.

Framework 3: Poverty – The Federal Poverty Line vs Self-sufficiency Budget

As a nation, we use the federal poverty line to set a threshold, an *economic floor*, for living standards.[31] The federal government uses this threshold in two ways: first to determine whether or not a person or family qualifies for assistance, and then again to calculate the number of people who live in poverty. In 2018, the federal threshold for poverty was a *pre-tax* income of $12,140 for an individual. For a family of two, the poverty line creeps up to $16,460; for a family of three it moves to $20,780; and for a family of four to $25,100. By this standard, nationwide about 40 million people live in poverty; of those, 18.5 million live in extreme poverty and 5.3 million live in conditions of absolute poverty that we associate with the developing world.[32] This is shocking to think about. And the reality of lived poverty is even worse. Anyone living and working in the United States knows the federal poverty line sets an unrealistic definition of poverty. Clearly the government has to know this, too.

The federal poverty line was developed for the government by Mollie Orshansky in the 1960s, when a family's food budget was thought to be one-third of their expenses. "Orshansky based her poverty thresholds on the economy food plan – the cheapest of four food plans developed by the Department of Agriculture."[33] She calculated the cost of groceries to meet those food plans and multiplied each of those costs by three to create the poverty line. Today the poverty line continues to be calculated the same way: as three times the cost of groceries for the cheapest food plan. There are at least three basic problems with this calculation. First, groceries have been a much smaller part of a family budget for decades. For many families, the costs of childcare, rent, and health care have outpaced groceries. In addition, expenses for transportation, phone, and internet are both substantial and indispensable. Second, as we just saw, most families spend considerably more than 30% of their income on housing. Third, national averages will always distort budget percentages. As incomes rise, wealthier households spend more money on food, but even so, the percentage of money spent on food is a smaller part of the household budget. Poor families spend less on food, but food costs are a larger part of their overall income.

The cost of food was never a good way to measure poverty; this calculation has clear problems with real consequences. Accurate measures of poverty are key to understanding the health of the economy.[34] Yet the federal poverty line provides an unrealistically low definition of poverty that *undercounts* the number of people who are struggling to make ends meet and limits the ability of people to qualify for assistance. Millions of families disappear into the chasm created by this standard: they are not able to pay basic bills every month and yet they are not counted as poor. This reality is complicated by the fact that in the US people do not commonly refer to themselves as poor, even when they are unable to reliably meet basic needs.

To get a better sense of people's experiences, let's look at how much money it takes to simply pay the basic bills every month – what is known as economic self-sufficiency, or just self-sufficiency. The Economic Policy Institute (EPI) is a nonprofit, nonpartisan think-tank created in 1986 to help ensure that the needs of low- and middle-income workers are included in economic policy discussions. In addition to conducting cutting-edge research, EPI provides an online Family Budget Calculator that calculates economic self-sufficiency for regions across the country. These calculations appear throughout this book, in each case generated on the EPI website. The calculator primarily relies on government data to determine the costs of housing, food, childcare, transportation, health care, and other necessities, as well as taxes for specific locations across the country. For example, the budget for food comes from *Official USDA Food Plans: Cost of Food at Home at Four Levels*, a report published by the Department of Agriculture's Center for Nutrition Policy and Promotion.[35] The housing costs are based on the Fair Market Rent calculations used by HUD for their housing voucher program. FMRs provide a standardized way to estimate housing expenses in specific areas of the country – which is of value, even if the estimates tend to run a bit low. Importantly, EPI provides a transparent estimate of what it costs to be economically self-sufficient – not a calculation of poverty levels.

From the EPI self-sufficiency calculations it's clear that taxes as well as rent vary widely from place to place. The EPI calculator accounts for regional differences beyond rent. For example, in San Francisco, California, a basic level of economic self-sufficiency for two adults with two children requires an annual income of $148,440. Just across the bay in Oakland, this same family would need to earn $123,310 to be self-sufficient. In Athens County, Ohio, the same family would

MONTHLY COSTS

2 adults *and* 2 children
San Francisco metro area

HOUSING	$3,121
FOOD	$998
CHILD CARE	$1,730
TRANSPORTATION	$1,114
HEALTH CARE	$1,152
OTHER NECESSITIES	$1,662
TAXES	$2,593
Monthly Total	**$12,370**
Annual Total	**$148,440**

MONTHLY COSTS

2 adults *and* 2 children

Athens County, OH

HOUSING	$768
FOOD	$721
CHILD CARE	$981
TRANSPORTATION	$1,152
HEALTH CARE	$1,113
OTHER NECESSITIES	$601
TAXES	$687
Monthly Total	**$6,024**
Annual Total	**$72,284**

need $72,284 to cover their basic needs. Keep in mind that the federal poverty line for this same family of four is $25,100 – regardless of where the family lives. In none of these communities is an annual pre-tax income of $25,100 for a family of four the *start* of poverty.

If these numbers seem high to you, consider that many families can and do get by on a lot less. They squeak by without health care or dental care, have a friend or family member watch the kids, skimp on groceries, "repurpose" gifts they've received, rely on used clothing, miss payments when they come due, and sometimes kite checks. And most families carry debt that doesn't even figure into these budgets. Keep in mind, this is *self-sufficiency* – it isn't based on going without. It's a budget that covers all the basics on the list. The EPI self-sufficiency budget does *not* include items beyond the basics – for example, there is no budget for existing debt, retirement, life insurance, or vacations. Taking a square look at the lives of working people brings the country's economic realities into perspective.

In 2017, half of all working people in the US earned *pre-tax* incomes of $31,561, or less.[36] To give this figure context, recall that in the same year, the federal poverty line for a family of four was $24,600. Wages have been completely disconnected from economic growth and from the cost of living. As a result, most people are working hard and having trouble keeping their heads above water.

The EPI self-sufficiency budget for that same family of four in the economically distressed rural county of Athens, Ohio, was $72,284 – *more than twice the pre-tax income earned by half of all US workers.* The broader context offers insight into the breathtaking number of struggling families and some indication of the extent of the financial fragility they face. Working for low wages denies struggling families the economic security that comes with a stable income and savings. It also drives families into debt that is frequently impossible to escape.

The United States has the highest level of wealth inequality among Western democracies.[37] Between 2000 and 2010 the nation reached a new level of inequality that was higher than that in India and South Africa.[38] Inequality was higher in the US in 2014 than it was in India under colonial rule (1920–30) or in South Africa under apartheid (1960–70).[39] Take a moment and let that sink in. The United States has a record level of income inequality that is probably higher than in any other society at any time in the past, anywhere in the world.[40] That doesn't sound like the country we like to talk about and yet it does reflect the country in which we live. There are a lot of struggling people and some very, very rich folks. And not much in between. If this seems doubtful, take a look at 2017 figures for annual income from the Social Security Administration:[41]

- 28% of workers earned less than $15,000
- 35% of workers earned less than $20,000
- 60% of workers earned less than $40,000
- 76% earned less than $60,000

These are the federal government's numbers, but they rarely make the news. At a time when 60% of workers were earning less than $40,000 a year, the poverty line for a family of four was $24,600. And that's without considering where they live or the impacts of racism and sexism. It's hard to claim that families are doing okay. But this book isn't just about people struggling to get by – it's also about the mechanisms that create poverty for the many as surely as they create wealth for a few. Our economy has lost so many mid-range jobs that it is now bifurcated between some jobs that pay very well and a majority that pay quite poorly.[42] Here are some of the upper income limits for 2017 that might be more familiar.[43]

- 0.1% earned $2,757,000
- 1% earned $718,766
- 5% earned $299,810
- 10% earned $118,400

These two sets of numbers on national income illustrate that the US middle class has virtually disappeared – unless you change the definition of middle class. The potential for class mobility decreases as the income gap expands. Importantly, our politicians have helped to ensure that the burdens of high tax rates are felt most acutely by the 76% of people earning less than $60,000 a year.[44]

Despite the glaring inequality and the profound economic struggles of fully employed workers, people in the US tend to believe that we have the best economic system on earth – even if it isn't working so well for them or for the people they know. It's a little like my family being convinced we were middle class, even though we had trouble keeping food on the table. We have a federal poverty line that is far too low to capture the reality of poverty and the lives of millions of people who might not be willing to call themselves poor, even though they have trouble providing for their most basic needs. And that suits the wealthiest people just fine.

The United States has a long tradition of trying to ignore or erase class differences. The stories we tell ourselves as families and as a nation about the "haves and have nots" shape the opportunities and the struggles of millions of people. *Living on the Edge* will bring class inequality into focus as we listen to people talk about their lives in ways that challenge existing measures of well-being. I have learned a lot from the people who generously shared their time and experiences with me. I believe readers will as well.

2

The Struggling Class

Across the US personal relationships are largely segregated by both class and race, even if our work relationships are not. As a consequence, it might be difficult to imagine what life looks like for the millions of people living on the edge. In this chapter, you will meet people whose lives and personalities could not be more different from each other: Michael Chase and Rose Taylor in Southeast Ohio; Ellison Thompson and Erika Brooks from the Standing Rock Sioux Reservation; and Vanessa Torres and Puppy Love (PL) from Oakland, California. The stories of the struggling class are not just stories about people. They are also stories about places. Where we live shapes our opportunities, our troubles, our aspirations, and our fears. The places we call home can give us a tremendous sense of identity and belonging and sometimes a depth of sorrow that escapes words.

Appalachia

In Northern Appalachia, my trip begins in West Virginia, and Southeast Ohio, just as autumn arrives.[1] The beauty of this region is breathtaking and seemingly unending. I take US 33, a two-lane road that winds through the wooded mountains of West Virginia. Much of the time there is a steep hill on one side and a drop off to the Little Kanawha River on the other. The narrow, winding mountain road is well-traveled by cars, pickups, and enormous coal trucks, all keeping pace with the 55 mph speed limit. For forty miles I search for a berm, a pullout, or a crossroad. There are none. My palms sweat every time I see a truck in my rearview mirror. Occasionally a small piece of land crops up between the road and the hillside, or between the road and the river. Single-wide trailers, and now and then a rambler, are nestled into these isolated patches.

This region was once home to many Native Americans, including the Shawnee, Cherokee, Manahoac, Monacan Chippewa, Delaware, Iroquois, Mingo, Miami, Seneca, and Wyandot. By 1843, all Native peoples had been forcibly removed from the region. By 1863, when West Virginia was founded, it was a racially segregated state in which it was *illegal* to register a child as "Indian" at birth.[2] And it remained illegal to indicate Native American ancestry on birth records until 1965, a year after the Civil Rights Act. In 2017, when my journey begins, census records identify the region as 90% white; the presence of Native peoples lingers only in the names of places – like the Little Kanawha River. There are no federally recognized Indian nations in North Central Appalachia today.

The winding mountain road is itself an historical site. Designated in 2015 as the Blue-Gray Highway, it became an official reminder of the numerous Civil War battles fought in the area. Although I don't see mention of the battles, I count three Confederate flags on this stretch of road – fewer than I had expected. Even so, I find them unnerving. Carried today by white supremacists on their marches, the flag is an emblem of the Confederacy and feels like a warning.

Eventually, the landscape opens to a crossroad, and the Little Kanawha River joins the wide and winding Ohio River. Where West Virginia and Ohio meet, an enormous coal power plant rises from the flatland along the Ohio River and looms over empty grassy lots that line the street. The place could be a scene from the old TV show *The Twilight Zone*. It looks as if the houses were plucked up, leaving driveways, patios and lawns intact. Smokestacks from the coal plant that look like nuclear reactors quietly churn out billowing clouds as a lawnmower drives back and forth across the empty landscape. This had been the village of Cheshire; the power company polluted the town so severely they paid $20 million to buy out residents.[3] I'll return to this in Chapter 3, but for now the journey continues northward toward Athens. In minutes, a beautiful cable-stayed bridge takes me across the Ohio River to Pomeroy, Ohio. The $65 million bridge is stunning both in its modern expanse and its dissonance in relationship to the former village of Cheshire and the economically distressed town of Pomeroy, which it connects.

Pomeroy, the county seat for Meigs County, was once a mining town producing both salt and coal. Its claim to fame rests on its

The Pomeroy–Mason Bridge connects the former village of Cheshire with Pomeroy, Ohio.

being the first town to load a coal barge onto the Ohio River. In the 1990s the mining industries shut down and the economic distress in Pomeroy is evident. Historic buildings with charming facades still line the streets, yet closed storefronts outnumber open businesses on the main thoroughfare. The town looks out onto the grand Ohio River and it's easy to imagine this as a tourist destination, the historic buildings filled with cafés, restaurants, and specialty shops. But just across the river, in Cheshire, the Kyger Creek and Gavin Power Plant burns about 35,000 tons of coal per day. It's rated as one of the most polluting power plants in the country.

Eventually, I reach Athens County, Ohio. It is one of eighty-three counties in Appalachia rated as distressed by the Appalachian Regional Commission (ARC), and one of six distressed counties in Southeast Ohio.[4] Counties designated as "distressed" face significant structural challenges and place economically in the bottom 10% of counties nationally. Before the pandemic, the poverty rate in Athens County hovered at 33%. In towns throughout the county the economic hardship is evident in the quality of housing, the number of cars that are falling apart, the number of shuttered businesses as well as in the kinds of businesses that remain open. Along some of the county's back roads, ramshackle trailers and dilapidated houses rise precariously in the hollows and hillsides. On the surface,

Athens County once prospered from its brickwork, including the renowned star bricks.

these communities resemble those I have seen on Native American reservations.

Unlike many Appalachian counties, Athens County is home to two colleges. Ohio University, located in the city of Athens, has approximately 23,000 students – equal to the number of local residents in the city and about one-third of the entire county population. The university has a big impact. Although the majority of students come to the university from red counties in Ohio, their presence at OU tilts the town toward more progressive politics than those of the surrounding communities. Out of eighty-eight counties in Ohio, Athens County is one of five blue counties. Students bring an influx of cash into the economy that supports restaurants and local businesses. They also push rents higher. Landlords can make more money by renting a house by the bedroom to students than by renting the entire unit to a single family. Affordable housing for locals in Athens County is rare. In addition, the large student body competes with locals for service industry jobs and arguably drives down wages in those jobs. As in most college towns, locals tend to view the student population as a mixed blessing. The town has a reputation for a drinking culture. On the main drag of Court Street, I count

With ARC support, Nelsonville, Ohio, is working to renovate and rebuild an historic town square in which they can host cultural activities for the communities in Athens County.

twenty-two bars in three blocks and quickly find fourteen additional places to go for a drink in side streets. All of them are successful businesses that operate all year.

Just twenty minutes up the road from Athens is the second largest city in Athens County, Nelsonville, home to 5,300 people. There I find an emerging arts community thanks to revitalization projects funded by the Appalachian Regional Commission. Although the ARC is slated to be defunded by the federal government, its contributions to this community are clear. With ARC funding the gorgeous old opera house on the town square is being refurbished to serve as an arts and music center for the community. And, thanks to ARC cash infusions and an industrious core of volunteer residents, the town hosts car shows and a smoked meat festival that draw people from around the county.

Nelsonville is home to Hocking College, a small, two-year technical college with majors in areas such as equine studies, nursing, construction, and food service. The college adds about 2,100 students to the local population. As in Athens, and other college towns across the country, landlords here push rents higher by renting houses by the bedroom to college students. If Ohio University in Athens has not been able to shake a reputation for drugs and alcohol, Hocking has not been able to shake a reputation for scandal generated by sexual assaults, race-based hate crimes, and administrative mismanagement.

Athens and Nelsonville are the largest towns in the county, which also includes eight small villages salted across 508 square miles.[5]

Michael Chase lives in Athens County and is working two part-time service industry jobs when we meet. With one white parent and one Black, Michael characterizes himself as American Black, "because when I say I'm Black, people ask me if I'm Ethiopian, so I'll just say American Black." Michael grew up in the area and has a high school degree. At age twenty-one, he is part of a generation that turns to the internet for news, social media, and impressive amounts of random trivia – like the history of straws. He is clearly a smart and engaged person, but college was never part of the plan for Michael. In his senior year, when he had his first conversations about college with friends, he realized he wanted to go, but he didn't know what he wanted to study. Some families spend thousands of dollars on college prep courses, others spend tens of thousands of dollars on college-counseling services, and still others expect their child to walk in the front door of an elite university as a "legacy" acceptance. There was none of this for Michael. No one seemed to have college in mind for him. Not his parents, not his teachers, and not the school guidance counselors. His future seemed to end with high school. Now Michael is more aware of the hazards he faces in life than of the opportunities he might have as a college student. "I'll say for right now, I'm only twenty-one. I don't have kids. I'm not in jail or prison. I'm not out here doing drugs or drunk driving or anything. I like to just work, hang out with friends. As for my future, I don't know."

Michael currently works a night shift at the front desk of hotel and a day shift at a nonprofit – both jobs are in the city of Athens. He thinks of himself as fortunate because although his work schedules vary each week, his hours never conflict. Neither job guarantees Michael a set number of hours or specific days. He might work weekends or weekdays – he discovers his days and hours each week when the schedules are posted. Since he never knows how many hours will be available to him in the future, he scrambles for all the time he can get. This means that on some days he works an eight-hour shift at each job. It also means he can go for days without working at all. There is no economic security, even though these are permanent positions. The constant variability of his work hours also makes it difficult if not impossible for him to schedule any personal appointments in advance.

Between his two jobs, Michael earns less than $16,000 a year; he doesn't have health insurance, sick leave, or vacation time. He shares an apartment with three other people – a situation he finds stressful – and still he worries at times about making his rent. When he works back-to-back eight-hour shifts for some length of time, Michael has been able to save as much as $500, which he tells me makes him feel quite rich. It also exhausts him. Days later he is still catching up on sleep. Despite his high energy and easy laughter, the dark circles under his eyes give away the pressure he is under. Almost everyone I meet in Southeast Ohio works *multiple* service industry jobs. In the area, it is common practice in the service industry to hire part-time workers. Locals believe this is intentional. It saves the companies a lot of money when they leave workers without sick time, health care, vacation time, or a retirement plan.

When I asked Michael how he would identify himself by socio-economic class, he said: "I would say for myself, I don't know, I'm fine. ... I don't consider myself poor. I would say ... I guess I would say I am struggling a little bit. I'm fine, I have all my stuff paid, I'm just not in a higher tax bracket. I guess I'm poor but I'm not – for me people who don't have food are poor. Or, someone who can't feed their kids, or you might not have running water or even electricity. I would say poor is when you just don't got anything. I think if you're poor, you don't have the right things you need to even survive."

The reality in Southeast Ohio is that everyone seems to know folks who are in far worse circumstances. For Michael and others, "being poor" means living in homes without running water or electricity or being unable to feed their children. A surprising number of Michael's neighbors live in exactly this condition. In 2017, Athens County had the highest rate of food insecurity in the state of Ohio. Almost 27% of children in the county lack consistent access to adequate food and about 70% of residents hover around the federal poverty line.[6] This sounds stark, and it is. In these circumstances, working families skip meals and/or reduce the size of meals, and/or rotate who gets to eat a meal, in order to make their food last.

Community food banks, once an emergency resource during difficult times, have become a weekly resource for families. As for access to running water, in 2014, when the US Census stopped collecting data on the number of households without running water, 1,000 homes in Athens County (1.5% of the population) lacked full indoor plumbing, while in neighboring Meigs County another 400 homes (1.7% of the population) had no running water.[7] Given this context, it might be clear why Michael does not think of himself as poor. The more serious issue is that the federal government does not think of him as poor either. The federal poverty line in 2017 for an individual was $12,060. In that year, 17.6% of African Americans fell at or below the federal poverty line. As you notice, Michael does not.

By working two jobs, Michael earns something below $16,000. He does not have stable work, lives paycheck to paycheck, and struggles to pay the rent on a shared flat. Yet the federal government does not count him among the nation's poor. This is exactly why it is important to understand the distinction between the federal poverty line and a self-sufficiency income. The Economic Policy Institute self-sufficiency budget puts Michael's experience in a very different context. As we saw in Chapter 1, the EPI self-sufficiency budget is based on basic monthly expenses in each region of the country. For a single person in Athens County, the budget is $34,545.

Recall from Chapter 1 that the EPI uses the Fair Market Rent (FMR) calculation established by HUD. FMR was established to standardize payments for low-income housing. In any given housing market, about 60% of local housing will be more expensive than FMR. There is a wide variety of housing in Athens County. Yet typical rent for a decent one-bedroom apartment runs between $800 and $1,300 a month – a long way from FMR. In this regard, the EPI self-sufficiency budget, which allocates only $605, is clearly low for the area. However, even using the FMR calculation, the EPI budget is more than twice what Michael currently earns.

I am confident that Michael would be shocked by this self-sufficiency budget. If he accepted the EPI figures as representing a

MONTHLY COSTS

1 adult *and* no children

Athens County, OH

HOUSING	$605
FOOD	$250
CHILD CARE	$0
TRANSPORTATION	$852
HEALTH CARE	$373
OTHER NECESSITIES	$345
TAXES	$455
Monthly Total	**$2,879**
Annual Total	**$34,545**

basic standard of living, he would see his income, and his efforts to get by every month, in a very different perspective. Like many others, Michael has normalized his inability to pay all of his bills all of the time, his inability to live alone, to take time off when he is sick or to afford health care. Not only is all of this ordinary to him, Michael is doing better than many around him. Basic self-sufficiency, as a standard of living, is not something he imagines as part of his life – and this suits his employers just fine. What has become ordinary for Michael is both completely unacceptable and unlikely to change.

Certainly, wealth and poverty are relative terms – there will always be someone earning less and someone earning more. Yet hunger and a lack of running water should not be the measure of poverty in any country – and certainly not in one that is among the wealthiest in the world. Michael did not end up in badly paid jobs because he lacks skills or intelligence. Nor because he chose a random "follow your heart" kind of dream. He applied for the entry-level positions that were available to him. If entry-level jobs once gave workers a leg up the proverbial ladder, the reality today is quite different. In the twenty-first century, low wage, entry-level employment often is what holds people in poverty. Part-time service industry work keeps people, and the families they support, in a very stressful and nearly constant economic scramble. Michael tells me he hopes to convert one of his jobs to full-time status soon, but even so he will still need to continue to work part-time at the other. The full-time salary won't pay his bills, let alone enable him to attain economic self-sufficiency.

The situation is similar for Rose Taylor, a white woman, who has lived most of her nearly thirty years in Athens County. She describes herself as among the more economically privileged in the county and it is clear that her friends think of her as fairly successful. "I have had friends borrow money from me, because they need to pay their rent, or they need food. The majority of my friends, I would say, barely make it every month." Despite Rose's desire to help, she finds the situation a little stressful because she too can find herself financially strapped at times.

Rose holds an associate degree and works thirty-six hours a week as a certified nursing assistant (CNA) caring for an elderly woman with Alzheimer's Disease. Her shift as a CNA is from 9 p.m. to 9 a.m. three days per week. If you know anything about Alzheimer's Disease, you know that there are no "easy" shifts in care giving. Dementia care at any time of day is full of unexpected challenges as well as surprising rewards. Like Michael, Rose especially values working the night shift because it doesn't interfere with the fluctuating schedule at her second, day job where she spends thirty hours a week doing body piercing. Typically, three days a week she is scheduled at both jobs, which leaves her just enough time between jobs to shower and go for a walk with her "fur child," a sweet dog that she cares for with her sister.

Rose describes her life as unsustainable but tells me that for now she has to make it work. Between the two jobs, she works sixty-six hours a week and earns less than $23,000 – before taxes. Rose has no benefits at either job. Her income is almost double the federal poverty line. That puts her well ahead of the 12.9% of all women in the country who lived at or below the federal poverty line in 2017. Perhaps most striking is that after state and federal taxes, Social Security tax and Medicare tax, Rose's income is less than $17,083 – and this is without any form of health care. Like Michael, she is above the poverty line of $12,140 but below the area standard for self-sufficiency income of $34,545.

With an after-tax income around $17,000, it's easy to see why Rose cannot afford to live alone – even though she works over sixty hours a week. If she became lucky enough to find a decent one-bedroom apartment for $800 a month, Rose would need to spend $9,600 per year on rent. Flats on the higher end ($1,300 a month) would cost her $15,600 a year. In order to get by, Rose shares an apartment with her sister, who juggles three part-time jobs – two as a nurse and one helping her mother at a diner. Rose and her sister tend to work opposite days/shifts which enables them to share custody of their "fur child." The dog provides great companionship for quiet walks in the woods, which have become an essential source of emotional support. "Life is incredibly stressful," explains Rose, "and the stress never goes away." Even without a crisis, life is a constant struggle for enough money, enough sleep, enough ease.

Rose has been trying to put money away each month. She tells me that if she can build a financial cushion, she'll be able to catch a break. What would catching a break look like? She tells me it would be staying home from work when she is sick or having time to do something she likes. Yet the ability to put a little money away each month depends on nothing going wrong – and something always seems to be going wrong. Last month, her savings were completely wiped out because she needed tires for her car. "It often feels like I'm doing really well. I have like a little tiny bit of savings. But then something happens, then it's like, oh, now I have to start all over again." As she talks, it's easy to see the deep exhaustion in her face. Rose's life is itself a contradiction: on the one hand she calls herself "lucky" because she could afford the tires and thus keep working, yet on the other hand, in her daily life, she doesn't feel very lucky. This is life in the struggling class.

"I recently went to the dentist. I have to have dental surgery next week, and I don't have dental insurance. And so, it's going to cost me like $600 to fix my tooth, and that's something that like I wasn't planning on obviously. Stuff like that stresses me out and it makes me like want to work more. But, at the same time, I need to protect my mental health as well. I manage anxiety a lot. I manage depression as well." Low-wage work exacts a high human cost.

Like many other folks working very long hours at multiple part-time jobs, Rose has no health insurance, sick time, or retirement benefits. "I had Obamacare last year. I tried to sign up again but ended up taking hours on the phone. I just didn't have time to like figure it out. Then the deadline passed. It was tricky because of my two jobs and two different incomes, and there was like a lot of questions." She'll try again next year but for now she's planning on taking out a medical loan to pay the dental bill. Rose reflects for a moment and says: "It's not even like a thing to ask about health insurance [when looking for work]. I know people that only have one job, they manage a bar or manage a restaurant, and they sometimes don't even have health insurance, I want to say like 50% of the time." Businesses with fewer than fifty employees have no legal obligation to provide health insurance. It's no wonder that medical loans are a thriving industry. We'll look at those carefully in the next chapter.

Rose is smart, hardworking, and broke. She describes her current level of work as unsustainable but even so she cannot afford the basics of being able to live alone, pay for car repairs, and cover medical bills. Rose worries about the future. "I don't need food stamps, but there have been times in my life where I've considered getting food stamps, but, as of right now, I don't need them." Rose pauses for a moment and takes a breath, "but if I were to ever have a child or have anybody else depend on me, that would have to be a possibility." It isn't an easy thought. It is a desperate one. Without access to reproductive health care – including abortion – an unplanned pregnancy would end her ability to work and force her and her child more deeply into poverty. As we will see in later chapters, for low-wage workers, marriage does not always offer a way out of poverty.

The experiences of Michael and Rose in Southeast Ohio are familiar to others living in the area. Like millions of others, they are caught in economic quicksand. For low-wage workers, it is impossible to work your way out of poverty. Without paid sick time, just a bad case of the flu will throw their ability to keep a roof over their head into question. More than 1,200 miles away, at the Standing Rock Sioux Reservation, things are both quite different and remarkably similar.

Standing Rock Sioux Reservation

When I land in Rapid City, South Dakota, on September 12, 2017, more than forty-eight wildfires are burning in Montana; they would go on to consume more than 1,295,000 acres before being contained a few weeks later.[8] Hundreds of miles from Montana, the fires were turning the South Dakota sky to ash. On my way to the Standing Rock Sioux Reservation in the northeast, I pass mile after mile of sunflowers – most of them damaged or destroyed by drought. For most of the drive, the car radio picks up only two stations: one playing country music and another broadcasting a Christian preacher. As I pass the enclave of Timber Lake on the Cheyenne River Reservation, the radio picks up Standing Rock's station, which plays a mix of community news, pop, rock, and traditional tribal music. And for the first time in hundreds of miles, my phone picks up a Wi-Fi signal, also coming from Standing Rock.

Although American Indian tribes are sovereign nations, the status of Native peoples in the US remains both unclear and precarious because a great deal of US policy rests on foundations of genocide, treaty abrogation, racism, and repression of tribal histories.[9] The US reservation system was initially established along the lines of concentration camps under a colonial occupation. Today, the far-reaching occupation includes geographical displacement, ongoing disregard for Native rights, appropriation of tribal land and resources, destruction of natural resources, contamination of Native land and water, prohibitions against religious practices, as well as geographic and political isolation.

The entire Midwest region was shaped by war and broken treaties that continually forced Plains Nations into smaller, more desolate areas, often separating cultures from their most sacred sites.[10] The Great Sioux Nation is composed of Seven Council Fires: Oglala, Brule, Sans Arcs, Blackfeet, Minnekonjou, Two Kettle, and Hunkpapa.[11] Today, members of the Great Sioux Nation live on five reservations across the Midwest: Pine Ridge, Rosebud, Lower Brule, Cheyenne River, and Standing Rock.

The Standing Rock Sioux Reservation was established by the federal government in 1889. Agricultural land that was owned by whites at the time was grandfathered into the reservation. In 2018, there were 454 farms on Standing Rock, only ninety-one of which were Native owned.[12] Today, the Standing Rock Reservation is home to Dakota and Lakota nations and spans 3,572 square miles across Corson County, South Dakota and Sioux County, North Dakota.[13]

The US government has consistently intervened in the lives of Native citizens in ways that are unprecedented elsewhere in the country. For example, in 1823, Supreme Court Justice John Marshall articulated a broad interpretation of existing law that unilaterally removed from Native people the right to sell their land. Tribal governments have no rights regarding the occupation of their land, unless the federal government agrees to those rights.[14] And, tribal health, law, and government remain contingent on federal bureaucracies and laws imposed upon them. Native people were not granted full citizenship, including the right to vote, until the Snyder Act was passed in 1924 – four years after the 19th Amendment granted women the right to vote and fifty-four years after the 15th Amendment granted Black men the right to vote.

Even today, the federal government retains the right to decide who is and who is not Native American and it continues to issue identity cards to Native people that certify the degree of "Indian Blood" they have.[15] Native people must prove the legitimacy of their identity through a federally set blood quantum – and many do not qualify. As a result of this racist imposition, Native people have been denied the rights of tribal membership, even when it is clear that they belong to the culture and community. This shocking practice calls to mind the race identity cards South Africans were required to carry during apartheid.

When I arrive in Standing Rock, the reservation is home to 8,616 people with a nearly equal number of tribal members living off the reservation. The population at Standing Rock is young; 46% of residents are below the age of twenty-four.[16] While the national unemployment rate hovers at 3.1%, at Standing Rock that number is closer to 79%.[17] And the poverty rate is 43.2%, nearly triple the national average. The scarcity of jobs and economic opportunities creates high unemployment and overcrowded housing. Most low-income residents live with family members, which can lead to overcrowded and unsafe conditions.[18]

On reservations, tribal and federal governments are the largest employers. At Standing Rock, the tribe owns and operates two casinos that employ almost 600 people, and several smaller businesses including restaurants, campgrounds, a convenience store, and a marina.[19] This level of development is impressive, considering that all Indian lands are held in trust and managed by the federal government. Nearly every aspect of economic development on Indian land is controlled by federal agencies. For example, companies must go through four federal agencies and forty-nine steps to get a permit that would take only four steps off of the reservation.[20] The occupation of Native peoples has been bureaucratized to devastating effect. The so-called guardian–ward relationship between the federal and tribal governments is not a trustee–beneficiary relationship, as is often claimed. Tribal governments are reduced to domestic dependent nation status and forced to rely on federal government agencies that are underfunded and difficult to access.[21] The federal management of Native resources and economies has created levels of poverty on reservations on a par with undeveloped nations.

Standing Rock is a sprawling community organized by Districts, eight in all, each with their own governance structure and many with substantial populations.[22] Many people at Standing Rock do not live in formally organized towns – even the two casinos/hotels are not part of towns. There are just three towns on the reservation, all about thirty miles apart: McLaughlin in South Dakota (population 679), and two towns in North Dakota: Fort Yates (population 200) and Cannon Ball (population 875).[23]

Fort Yates is home to Sitting Bull College and to the Standing Rock Tribal government. The beautiful college campus stands as a promise to the future in a community that prizes its children. The tribal government works hard to support youth, and just down the road from the college is a modern public school campus that contains buildings for elementary, junior high and high schools. Fort Yates itself is a crossroads with a grocery store, gas station, post office and bank. Just north from Fort Yates is the town of Cannon Ball. Half of the families in Cannon Ball have incomes *below* the federal poverty line; and, nearly half of the residents are children under eighteen.[24]

By morning on my second day at Standing Rock, a cloud of smoke from the Montana fires settles like a thick fog over the entire area. I can no longer see the rolling meadows stretching to the Missouri River, much less the expansive bridge that spans it. Beads of headlights travel on a slim thread of road moving across the reservation. I join the line of cars leaving the reservation and heading into Mobridge – a town that was built on land taken from the Lakota Sioux in 1906 for the construction of a railroad.

In Mobridge I find a gas station – and things quickly become confusing. The pump has a range of five options, all with various grades of ethanol. I have no idea which one the rental car needs and no way to make sense of all of the choices. I wait as an older white man washes the windshield on a woman's truck; as he works, he calls out to everyone entering the station by name. The white woman behind the wheel of a very tired-looking Ford engages him in easy banter. It was a banter that I came to recognize as both a kind of community and a kind of wall. The banter isn't open to everyone. I would bump up against it many times when dealing with white people in the area. After some time, I signal and make it clear that I'm waiting for help. In return they both look away, making it equally clear that they would finish their conversation without hurry. When the woman finally starts her engine and pulls away, I still seem to be invisible to the attendant and so I ask for help. Without a word, and without looking at me, the man picks up the nozzle for the 87 octane and begins to fill my gas tank. Then, with a sweeping gesture toward the gas pumps, says: "These are a gift from your Black president. Or I should say your former Black president." I wonder how this older, white man sees me.

When I want to convey a sense of ease that I really don't feel, as I did in this moment, I imagine someone I love before speaking. I smiled and shifted my weight to a relaxed posture. But then out of my mouth comes:

"What gifts are we getting from your white president?"

"Oh, so you're going to be like that." He takes a step back. Obviously, my smile isn't always enough. But the exercise is helpful, and I don't give up easily on the strategy.

"No, no," I laugh. "I asked because of how you said it. Are you a Trump fan?"

"Definitely not. That election didn't give us any choices. I know some think she would have saved the world. That woman is just … well, let's just say neither one of them are looking out for us. They keep getting richer and you and I keep getting poorer. Nothin' going to change that." Maybe my strategy has worked. I seem to be on his side of the fence now. I don't know how this happened but I'm grateful. I take care not to mention the name of "that woman" (Hillary Clinton) in our conversation about politics.

There are two main roads in Mobridge, one that is a throughway for traffic heading in and out and another that resembles the sleepy main streets of business districts in many midwestern towns. It's about 10:30 in the morning when I drive down the main street in Mobridge. It's a few blocks long and mostly empty, except for a string of pickup trucks parked in front of a local bar.

In my phone calls home, my family complain about the photos I send them: "Why don't you take photos of places that have people in them?" The truth is that in struggling communities a lack of disposable income can make a town feel completely empty. This

Downtown Mobridge, South Dakota.

is certainly the case in Mobridge. Although noticeably larger and wealthier than the towns on the reservation, it is also clearly a struggling community. Most of the businesses are shuttered. The storefronts that are open do double duty: a single storefront serves as a craft shop, a florist, and a café. There are no bookstores, department stores, movie theaters or bowling alleys. As is typical among the Midwest towns I visited, the Ace Hardware store is the largest and most well-kept building in town.

Mobridge is remarkable in that it has a restaurant and two full-size grocery stores. I shop in both on weekday afternoons and find that I am the only woman unaccompanied by a man as I wander the aisles.

All of the women appear to be shopping with their husbands. In a town where everybody seems to know everybody else, I stand out – perhaps for more reasons than I can imagine. In the dairy section, I stand for a moment staring at an ordinary pound of butter that sells for $6.50. I can't help but wonder why, after all of these years, I still expect groceries to be less expensive in poor communities. It has never been the case. The butter here is more expensive than in Whole Foods in Washington, DC. In this rural South Dakota community produce is more limited and less robust than in the DC area, and there are fewer options on the shelves. Add to these difficulties the fact that people on Standing Rock have to travel thirty or forty miles *one way* for a weekly shop. I wonder what that trip would be like in a South Dakota winter.

The next day I drive out to McLaughlin. Routes 12 and 9 intersect in McLaughlin and the intersection has the bustle of an agricultural hub – grain silos and massive trucks sit just off the crossroads. The town's main street is a couple of blocks long, and is home to a small café, a gas station, and a senior center. McLaughlin has a population of about 670. In the 2010 census, white people were almost one-third of the population; by 2019 that number had fallen to 25%. Although a lot of Native people live there, there is an overwhelming presence of white people that makes McLaughlin feel like a white enclave on the reservation. Unfriendly doesn't begin to capture the feeling I get from other white people in the town. White people consistently dismiss my interest in the place, interrupt my conversations with Native people, and question me intently. I am too far outside of local culture to understand any of this with confidence, but it surely stands out in my experience.

At the local senior center, I am greeted by an older white woman who sits at a Formica table. All four walls of the faux wood paneling have been covered with lacquered jigsaw puzzles completed by people who attend the center. As I quickly survey the room, I notice that the clock is one hour *behind* the time on my phone. When I ask her about this the woman explains: "No it's not behind. We use *Mountain* time here." A simple enough statement but said with such intensity that it seems to have a pointed significance that I don't understand. Later, in Fort Yates, Two Lance Woman explains: "Only white people use Mountain time," she tells me. "Indians do not recognize the Mountain time zone – everyone on the Cheyenne and Standing Rock reservations uses Central time." This was the point the woman in the senior center was making. White-people time. It's a very intentional assault on Native sovereignty even from within the borders of the reservation.

Ellison Thompson is a Lakota woman who lives in McLaughlin. She and her husband were both unemployed when she got pregnant. That's when they made a deal that whoever got a job first would take it – the other, by necessity, would be the stay-at-home parent when the baby came. Ellison got the first job; her husband is now a stay-at-home dad caring for their ten-month-old baby. With a second child on the way this arrangement is unlikely to change. Ellison would like to go to back to school to complete a degree but there's never enough time for everything that needs to get done as it is.

Ellison works full-time as a clerk in the hospitality industry to support her family. "I'm really thankful for my employer because they do provide really good health insurance and a steady paycheck, and that's what I need. It's hard for a lot of people to find a job around here." In 2016, 16.4% of the Standing Rock population earned less than $10,000 a year.[25] As on other reservations, life expectancy and quality of life rates are among the lowest in the Western Hemisphere; Native children face premature death rates that are three to four times higher than the national average.[26]

Ellison's pre-tax income of $14,000 a year means she brings home just about $1,000 a month. She is well below the 2017 federal poverty line for a family of three set at $20,420. For comparison, the EPI self-sufficiency budget for a family of three living in Corson County, South Dakota is $62,502.

MONTHLY COSTS

2 adults *and* 1 child
Corson County, SD

HOUSING	$660
FOOD	$654
CHILD CARE	$416
TRANSPORTATION	$1,248
HEALTH CARE	$1,123
OTHER NECESSITIES	$530
TAXES	$578
Monthly Total	**$5,209**
Annual Total	**$62,502**

How does Ellison manage given the gap between $14,000 and $62,502? She depends on help from her family. Her salary covers the phone bill, half the electricity bill, heat, food, clothing and household items, the car payment, and baby expenses. In addition to having a husband who provides childcare, Ellison's mom provides critical economic support: "My mom, even though she doesn't live at our house, she still splits the bills with me and pays the rent."

The arrival of her baby has had a big economic impact. Ellison tells me with some surprise: "Babies are really expensive!" The cost of raising children surprises a lot of people but no one more than new parents. They can count on spending about $200 a month on diapers, formula, and baby food alone.[27] On top of basic expenses are the costs of clothing, furniture, a car seat, a stroller, childcare, and medical care. And the costs keep rising as children age. Ellison relies a lot on her family. "There's a lot of single mothers here. I'm thankful that I have my husband, because he helps me so much. I don't think I'd be able to do it as a single mom. We are just trying to get by, and that's all we're all really doing is getting by."

When Ellison's second child arrives, they will be a family of four, and in the best case her husband will continue to provide childcare, she will keep her job, and her mother will continue to help with family expenses. The best case means keeping already limited resources stable. The best case also means hoping that Ellison's child will be born in good health and at a normal birth weight.[28] Even if everything is the best case, life will become harder. This unexpected but very much wanted pregnancy will further strain already inadequate resources. The federal poverty line for a family of four in 2019 was $25,750. The EPI self-sufficiency budget for a family of four in Corson County, South Dakota was $74,098.

Ellison remains hopeful, pragmatic, and diligent. "A lot of the stuff I get is from rummage sales and [store] sales. I'll wait until something goes on clearance before I get it, or I'll wait so far along the line until it goes on sale vs. buying it at a high price, or I'll order on Amazon, so I don't have to waste gas. Because I live in a small town, I don't have a whole lot of shopping options." Without Amazon deliveries, Ellison would have to make the 160-mile round trip to Bismarck, North Dakota, to buy clothing and household items. It's impossible to get anywhere without driving a considerable distance and this becomes an even bigger problem in the long and snowy North Dakota winters.[29] The internet service that makes it possible for Ellison to buy goods online is provided by the reservation and is itself evidence of visionary leadership. Across the country nearly 15 million

MONTHLY COSTS

2 adults *and* 2 children
Corson County, SD

HOUSING	$660
FOOD	$827
CHILD CARE	$868
TRANSPORTATION	$1,263
HEALTH CARE	$1,345
OTHER NECESSITIES	$600
TAXES	$612
Monthly Total	**$6,175**
Annual Total	**$74,098**

people live in sparsely populated rural communities with no access to a broadband internet service.[30]

Like many people in struggling families, Ellison does not have a savings account. She tells me "I don't even know how to save. I can't save for my life, because we always need something. I always need something, whether it be an oil change, diapers, wipes, food. There's always something." It's a daily struggle for her to sort out what they can and can't afford, but even so, Ellison is quick to say that she has more privilege than others in her community. Not only does she have the support of her husband and mother – she also has a car. While you might be able to hitch a ride with a neighbor or friend to a grocery store, owning a vehicle is essential to holding a job. The distance between home and work can easily be thirty to forty miles one way.

Yet for low-wage workers owning a vehicle is a catch-22. "I have a vehicle that I'm paying off, so I have car payments that come out of my check," explains Ellison. "The car is just really another baby. It's equally as expensive to take care of." The Dakota weather and the long-distance driving take their toll on vehicles. While Ellison is among the wealthier people on the reservation because she owns a vehicle, she can't really afford to have something go wrong with her car. On Ellison's budget there is no such thing as a small car repair. Even a small problem could start a cascade of events that will threaten both her budget and her livelihood. Worse yet, a mechanical breakdown would require a tow to a repair shop and leave Ellison with no way to get to work. With reduced work hours, it may take a while for her to be able to pay for the repairs – assuming she doesn't get fired for missing work. "Even though some of us have more than others," says Ellison, "we're still struggling." This is clearly true and, as Ellison points out, not everyone struggles in the same way.

Erika Brooks identifies herself as a member of the Standing Rock Sioux Tribe; she holds an associate degree and has worked her way up in Head Start from an initial position as an aide, to becoming a teacher, and then to her last position as a supervisor of several centers. She has traveled more widely than most people I meet. As a member of a religious organization, she traveled to Germany, Romania, and Russia doing service work. But when we met, a lot had already gone wrong in Erika's life. When her siblings struggled with substance abuse issues,[31] Erika came home to South Dakota to help with their children. For the last ten years she has been caring in some way for nine children, four of whom live with her. She arrived to meet me in a restaurant with the two youngest. Without romanticizing the challenges, she says the children give her life both meaning and satisfaction.

Now at age fifty, Erika is unemployed and filled with worry for the children. While she supports herself and four children on an income of less than $16,000, Erika never described herself as poor. "It's pretty stressful, because we're on a really limited income, but I make sure that, you know, we do everything on a tight budget so that we have enough." In 2017, the federal poverty line for a family of five was $28,780. Like all federal calculations of poverty this number is completely unrealistic. In the same year, the EPI self-sufficiency budget for a family of five living in Corson County, South Dakota, was $82,524.

As seems obvious, Erika cannot afford childcare – actually, she can't afford most of what is on the EPI self-sufficiency list. Several years back Erika was working full-time and living in an apartment in Mobridge. Things were good and she was able to help care for her family. "I was pretty involved with buying groceries for them and paying bills for them, along with my own bills, just doing that." One day her sister brought her daughter to Erika's apartment and said, "'You can have her.' And I said, 'For the weekend?' and she said, 'No, you can have her,' and I said, 'You mean permanently she's mine?' She said, 'Yeah, take her,' and she had her clothes packed in a wagon. So, I kept her. I raised her." That was eight years ago. Since

MONTHLY COSTS

1 adult *and* 4 children
Corson County, SD

HOUSING	$909
FOOD	$1,009
CHILD CARE	$1,007
TRANSPORTATION	$1,159
HEALTH CARE	$1,339
OTHER NECESSITIES	$774
TAXES	$680
Monthly Total	**$6,877**
Annual Total	**$82,524**

then, three more nieces have come to live with her. It wasn't easy, but Erika stretched to work full-time and care for the four girls. Then one day the new building manager asked her for paperwork that would prove she had legal custody of the girls. On the reservation, that would never happen. But she lived in Mobridge and now she was being asked by a non-Native building manager for custody papers.

Erika went to the tribal courts to apply for custody of the girls, a process which requires a six-month waiting period. She had lived in the building without incident for years, but the new manager began threatening her and citing her for building violations. Erika tells me she watched him treat other residents with kindness but with her he was always rude. She has one word to describe what happened: prejudice. "I tried to explain my side of things. I had been a good tenant for five years, and how could this, all of a sudden, be such a problem? It was traumatizing for me. He didn't just come and knock on the door or give me papers. He would bang on the door hard and say, 'Open up,' and scream and yell and be hysterical about it every time he came. It just scared the crap out of me. I don't know why, but I was so intimidated by him." Within months, Erika and the girls were evicted. She had four kids and no place to live. And soon no job. The story gets worse. The manager claimed they had left the apartment in a mess and charged them $4,000. "We had washed walls and cleaned carpets," explained Erika. "I took pictures of it to prove that we had left it in really good condition, and they still charged me."

"I've lived pretty much an isolated life with going to school and working. I've been bringing the girls into my home one by one and raising them in a really quiet, stable environment. I've done everything to protect that way of life, and now we're thrust into this whole other dynamic. You have to be really cautious and careful and watchful, because the children are the ones that suffer the most." After being evicted, Erika's best option was to take the girls to a shelter. "We ended up staying there for five months, and then we were asked to leave, because they couldn't help us anymore."

Erika and the four girls have been living in the basement of a two-bedroom house. Her sister, her sister's boyfriend and his brother live on the main floor. "They drink a lot," says Erika. "Like five days out of the week they're drunk." And when they drink, Erika and the kids become targets for abuse. "We basically live downstairs and have our meals and stuff in the basement and just kind of keep to ourselves, or we go for drives or go to the park a lot. So, we kind of, you know, keep a low profile in the home, and we've been living like that for about two-and-a-half years."

Their possessions had been stored in an empty house in the country that was recently rented out. Erika didn't have gas money to get to the house and pleaded for time to get her things out – it was a lot of memorabilia. But her pleas went unheeded and she lost everything. It's a huge emotional loss for Erika but, at the moment, she sees it as the least of her troubles. Her thirteen-year old was recently raped by a trusted family member. (More on this in Chapter 7.) Erika decided to let go of her possessions and focus on the future.

Erika has applied for housing on the reservation. Standing Rock housing policies prohibit drug use and she is hoping that the fact that she doesn't drink, smoke, or do drugs will help her. But even so, the waiting time for affordable housing on the reservation is years long. Erika is working with the tribal leadership to get their case expedited to stabilize life for the children. She is afraid to rent an apartment off of the reservation, even if she could afford it. "I'm still so frightened by confrontations with landlords. I mean, I'm amazed at myself, because I've been a really strong person all my life, very independent, very straightforward, and now I cower. I just shiver every time I think about dealing with a landlord. I'm scared they're going to kick me out, or something's going to happen, and I'll be on the street with four girls again and a very limited income. So, it's really frightening. I know that I'm at the disadvantage, because I'm Native. They think automatically that I'm stupid or I'm uneducated, that I'm not an equal, and don't deserve the same respect that someone else might. I see that everywhere I go."

The sense of Erika as a capable, professional person is palpable to me as we talk, as is her paralyzing sense of vulnerability. "My life is like a yellow caution sign, because I'm just always so concerned with the girls' safety and their well-being from the time we wake up." The daily routine for Erika and the girls starts early. The school bus arrives at 7 a.m. for the older girls in junior high and Erika is there to meet the driver every day, to make sure the driver knows her, as she sends the girls off for the ten-mile trip to the nearest school. In South Dakota, thirty-four school districts have opted for a four-day week to save money on transportation. This means that Erika's two older girls are picked up for junior high at 7 a.m. and returned home at 4:30 or 5 p.m.

Her youngest child has just started at a local kindergarten and Erika hopes this will enable her to get back to work and so be able to provide a better living situation for the children. For now, while the girls are in school, Erika runs an informal taxi service. "Someone might hire me to drive to McLaughlin. That's how I get my gas money. It's $10 a ride to McLaughlin and back." She also acts as an informal taxi for neighbors when she makes the sixty-mile round trip to Mobridge for groceries and household goods. The thought of car trouble is too distressing to even talk about. So much depends on having a vehicle that runs – even if it is held together with Bondo and duct tape.

This is what it means to be part of the struggling class: to work consistently in a breathtakingly vulnerable situation, with few resources, and with an unfounded hope that you can build a better life. If the isolation of the rural landscape suggests some similarities between Appalachia and Standing Rock, few places could be more different from this reservation than Oakland, California. And yet, even here, the daily lives of the struggling class bear remarkable similarities.

Oakland, California

Oakland, California is a racially diverse city with demographics that are roughly 29% white; 26.5% Latinx; 22.5% African American; 15.2% Asian.[32] Wealthy neighborhoods, like those in the Oakland hills, are home to families of color as well as white families. The city's poor communities, however, are overwhelming Black and Latinx. Home to 429,082 people, Oakland has a population density of

7,676 people *per square mile*. (By contrast, Athens County has 130.7 people per square mile and Standing Rock has about nine people per square mile.)

The Oakland commercial district is an eclectic mix of old and new storefronts that give this part of the city a working-class bohemian reputation. Lakeshore Avenue is home to multiple cafés, bakeries, and small restaurants. Peet's Coffee operates a large café just a few hundred feet away from a Starbucks. The upscale Peet's is designed to invite people to linger – for the price of a cup of coffee, patrons settle into books or conversations that can last hours. The neighborhood is home to an old-fashioned donut shop, an artisanal bakery, a small greengrocer and a trendy gift store. Yoga studios and high-end hair salons (for women and men) take up significant real estate. Just one block over from Lakeshore Avenue on Grand Avenue, the picture is a little different. The high-end chains have not invested in Grand Avenue as they have on Lakeshore Avenue. The storefronts show signs of wear and age, and closed stores are prevalent. For an outsider, this makes it hard to tell if the community is gentrifying or collapsing.

The Lakeshore district is ringed by hills to the east. A maze of narrow streets winds past bungalows as it climbs up the hillside to increasingly expensive homes. Slightly to the west of Lakeshore and Grand Avenue is Lake Merritt – an amazing tidal lagoon and wildlife refuge. People without disposable income generally lose access to public space. (Libraries in urban areas remain one of the last bastions of community space but a very circumscribed one.) Lake Merritt is an urban jewel surrounded by parkland. The lake is a regular destination for school field trips to analyze water samples or visit wildlife recovering from injuries at the Nature Center.

The parkland includes a playground for small children surrounded by picnic tables, a bonsai garden, a children's fairyland, and a boating center. Not all of it works well, not all of it works all of the time, but it is a tremendous community resource. Indeed, in a country radically segregated by class and race, one of the most striking things about Lake Merritt is the willingness of people in the community to share it. Schoolchildren, families, lovers, sunbathers, students, fitness buffs, picnickers, and temporary housing encampments all coexist around the 3.5-mile shoreline. In a city where a two-bedroom apartment might rent for $5,000, it's not surprising to see a small tent encampment beside the lake. When the city authorities moved port-o-johns into the park for people living in the tent encampment, it became obvious that things were not going to change any time soon. This is not to say that everyone is

Lake Merritt, Oakland, California.

happy about it, but the park continues to serve a wide and diverse community.

Oakland, once called the Harlem of the West, has been experiencing an influx of young, white, wealthy tech workers and an explosion in housing prices. The changing demographics are also affecting the park use. As white families move into Oakland in increasing numbers, complaints to police about people "living while Black" have also increased. For example, in 2018 Oakland made the news when a leisurely picnic turned into a nightmare. A white woman, Jennifer Schulte, called the police on a Black family using a charcoal grill at their Lake Merritt picnic. As she summoned the police, Schulte reportedly told Kenzie Smith and Onsayo Abram, who were barbecuing, that they would be going to jail. Smith told the *Guardian* he couldn't get her voice out of his head. "I honestly thought that I was going to die."[33] Jennifer Schulte became a potent symbol for the ways in which white people target Black people engaged in ordinary behavior. She was quickly dubbed "BBQ Becky" in memes that went viral. Later in the month, hundreds of Black residents showed up at Lake Merritt for a "BBQ'n while Black" cookout/protest.

There is much more to Oakland than Lake Merritt. A short drive from downtown Oakland, several communities are laboring under the weight of deep poverty, including Acorn, Ghost Town, and the

Deep East. Today, these communities can only be described as the homelands of American apartheid. Their reputation for violence makes it easy to forget – perhaps encourages people to forget – that people live here, raise children here, and call these communities home. The media refers to them as "areas." No one lives in an "area." Even the poorest of us live in communities and neighborhoods – even when those communities carry a more dangerous feeling at night.

Once envisioned as part of a redevelopment plan, the Acorn neighborhood, at the edge of West Oakland, stands as a weary testimony to the old housing projects of the 1960s. Today, the community is not just bordered by Interstate 980 – Interstate 880 runs right through it. Small yards in front of homes have been paved with concrete and delineated from each other and the sidewalk by chain link fencing. Every home I saw was protected by bars on the windows and security gates on doors. As I wander through these streets on foot, the overwhelming presence of concrete and home security is harsh and unrelenting.

Just a short distance away in West Oakland, another development project created the neighborhood of Ghost Town. Hundreds of families, nearly all Black, lost their homes to eminent domain claims that cleared the way for three freeways, a massive freeway interchange dubbed "the MacArthur Maze," and the Bay Area Rapid Transit (BART) system, all of which cut through the low-income community. The MacArthur Maze marks the south border of Ghost Town, that stretches roughly from 27th Street to 35th Street. Under the knot of freeways that form the Maze, the sidewalks are filled with encampments of people – an informal community of its own, with cardboard architecture, a few shopping carts, and mounds of belongings wrapped in trash bags.

In the midst of the sidewalk encampments and broken-down buildings are schools and children. In this neighborhood half of all families live below the federal poverty line. Despite the number of boarded up buildings, however, it is a neighborhood with a strong identity.

The community is home to a small garden known as Ghost Town Farms, as well as the local Ghost Town Brewery, and it once attracted artist collectives that sprung up in converted warehouses. A tragic fire in the artist's collective known as the the Ghost Ship in 2016 took thirty-six lives and led the city to condemn many of these properties.

Viewed from Ghost Town, Oakland's high-rise office buildings form a horizon that looks like the Emerald City of Oz. So perhaps it is telling that the history of Ghost Town has been replaced with local lore. One story claims that there were so many killings in the

Ghost Town, Oakland, California.

neighborhood it became known as a Ghost Town, another that the name derives from the fact that two casket makers were once located side by side in the neighborhood, while a third attributes the name to a drug kingpin who referred to the area as a Ghost Town because he had eliminated all his rivals. The scariest story of all is the real history. It has nothing to do with gangs – it's a story of how collusion between government and business betrayed entire communities; first through redlining practices, and then through eminent domain claims.

Across town, the Deep East is a neighborhood roughly defined as running southeast of 73rd Avenue to the San Leandro Border. I stop for gas on 106th Avenue – deep in "the Deep East." I am immediately and obviously out of place as an older, white woman, in a community that seems to be younger and without white faces. As in Mobridge, I don't understand immediately how the gas station works. Familiar things can be so different. Here, the pumps do not take credit cards. I ask a young man sitting in a car on the opposite side of the island for help. He slowly, and wordlessly, points to a small bullet-proof booth with an attendant. I join the small but steady flow of people to the booth. A young woman arrives ahead of me and with a hand gesture offers me the opportunity to go ahead of her. No eye contact, no smile, not a word. Her face is closed to me and I don't know how to read the interaction. I decline her offer and get a silent shrug. She leaves without speaking or making eye contact.

On the road beside the gas station an old van is parallel parked. The hood is open and the engine exposed. Enough engine parts are scattered around the vehicle that it looks like a long-term repair project in process, yet no one is in sight. Not far from the van, on the chain link fence that surrounds the gas station, a man growls and snarls – I've never heard a person make sounds like this. He is splayed spread-eagle across the fence, his body twisting and turning. Although he is writhing, he remains so attached to the fence that I have to look closely to be sure he is not actually tied to it. He is not, but his grip is powerful. A line of men and one woman sit on a curb inside the parking area of the station. No one engages the growling man, no one stares, or even seems to notice.

I follow their lead, pump my gas and return to collect my credit card. This time, a young man offers for me to go ahead of him. I decline but he insists with such firmness that I can only say thank you and accept. While waiting for the clerk to process my card, I turn around and start a casual conversation with this man. I talk about the weather; yesterday was unbearably hot and today is a breezy spring day that feels perfect. He agrees. I make a comment about the unpredictability of the weather that gets a laugh. He has a beautiful smile and for a moment I make eye contact. And then his face closes and I know to return to my business. I realize much too late that, in some communities, survival can depend on learning to see nothing and say nothing. That in some places in the country, eye contact might get you killed. Is this where I am? If so, it is all the more amazing that ordinary acts of kindness seep through in daily interactions. I collect my card receipt and leave.

Signs of an informal economy are everywhere – in the particular presence of young men on street corners, in the sparkle of polished rims on new cars, and in the very serious young men scanning the environment as they drive slowly past. I wonder if the gas station, or the area around it, is some sort of drop point. As I type up my notes, I wonder if I should have used cash. Could my card have been skimmed while I pumped? The corrosive power of doubt seeps in as I reflect. My card was not skimmed, and it is worth noting that when it has been in the past it was always in wealthier, whiter places that I had not learned to see as dangerous. This is not to minimize or deny that violence that has come to characterize the communities around 106th Avenue, but to acknowledge the humanity of people living there and the prejudice that outsiders bring to it – intentionally or not.

Vanessa Torres is one of the more than 15,000 people who live in the Deep East. Vanessa grew up with her parents and four siblings in a two-bedroom apartment they rented for about $1,700 a month. As the oldest of the five children, she has had a lot of responsibility in the family. She began translating for her parents at age eight, and now at twenty-four describes herself as something of a parent to her parents, who rely on her to help navigate technologies as well as bureaucracies. "Something that is sometimes frustrating is that they think we know how to do everything." It's a common generational issue for immigrant families.

Vanessa, like many others, feels the impact of gentrification in Oakland. In 2019, the mid-point for monthly rent for a one-bedroom apartment in the Deep East was $2,300.[34] I hear the stress in Vanessa's voice as she leans forward: "This is the '*hood*.' If Latino, low-income communities can't afford it anymore, well, shit, where do we go? We obviously can't afford to live in nicer, affluent communities. If we can no longer afford to live in low-income communities that are considered dangerous, that are considered poor, then where do we see ourselves?" Vanessa answers her own question. She's been watching Black and Brown families move from the Deep East to Tracy and Stockton, "cities where there's essentially nothing," sighs Vanessa.

"My mom sells tamales once a week, and my dad's a laborer. I'm the one who has the job, a good social.[35] So I think that's kind of pressure on me too to make sure that I stay well off so I can support myself and support my family. I am already at a big advantage: I speak English, I was raised in this country, and I have a four-year degree." Vanessa works for an educational nonprofit that serves Latinx high school students. It's a professional position that comes with health insurance and a salary that she ballparks between $45,000 and $59,999 a year. This puts Vanessa in the ballpark for the Economic Policy Institute calculations for self-sufficiency for a single person. By these numbers alone, she seems solidly middle class. But life is always more complicated than numbers. On paper, Vanessa is single. In reality she is responsible for her parents and younger siblings. Vanessa tells me: "If I wasn't supporting my family, then I wouldn't be considered low income, but a chunk of money and resources goes toward my family and it's definitely more challenging." There's more to be said about this later. For now, it's also worth noting that she remains tethered to the struggling class in other ways. For example, although she has health insurance, the Deep East is isolated from health-care providers. To get health care, she needs to take public transit, which can mean taking multiple buses to a different part of

Oakland. For Vanessa and her family, there is no such thing as an easy, or a short, trip to the doctor.

Again, keep in mind that Fair Market Rent (FMR) – the standard calculation used here – is quite different from *actual* housing prices. Sixty percent of local housing is more expensive than this. The reality of the rental market in 2019 meant that *studios* in Oakland went for $1,761 a month ($21,132 per year). We saw in Chapter 1 that HUD's definition of *affordable* housing, includes utilities and costs no more than one-third of your pre-tax income. While most rentals do not include utilities, let's bracket that issue and look just at the monthly rent. Using HUD's parameters for assessing affordable housing, a renter would need to earn *at least* $5,283 a month or $63,396 a year to be able to consider a studio in Oakland affordable. Vanessa's salary is not enough to enable her to afford this studio without becoming what HUD calls "cost burdened." That is to say, she would have to pay more than 30% of her income for housing. The lack of affordable housing is the source of a lot of misery. A person living at the federal poverty line ($12,140 per year for a single person) could put 100% of their income toward rent and still not cover the cost of an average studio apartment. The federal recognition of poverty comes *long* after the point when housing in Oakland becomes unaffordable.

The self-sufficiency budget of $57,383 for a single person is in the neighborhood of what Vanessa earns – but it's hard to say precisely,

MONTHLY COSTS

1 adult *and* no children

Oakland/Fremont metro area

HOUSING	$1,540
FOOD	$310
CHILD CARE	$0
TRANSPORTATION	$853
HEALTH CARE	$361
OTHER NECESSITIES	$746
TAXES	$971
Monthly Total	**$4,782**
Annual Total	**$57,383**

since we only have a ballpark figure for her income. To fully support herself and four others (two parents and her two youngest siblings), Vanessa would need to earn $156,717 a year. It isn't clear to me just how fully she supports her family, but it becomes easy to see how quickly circumstances move Vanessa from middle class to low-income. This is exactly why income alone never tells the full story.

Even so, when I notice that Vanessa has $20,000 in savings, I am ready to cancel the rest of the interview. And then she explains that she and her family cut corners to save money as if their lives depend upon it – because they do. "I feel like me and my family have tried really hard to save money," explains Vanessa, "because I'm undocumented. My parents are undocumented. My brother's undocumented, so I know that there's no safety net for us. For example, my parents are not working right now [because of the pandemic], and they can't get unemployment. I want to make sure that I try to save up every penny as possible, because we don't know if there's going to be a situation within our family." Vanessa's income is critical to her family, which includes a younger American-born sibling who would be left alone if the family was deported. According to the Marshall Project, there are about 10.7 million undocumented immigrants in the United States, and, nationwide, "about 908,891 households with at least one American child would fall below federal poverty levels if their undocumented breadwinners were removed."[36]

In 2000, Vanessa was just four years old when her mother and father brought her and her one-year-old brother to the United States from Mexico in hopes of finding employment and educational opportunities. "It's frustrating to hear the backlash from people [who say] 'well, if you'd wanted to come to this country, then you should do it the legal way.' Sometimes our families don't have time to wait for the legal way. It's a do or die type of thing. But people love to throw around, 'if you want to come to this country, come here the legal way. Apply for a visa, blah blah blah.' My family is still in the process of – " Vanessa pauses with exasperation and draws a breath. "We applied to get citizenship through an uncle for the four of us in '99. It's 2020, and we still have not heard anything back, and we look at the visa bulletin board – it's a really slow progress. It's very slow progress." A legal immigration policy that takes more than two decades to process an application is actively encouraging illegal immigration.

Vanessa and her brother are among nearly 700,000 youth who have received Deferred Action for Childhood Arrivals (DACA). DACA is an immigration policy that protects children brought to the

US without documentation from immediate deportation. It enables them to obtain a social security number and is contingent upon regular renewals. However, DACA does not provide a pathway to citizenship, which leaves recipients vulnerable to changing administrations. "It's challenging, but I think, at the end of the day, you kind of have to live day-by-day, navigate day-by-day. When people ask questions like, where do you see yourself in five years, I'm like, I don't necessarily like that question. Who can guarantee me that I will be here? I'm talking about will I be in this country in five years? So, it's kind of hard to think about the future when I'm trying to live day-by-day, month-by-month here."

While the temporary protection of DACA has enabled Vanessa to obtain a professional job, both of her parents, like many in her community, are part of an informal economy of undocumented workers. Vanessa continues: "especially for the working folks, they are not compensated enough for their labor, like farm workers, construction workers. They are putting their bodies, their health on the line and at risk, and a lot of these are Latinos who are working on the fields, who are working construction. If you're working construction and you mess up your back, you're screwed. How are you going to continue working this job that you have? Now you have to look at other forms of working when you've been so used to working construction and making this much money? If you get hurt on the job and you have to take another job, that could be a pay cut essentially. Then that could be a cut within your life. You have to make ends meet and narrow things down, [which] essentially means moving out to somewhere cheaper. They would have to move out to places where there's more poverty."

The Pew Research Center estimates that more than 40 million people living in the United States are immigrants – 35.2 million of them (roughly 77%) are here legally and about 10.5 million (around 23%) are here without authorization.[37] About 25% of all immigrants to the United States come from Mexico and, like Vanessa's parents, they come for work. According to Pew, industries that depend on the labor of unauthorized immigrants include agriculture, food production (slaughterhouses and canneries), construction, manufacturing, and hospitality (as maids and custodial workers).[38] Families like Vanessa's live in fear of getting caught up in raids and deported without notice. The Pew Research Center reports that from 2001 to 2017, a majority (60%) of immigrants deported from the United States had not been convicted of a crime.[39] Despite Oakland being a sanctuary city, Immigration and Customs Enforcement (ICE) are using the city airport as a staging ground for thousands of flights.

Between 2010 and 2018, the ICE air operation flew nearly 43,000 people in and out of Oakland.[40] Of these, almost 27,000 were being deported; the other 16,000 were being transferred as part of a detention and relocation system that seems designed to cut people off from legal and community support that could help them stay in the country.[41]

While the Trump administration refocused national conversations about immigration in very hostile ways, the truth is that as a nation we have never been willing to address the fact that unauthorized workers have long been central to US business. Immigrants and their families have been caught between the pull from businesses that rely on unauthorized immigrant labor and the push of immigration policies that result in deportation. Immigrants and their families pay a steep price.

In 2019, President Trump ordered ICE agents to conduct mass roundups of immigrant families across the country. His administration also sought to rescind Obama-era protections for immigrants, including the DACA program. "I think there's not a single time," says Vanessa, "when I am not afraid of something happening to my father or my mom or me that we're no longer with each other. We're afraid of deportations or removal proceedings, so just being with my family, spending time with them, absolutely brings me joy, because we could be here and in the split of a second … then we're not." And of course, this means saving every penny in case the day comes when her family is torn apart by a raid. In early summer 2020, the Supreme Court rejected the Trump administration's effort to end DACA, but the government was able to change the reporting requirement for recipients from once every two years to once a year. For Vanessa and the DACA recipients like her, the battle continues.

Vanessa isn't the only person in Oakland with a professional job and financial struggles, although the struggles all look a little different. Puppy Love (PL) is the name chosen by an African American man living in Oakland to serve as his pseudonym. He is in his fifties and has one child, who is now an adult. PL might be more of a homebody than people expect and spends a fair amount of time at home doing chores. For relaxation he works out and tries to go fishing at least twice a week. PL has steady, full-time employment as a manager in a nonprofit providing adult education to people with developmental disabilities. He cautiously refuses to talk about his salary, but volunteers that he has no savings, retirement plan, or assets. PL is one of only two men in the entire organization, about which he says diplomatically: "It's definitely a challenge on some days; things aren't thought about from a man's perspective as easily as they are in this organization from a woman's perspective."

As a supervisor, he spends his days troubleshooting problems and likes the variation that problem-solving brings. "I don't control what happens to my consumers when they're not in my care, but when they are in my care, I need to provide the best welfare, safety, and security possible. That's important to me. I don't think that's important to everybody else in society when it comes to this population. They're very neat folks. They're loving. They're caring. They're intelligent."

PL has worked incredibly hard for the success he has had. He has held the same full-time job for more than five years; it's work that he finds rewarding and which provides basic health care and vacation time. While he appreciates that he is fortunate to have a job that provides vacation time, PL can't afford to take a vacation: like millions of others, he lives paycheck to paycheck. Despite having steady, full-time work that he loves, PL is a long way from economic security. "You know, my worries are that, you know, am I going to have a place to lay my head at the end of each night? I'm always worried about, you know, is my truck going to make it home? The cost of living in California goes up every day. The cost of health care goes up every day. Living in the Bay Area is quite expensive. Rent is raised dramatically from year to year. I work in a nonprofit organization, so I don't get a raise every year." In the last three years, PL's monthly rent has increased by $250, yet his salary has remained static. He explained: "that $250 that I'm now paying extra on rent was going toward the grocery bills, the gas bills. Now I'm having to scrounge that money up. You know, it's got to come from other places … It is definitely a hard place for me to live due to the rent."

Oakland has been described as the new ground zero in the affordable housing crisis. The city's weak rent control laws have failed to effectively stabilize rents in the city. It feels wrong to even call it rent control if a landowner can increase rents by 10% or more just by providing tenants with a written notice sixty days in advance. Locals are well aware that the city has long protected landowners over tenants. But the current housing crisis now feels like a betrayal to many who say the city has not only pandered to tech companies with tax breaks, but is also encouraging the rapid gentrification that pushes long-time residents out of the city.

Clearly, PL is not alone in his worries about rising rents; in 2018, 4,000 people competed for just twenty-eight spots in a new affordable housing development in Oakland.[42] For people in the struggling class, rent is never one-third of their monthly expenses – everyone is "cost burdened" and the going rents are well beyond what many can manage. Between 2017 and 2019, Oakland experienced a 47% increase in residents unable to afford housing.[43] A national renter survey in 2017 showed that one in five households had been unable to pay their rent in full within the past three months, and that roughly 3.7 million people had experienced an eviction as a result of non-payment of rent.[44] The high cost of housing is forcing many older people into homelessness. According to HUD, people over the age of fifty make up 31% of those living without housing.[45] Affordable housing is critical to keeping individuals and families out of poverty.

PL tells me that retirement is out of the question – he couldn't afford to live in Oakland without a job. Although the East Bay is home, PL will need to leave if he is going to retire. However, like many people living with economic uncertainty, he can't even imagine a place to move to. He has family in South Carolina and although it is less expensive to live there, he doesn't think he could go back. "I couldn't live in South Carolina, because the racial overtones are so prevalent there that it doesn't work for a young man that's grown up in California." Yet California is changing in ways that make it harder for him to get by.

PL still experiences a lot of racism in the East Bay: derogatory comments, people crossing the street when they see a Black man coming toward them. "Sometimes you walk into service stations or you walk into an organization and you don't get service as quick as other people, or you're ignored, so that happens a lot in the Bay Area." Even while PL experiences racism, he considers it as related to class as well. "If you're in the upper, top middle class of Americans, I think a lot of these things are not issues for you, because you have the money, the financial backing to do what you want. But when you don't, you know, you live in a certain neighborhood, you have to drive a certain car, you have to wear certain clothes, and those things are identifiers for certain people in America of difference, and difference is a scary thing in this country right now."

Life as a Flashing Yellow Light

The people introduced in this chapter are quite different from each other, yet their experiences share something in common. They are hardworking people who have been pushed into the struggling class. Some by the underemployment of long hours at low-wage jobs, and some by stagnant wages in the face of rising housing costs. Even so, the people who struggle to cover their bills each month are invisible when politicians and the media celebrate gains in the stock market. As a nation, we still haven't opened a conversation about economic self-sufficiency for workers.

We have a federal poverty line set so low that it excludes millions of families who are unable to afford basic necessities each month, even people who literally cannot afford housing. The "fair market rent," established by HUD as a guideline to ensure that families pay no more than 30% of their income in rent, is all but meaningless. Yet this guideline is used in every calculation of economic need. Clearly, the government uses skewed measures that minimize the reported numbers of people who are struggling. We can't begin to have an honest, national conversation about class unless we confront the real numbers and recognize that it's no accident that millions of people have trouble making ends meet. Through a collusion of business and government, the economy systemically creates vast profits for some, through low wages and high rents. Even beyond the cost of housing, there is a lot of money being made off the backs of struggling families. In the next chapter we'll look at just how business manages to pull that rabbit out of the hat.

3

A Hazardous Life: The High Price of Being Poor

Who could have imagined that a store that sells most items for a dollar (and none more than ten dollars) would become an economic powerhouse? On June 5, 2019, CBS News announced that Dollar General was the number one retailer in the US. In the first quarter of 2019 alone, the company had made $6.2 billion in sales.[1] At a time when retail stores are closing across the country, dollar stores have become a thriving industry. By the close of 2019, there were more than 33,185 "dollar stores" across the country.[2] By comparison, Walmart, the largest US retailer, runs 4,700 stores, McDonald's operates just under 14,000 restaurants, and Starbucks has 14,600 locations.[3]

Garrick Brown, director for retail research at the commercial real estate company Cushman & Wakefield, told *Bloomberg Weekly:* "Essentially what the dollar stores are betting on in a large way is that we are going to have a permanent underclass in America. It's based on the concept that the jobs went away, and the jobs are never coming back, and that things aren't going to get better in any of these places."[4] Because dollar stores thrive in the poorest communities, they are often characterized as being recession proof. If you stop to think about the number of stores and the amount of profit they make, you have to ask yourself: How in the world do businesses in the poorest communities make this kind of money?

The Center for Science in the Public Interest (CSPI) illustrates how the dollar stores' strategic business plan maximizes profit by creating captive consumer markets. The chains typically target rural areas that are currently 15–20 miles from a big box grocery store.[5] To put this into perspective, in 2014 the US Department of Agriculture considered areas to be "food deserts" if residents were one mile or more away from a store where they could buy fresh and nutritious food. Struggling rural communities are an extreme version of what the government calls food deserts. In cities, dollar chains target racially segregated Black and Brown communities that are struggling economically.

After identifying an area, the company builds clusters of stores, which effectively inhibits large box stores from moving into the area.[6] This practice also undercuts the prices at small, locally owned family businesses, quickly forcing them to close. According to CSPI, the chains also negotiate with local governments for hefty tax breaks, and deal sweeteners that often cover both the cost of store construction and utility bills. In order for local governments with already limited resources to subsidize these stores, they must cut public services to residents. Given the need for retail, the promise of an eventual tax revenue stream, and few alternative options, these deals too often feel inevitable for local leaders.

Once a dollar store opens, they offer people lower weekly grocery bills at higher costs. Yes, you read that right: lower bills and higher costs. Just how does that happen? It's a familiar story in struggling families: you buy what you can afford, even if larger quantities would work out cheaper. For example, in a dollar store a 16 oz carton of milk that sells for a dollar makes it possible for someone on a limited budget to put milk on the kitchen table. However, paying $1 for 16 oz of milk is the equivalent of paying $8 a gallon for milk. In grocery stores, a gallon of milk typically sells for $3.50. Not only do locals pay more for goods, dollar store business plans to block competition actually limit the amount of access communities have to cheaper and fresher food. In turn, poor nutrition contributes to poor health and the cost to struggling families rolls forward. While dollar stores can fill a need in communities, there is growing evidence that these chains are not just a byproduct of economic distress, they also cause it by stunting possibilities for economic growth.[7] Dollar stores are one of several predatory businesses that flourish in struggling communities. There is a lot of money being made off of the backs of struggling people. Industry executives refer to it as monetizing poor people. I refer to it as predatory. Predatory practices turn a profit for businesses while causing serious harm to consumers.

Included in this hall of shame are payday loan companies, many banking practices, many health-care practices, for-profit colleges, rent-to-own furniture stores and over-priced mobile homes. Predatory practices are one of those topics that has no end to worse – it would be easy to make the argument that nearly every business that has ever touched a poor community has left a negative footprint. Given the virtually unlimited instances one could consider, this chapter focuses on just two issues that came up over and again in conversations: banking and health care. In this chapter you'll hear the familiar voices of PL in Oakland, Ellison Thompson in Standing Rock, and Rose Taylor in Athens County. You'll also be introduced to Jenna Terry in Eastern Kentucky, Peter Walker and Tommy in Tennessee's Cumberland Plateau, and Jenny Gaines in Ohio.

Payday Loans

Life is full of problems – large and small, expected and unexpected – that's just the nature of life. But problems fall harder on people and families without the basic economic buffers provided by a reliable living wage, affordable housing, and health insurance. The people who shop at dollar stores. Unexpected expenses for these folks also mean they are facing a lot of other bad options including payday loans, medical loans, and high-interest loans for high-risk borrowers. All of the people who agreed to in-depth interviews for this book had a checking account, some also had a savings account. In this sense, they were a leg up from the millions of Americans who rely on check cashing outlets because they cannot afford a checking account. Even so, most of those I talked with had experience with predatory businesses – most especially predatory lenders.

Payday loan companies are high-interest, short-term lenders that tend to set up shop in low-income communities. Although payday loans are generally made for amounts of $500 or less, they are the most expensive *legal* loans on the market.[8] The interest rates vary, but the national average APR is 400% (in some states it is as high as 660%), and the repayment is typically made in a lump sum between seven and thirty-one days later.[9] The average payday loan term is two weeks. In this timeline, an APR of 400% works out as $15 interest on every $100 borrowed.[10] If you borrowed $300 with a 400% APR, you would pay back $345 when the loan comes due in two weeks. If you cannot pay the loan in full, you would owe the original $300, plus interest, and a fee. On the surface, this may not seem like a bad deal – especially if there are no other viable options. In this sense, payday loans are like that bottle of milk at the dollar store. However, the high interest rates and lump-sum payments are an economic double-whammy for borrowers. If your paycheck isn't enough to cover regular expenses, it likely isn't enough to enable you to make a lump-sum loan repayment. By some estimates, 80% of people who take out a payday loan remain trapped in repaying that loan for a year or longer.[11]

With limited options, survival in the struggling class requires periods of unrealistic optimism – the belief that things will work out, the money will be there, and the debt will be repaid. That's just how Ellison Thompson from Standing Rock was thinking when she took out a payday loan to patch through between paychecks. She agreed to the standard terms of the payday loan, which included giving the lender direct access to her checking account to ensure the loan payment was deducted before other bills were paid. But in the weeks before the loan came due, she lost her job. "I couldn't keep up with the payments, and then it turned into a court order."

Ellison's experience is shared by others in this book. If you have never been in this spot, you might imagine that suing customers for a failure to pay would be like wringing blood from a stone. Here's how it works. The lawsuit forces a court-ordered judgment against the borrower. Ellison could ignore the order and go to jail or show up in court. Once in court, there are two options: the court can garnish wages and/or seize property. In the case of struggling folks, few own anything beyond a car, and in rural areas cars are essential for employment. So, most people are *hoping* the court will garnish their future wage rather than take their vehicle. Think about this: the best outcome for Ellison was to commit to having wages on her next job garnished. As she looked for work, the interest continued to compound – which meant she would have to pay the loan, the interest on the loan, and interest on the interest that was accruing. And it continues to compound as the loan is repaid. The lender can't lose. Payments are automatically deducted from every paycheck before they are even issued to the worker. "I'm still recovering from that," Ellison tells me, "things are okay now, but it was a really hard lesson." That word "okay" pops up a lot in my conversations with struggling folks. When someone tells me that things are okay, I understand that to mean they are not in an *immediate* crisis, which was the case for Ellison. In order to take out a payday loan, struggling folks have to be in a desperate situation and yet be hopeful about their future.

According to a 2018 report from the Office of the Comptroller of the Currency (OCC), about 12 million people use a payday loan service each year and loans typically range from $300 to $5,000.[12] As working people are submerged by swelling debt, lenders are making a fortune. Every year, people using payday loans pay about *9 billion dollars* in interest and fees.[13] In 2017, there were 14,348 payday loan storefronts – about the same as the number of Starbucks locations.[14] Payday loans are regulated by states. In some states, a person who borrows $300 for five months would end up repaying $980 when interest and fees are added. And by far, this is not the worst case. In other states it is possible to borrow $700 and wind up repaying $3,000 because of the escalating debt incurred by interest and fees.

Payday lenders often argue from both sides of their mouth when defending their exorbitant interest rates. From one side they say that APRs don't matter since payday loans are, by definition, short-term loans. From the other side they say they have to charge high APRs because they serve financially vulnerable communities. The reality for many borrowers is that they become trapped in cycles of increasing fees and interest that keep them paying on the loan for a very long time. It isn't uncommon to hear of folks taking out a payday loan because they can't afford the payments on an existing payday loan. (Yes, most states do allow folks to do that. Some states allow up to four "rollover" loans, and others set no limit on them.) According to Alex Horowitz, a senior research officer with Pew Charitable Trust's consumer finance project, "Right now, 80 percent of payday loans are taken out within two weeks of a previous payday loan because the loans on average take up one-third of the borrower's next paycheck."[15] This burden grows with each new loan. "The average payday loan customer pays $520 a year in fees to repeatedly borrow $325 in credit."[16]

As you would expect, in states that do not cap interest rates (Idaho, South Dakota, Texas, and Wisconsin), borrowers pay the highest rates. More recently states have begun to introduce caps on payday loan amounts and interest rates.[17] When the California legislature attempted to cap interest rates, they faced fierce opposition from payday loan lobbyists. The state failed five times in their efforts before finally succeeding in 2019. The new California legislation caps payday loans at $300 and interest rates at 460% APR.[18] Really. That's the good news after five failed attempts. This should offer insight into the amount of money being made and the power of the payday loan lobby. But the fight isn't over, and California legislators continue to advance plans to support consumers.

In Oakland, California, I talk with PL in his office at the nonprofit agency. He smiles as he takes in the boisterous laughing and clapping from a talent show in the next room that punctuates our conversation. As our conversation turns to payday loans, he rocks forward in his chair and draws a breath. "Emergency bills come up. Your car breaks down. A loved one gets sick. A family member needs some financial backing to get out of a bad situation." PL pauses and looks at his hands. "I don't have currency for that. So that, you know, entails me having to borrow money or get a payday loan." I ask PL what this is like for him. "It's been frightening. It's been disastrous, because I'm spending money that I already don't have, so it's been scary. It's been traumatic. I would not encourage anyone to do it." Lenders make their profit by counting on the reality that if people have no savings, chances are slim they will pay the loan off when it's due. "You could be paying double of what you borrowed just in two weeks" says PL. "That's why it's so hard to get out." Even the national trend among payday lenders to offer installment payments as an alternative to lump sum payments isn't necessarily the saving grace being promised. For example, Enova (with branches in more than thirty states and abroad in Brazil) advertises a $1,000 loan with thirteen payments at a 172.98% APR, which requires a total of $2,225.18 to pay off.[19] No one who has a choice would borrow money on these terms.

In 2019, Ohio legislators also fought back against the predatory practices of payday loan companies. Despite being outnumbered by industry lobbyists in the fight, the state prevailed and introduced comprehensive reforms. They reduced APR on payday loans from 677% to 28%; capped fees and interest at 60% of the loan principal; capped short-term loans at $1,000, and extended the repayment period to a ninety-one-day minimum and a one-year maximum.[20] The state also limited the outstanding principal a borrower can carry across several loans. This was a huge accomplishment, especially in light of California's reform. Yet campaign contributors and lobbyists continue to spend millions to resist meaningful change, precisely because they've been making so much money. Predatory loan practices target struggling communities, where people have few options. Like that $1 container of milk, what gets a family through in the short term can keep them stuck in hardship for the long run.

High-Interest Loans

Cars are expensive, whether you have a new car with a hefty payment schedule or swap out car payments for the inevitable repairs that come with older vehicles. In rural areas, folks face a catch-22: it's nearly impossible to get a job without a car and impossible to buy a car without a job. It's not just that the rural terrain makes owning a car a necessity. A century ago, the country abandoned investment in public transit in favor of private vehicles.[21] Since then, the high cost of car ownership has forced millions of people into debt. More people in the United States carry auto debt than ever before, and we owe more on our loans than ever before.[22] Nine of every ten vehicle purchases are financed.[23]

Auto debt has grown fastest among people between the ages of eighteen and twenty-nine.[24] Yet the cost of car ownership doesn't fall evenly. Shawn Rochester, a personal finance consultant, estimates that a Black driver will pay $1,100 more in purchase price, $500 more in loan interest, and an additional $500 a year on insurance premiums.[25] In addition, the costs fall hardest on people who are classified as "high-risk borrowers." Banks classify people as such if they have no credit, bad credit, or a high debt-to-income ratio. In consumer finance, when your debt is 33% of your income you are classified as a high-risk borrower. Since struggling families have low incomes, they are particularly vulnerable to having a high debt-to-income ratio. This classification means once again that you will pay more for less. And too often, you will pay yourself right into a deeper hole of debt.

My research for *Living on the Edge* takes me to Eastern Kentucky, the heart of coal country and some say of country music as well. Highway 23 in Eastern Kentucky is known as the Country Music Highway. The Sandy River Basin has been home to a dozen of country music's most famous artists including Loretta Lynn, Crystal Gayle, the Judds, and Chris Stapleton. The Sandy River is a tributary of the Ohio River that runs from Ohio to Kentucky and forms a state boundary between West Virginia and Kentucky. It wouldn't be an overstatement to say the Sandy River Basin defines the region both symbolically and geographically.

There are twenty-one counties in Eastern Kentucky that have struggled against persistent poverty for half a century.[26] They are classified by the Appalachian Regional Commission as distressed counties and all have 30% or more of the population living at or below the poverty line. From Floyd County I would need to drive *150 miles* to get out of deep poverty.[27] The median household income in this region is $18,711 – 66% lower than the national average.[28] If people of color are the face of poverty in urban areas of Kentucky, in rural communities, white women and children are the face poverty. In both cases, poverty is not always the result of unemployment. For example, in Prestonsburg, the seat of government for Floyd County, the U-3 unemployment rate was 7.5% before the pandemic, about twice the national average.[29] Yet *underemployment* is a serious issue driven by service industry jobs.

Jenna Terry is among the service industry workers in Eastern Kentucky. She was raised in Eastern Kentucky and has lived here for her entire life. She lives with Doug, her boyfriend of four years, and their two-year-old daughter. She beams with relaxed pride whenever she mentions their daughter. Jenna is in her late twenties and earns a pre-tax income of about $20,000 a year waiting tables five days a week – almost full-time. In Kentucky, this means she brings home about $16,851. Perhaps it goes without saying that she doesn't have health insurance, paid sick leave, vacation time, or a retirement plan. Although Jenna regularly works until 9 p.m., when the restaurant closes, she is lucky to have some flexibility in her hours. Depending on her childcare needs, she might start as early as 2 p.m. or as late as 5 in the afternoon. Doug has a job selling cars; he earns a base pay and commission. On the conservative side, their *combined* income is slightly above $40,000. This is twice the federal poverty line for a family of three ($20,780), but once again well under the self-sufficiency budget of $53,818 for a family of three in Floyd County.

It is especially worth noting that a self-sufficiency budget does not provide an allowance for debt. Like many struggling families, Jenna and Doug are struggling with mounting debt.

Even though they have trouble paying all of their bills each month, and haven't been able to accumulate any savings, Jenna describes her

MONTHLY COSTS

2 adults *and* 1 child
Floyd County, KY

HOUSING	$620
FOOD	$584
CHILD CARE	$452
TRANSPORTATION	$1,088
HEALTH CARE	$663
OTHER NECESSITIES	$486
TAXES	$592
Monthly Total	**$4,485**
Annual Total	**$53,818**

life as more economically stable than ever. This doesn't seem odd to her and I listen closely to try to understand. Jenna leans across the table and tucks a strand of curly blond hair behind her ear as she tells me, with a mix of pride and amazement, that she and Doug recently were able to secure enough financing to buy *two* cars. "I feel like this is a really big step, being able to purchase a car – let alone two, together. Our financial constraints have kind of been lifted a little bit in the last little while. We're not struggling as bad as we were before. We've kind of learned to somewhat budget a little bit, even though things happen. It kind of can ruin it sometimes, but I just think financially things have changed some, and it's a big weight off our shoulders when you can breathe for a minute financially." The sense of relief that Jenna feels is tangible. On this early Sunday morning, she looks both young and worn out. Seeing her relief, I am instantly happy for her. With two cars, they can manage two jobs between them and childcare arrangements. Yet the more Jenna talks about the cars, the more I begin to worry for her.

Jenna and Doug bought their first car a short while back. Like most other people with no credit or bad credit, they had limited financing options. They accepted the compounding, high-interest rate of a *personal* loan with OneMain Financial. "Oh, God, I hate it" Jenna tells me. "I wish we would have never done it." Jenna and Doug got into a financial bind and had trouble keeping up with the payments. As a consequence, they had to renew and renegotiate the terms of their initial loan. Then Doug got into an accident that totaled the car. They needed to continue to pay the loan on that car but now didn't have any way to get to work. "That's when we had to get our cars. I hate doing that because we've been in a couple of binds where we didn't know if we were going to pay our rent bill, or get groceries, that type of thing." Their income is the same as when they had trouble with payments on the first car loan. Now they are carrying three car loans – the first one that was refinanced and two more for the cars they just purchased. Again, Jenna and Doug weren't in a position to refuse whatever terms were offered to them. They worried that without the vehicles they could end up "living in really run-down places back in the hollers selling drugs to make money." It's a frightening reality for many and it made the loans seem worth a try.

Loan companies are typically called predatory lenders when their business is based on making high-interest loans to high-risk borrowers. These lenders often provide incomplete or confusing information to borrowers and charge inflated fees and added costs for their services. Predatory car loans can be economic quicksand even when everything goes right; for most families, everything does not go right for very long. Predatory lenders will push people further into dangerous levels of debt by offering them a chance to roll over their debt into a new loan.

In the short term, predatory lending practices provide immediate relief for people who are in desperate straits. The lenders count on the short-term thinking that financial stress creates. "I wouldn't ever suggest anybody do it," explained Jenna. "You're stuck with this payment for so long, and the interest is outrageous. It just isn't worth it. And then we took *another* loan because once you have made so many payments, you can borrow again, so the debt just keeps piling and piling and piling." OneMain Financial targets people who want to consolidate loans or purchase a vehicle.[30] Before the pandemic, they advertised "same day" loans up to $30,000 but in 2020 the website showed loans capped at $20,000. The company requires an origination fee on the loan and offers small monthly payments with compounding interest rates as high as 35.99%. In order to keep the monthly payments low, they extend the length of the loan – and increase their own profits. On the OneMain Financial website calculator, a sixty-month $5,000 loan at 35% interest repays $10,620. Jenna and Doug carry a loan rollover for the first car, two car loans for the subsequent cars, and under the weight of debt they took out another loan to help them make ends meet.

Loans from predatory lenders do not strengthen borrowers' credit as much as they bury them deeper in debt. Folks who are struggling on the economic margins are especially vulnerable to predatory lenders – which is exactly why so many of them set up shop in low-income communities. The rate of car loans in low-income communities has increased faster than car loans in any other community; between 2005 and 2017, loans in low-income neighborhoods increased by 49%.[31] In the fall of 2018, US households owed $1.26 *trillion* in auto loans; much of this debt belongs to people with weak credit ratings.[32] In the twenty-first century, forcing people into debt is a remarkably profitable business plan.

Auto loans have been essential for Jenna and her family; at the same time, these loans have compounded their economic vulnerability. Without an economic buffer, it is impossible to separate health issues from financial ones. In a world where the flu or a broken leg can threaten employment, Jenna lives with a diagnosis of lupus, an autoimmune disease that creates uncertainties of its own. In the struggling class, disaster seems to loom around every corner. But it's impossible to live with that kind of worry – no one can afford the burden of tomorrow when keeping food on the table is stressful enough today. And so, people in the struggling class decide they have to trust in the future – they have to have a sense of hope that makes no sense whatsoever on most days. Jenna and Doug didn't make bad choices from among a range of better, or even good, alternatives. They made the only decision they could that would allow them to continue to work. Predatory lenders are literally banking on exactly this.

The Devil's Bargain: Health Care

If the nation once saw Appalachia as a place out of time, Evangelical missionaries understood the people of Appalachia as being in need of spiritual, social, and economic uplift. They flocked to Appalachia driven by an understanding of the region as southern, white, and "unchurched."[33] Over decades, they have made an impact. To take a break from driving, I stop at a shop in a small town in Tennessee. The shopkeeper greets me and proudly explains that her store belongs to God. "I just mind it for him," she says with a great smile. Before I could blink twice, we are in a conversation about faith and I am asking about her relationship to the Bible.

"The Bible – start to finish – is the word of God."

"Old Testament and New?"

"Yes, word for word."

I'm a little unsettled by this but not surprised. She tells me she can see the spirit in me and asks about my own faith. I say I am Buddhist and I see her freeze. At first it looks like fear and then her face softens.

"Who do you pray to? What happens to your soul when you die?" Her questions tumble out. I answer them as best I can and then ask her my own question. "What is a soul?" She looks perplexed and pauses.

"The soul is what goes on when we die – it goes to heaven or to hell." I find this curious and ask, "Does the soul have a personality?" She is puzzled. Then decidedly answers that the personality is part of the body so must die with it. "Then what goes on?" She seems less certain and her answers grow vague. I see that each of us is equally unsatisfied by the answers to the other's questions. And still the conversation continues. Before I leave, she asks if she can pray over me. I agree and there in the middle of the afternoon, a few feet from the front door of her small store, she offers a prayer as kind and thoughtful as it was heartfelt and encompassing. I leave her store with a sense that I have arrived in Tennessee.

As in other places in Appalachia today, the presence of Native people in Tennessee is evident only in the names of rivers, lakes, and land they were forced to leave behind. The 1830 Indian Removal Act created The Trail of Tears, a 1,000-mile forced march from their homelands to Oklahoma. Today there are no federally recognized tribes in Tennessee or Kentucky. My first trip to Tennessee is in late spring. The poverty and the beauty of the region are both stunning.

It's not hard to find struggling communities. I spend time in counties that the Appalachian Regional Commission (ARC) classifies as "at risk." Logically, you might think this means "at risk of poverty," but you'd be wrong. They are already poor and at risk of becoming "distressed," a classification carried by the poorest 10% of counties in the nation.[34] In the "at risk" county of Overton, 17% of the population is at or below the federal poverty line but 71% of the population hovers just over the federal poverty line.[35] Throughout this county and many others, churches have stepped in where the government has left people behind, offering social activities, playgrounds for kids, family counseling, and sometimes economic assistance. I heard more than one Christian radio show taking up donations for a family in which the breadwinner had been in an accident and was unable to work.

There are 141 counties in Appalachia designated as "at risk" counties.[36] Fentress County is among them. The Fentress county seat of Jamestown is nestled in rolling hills covered with canopies of hardwood forests, just beyond the slow-moving Cumberland River. In Jamestown I am surprised by the presence of the West End Café

Cumberland River, Tennessee.

and I stop for coffee. It's a large room with long rows of tables and chairs that make it feel more like a church basement than a café to me, despite the presence of a few booths. Just behind the register stands an ordinary kitchen fridge with the Ten Commandments taped to the door. After taking a seat and waiting for my order, I overhear a woman in the booth behind me encourage another to file a complaint with the local school, because "it is against the law to teach children things that go against their faith." I draw a deep breath and head to the restroom.

Although there are two single-use bathrooms, one clearly marked for men and the other for women, an additional handwritten sign is taped to the women's room door: "Women only! NO MEN." Clearly, it's a political statement – one that fits in with the Christian slogans on T-shirts and posters that fill the café. Christianity seems to pervade even the most routine aspects of social life in this part of Tennessee – so much so, that even when I meet people who are not churchgoers, they still hold a worldview that is consistent with the social values of the local religion. Small-town life can have big consequences in personal relationships.

Across Tennessee, I met women who talked about the problems with their local school, their pride in the US military, and their anger

Café in Fentress County, Tennessee.

at NFL players who "take a knee." They also speak loudly about their antipathy toward President Trump and their resentment that responsibility for his election was laid at their doorstep. Some are still bitter that Al Gore lost to Bush junior in 2000 through a court decision rather than a clean election. I met men and women who were four or five years younger than me but who looked easily ten years older. The hardship of their lives was never the focus of any conversation but seem to lurk everywhere. In Tennessee, I spend a lot of time talking with people who did not want to talk about their lives.

Peter Walker agreed to talk with me in a taped interview. He is a thirty-two-year-old white man who lives in a county classified by the ARC as economically distressed. Even the main town in the county, like other towns in the region, has no grocery store, pharmacy, movie theater, bowling alley, or laundromat. Younger folks who want to have fun go out to the surrounding mountains, rivers, waterfalls, and lakes of the Cumberland Plateau.

Peter has a full-time job as a setup man in a stamping factory that makes things like big car parts. Being a setup man involves managing ropes of coiled steel as they go into and out of the dye press. "You've got to measure and put them in there, and you pull it through the decoil up at the press, and you put it inside the dye, and you hit 'em hard with stuff." Both of Peter's parents were factory workers and they tried to steer him away from it because the work was so hard on their bodies – the work comes with a lot of risks. But factory and mining jobs are the best paying in the region. The going rate for the work Peter does is about $18 an hour – in Tennessee that translates to about $37,440 before taxes, which puts him slightly above the EPI self-sufficiency budget of $33,197 for a single person in his county.

Peter's work pays well, but being a setup man is a dangerous job. "You get cut a lot, and I get metal shavings in my skin, hydraulic fluid [on me] – I'm allergic to that," he explains. "If you don't watch what you're doing, you can get killed or seriously hurt. One little slip, you could smash your finger, get your fingers cut off, anything, stuff flies and hits you in the face. I've seen a bunch of that happen to people. I've seen people get their hands caught in conveyer belts. A part will come down and clamp their hand in the belt and twist it and have their hand be cut open. It's dangerous."

Peter has been having a lot of pain that he thinks is the result of the machine he operates at work. Yet months after this pain came on, he is still refusing to see a doctor. "I have all kinds [of doctors] to choose from, but I'm a little hardheaded and stuff about going to doctors, because I like sticking it out. That's just a habit I got."

He has health insurance; he has access to doctors, so why not go? Peter explains that seeing a doctor requires making an appointment during business hours, which isn't easy to do for people who work in mines and factories – it generally means taking a whole day off work, which is either unpaid or vacation time. The nearest doctor is about forty-five minutes away – as is the nearest hospital. Once you see the doctor, you might get sent for tests, which means more time off work. Then there are co-pays (for Peter some of these are as high as $100) and insurance policy exceptions for tests, which may or may not make them unaffordable. After all the tests, there is then another day off work to go back to the doctor for the results. All of that happens before anyone starts to think about what the problem is or how to treat it. And then there is the fear factor: what if something is really wrong and he can't work anymore? Peter has enough sick time to cover the flu but not much else. "Everybody's like, you need to go and check yourself out, because you never know." Still, he refuses. Sometimes it's just easier to be hardheaded. To survive in the struggling class, you need to be self-reliant and resilient. A big dose of stubbornness also helps. But this isn't just an issue for Peter. Health care is hard to access for most people living in struggling communities.[37]

Our system of medical care makes it hard – if not impossible – for hospitals serving struggling communities to stay open. In rural areas throughout Appalachia, hospital closures are also rising. And of course, with every closure, thousands of workers are laid off. In Tennessee alone, eleven hospitals serving rural communities closed between 2010 and 2018.[38] As of this writing sixteen of Kentucky's rural hospitals are at risk of closing. Across the United States, 102 rural hospitals closed between January 2010 and March 2019.[39] And the rate of closures has worsened, with nineteen rural hospitals shuttering in 2019 alone.[40]

In a small rural community in Tennessee, I talk with Tommy, a white man in his mid-sixties; he's separated from his wife and has two grown up children. Over the course of his life, Tommy has had some very good jobs. One of them – working on oil rigs – gave him a chance to travel the world. Tommy quit the rigs when he nearly died from a severe illness. After a long stint in a hospital, he decided to go to school for a degree in nursing. Eventually, he found his way back to Tennessee and the land that has been in the family since the mid-1800s.

When we meet, Tommy is financially supporting four people in addition to himself. He doesn't elaborate on what this entails and I don't push. Tommy earns somewhere between $45,000 and $60,000 a year. In 2018, the federal poverty line for a *family of five* is $29,420 – but the self-sufficiency budget for a family of five in this county is about $83,000.[41] The county is economically distressed; more than 22% of the population live *below* the federal poverty line. Tommy has just opened a small business in a town of about 950 people – making it the fourth business in the community. In some ways it looks like he has a low-stress job – especially when compared to rig work and nursing. In other ways it looks very stressful. Tommy isn't sure he will be able to hang on to the business.

"We used to have a hospital in this little town, but it went bankrupt," Tommy squares his stance and places hands on hips as he talks. "There have been several companies that came in and bought the hospital. They were for-profit companies. The last company that owned it, they basically stripped the hospital of anything it had. That is one of the reasons why they have a hard time recruiting factories into this area." In communities where dollar stores seem to be everywhere, hospitals are always hard to come by. Without a local hospital, people in Tommy's town rely on the nearest regional medical center about twenty-five miles away.

Health troubles often strike in unpredictable ways, and in struggling communities the lack of access to health care is compounded by the increased risks of life-threatening illness. Obesity, diabetes, heart disease, kidney disease and liver disease are two to three times more common in people who have a family income less than $35,000 compared to those with family incomes of $100,000 or more.[42] Struggling communities also experience high risks for cancer, black lung disease, and asthma, diabetes, as well as drug addiction and substance abuse. The stress – not just the debt – compounds, contributing to a lower quality of health and to shorter lives.

Emergency medical services (EMS) are also closing in record numbers, making it harder to get to a regional medical center. Across the country, thirty-nine state health departments (including those in largely rural states) have declared EMS to be a non-essential service.[43] This classification enables counties to defund these services, making it even harder for people to access emergency care. For many women, even the ordinary event of pregnancy can hit hard. Recall Ellison Thompson from Standing Rock. Ellison ran into trouble with her first pregnancy and thought she was losing her baby. After calling for an ambulance, she waited a full hour for it to arrive. There just are not enough emergency service vehicles to cover the entirety of Standing Rock. The nearest emergency room for Ellison is a medical center at Fort Yates – just under thirty miles from her home. Ellison counts herself and her baby lucky to have survived.

Almost a thousand miles away from Standing Rock, Appalachian communities face similar circumstances for different reasons. Jenny Gaines worked as secretary for an organization in Ohio until it folded. More recently, she had the chance to do what she calls her "dream job" of running a small general store. The store sells work by local artisans, food made by local businesses as well as freshly made sandwiches and sides. Her husband also works and together they support two children on a pre-tax income of under $45,000. To put this in perspective, the federal poverty line for a two-parent, two-child household in 2018 was $25,100; a self-sufficiency budget for the same family in Athens County was $72,284. In Ohio, a gross salary of $45,000 produces an after-tax income of around $36,000. There's not much wiggle room in that budget, but even so Jenny and her husband have managed to save almost $1,000.

In struggling families, no one spends money without thinking. Jenny is careful with money and skilled at making the best use of what they have. Her days start early with walking the family dog, getting her two kids to school, and then swinging by the local grocery store to pick up last-minute items to supplement her regular produce delivery. She opens her small general store by 9 a.m. and by 2 p.m. is back on the road to collect her kids from school at 3. Jenny and

MONTHLY COSTS

2 adults *and* 2 children
Athens County, OH

HOUSING	$768
FOOD	$721
CHILD CARE	$981
TRANSPORTATION	$1,152
HEALTH CARE	$1,113
OTHER NECESSITIES	$601
TAXES	$687
Monthly Total	**$6,024**
Annual Total	**$72,284**

the kids then come back to the store where the children do their homework and hangout until closing. Business is slow and Jenny uses the store kitchen to cook dinner for the family, which she brings home when she closes shop at 8 p.m. It's a long day but Jenny has a talent for making the store a fun place to be, even as she strategizes to make resources go further.

Jenny tells me that yard sales are the department stores of the county. "We like to go to the yard sales. Yard sales are awesome, because down here like that's the clearing house of other people. You can get on to a good circuit of people who are just a size above your kids, and, you know, you can use some of their things, so we get a lot of hand-me-downs." To get to an actual department store you would have to drive about seventy-five miles to Columbus.

Jenny and her family prefer to make the 200-mile drive (one way) to Cleveland. "I'll tell you stories of the little kids going to the mall, and these are the big malls in Cleveland. I took my daughter to the mall the one time, and she said, 'Oh, my goodness, look at all these coats. Look at all these dresses. I'm in heaven,' and she's spinning around, and the ladies looked at us and said, 'Where are you guys from?' I said, 'Well, we're from southern Ohio.' They're like, 'Don't you have malls there?'" Jenny's daughter had never been in a department store, much less a shopping mall. They just don't exist in Southeast Ohio. Jenny explains: "I've had the same pair of jeans for the last seven years, you know. It doesn't matter, but if you go to Cleveland, that may not be the acceptable outfit."

In the days before Obamacare, she and her husband had medical insurance – maybe not the best, but the best they could afford. Having health insurance at that time distinguished them, by community standards, as part of the upper economic tier. "When I was having my daughter, I was old," says Jenny. This catches me off guard, her daughter is now in elementary school and Jenny is clearly not what I would call old. "I'm having my daughter at 35, and in the hospital in the room down from us there was a girl – she was 12 or 14 having a baby." Jenny tells me this is a familiar fate for children who are raised without enough – not enough food, not enough love. Living in a community where everyone knows everyone, Jenny pauses before deciding to go on. "She named her daughter Tequila." Jenny tells me she would see Tequila around town, her baby bottle filled with Mountain Dew and a sucker serving as a pacifier. "The dad maybe, boyfriend, would ride a bike down the street with the little baby under his arm like a football. You can get the visual, right?" Jenny shakes her head and sighs. Neither parent is old enough to drive yet they are living on their own. What options do they have? "But you know what? They're doing the best they can." This is a common mantra of the struggling class: doing the best they can. Yet rarely are these efforts enough.

Jenny sighs and starts again to tell the story of her own daughter's birth. She and her husband were planning for a future and working hard. Despite the fact that they were paying out of pocket for private insurance, the company made them jump through hoops at every turn. They didn't always know something wasn't covered until they looked at the bill. And then, Jenny tells me, there are the "things that you need but you can't get." Her family hasn't needed much, but sometimes even that little bit has been hard to come by. "Even just trying to have a baby was difficult, you know. I went into regular labor for like twenty-eight hours; then I had to have an emergency C-section, because the baby wouldn't come out." This was a success, but the insurance company declared it was a *scheduled* C-section – not an emergency one – and therefore was not covered by her policy. The cost of her daughter's birth was $30,000, and the family was left to negotiate that payment with the hospital. As many families know all too well, when the chips are down, insurance companies often walk away.[44]

While Obamacare helped to expand the number of people with health insurance, it was not intended to reform insurance plans or to address the rising costs of medical care. Between 1996 and 2016, health-care costs in the US doubled, and families are feeling it. Perhaps nowhere is this more obvious than when women give birth. Jenny's experience of being left with an enormous hospital bill after the birth of a child is not unusual – it isn't even the worst that can happen. In 2016, the *Guardian* reported on the Cavatore family in Houston, Texas. Elle Cavatore gave birth to twin premature baby boys who needed care in the neonatal intensive care unit. One of the twins required extensive medical care and died in a hospice at just seven months old. The loss of a child is horrific in any circumstance. While grieving their loss and caring for the twin who survived, the Cavatore family faced an avalanche of bills – one of which was for $1.1 million.[45]

According to the Centers for Disease Control and Prevention (CDC), more than half a million babies in the United States are born prematurely each year – that's about one in every eight births.[46] The key factors that increase the risk of having a preterm birth include poverty, late or no prenatal care, stress, and long working hours with long periods of standing. A mother's age and race are also factors, with African American women younger than seventeen and older than thirty-five being most at risk for having a preterm birth.[47]

African American women are also less likely to be taken seriously by doctors. Racism is a public health crisis that struggling families face in addition to medical debt. According to the Ohio Department of Health, the mortality rate for Black infants in Ohio is three times higher than for white infants.[48]

The medical debt incurred by having a baby can push a family into poverty and hold them there. A study published in the *American Journal of Public Health* found that two-thirds of all bankruptcies are related to medical care – that's 530,000 families going bankrupt each year because of illness or medical bills.[49] Obamacare has made no impact on this figure. This is a very hard reality even for families that have planned to have a child. Many others face the burden of an unexpected pregnancy that threatens an already vulnerable existence. In this context, it is notable that several states, including Texas, Arkansas, Kentucky, Mississippi, Indiana, and Utah, have sought to use the Covid-19 pandemic as an excuse to limit or completely curtail women's access to abortion by declaring service providers to be non-essential businesses and so forcing them to close.[50]

People in struggling communities also face obstacles to affordable treatment for medical problems that don't require hospitalization. In 2017, 61% of Americans could not meet a $1,000 emergency without going into debt.[51] You might recall from the Preface that in 2018 polls showed that between 65% and 80% of the population were living paycheck to paycheck. Before the pandemic, Federal Reserve reports on financial stability consistently found that 40% of the country could not afford even a $400 unexpected expense – not many medical problems are resolved for less than $400.[52] As a result, medical loan companies – which operate like payday lenders – flourish in struggling communities as families turn to them to cover medical expenses large and small.

Rose Taylor also lives in Ohio. You might recall her from the previous chapter. She works sixty-six hours a week split across two jobs, one as a certified nursing assistant and another doing body piercing. When we met, she was about to take out a medical loan for a dental problem. Rose is in good company when she calls medical loans "a necessary evil." Like payday loans, medical loans enable her to take care of health treatments she otherwise couldn't afford. "So the dentist office that I go to is aware of the economic situation [in Athens County]." As a consequence, Rose's dentist provides patients with medical loan information to help them with expenses. "Basically, it's like a credit card," says Rose, "but it's for medical expenses only. So you can call them, and they pull up your credit report and go through payment options." Rose, like many others, will use this line of credit to pay for her dental work.

There are two companies that provide medical loans in Northern Appalachia: OneMain Financial (the same company that financed Jenna's and Doug's car loans in Kentucky) and CareCredit. Since we already have an idea of how OneMain Financial operates, let's look at the CareCredit Health Care Credit Card. The company works with over 200,000 medical providers nationwide and offers medical loans starting at $200. Its credit card can be used for a wide range of expenses including dental, primary care, and diagnostics. According to the company's website, it can also be used for expenses including pet care, fitness, and spas.[53] When I read this, I think about Rose making that phone call from her dentist's office before she schedules her next appointment to fix an increasingly painful tooth.

As with all short-term, high-interest loans, the details are confusing – even if you are not in the middle of an emergency. And that's not by accident. In 2013, the Consumer Financial Protection Bureau ordered CareCredit to refund $34.1 million to borrowers because of "deceptive credit card enrollment practices."[54] CareCredit advertises so-called promotional periods that range from six to eighteen months, as well as financing up to twenty-four months. If Rose is offered a promotional period of six months, she will pay no interest if she makes her monthly payments and fully repays the loan within six months. This is, of course, exactly how Rose is thinking about the loan. Six months, interest free.

What is advertised as a promotional period is in fact a deferred interest plan – that's a very big and very bad gamble for struggling folks. If Rose borrows $900 for six months and can afford to pay $150 a month every month for six months, she pays no interest. As we have seen from the previous chapter, this is extremely unlikely. If Rose could do that, she would also have money in a savings account; she just doesn't have that much fat in her monthly budget. So, she likely will do what millions of borrowers do. She will make every single one of the *minimum* monthly payments during the "promotional period." These might be as low as $35, but those minimum payments mean that at the end of the six months she will not have paid off the loan in full. She will owe the outstanding balance, a late fee and retroactive, compounding interest of 26.99% *from the date of the loan origination*. You don't have to be a gambler to see that this is a stacked deck. With $23 billion in revenue in 2018, medical patient financing is projected to continue to grow.[55] I have to say again, there is a lot of money being made off of the backs of struggling people, all of whom get pushed deeper into debt as a result. This is just a snapshot of the health issues that come into view in casual conversations about ordinary lives.

It's impossible to separate the predatory businesses that target struggling communities from the economic and health struggles faced by people living in those communities. This chapter has offered a narrow look at some of the common business practices that prey on people by exploiting their financial distress. The problems however are even larger. Struggling communities not only suffer disproportionate instances of predatory lending, they also face greater instances of consumer fraud and unfair labor practices. Not only are people in struggling communities more likely to be the targets of abusive practices, they have less bargaining power and are less able to protect themselves. They are also least able to afford attorneys to take employers and businesses to court.

The High Price of Being Poor

Everyone makes poor decisions from time to time. Yet struggling families most often face a choice between two or more bad options. They can't *avoid* a poor decision. Being cash-strapped means the impact of those bad decisions cuts deeper, lasts longer, and makes both the choices and the consequences more visible to public view. In short, predatory practices ensure enormous profits for corporations by putting hardworking people in economic quicksand.

Poverty is a *product* of the current economic system – a product that makes a small group of people very rich. This reality is as old as the nation. It brings to mind an old story that I often heard told in Appalachia. A boss tells a coal miner to make sure he brings his mule out of the mine alive. The miner asks: "what about me?" To which the boss responds: "If the mule dies, I have to buy another one. I can always hire another worker." Workers are as disposable as the products they create.

The next chapter examines how predatory practices have contaminated the water, land and air in struggling communities, in order to generate massive profits for a small number of people who live in other parts of the country – sometimes in other countries entirely. In nearly every interview, environmental pollution was mentioned without prompting, and yet it was never a topic that people lingered over. In some ways it is easier to ignore than other more immediate issues, like keeping food on the table.

4

Sacrifice Zones: The Places We Call Home

"We don't want to talk to anyone," Two Lance Woman folds her arms. "We've talked enough." I've just arrived in Fort Yates on Standing Rock and Two Lance Woman is the first person I meet. She is weary from the long, arduous assaults on the Water Protectors at Standing Rock. Weary from the attacks by dogs and armed troops. Weary from battles in biased courts. Weary from the media barrage that seemed to change nothing. I nod and wait quietly. Perhaps it is the force of her anger that leads her to break the silence: "Why do we have an environmental justice movement?" I keep eye contact but say nothing. "Because there is no concern with justice in the government or corporations. Imagine living in your ancestral homelands and you see fracking and uranium mining. The agencies that are supposed to protect us don't think about our exposure to toxins. Our views are not held as valid or as important. We live in a sacrifice zone – I live next to a nuclear weapons plant. Because we are poor, we are less likely to resist anything that creates jobs." She is exactly right.

Across lands including those of the Lakota, Shoshone, and Arapaho nations, water aquifers are contaminated by fracking and oil pipelines. In other parts of the country, uranium and copper mining industries have dumped uranium, arsenic and heavy metals into landscapes and aquifers. In Appalachia, entire towns have been lost to toxic waste. And in Oakland, California, lead contamination poisons children at rates higher than those of Flint Michigan.

If it seems surprising to find a chapter on environmental contamination in a book about families trying to make ends meet, consider that the most toxic environments in the country are consistently those that struggling families call home. This isn't an accident, and it can profoundly affect the health and well-being of residents. This chapter takes a look at the background of environmental degradation and contamination that undermines the health, well-being, and safety of people who live in struggling communities – as well as those who live downstream from them.

Lead Contamination in Oakland, California

Once home to both General Motors and Chrysler, Oakland was the Detroit of the West. It was home to companies producing engines, cars and tractors, as well as to shipping and canning industries. Manufacturing plants in Oakland provided blue-collar jobs with wages that could support a family well. But after the Second World War those industries began to leave, and by the 1980s the city had become unrecognizable to many. Oakland continued to lose industrial jobs over the next thirty years, leading to high unemployment rates and leaving behind toxic chemicals as well as carcinogens found in paint, solvents, and asbestos. All of those toxic contaminants remain. This section will focus on just one: lead.

There is no safe amount of lead. It can cause learning and developmental disabilities, decreased IQ, behavioral problems, stunted growth, and kidney problems, among a host of other complications.[1] So, when Irina Dessaint found her eighteen-month-old daughter with paint chips in her mouth, she immediately asked her pediatrician for a lead test.[2] When the results showed a blood level of 59 micrograms per deciliter, Irina and her husband rushed their daughter to the hospital. Irina's family was lucky in that the hospital was able to reduce her daughter's lead levels quickly, although months later, at 8 micrograms per deciliter, it is still too high. Children with a blood lead level as low as 5 micrograms per deciliter – the acceptable level of toxicity set by the Centers for Disease Control and Prevention – still show signs of lead poisoning.[3]

In Oakland 6% of children have elevated levels of lead in their blood – that's almost twice the national average. According to the Alameda County Health Department, in Oakland's Fruitvale District, 7.57% of children have elevated levels.[4] The Fruitvale District, just southeast of downtown Oakland, is home to the city's largest Indigenous and Latinx communities. It is one of 3,000 neighborhoods in the country with higher levels of lead contamination than Flint, Michigan.[5]

The dangers of lead have been well known and widely documented for at least three centuries. Benjamin Franklin wrote about lead toxicity in the 1700s; in the 1800s lead pipes used in plumbing were identified as a source of poisoning, and by 1859 the first widespread health concerns were raised.[6] The Sherwin Williams Company published a study in 1904 that demonstrated the toxicity of lead in paints.[7] Leaded gasoline was known to be poisonous the day it was invented in 1921, yet companies used it despite there being an ethanol option.[8] Prominent research produced concerted efforts to ban the use of lead pipes in the 1920s, and many cities began to prohibit or restrict their use.[9] In response, in 1928 manufacturers formed the Lead Industries Association, which soon became a powerful lobby that ensured lead products *would* be used, despite the scientific evidence of its health hazards. As a result, lead pipes were not banned until 1986.[10]

The toxicity of lead has never been a secret, and the continued use of it despite this knowledge reflects a set of values shared by businesses and government. The use of lead reveals more than collusion between government and industry to place profits over public health. If it was about just greed and disregard, we would find levels of lead toxicity spread relatively evenly across the nation. But this is not the case. A growing number of studies show that low-income communities, especially those of color, are exposed to higher levels of lead paint, air pollution, hazardous waste, and Superfund Cleanup sites than their wealthier white counterparts.[11] Highly polluting industries avoid communities that have the political capital to challenge them.

In 2017 Oakland tested forty-seven of its eighty-seven school sites and found that lead contamination levels exceeded federal standards in seven schools.[12] Lead plumbing, common to old buildings, contaminates all of the water that runs through it. In 2018 Oakland Unified School District estimated that it would cost $38 million to address the problems with faucets and water lines in schools.[13] However, by 2019, elevated levels of lead were being found in the buildings themselves, in soil under the buildings, and even under pavements around the schools. Estimates of how many billions of dollars it would take to gradually remove lead from schools vary widely, but some experts believe that doing so could *save* as much as $84 billion annually in relation to the health care, education, and behavioral problems of children harmed by lead each year.[14] In Oakland, lead contamination is part of the ordinary landscape, like the air. Struggling communities suffer the brunt of contamination and receive the least amount of remediation. Companies have made a lot of money by using lead in their products. Not one of them is financially responsible for the enduring public health crises they've created. Government intervention has been both slow and limited.[15] Struggling families are left on their own to deal with the health consequences.

Extractive Industries

For centuries, the federal government allowed companies to extract natural resources at little or no cost to themselves and without responsibility for the environment. Most people know this happens on publicly held lands; for example, the government has long allowed drilling for oil in some coastal waters. Less commonly known is that in Appalachia, so-called "broad form land deeds" have enabled companies (most of them out of state) to own all of the mineral wealth beneath the surface of the land, while residents simultaneously own the surface land. Since property taxes are assessed on the surface land, broad form deeds gave corporations tax-free access to the minerals below.[16] Most significantly, this arrangement allowed corporations to remove the resources under the surface *by whatever means necessary*. The deeds included clauses that exempted corporations from all harm to streams, flood plains, and aquifers, and left owners of the surface land to cope with the mess of toxic pollution and environmental degradation caused by mining.[17] Broad form deeds are no longer used, but the coal industry's past use of them laid the groundwork for the oil and gas industries.[18]

Today, legislation that separates surface rights from mineral rights has been advanced by the oil and gas industries, but under a new name and with slightly different rules. The US Bureau of Land Management (BLM) now refers to these arrangements as split estates or co-tenancies. The corporations that lease or purchase mineral rights are allowed to occupy as much of the surface land as is needed for extraction. The laws allow them to frack and drill in a region as long as 75% of the people who own the surface rights in that region agree – the remaining 25% of landowners are thus forced to allow drilling and fracking.[19] This is the case regardless of how much property is owned by each of the landowners. Consequently, people who live in affected areas are more likely to refer to "forced pooling" rather than split estates.

It's easy to see the appeal of leasing or selling mineral rights among vulnerable people in low-income communities. But the costs are often unimaginable. Resource extraction often leaves communities without access to clean water and in some cases makes entire towns uninhabitable. In 2020, Donald Trump nominated William Perry Pendley, then acting head of the BLM, to serve permanently. In the five books he has written, Pendley argues against so-called "environmental extremists," endangered species protections, and Native treaty rights and in favor of private property and private industry. According to the Western Values Project, a public lands and accountability nonprofit, in the early 1980s Pendley as acting assistant secretary for energy and minerals under President Ronald Reagan sought to delay the oil and gas industry royalty payments owed to Indigenous people.[20] The problems with the BLM didn't start in 2020 and they are not the exception to the rule. We'll take a look at a few practices on the Wind River and Standing Rock reservations as well as in Appalachia.

Wind River Reservation

The 600-mile drive from the rolling plains of Standing Rock to the Wind River Reservation in Wyoming passes through parched, high mountain desert spotted with dry buttes and oil rigs. The natural landscape is sparse and gorgeous. The land feels as open and as limitless as the sky. In the distance, the Wind River Mountain Range rises abruptly from a broad, flat valley. Horses calmly graze in pastures below the snow-tipped mountains. The first snows reach the mountains in mid-September; in another week snow will fall in the valley as well. The beauty of this land is as dramatic as it is stunning, and the history of the area is as important as the landscape.

It's impossible to talk about where Native peoples live today without going back to the more than 500 treaties made between the US government and the governments of Indigenous nations. The treaties were legal agreements regarding land boundaries, sovereignty, and freedom. The US government broke every single one of them. It isn't just that Native people ceded land lost in battle; land theft has been an ongoing and strategic practice of the federal government.[21] And it is not a practice relegated to the past.

Initially the US military forced Native people into areas that were thought to be desolate and barren. As it turned out, many reservations were established on land that has rich deposits of oil, gas, and minerals. However, the US government holds what is called plenary power over all Native tribes or nations. Plenary power divests parties other than the federal government of all rights. For example, it gives the government the right to break any treaty with Native tribes without review or consent.[22] It is a political power that has been

Wind River Reservation, Wyoming.

exercised by Congress since the formation of the US government and is supported by the Supreme Court.

In 1867, three years after the horrific Sand Creek Massacre,[23] the federal government forced the Eastern Shoshone onto a reservation in the Wind River Valley in the hope that the raiding tribes would attack the reservation rather than the mining camps.[24] By the treaty of July 3, 1868, the Shoshone relinquished a larger reservation that crossed Colorado, Utah, Idaho, and Wyoming and accepted the land known as the Wind River Reservation.[25] However, in 1878, the federal government broke the treaty by relocating all Northern Arapaho onto the Wind River Reservation and forcing all Northern Arapaho children into a boarding school on the Shoshone Reservation – a move they claimed to be temporary. Members of the Northern Arapaho and the Eastern Shoshone will happily tell anyone who is interested that they have a very long history of being fierce enemies. For example, Oralia, an Arapaho, explains as a matter of fact: "I think the federal government hoped that the two tribes would actually kill each other off, because we were mortal enemies. They've [the US government] always tried to kill us off."

The Shoshone believed the federal government wrongly gave their land to the Arapaho and took their case to court. In 1938, the Supreme Court ordered a multi-million-dollar settlement for lands ceded north of Wind River.[26] A subsequent land deal solidified the Arapaho claim to land on the Wind River Reservation. Even now, boundaries remain in dispute and the implications may be more important than ever, given rights of taxation and criminal justice, as well as water rights.

In 1887, the US government illegally applied the General Allotment Act, also known as the Dawes Act, to the Shoshone Reservation, which enabled the federal government to assign parcels of reservation land to white homesteads.[27] On the surface, the Dawes Act claimed to promote individual family-based economic independence and break up more communally-based tribal relationships. In reality, more than half of all reservation lands were sold to non-tribal persons.[28] Having lost a substantial amount of their land-based resources, people on the reservation also faced hunting prohibitions, meager rations, and deadly epidemics of tuberculosis and measles. By 1905, a second McLaughlin Agreement allowed an influx of white settlers to establish the town of Riverton on reservation land.[29] The settler towns and farms of Pavillion, Kinnear, and Midvale were also established on land designated by the 1868 treaty. In 2018 the Supreme Court reviewed a case in which the Eastern Shoshone and Northern Arapaho tribes argued that Riverton was within the boundaries of the Wind River Reservation and therefore a part of it.[30] The Court, however, preserved the boundaries of the 1905 agreement which allowed white settlers to claim this land.[31] This history is far from complete, but it sets the context for the way towns have developed and extractive industries, particularly oil and fracking, have encroached.

Today, the Wind River Reservation has a population of about 26,000. Most homes in Wind River are scattered across a wide valley. The area is also home to small towns of about 500 people;

Wind River Reservation, Wyoming.

Riverton, with a population just over 11,000, is the biggest town around. Even so, I arrive in Riverton to the news that the town's only chain grocery store, Safeway, is closing its doors. For the foreseeable future, the town will rely on a Walmart and a large local market for grocery shopping. I leave the wide lanes and traffic signals of Riverton behind as I drive north on Route 132 to the town of Ethete. Ethete is a young community (median age twenty-six) with about 1,500 residents.[32] However, before I actually see the town, the map program on my phone chirps to tell me I've passed it. I would drive through Ethete three more times before seeing it. On my fourth approach, I pull to the side of the road to check the map. My car idles in front of an old wooden house that seems to be collapsing where it stands. The doors and windows are boarded over; the land around it looks like a local junk yard. But before I can sort out my map troubles, a very aggravated man pulls up behind me – this is his home, and I am blocking his driveway. I apologize and move on, still looking for Ethete.

The community that my map program located as the heart of Ethete turns out to be a small circle of boarded up homes – some in use and some not. Across the street stands the real heart of Ethete: a large parking lot with a laundromat, a gas station/convenience store, and a check cashing outlet that also serves as an embroidery store. Nearly 20% of Ethete residents live at or below the federal poverty line.[33] For perspective, according to the US Census the national poverty rate in 2019 was 10.5%.[34] As I continue on from Ethete toward Fort Washakie I pass a church, a Shoshone Cultural Center, and small communities of newer prefab homes with metal roofs and single-wide mobile homes. Fort Washakie looks more prosperous than Ethete, even though it has a much higher poverty rate of 30%.[35] The population of 1,823 people is young, with a median age of twenty-five.[36]

I reach a small cluster of businesses on Highway 287: The Wind River Trading Company, a post office, and the Hines General Store. The businesses feel like a prosperous oasis, with local shoppers from the reservation using the General Store and post office and tourists enjoying the Trading Company. I imagine that Highway 287 gets a significant amount of traffic heading southwest to Lander, a town of about 7,500 people that serves as a hub for tourists exploring the nearby national park and for people with expensive second homes in the foothills.

In addition to the shops at Fort Washakie, the reservation is home to two small casinos. Employment options are extremely limited, even in the surrounding towns of Landers and Riverton. When people face extremely limited economic opportunities, extractive industries offer the promise of survival, if not growth. For more than seventy years, oil and gas leasing has been a source of income for the Wind River Reservation. Arapaho and Shoshone lease parts of the reservation land to about thirty oil companies. Though few tribal members have prospered from the leases, the uneven source of income has been critical to the economic survival of some families. Among tribal members, rumor and suspicion of oil theft as well as claims of government mismanagement have been nearly constant. This is no wonder, given both the history of the federal government and its function in overseeing leases. The US government is a trustee of the tribes, which means it is responsible for managing all reservation lands. Federal law requires that Wind River leases be approved by the federal government; the US Geologic Survey then collects royalties, and the Bureau of Indian Affairs distributes them.[37] While this might sound like a paper nightmare from the start, it's also logistically next to impossible. In this division of responsibilities, the US Geologic Survey is charged with supervising production to detect theft, but their grossly understaffed office is nearly 200 miles from some of the drill sites.[38]

Resource theft of Native land, water and minerals has been both common and relentless. In most complaints, the federal government moves so slowly that it appears to be stonewalling. Corporations deny all claims, leaving tribal members to either drop the matter or hire their own investigators. The Arapaho and Shoshone tribes have done just that whenever possible. The work of one private investigator lead to an FBI investigation and a subsequent lawsuit in 1979 claiming federal mismanagement of their mineral rights.[39] The tribes charged that the federal government failed in its oversight in multiple ways, including undervaluing minerals, failing to terminate leases that weren't producing, failing to collect rental payments, improperly spending the money that was collected, and failing to compensate the tribes adequately for the resulting environmental degradation.[40]

Decades later, in 2014, they received a settlement of $157 million.[41] For the Wind River Reservation, the settlement went to legal fees, payments to tribal governments, and the creation of a $10 million fund to clean up the pollution caused by the oil and gas companies. Tribal members each received between $6,000 and $15,000, which was largely spent off of the reservation in businesses owned by non-Natives.[42] While this lawsuit was an enormous victory, an investigation by *The Arizona Republic* in 1987 found that between the years 1979 and 1986, the federal government allowed oil and gas operators to report their estimated production based on an honor system, which cost tribal nations an estimated $5.8 billion in royalties.[43] If that money had gone into the settlement of the case, it would have increased the award by a multiple of four.

Given the way the federal government oversees Indian affairs and the way white settler communities have been established on reservation land, it's easy to understand why tribal members are in constant conflict with the federal and state governments over land and water rights. In Riverton, I meet a white woman named Marge who tells me that she lives in Pavillion and makes a forty-minute drive every day to a housekeeping job. Marge says with great pride that I really need to see Pavillion. "It's a real cowboy town!" she beams. Foolishly, I ask what she means. Marge flashes a look that lets me know immediately this is a really dumb question. "Well once a year they have a cattle drive that goes right through the middle of town." I smile and nod. It is one of the many times that I emerge as a somewhat hapless outsider. But it wasn't the cattle run that caught my attention.

Pavillion is a small town, home to 421 people according to the local welcome sign; 230 according to the 2010 US Census figures.[44] In either case, the population appears to be 95% white. In a community filled with well-kept single-wide trailers, it also has a post office, a school and a store. What really sets Pavillion apart from comparable communities I have visited is that the store has a restaurant/café – a small sign of disposable income that can be hard to find in struggling rural communities.

Even more surprising perhaps is the fact that the town is ringed by four churches and there are nine more just a short distance away. Pavillion takes up only about twelve square miles but is the site of 169 gas wells. Some of these are within 500 feet of homes.[45] In the 1990s, when oil and gas development began to boom in the area, residents of Pavillion started complaining about tainted water, attributing numerous health problems and the deaths of their animals to fracking contaminants. Many years later, in 2011, the Environmental Protection Agency (EPA) released an *initial* study reporting that the water supply to the town and the surrounding area was contaminated. However, the state of Wyoming quickly intervened and forced the EPA to shut down its study and turn over all water samples.[46] The state subsequently issued a report claiming there was no proof of contamination. Both the Northern Arapaho and Eastern Shoshone tried to intervene to stop the EPA from relinquishing the investigation, but to no effect.[47]

In 2012, the Wyoming legislature agreed to provide $750,000 for cisterns for residents who request them, and the gas company Encana provided $72,000 for potable water to fill them.[48] Marge uses water from a cistern for her house but continues to use the groundwater for her chickens, horses and garden. With that sparkle of pride, she tells me that Pavillion residents will get free water delivery for five years. I ask what happens in five years. "Well, then we're on our own." Wes Martel, a member of the Eastern Shoshone Business Council, isn't ready to stop fighting. "We can live without oil and gas," said Martel. "We can't live without water."[49]

A private study by Stanford University in 2016 confirmed that fracking had indeed contaminated Pavillion's groundwater with dangerous levels of toxic chemicals.[50] The Stanford study also found that the fracking in Pavillion is being conducted in shallow areas – despite public claims to the contrary. Shallow fracking injects millions of gallons of highly toxic chemicals very close to public aquifers. The Wyoming Oil and Gas Commission conducted its own study of gas wells in the Pavillion area and offered a competing explanation of the contamination: more than half of the 169 wells have incomplete casings. While the fracking and oil industries debate which source is to blame for the contamination, the Wind River Formation aquifer is so filled with contaminants that some scientists believe it cannot be cleaned up.

Northern Appalachia

The environmental and public health devastation in coal country is hard to overstate, yet it rarely makes the news in any prominent or consistent way. Mountain top removal, strip mining, and coal-fired power plants have destroyed land, water, and air quality in the region. Slurry ponds frequently create devastating and immediate crises. Sludge or slurry is the name for toxic waste created when coal is washed to separate it from rocks and dirt. The slurry is a mix of rock, water, and mud that carries arsenic, mercury, chromium, cadmium, and selenium – for starters.[51] These are the same heavy metals that are present in coal. Coal mining generates millions of tons slurry each year and coal industries use the cheapest way of handling it, which is to build containment ponds. Because the ponds are not lined, these heavy metals inevitably seep into groundwater and local waterways; and, of course, the dams holding the ponds fail with some regularity. For example, in 2014, a coal slurry spilled in the Elk River, West Virginia, and made its way into the Charleston main water treatment plant.[52] This spill contaminated the entire water supply of the Kanawha Valley, spanning five counties and affecting one sixth of the population of West Virginia, leaving everyone without potable water.[53]

In another of a long line of coal slurry breaches, the West Virginia breach of March 2017 spilled 5,400 gallons of slurry into Drawdy Creek.[54] This spill left everyone in St. Albans and Lincoln counties without potable water. Even a few hours away in Washington, DC, news of these spills never seemed to enter public awareness. They received little national or regional attention even though they devastated entire communities. Studies like those by Michael Hendryx, a public health researcher at Indiana University, consistently find that residents of West Virginia's mining counties were more likely than folks in non-mining communities to suffer from cancer, kidney disease, obstructive lung diseases, birth defects, high blood pressure, and a shortened life span.[55] The coal mining industry not only contaminates the local watershed, it also contaminates the air with heavy metals.

You might recall from Chapter 2 that on my way to Athens County, just north of the large S bend in the Ohio River where Ohio, Kentucky, and West Virginia meet, I found a scene that looked like it came from *The Twilight Zone*. This was once home to the village of Cheshire and over 450 people. In 2000, just over 200 remained,[56] when a toxic, blue haze of sulfur trioxide from the coal plant descended on the village.[57] The haze would settle over Cheshire for days, causing headaches, sore throats, and respiratory problems. The CDC found sulfur compounds in the air that were five times the level that will cause an asthma attack.[58] In 2002, after years of complaining and a pending lawsuit, American Electric Power, the company that operates the large coal-fired power plant, offered to pay residents up to three times the value of their homes – on the condition that they signed away their rights to sue the company for health problems.[59] Most people took the deal. American Electric Power bought the riverside village for $20 million. It was not made to stop polluting or to compensate for the pollution it produces.[60] The company did not admit any responsibility and claimed it was motivated only by a desire to expand the plant – which it never did. The plant continues to burn about 35,000 tons of coal every day.[61] Corporations have a long history throughout the nation of exactly this kind of unaccountable behavior.[62] It's cheaper for companies to pay fines than to follow the law and fix the problems.

Ohio alone had at least twenty-five more towns that were destroyed by the industries that built them.[63] In West Virginia, the coal industry also built and destroyed a similar number of towns.[64]

Five of the older sites are now advertised by the state as tourist attractions: "ghost towns" in the "wild wonderful west." Ironically, yet predictably, Ohio and West Virginia were among the twenty-one states that challenged the EPA's efforts to *limit* power-plant emissions of dangerous toxins such as mercury.[65]

The case was heard in the Supreme Court, which in 2015 ruled against the EPA and in favor of the states.[66] In a divided Court, the conservative majority set aside the EPA regulations on plant emissions because the EPA didn't balance the costs nearly enough in their rule-making process. Justice Scalia, writing for the Court majority, argued: "One would not say that it is even rational, never mind 'appropriate,' to impose billions of dollars in economic costs in return for a few dollars in health or environmental benefits."[67] In other words, the conservative justices sympathized with the corporations and seemed eager to find ways to protect them from costly regulations designed to prevent life-threatening illness and lasting environmental contamination.

Justice Elena Kagan's dissent explained that the EPA had conducted a formal cost-benefit study and found that the benefits of its regulation included as many as 11,000 fewer premature deaths annually, along with a far greater number of avoided illnesses. These benefits would exceed the cost to power plants by as much as $80 billion each year.[68] However, the Court's decision left it to the *local communities*, not the corporations, to deal with the health and environmental costs. The case was sent back to the lower courts with a demand that the EPA account for business costs, which it did. Instead of backing up the EPA regulations, however, the Trump administration used the case as an excuse to weaken Obama-era rules that had limited mercury emissions from coal power plants. As a presidential candidate, Trump promised: "My first day in office I am going to order a review of every single regulation in the last 10 years – all needless job-killing regulations will be cancelled."[69] While there is little evidence that regulations "kill jobs," Trump kept his promise to cut regulations.[70]

It's clear to see that elected officials and courts – even the Supreme Court – have served the interests of the mining industry over the interests of residents and the environment. The people who can least afford health care, and have the least access to it, are made to live in the most polluted environments. There's a temptation to blame struggling community members for voting in favor of the politicians and judges who allow this. In regions where there is very little work, people have always pragmatically supported industries that provide employment – perhaps with the belief that corporations, government or the courts would protect them from the hazards of the industry. Or perhaps they simply don't have the luxury of a better option. In any case, the nation has remained silent as entire populations have been rendered disposable.

Central Appalachia

Tennessee is a gorgeous state characterized by three distinct geographical features: Eastern Tennessee by the Blue Ridge Mountains; Central Tennessee by the Cumberland Plateau; and Western Tennessee by the Mississippi floodplains. Both the Blue Ridge Mountains and the Cumberland Plateau are dominated by breathtaking mountains covered in hardwood forests, winding roads that hug rivers and lakes, and waterfalls tucked into all of it. If you haven't been to Tennessee, it's impossible to anticipate its natural beauty. Beneath the stunning beauty of the region are vast natural resources that drew extractive industries to the area. Although the Cumberland Plateau is state land, the Tennessee Valley Authority and mining companies hold the underlying coal rights. Very few landowners also own the mineral rights to their property.[71] As a result, the ecology of the Cumberland Plateau has been profoundly threatened.[72] "Mountaintop removal has cost the region 500 mountain peaks and destroyed or damaged more than 1,500 miles of streams."[73]

Coal ash is among the many forms of pollution created by the coal industry. When coal is burned to create electricity, it generates enormous amounts of residue, called ash. As with slurry, the industry has chosen the cheapest way to deal with this toxic waste: they mix it with water and pour it into ponds. Like slurry ponds, ash ponds contain heavy metals that seep into the groundwater and local waterways. There are about twenty-five coal ash ponds in the southeast that are classified by the EPA as high hazard – meaning that if the containment wall breaks, there is a high likelihood of fatalities.[74]

In 2008, the largest coal ash disaster to date happened at the Kingston Fossil Plant in Roane County, Tennessee, when a retaining wall collapsed releasing *more than a billion gallons of toxic material* into two rivers.[75] The disaster was declared a Superfund Cleanup Site and cost the federal government over one billion dollars to clean up. Regulations to secure coal ash waste were finally implemented in the Obama years but were rolled back by the Trump administration, which no longer requires groundwater monitoring at all sites. In 2019 Tennessee had over thirty water systems with unsafe levels of contaminants.[76]

The mineral-rich Cumberland Plateau extends from Tennessee northward through Eastern Kentucky. In Kentucky, where 800,000 adults and 25% of all children live in poverty by federal standards,[77] coal promises prosperity – at least for some. The annual salary for coal miners in this region is about $83,000.[78] But according to state figures, in the first quarter of 2019 there were just under 4,000 working miners in Eastern Kentucky, down from more than 15,000 just a decade ago.[79] The loss of these jobs has meant that most people in Eastern Kentucky now work in low-wage jobs. It's easy to see the appeal of mining for local workers.

It isn't just that coal miners are losing their jobs, entire communities go down with them, and with the communities, entire regions. As opportunities are lost, so are generations, who no longer see a future for themselves. High rates of teenage pregnancy, poor access to prenatal care, and a host of problems around substance abuse flourish in environments where people lack the dignity of decent employment. In this context, voters in the region think about the interests of their potential employers when they cast their ballots. People vote in favor of political commitment to industry in hopes of gaining employment. But the relationship between politicians and corporations in any region also undermines regulations regarding health, safety and the environment, at great cost to workers and generations of residents.

The region is known for its coal fields and country music. But it might also be defined by its lack of regulation and environmental protection. The absence of logging regulations on private land, the lack of zoning ordinances, and the expansion of strip mining have created periodic flooding and persistent disasters.[80] The region continues to suffer from the destructive effects of mining, most especially on water. Meanwhile, residents continue to complain about the ineffectiveness of legislation. The failure of regulators to enforce existing mining laws has been tragically illustrated throughout history. In October 2000, a 2.2 billion-gallon coal slurry pond owned by Martin County Coal Company/Massey Energy (MCC/ME) in Martin Country, Kentucky, collapsed and spilled 300 million gallons of toxic coal sludge containing heavy metals (including mercury, lead, arsenic, copper, and chromium) into the Big Sandy River and Tug Fork, contaminating the drinking water for eighty miles downstream.[81]

The spill was thirty times larger than the Exxon Valdez disaster that dumped 12 million gallons of oil into the ocean.[82] Yet unlike the Alaskan disaster, few people have heard of it. Most locals didn't even know there was a coal slurry reservoir in the mountains until

Downtown Paintsville, Kentucky. Legendary country music singer-songwriter Chris Stapleton grew up in a small community just outside of Paintsville. I wasn't in town for five minutes before locals were telling me about Stapleton's high school days and recent sightings of the megastar.

it broke. It turns out to be one of hundreds of slurry ponds in the local mountains. The Union of Concerned Scientists accused political appointees in the Bush administration of preventing a full investigation and of covering up the damage.[83] MCC/ME had received eight or nine outstanding mining violations since 1994, three of which had been classified as "willful or negligent."[84] Yet in 2000 MCC/ME declared the Martin County rupture an unpredictable "Act of God." Elaine Chao, wife of Senator Mitch McConnell (R-KY) was appointed by the Bush administration as Secretary of Labor to oversee the Mine Safety and Health Administration (MSHA). Under her leadership the number of violations for this spill was reduced from eight to two (one of which was dropped); MCC/ME paid a federal penalty of $5,600.[85] In 2018 residents affected by the spill still couldn't use tap water.[86]

The Natural Resources Defense Council had reported in 2015 that 53% of people across Kentucky were getting water from utilities that had at least one violation of federal safety standards – making it second in the nation only to Puerto Rico (69%).[87] Counties in the eastern coalfields rank in the lowest 10% for life expectancy in the United States.[88] For all the corporate profit that's been skimmed off of this land, it's a bitter way to leave the people who live there. Everyone living in the region is left to cope with the environmental contamination and the illnesses it creates.

In face of the job losses in the coal industry, prisons have sold themselves as an economic savior to counties with high rates of poverty and unemployment. But there is little about prison systems as opportunities for economic growth that makes any sense – outside of the pork barrel environment of Washington, DC. Eastern Kentucky was planning its fourth federal prison, the 2,100-bed US Penitentiary Letcher.[89] Even as the US Penitentiary Big Sandy began to sink – because it was built directly on top of a former coal mine – plans were underway to build USP Letcher on top of an old coal mine.[90] People incarcerated in prisons are invariably too far away from family. Yet rural prisons are built far from airports and in regions without any form of public transportation, making it very difficult for family to visit. According to the Sentencing Project, national statistics show that 63% of the 1,200 beds at USP Letcher would have been filled by parents with children and 84% of inmates would have been more than 100 miles from home.[91]

Activists in Eastern Kentucky responded to the prison projects with several prison abolition movements as well as a media arts and education project at Appalshop, "Holler to the Hood," that connects the communities where prisoners are housed with the communities where prisoners lived. A mix of local activists in the prison abolition movement, environmental groups, and their attorneys successfully shut down the plans for USP Lechter. In 2021, the federal government withdrew all funding.[92]

The budgeted cost of Letcher prison was $510 million, which would have made it the most expensive federal prison ever built.[93] We need to be clear that these prison projects are about the well-being of corporations and politicians. The state websites for Kentucky, Tennessee, Virginia, and West Virginia advertise salaries for correctional officers ranging between $22,584 and $26,028. Keep in mind that in Northern Appalachia the poverty line for a family of four is $25,100 and a self-sufficiency budget is $72,284. In Eastern Kentucky, the counties with federal prisons (Martin, Clay and McCreary) remain among the poorest in the US.[94] Prisons do not stimulate economic growth any more than they rehabilitate the incarcerated.

The nation has not yet had a conversation that adequately addresses both climate change and support for economically devastated communities. The struggles of people living in Appalachia are too often ignored, disdained, or romanticized. Books like J. D. Vance's *Hillbilly Elegy* continue to reinforce a deeply rooted myth that Appalachian poverty is the result of cultural factors and personal choices – a "culture of poverty" passed from one generation to the next.[95] These stories focus the national conversation on personal responsibility and away from the systematic underdevelopment of the entire region by extractive industries. This is why, when Vance attended the Appalachian Studies Association conference in 2018, young members of the Association turned their backs on him, singing "Which Side Are You On?," a 1931 protest song written by Florence Reece during the bloody Harlan County Mine War.[96]

Generations of Appalachians are accustomed to being misrepresented by outsiders, and locals have not forgotten the ways in which they have been done wrong. Appalachians have been exploited by industry and marginalized in the media and politics for hundreds of years. In Eastern Kentucky, the locals had no shortage of stories to tell about the bad press they receive. In many of the places I visited for this book, people were reluctant to talk with me, but nowhere was it as hard to get folks to agree to an interview as it was in Eastern Kentucky. Among older people, the easiest conversations began at farmers' markets over jars of pawpaw jam, mashed potato candy, and handmade quilts. Yet in Eastern Kentucky, it was the younger generation who were much more willing to talk. And more eager to leave.

Standing Rock Reservation

Oil production in the Bakken fracking fields, 160 miles from Standing Rock in North Dakota, has increased 600% in recent years.[97] It has been accompanied by an increasing number of environmental catastrophes. For example, between 2006 and 2014 an estimated 5.9 million gallons of oil were spilled in North Dakota, along with 11.8 million gallons of fracking wastewater called brine.[98] While "brine" might sound harmless – like something you'd use for making pickles – it isn't. Fracking brines contain over 200 toxins including arsenic, benzene, formaldehyde, lead, and mercury.[99] All of which have harmful impacts on health, ranging from lowered IQ levels and behavioral issues in children, to kidney, brain, and central nervous system damage in adults. Fracking brine also has been documented as containing abundant amounts of radioactive contaminants, including radium-226 and radium-228, that are linked to bone marrow and lung cancers.

The Nuclear Regulatory Commission requires industrial discharges of radium-226 and radium-228 to remain below 60 picocuries per liter, yet they have been recorded as high as 28,500 picocuries per liter in some brines.[100] However, state and federal governments continue to protect the companies that contaminate the environment at tremendous cost to the health of residents and the well-being of future generations, the environment, and wildlife. Thanks to the expansion of federal exemptions in 1980, oil and gas companies are not required to treat their waste products as hazardous waste.[101] Consequently, fracking brine is unregulated and is used across the country to de-ice winter roads and in rural areas to tamp down dust on unpaved roads in the summer. It is even sold in hardware stores as a de-icer. Brine-spreading is legal in thirteen states, including the Dakotas, Colorado, much of the Upper Midwest, northern Appalachia, and New York. Some states are going even further and advancing legislation to *protect* the practice of brine-spreading.[102] The oil and gas industries rely on the government and the banking industry to advance their interests. Between 2016 and 2018, JP Morgan invested nearly $196 billion in oil and gas, which was nearly a third more than the next biggest bank investor in fossil fuels; it is also among the biggest backers of fracking.[103]

At Standing Rock, the Keystone Pipeline System offers one more example of collusion between business and government at the expense of people and the environment. A system of three pipelines carry tar sands over thousands of miles. When the pipelines were proposed, developers told residents that spills would occur about once every forty-one years.[104] However, tar sands, which are thicker, more acidic, and more corrosive than conventional crude oil, make pipelines prone to leaking.[105] A study in 2011 by the Cornell University Global Labor Institute found that pipelines moving tar sands oil in Midwestern states between 2007 and 2010 spilled three times more per mile than the US national average.[106] The original Keystone pipeline commissioned in 2010 runs 1,600 miles from Canada to the Texas Gulf Coast. It has a long history of spills and leaks, including nearly 400,000 gallons of oil in North Dakota wetlands in 2019.[107] The Keystone XL also runs from Canada to the Gulf Coast by a slightly different route. In its first year of operation it had twelve leaks that resulted in significant oil spills, one of which poured almost 407,000 gallons of crude oil into the ground.[108] The third pipeline is known as the Dakota Access Pipeline (DAPL) and runs 1,200 miles from the shale oil field of the Bakken Formation of North Dakota, southeast through South Dakota and Iowa, to refineries in Illinois. DAPL was initially routed through the wealthier, largely white community of Bismarck, North Dakota. People in Bismarck complained and in 2016 it was rerouted through historic and sacred sites on land accorded to the Standing Rock tribe by the Fort Laramie Treaty but not recognized in the current legal configuration of the reservation.[109]

The decision to reroute the pipeline meant that it would come within 1,500 feet of Lake Oahe, Standing Rock's water supply, and pass under the Missouri River.[110] The Missouri is the longest river in the United States and has a drainage basin of 529,350 square miles.[111] The Standing Rock community, along with the 17 million people who live downstream and all wildlife that live in the basin, are at risk from leaks in the pipeline. Yet, as in Appalachia, politicians and corporations continued to pitch the pipeline in terms of jobs – not in terms of risks.

The pipelines came with the TransCanada promise of generating 119,000 jobs. According to a US State Department report, they have created thirty-five permanent jobs and 3,900 temporary construction jobs.[112] No estimate can be that far off without a lot of politicians colluding with the corporation. From the beginning, the Standing Rock community saw through the deceit and battled the fossil fuel industry through research, prayer, lawsuits, and protest to block construction. The Lakota have a prophecy in which a great black snake will come to the Lakota lands and devastate the earth.

Cannon Ball is the community on Standing Rock that was closest to the Oceti Sakowin Camp, the site of the #NoDAPL protest. The Missouri River is slightly visible in the background.

According to the prophecy, it will be the young who will rise up to slay the black snake – a detail not lost on the Standing Rock Sioux youth, who were the first to set up camp against the pipeline, along with LaDonna Brave Bull Allard, in April 2016.[113] The #NoDAPL hashtag spread through social media and the protest quickly grew into a multinational encampment of thousands of people, including Native and non-Native folk from across the country.[114]

Initially, the peaceful protest was met with a militarized response when the National Guard and private security forces joined forces – which was frightening in itself. But when the Federal Bureau of Investigation decided to identify environmental groups as possible terrorists, federal counter-terrorism officials joined forces with the National Guard and private security companies to confront what they claimed were threats to infrastructure.[115] Personnel and equipment from over 75 law enforcement agencies confronted what had been a peaceful protest.[116] Together, the agencies deployed armored vehicles and used tear-gas, pepper spray, tasers, water cannons, rubber bullets, and dogs against protestors. Leaked documents from TigerSwan, a private security firm hired to break the protest, describe the Water Protectors as "an ideologically driven insurgency with a strong religious component" and compare them to jihadist fighters.[117] The documents also confirm that the protestors faced military-style counter-terrorism measures from private contractors working with law enforcement agencies.[118] This extreme use of violence against Native people was all too familiar.[119] The attack resulted in widespread injuries and more than 700 arrests.[120]

In September 2016, President Obama vetoed the pipeline construction, citing the pervasive threats to ecosystems, drinking water sources, and public health. Kelcy Warren, the billionaire head of Energy Transfer Partners that developed the pipeline, donated more than $720,000 to Donald Trump's presidential campaign, and upon entering office Trump immediately signed an executive order reversing the Obama decision.[121] Then things got worse for the protestors.

Using Trump's former law firm, Energy Transfer Partners filed a billion-dollar lawsuit against Greenpeace and its partners for engaging in "a criminal network of fraud and misinformation."[122] The suit used the Racketeer Influenced Corruption Act (RICO) to allege that Greenpeace and other defendants engaged in an illegal enterprise to *persecute* Energy Transfer Partners. The Trump administration advocated that protestors receive twenty years for *inhibiting* the operation of an oil or gas pipeline.[123] Native and non-Native activists have faced a range of unprecedented federal charges that carry between fifteen- and twenty-year sentences.[124] Since 2016, at least seventeen states have introduced legislation to criminalize pipeline protests.[125] As of this writing, these states (including North and South Dakota) have cast peaceful protestors as economic terrorists and made both planning a protest and the act of protesting the pipeline a felony – even if the pipeline is on your own land.[126] New laws are also evolving that would transfer the costs of policing protests to protestors. In 2019, South Dakota passed legislation allowing third parties to sue "for up to three times the damage estimate to cover extraordinary law enforcement costs related to a pipeline's construction." [127] This penalty is in addition to jail time and fines.[128] The Oglala Sioux tribal council responded by banning Gov. Kristi Noem from the reservation.[129]

Chase Iron Eyes, an activist, politician, and attorney, told BuzzFeed: "We're in this state where water has no value – many of these things we see as natural resources also are seen as having no intrinsic value. What I've learned through the pipeline fight is that Indigenous Peoples have a role to play in helping this place transition from a colonized state to re-civilizing the world. What has been sold to us as civilization … it is not civilized."[130]

The Standing Rock Sioux Tribe, the Cheyenne River Sioux Tribe, and their legal team at EarthJustice have continued to fight the pipeline in court. In late spring 2020, President Trump used the pandemic as an opportunity to fast track the pipeline.[131] But Native people are winning in court. District Court Judge James Boasberg found that the Army Corps of Engineers failed to fully consider the environmental impacts of the pipeline, and that there were too many safety concerns to allow its continued operation. He ordered DAPL to be shut down within thirty days for a thirteen-month environmental and safety assessment to be completed by the Army Engineers.[132] The case went to the Supreme Court, which in July 2020 let the decision stand. The following day the Court effectively halted construction of the Keystone XL pipeline when it upheld a lower court ruling preventing it from crossing waterways.[133] In January 2021, President Biden issued an executive order that revoked the permit for the Keystone XL pipeline.[134] Many would like to see the permits for DAPL and the original Keystone pipeline revoked as well. You don't have to be psychic to know the fight isn't over.

Sacrifice Zones

When you look at struggling communities, there is always someone – living somewhere else – who has gotten rich from their labor or their land. Meanwhile the people in those communities are left with the burden of environmental contamination that will harm generations. Contamination that affects children's ability to learn. Contamination that results in high rates of cancer, kidney disease, and birth defects. Government too often aids corporations across the country to suppress evidence, stall inquiries, minimize regulations, and decrease penalties for harming public health while increasing penalties for peaceful protest.

To the person left with undrinkable water due to environmental contamination, the oil industry and the coal industry are not fundamentally different from one another.[135] What their corporate practices have in common is that they offer the illusion of choice and the false promise of hope for people living in desperate times. Heavy-metal contamination in Appalachia, Standing Rock, Wind River, and Oakland, California devastates low-income communities. Again, this isn't the result of a lack of knowledge. Business and government know the dangers. All of the practices in this chapter have been met with protests for generations. Few people in these communities are duped. They know that both business and government have opted for higher profits over public safety. If there is a single bad decision that people have made and continue to make it is believing that their government will protect them from profiteers.

At the end of the day, low-income communities are faced with limited employment opportunities, pervasive poverty, and a political leadership more invested in profit and power than in the well-being of the people they represent. It isn't working families who are filling the coffers of political campaigns. Entire watersheds and ecosystems have been polluted and whole towns have been destroyed because it is more profitable for companies to move people out than to stop polluting. In the face of this massive betrayal of public trust, business continues as usual. And the media enable all of this with their minimal coverage, inaccurate coverage, and at times total silence.

Wealth and poverty are about much more than money. So far, we've looked at the economic struggles and environmental dangers that pervade daily life in struggling communities. The next chapter looks at the kinds of violence and other threats that can only happen in communities that have become sacrifice zones.

5

Ordinary Things That Can Only Happen Here

Almost everyone lives with some level of safety concerns: parents worry about the safety of their children, women organize their days to avoid being out alone at night, and families purchase security systems for their homes and vehicles. But while we all have such concerns, the "ordinary" safety concerns of people in struggling communities are quite different from the "ordinary" safety concerns of people in wealthier ones. For example, while substance abuse and addiction exist in every economic class, wealth can provide privacy that hides the problems from public view – you won't see empty bottles or needles on the sidewalk. Wealth can also put top-notch treatment centers within reach if needed. An important aspect of socio-economic class is what we experience as ordinary – the kinds of activities, events, people, and problems that we can reasonably expect to encounter in our day-to-day lives.

All the struggling communities I visited, rural and urban, faced serious issues with substance abuse and drug addiction. Some events related to these issues would be truly shocking for any community. But in reality they could not happen in just any community. They happen in struggling communities. Recall, for example, Jenny from earlier chapters. She is a mother of two children who lives in Ohio. She tells me, "I worry for some of the people who live down the street from me. I worry about these little children who don't have winter coats or don't have something to eat. There's a lot of that around." Jenny is acutely aware of the suffering of people around her and very engaged in trying to make a difference. She's had some much harder times in the past, which seems to make it easy for her to identify with people who are worse off than she is. "I've been there when you don't have $10," she says. "Ten dollars is a lot of money when you don't have a dollar, when you don't have food." Jenny helps wherever she can. "A lot of people down here carpool. A lot of people down here ride bikes places. You might not be able to get to everything you want to, but maybe a neighbor or a friend will take you." Jenny knows what it means to live without a car and as a result made a regular habit of picking up hitchhikers – until she had an argument about it with her husband. Jenny relented. A little. "Now I only take old ladies home from the grocery store."

In a late afternoon conversation, Jenny recounts an incident that brings her to tears as we talk. A while back, a neighbor who lived down the street asked for a lift into town. Jenny had given this man rides before but this time she wasn't able to do it. Her refusal made him so angry that it confused Jenny. It also raised a flag for her, but she wasn't even sure what kind of flag. The next day the meth lab in his house blew up. "I woke up, and there was fire engines and everything. He died." Jenny pauses and looks blankly, as if she is still in disbelief. "I cried," she says as her tears well up. Even now she second guesses what might have happened if she had said yes and given him a lift. "I don't know if I would have changed his life, if I would have helped him – or, if I would have been a part of that."

Jenny didn't know her neighbor had a meth lab in his home. But she does know that there are meth labs in the community around her. "I mean, that's happening still like to the left or the right. I worry about things like that. Those are things I worry about." While meth might make its way into any community, meth labs do not. Jenny, in many ways, is the best kind of community member any town could have. It's important to her to be a good neighbor; she is actively engaged in her local schools and in community improvement projects. Yet an exploding meth lab a few doors down from her home is also part of her daily reality. She talks a lot about balancing her desire to help her neighbors and her fear of jeopardizing her family. All too often, Jenny finds herself asking, "What's the right thing to do?"

The question "what should I do?" comes up in large and small ways across struggling communities. Nothing seems to prepare one for the ordinary events that occur in them. This chapter will give readers some idea of just how different "ordinary" reality is for the people who live in these communities. We will hear from Vanessa, Angel, PL, Honest, and Tom in Oakland, Michael and Rose in Athens County, Tommy in Tennessee and Jenna in Eastern Kentucky about the concerns they negotiate every day – concerns that have nothing to do with their own financial struggles and everything to do with the various forms of violence and substance abuse that can become embedded in struggling communities.

Things Can Happen

Across the country, every community contains economic spectrums; there are always people better or worse off. So, I want to emphasize that the stories related here are not representative of entire communities. For example, Oakland is one of many US cities characterized by both extreme poverty and exceptional levels of wealth. Concerns about potential gun violence are widespread across all neighborhoods. Yet *shootings* don't happen in every neighborhood. They are concentrated in struggling communities. Even when children in Oakland have strong, supportive families, they can fall victim to gang shootings.

You might recall Vanessa Torres from Chapter 2. She works at a nonprofit helping Latinx youth plan for, and succeed in, college. "I really try to work really hard with them to make sure they feel like they have a voice, they have the space where they can talk about issues that are affecting them outside of school and inside of school, and I've been very successful. I feel like it really matters that I came from this community so they can really relate to me."

Vanessa has lived in Oakland for twenty years and went to the same schools these students now attend. When I ask Vanessa what school was like for her, she begins with a story of walking to high school in the Deep East. "Walking from my house to school, it's the fear of 'What if I get robbed?' You could be walking to school and there's someone sitting down shooting up drugs. There would be needles around, and that's really unsafe. There's a lot of gang violence, and it's just overall really unsafe to be walking. There's just people out there." Deep East Oakland is in Police District 5 and has a disproportionate amount (27%) of the city's violent crime[1] – a reality children as well as adults navigate every day.

If walking to school sounds like running a gauntlet, taking the bus wasn't any better. "I had a bus pass that was given to me for school, but it just wasn't safe sometimes to be riding the bus." Vanessa recounts "a little altercation" between a passenger carrying a gun and the bus driver. "I was like, wow. I didn't tell my parents at the time. I just held it in, because that was such a scary experience. You see a lot of things. You see a lot of homeless people. You see people on drugs, people just laid out in the street. My first day in high school during lunch there was a shootout outside the school. So, we were on lockdown right away." As a child going to school, Vanessa also constantly worried about ICE raids and the potential deportation of her family.

As an adult, Vanessa still worries about ICE and faces a world that is still filled with risks. "I am a woman. I'm alone. I'm always afraid of something happening to me, being kidnapped is the most horrible possibility. I think that's what sometimes worries me, but I'm 'Okay, Vanessa, you've got to carry yourself strong. Make sure you're always aware of your surroundings.' But I know that's not a possibility always. There's tons of women that go missing every year. I'm afraid for my safety and sometimes for the safety of my parents – being at the wrong place at the wrong time and just many things happening." According to the California Department of Justice, 3,395 adults and eighty-eight children disappeared from Alameda County in 2019.[2] The reality of abductions is even more harsh in other parts of California.

Angel Perez also grew up in the Deep East. He is in his mid-twenties, but his boyish face and shy demeanor make him seem much younger. Angel left Oakland to attend college and had plans for law school after graduation. "I was interested in law school at a time, specifically because I wanted to get into immigration law. That's something that I've always been passionate about." Initially, he had trouble finding affordable housing off campus and struggled with school. Then his plans were upended when his mother died unexpectedly. "The thing is that my family at home needed help trying to keep up with the cost of living. I've always been someone that likes to help out my family, so the immediate thing for me was just to come back to Oakland and come live with my family." For Angel, this meant working and commuting from Oakland to a college about seventy-five miles away to finish his undergraduate degree. His grades dropped and his dream of law school vanished. Angel persisted and graduated within five years – with $2,000 in student loans and $9,000 in credit card debt.

Angel currently holds two part-time jobs, works less than half time and earns under $16,000 a year. Sometimes on weekends, he helps his Dad with painting jobs. "I've been wanting to get my teaching credential to be able to teach full-time. I've worked in afterschool programs and as a teacher assistant doing the paraprofessional work. I've been wanting to continue to the next step to be able to get a teaching credential, and then being able to go full-time in the classroom." As he talks about teaching, Angel becomes animated with a big smile and an easy laugh. In those moments, I can imagine him being a teacher that students love and remember years later. But he hasn't been able to move forward with his plans for a teaching credential. He freezes when he thinks about the future.

Angel is a DACA recipient. "We don't know exactly when and what's going to happen, if they're going to take it away, or if they're going to continue to allow us to renew." He wonders out loud what will happen if he pursues a teaching credential and DACA is rescinded. But in reality, he knows what would happen. His dreams would be over. "I do know that. I have heard that there's people who did not qualify for DACA but who work as independent contractors. So, I do know that there's a possibility to work that way." As he imagines working off the books in painting or construction his entire body collapses.

Angel came to the United States with his parents when he was two years old. "I've been living in Oakland since I was in elementary school." He seems both sad and reluctant when I ask him to help me understand what he experienced growing up in the Deep East. "Just things like violence and the lack of resources as well, all the trauma and the violence I've seen." He pauses and looks at the kitchen table. "There have been events," he tells me. "A car was being burned one morning not too long ago. People drop off quite a lot of cars in the middle of the night, take off the wheels, take out whatever parts are good enough to sell, and then abandon [the car]." The burned-out cars on the street and the security bars on windows and doors can make it easy to forget that children live here. Angel lives with the pervasive threat of violence in his community as well as knowing that at any moment his family could be caught up in a raid. The reality of violence and trauma in struggling communities is intensely destabilizing.

Over the last fifty years, the city of Oakland has had 5,142 homicides.[3] It has been under federal oversight for more than seventeen years to ensure police compliance with fifty-two required reforms.[4] In 2012, the Oakland Police Department reported that 70% of the 126 murders and 577 of the shootings that year were gang related.[5] Unable to eliminate gangs, the city changed its strategy and focused on eliminating gun violence. The efforts have taken some time. In 2016 the reported violent crime rate in Oakland was still 259% higher than the national average. Two years later in 2018, the city reported sixty-eight murders. This was its lowest murder rate since 1999.[6] Yet even as I write, Oakland is still trying to beat its reputation as one of the most dangerous cities in the US.

The potential presence of gun violence affects everyone. This reality is made most clear to me in the bright skies of a fall day. Sitting across the street from a local school in the Deep East, I watch children bubble out of the school doors into the warm afternoon sun as they do everywhere – with laughter and shouting as they giggle and shove their way down the sidewalk. This school serves a struggling neighborhood that is largely Black and Brown – a neighborhood with some of the highest crime rates in the city. The children's laughter is a kind of testimony to the strength of the families in this community. Yet, among the older children the laughter doesn't flow as freely, and the games are not as innocent. A child of about twelve years old takes aim and mimes shooting his classmate. What catches my eye is not the pretend shooting but the performance of it. It has an informed intent that is neither naïve nor careless.

Everyone I talked with in Oakland mentioned the threat of gun violence. What really struck me was that no one mentioned it as a major concern, just as a part of ordinary life. Recall PL from earlier chapters. He is a Black man living in Oakland who has a full-time professional position at a nonprofit. PL explains his safety concerns to me this way: "I'm in the Bay Area. You worry about ... things. You worry about driving home and getting shot at on the freeway. I live in a neighborhood that probably isn't the most accommodating neighborhood, so, yeah, I worry about those things every day." PL stops and reflects for a moment and corrects himself. "Well, no, I don't worry about them every day. I'm just *conscious* of them every day. I'm kind of numb to them. They're everywhere." Indeed, for most people it is impossible to live with a constant fear of getting shot or of break-ins and still go about the mundane business of life. And yet, it may be impossible to survive in high crime areas if you don't have a constant awareness of the potential risks and how to minimize them.

This was true for a young Black man named Honest, who had first-hand experience of gun violence. Honest holds an associate degree and is patching through a period of unemployment by doing small modeling jobs for clothing ads and looking for work in the music industry. He shares a flat in Oakland with five other men. If a single word could capture the spirit of a person, for Honest it would be "gratitude." His sense of gratitude comes up over and over again in conversation. Gratitude for his life today, despite his economic struggles. Gratitude for what he learned from the hardships of spending nine years in a children's group home. Gratitude for the opportunities that come with a new day. "I can see now how I can make my future – because now, the future doesn't really exist. It's about executing, you know what I'm saying?" He turns to make sure we have eye contact and says with emphasis "Right now, right here, you have a choice."

Honest is both philosophical and resolute in taking responsibility for the quality of his life. Yet he is not naïve. "There's problems out there. Like, I'll give you an example. Me and my dad are driving down the street. My dad was driving – we were going to take him to work and I was going to take the car. He's driving down this little, skinny street. We make a left at the light." Honest animates the story with his hands, indicating the narrow street and the positions of cars. "Okay, a car comes out of nowhere from behind us and scratched us on the side [as it passed]. Then another car's coming [down the street toward us]. Like I said, it's a skinny street and they hit each other so hard!" His fists represent the cars colliding; they hit and fly into the air as he raises his voice. "It was so crazy. Boom! They should have flown out the window. Like it was that hard." Honest pauses and shakes his head. "One dude got out of the car. The other one couldn't get out of the car. He was stuck. The airbag popped him and everything. Four dudes hopped out of the other car with pistols and long guns and everything. I'm talking about shotguns, AKs – I'm talking about big ass guns. The scariest ones you see in a movie or something like that. It didn't even look real. Honest and his dad abandoned their car and ran as weapons fired and smoke filled the air. "We, we were trying to get to safety. It was so crazy. But anyway, my dad didn't even go to work that day." That's exactly how the story ends: "But anyway, my dad didn't even go to work that day," and then he changed the conversation.

Recall that we had been talking about being responsible for making your own life, when Honest offered this example of one of the "problems that are out there" – the way that trouble can find you. The impact on Honest today? Anxiety. He stays vigilant whenever he is in a car and becomes extremely anxious when boxed in by other cars. Life in the struggling class isn't just about paying bills, it is also about the kinds of trauma that can happen for no apparent reason. For people with children, the impact is even greater.

Tom Sam's sentiment echoes that of PL. Tom Sam is a Diné/Comanche man in his thirties who lives in Oakland with his wife and their two small children, aged three and five, as well as his twenty-year-old niece. Tom and his wife homeschool their children. Within minutes of meeting Tom, it's clear to me how much he loves being a father. Equally clear is that it's important to Tom that he contributes to a greater good, rather than amassing his own personal wealth. "I want to be that solution-driven individual to try to help just create better opportunities. That's my passion and with the addition of my kids, it becomes even more of my life passion. I want to ultimately create a better world for them and their children and their children." His concern for future generations threads through all he does. "I believe that whenever you serve the most underserved, then everybody else prospers and gets the benefits of that as well." Tom's work with a nonprofit helps Native children in local schools by providing them with appropriate cultural, academic, and mental health support as they go through a system that seldom recognizes their existence.

Tom has a four-year college degree and a steady job. He tells me he feels middle class – but he knows the reality is something else. He picks up a little additional income from time to time by singing at graduations, birthday parties, and powwows, and supports his entire family on a salary of between $50,000 and $60,000 a year. Despite what might sound like an enviable income, Tom is uncertain of his ability to pay all of their bills each month and has trouble keeping $500 in the family savings account. To appreciate why this might be, consider that when I met Tom in 2018, the poverty line for a family of five was $29,420; the EPI self-sufficiency budget for this same family in Oakland was $156,701. The stark contrast between these two figures highlights the tremendous gap between the way the government talks about financial need and the levels of economic need that people experience.

MONTHLY COSTS

2 adults *and* 3 children
Oakland/Fremont metro area

HOUSING	$3,219
FOOD	$1,094
CHILD CARE	$1,676
TRANSPORTATION	$1,321
HEALTH CARE	$1,278
OTHER NECESSITIES	$1,740
TAXES	$2,730
Monthly Total	**$13,058**
Annual Total	**$156,701**

Notice in the accompanying figure that the FMR rent estimate is $3,219 ($38,628 per year). In the very best case, that would be 60% of Tom's pre-tax income – that's twice the bite that fair market rent is intended to have. Remember here again that 60% of rental units are priced *higher* than FMR.

Living in California, Tom's salary (between $50,000 and $60,000 a year) means he can expect a total tax burden of 21.94% (federal, state, FICA, and Local) or $12,945, if he earns on the high end ($59,999), leaving them about $46,055 per year – which makes even FMR housing unaffordable. If he earns on the low end ($50,000) his overall tax burden of 18.92% would leave him with $37,296 in take-home income – less than fair market rent for his family. With a college degree and a stable, full-time professional job, common sense would seem to place Tom in the middle class. Yet, the lived reality of his life places him in the struggling class, unable to count on covering all of his bills each month. And that is with nothing going wrong.

Financial issues are not all that worry Tom. "I mean, there's constantly like the concerns of just like violence within the city that we live in," explains Tom. "It's not a fear. It's just about an awareness or a presence of the potential for violence, violence in all forms of the word." It's also more than awareness. It's a possibility that can reach into his life at any moment. "I'm going to participate in a funeral in a couple of days here for a young man who passed away, just kind of unexpectedly. A victim of street violence." As he talks about the upcoming funeral for a young man he knew, sadness falls like a shadow across his face. The funerals that Tom attends force him to think a lot about his own death and what would happen to his family. "I let my children and my family know that I love them, and I not just love them; I think love undermines like what I truly mean. I really appreciate them, and I value them, and I honor them, and I respect them, because of the way that they are and the way that they make me feel."

The dangers of violence are not abstract for Tom. Indeed, they are too often all too real, too present. Tom relies on indigenous cultural practices to cope with the stress, but the threat of violence comes from a lot of directions. As a man of color, Tom counts the police as an added source of danger. He tells me, "I get more anxiety around police than I do around what could be potential thugs or even street violence because they are able to do it [commit acts of violence] under the auspices of legalities." In communities of color, police do not often serve as a source of comfort and protection. Tom tells me that police can do things "that others are criminalized for. And so, I feel safer if I see like street crime happening than I do if I see police-agitated crime happening."

In 2019, police killed 999 people in the United States; of these 135 were in California and of those only 24% (thirty-three) victims were identified as white.[7] The realities of police brutality have emotional as well as physical costs. In a life filled with economic uncertainty and the threat of gun violence, families of color like Tom's also face a very real threat of police violence – for which there is little recourse. To live in a struggling community is to have a very different sense of what might happen in any given day.

More Than Needles on a Sidewalk

In Tennessee, Tommy runs his hand over his neatly clipped gray hair and sighs as we talk. You might recall him from Chapter 3. He is a white man in his sixties who returned to a small rural community in Cumberland Plateau. Among Tommy's past jobs was a stint as a nurse at the Vanderbilt University Medical Center in Nashville. As a nurse with emergency room and burn unit experience, he had too many encounters with young people from urban and rural communities who had turned to making meth when their economic opportunities shrank. He tells me: "You would see people in a very desperate situation, and they would go and make meth."

In my travels, I also encountered meth addicts and recognize the familiar devastation of gray skin, sores, ruined teeth, and wasted bodies. So I am surprised by how Tommy starts the story; the woman could not have been an addict for very long. "I was taking care of a young lady," says Tommy. "She was twenty-seven, twenty-eight years old, beautiful young girl, and she was from a rural part of Tennessee. She was making meth in a home, and she was high. She said, 'So I'm making this meth, and I set myself on fire, and I'm like, oh, I'm on fire! I run out of the house and I'm trying to take my pants off. My pants are on fire. I'm taking my pants off, and I get them down to my ankles, but I've got boots on, and I can't get my pants off, and my pants are burning around my ankles, and I can't get them off.'" Tommy grimaces and tells me that when she came to the hospital her skin was burned off completely and her tendons were exposed.

Tommy recounts that he told her, "You know, you don't look like the typical patient that you get using meth. Why would you do this? And she said, 'Well, I had an old boyfriend that taught me how to make it and I make it pure. I've lost my husband. I've lost my kids. My parents won't talk to me. I've lost my home. And my biggest fear is that when you guys put my skin back on, I'm going to go out and make some more.'" Tommy was completely floored and years later it shows in his face as he retells the story. He reflects on her explanation: "'Think of the most pleasurable thing that you've ever done,' and I said, Okay, and she said, 'Now multiply it by ten,' and I said, are you kidding me? She goes, 'I'm not. That's how much you crave it.'" Tommy pauses and it seems clear the story still shakes him to his core. "So that's the kind of drugs they're making in the rural areas. The burns were so bad that, at one time, [hospitals] were spending millions of dollars during the meth epidemic on wound care and skin grafts, and they were afraid it was going to bankrupt them." Meth offers a relatively cheap high that can last for days – and it's extremely addictive. The intensity of the addiction in Tommy's patient is what distinguishes meth from other drugs.[8] Across the nation, meth-related hospitalizations jumped by 250% between 2008 and 2015.[9] The Missouri State Highway Patrol ranked Tennessee among the top ten states for meth-related seizures in 2018.[10] Yet as dangerous as meth is, the chances of overdosing are even greater with opiates. In 2017, 47,600 people died from opioid related overdoses.[11]

As it turns out, drug trafficking comes into a particular focus for me as I drive from Tennessee to Kentucky. Interstate 75 takes me through open meadows and wide vistas reaching to the horizon. The dense forests have been clear cut and the view is salted with strip mines and blasting sites. On my trip northward Michigan plates abound on cars and trucks. I don't see families or even a vehicle with passengers – just white men behind the wheel. This strikes me as being so odd that I wonder if this is the drug corridor that people in Southeast Ohio talked about. You know the saying, if it walks like a duck, quacks like a duck... And so it is with Interstate 75, which the National Drug Intelligence Center identifies as a drug-trafficking corridor that extends all the way from Miami to Michigan.[12]

Pain clinics in Florida have helped to make the state the epicenter of prescription drug abuse by prescribing more than ten times the amount of oxycodone *than all of the other states combined.*[13] As a result, Interstate 75 became the "Oxy Express." That's one part of the equation. The other is that drug companies target struggling communities. In 2017, the CDC reported that Kentucky issued nearly eighty-seven opioid prescriptions for every 100 people[14] (and Florida, to repeat, prescribed more than *ten times* the amount of oxycodone than all other states combined).

Oxy, heroin, and fentanyl have all swept through Appalachia. If you have ever wondered why most opioid addicts are white, you only need to look at the regional saturation of opioids. Between 2007 and

2012, *780 million* hydrocodone and oxycodone pills were delivered to West Virginia alone – a state with a population of 1.8 million.[15] In some counties, every family knows someone involved with opioids in some way. Sometimes the least imaginable people. Michael Maloney writes: "My mother had been an ironing lady. She developed arthritis and could no longer iron. The doctor put her on pain medications. Her social security was three hundred a month, not enough to cover rent, food, and utilities. She found she could take half of the medications, sell the rest and double her income."[16] Mrs. Maloney wasn't alone in trying to subsidize her income, but she and those like her were not the heart of the problem.

For years, drug manufacturers claimed Oxy was a good drug that was finding its way into the hands of bad people. Yet their actions tell a different story. For example, Purdue Pharma's promotional campaign for OxyContin was aggressive and targeted. In Mingo County, West Virginia, three small pharmacies in towns with populations ranging between 280 and 3,000 received a total of 30 million opioid pills from distributors; a pharmacy in one of these towns (population 400) dispensed *9 million opioid pills in two years*.[17] The company produced false and misleading information about the drug and instructed their sales representatives to discount physician concerns about patients developing a tolerance for OxyContin.[18] By 2001, sales of OxyContin made up 80% of Purdue Pharma's revenue.[19] They were not alone.

It is clear that drug manufacturers, distributors, doctors, pharmacists and other licensed medical professionals participated in the creation of a national epidemic, largely by targeting people in struggling communities. The drug's distributor McKesson Corporation is the sixth largest company on the Forbes 500 list. In 2019, McKesson agreed to pay West Virginia $37 million to settle a lawsuit over its flooding of the state with millions of opioid pills.[20] For distributors and pharmaceutical companies, OxyContin sales are a billion-dollar business, well worth the million-dollar fines they intermittently receive.[21] Sound familiar? Here again is the collusion of government and corporate interests to generate wealth for a few at the expense of many in some very poor communities.

According to the Centers for Disease Control and Preventions, between 1999 and 2018 more than 450,000 people in the US died from opioid overdose.[22] By contrast, there were 58,220 US military deaths in the Vietnam War.[23] In 2018, 32% of all opioid deaths involved *prescription* opioids.[24] Throughout the opioid crisis, the US Drug Enforcement Administration (DEA) complained that no one was reporting – or tracking – the millions of suspicious orders for Oxy.[25] How could that be possible in the midst of a massive opioid epidemic? Here's part of how it happened. Representative Tom Marino (R-Pennsylvania) sponsored legislation that *prevented* the DEA from investigating the suspicious drug orders at the heart of the opioid epidemic.[26] Senator Orrin Hatch (R-Utah) put the final touches on the bill and Congress passed it into law. "Political action committees representing the industry contributed at least $1.5 million to the 23 lawmakers who sponsored or co-sponsored four versions of the bill, including nearly $100,000 to Marino and $177,000 to Hatch. Overall, the drug industry spent $102 million lobbying Congress on the bill and other legislation between 2014 and 2016, according to lobbying reports."[27] If this isn't shocking enough, President Trump wanted to appoint Marino as his "drug czar."[28] Marino was forced to step back from the nomination when his efforts to hinder the DEA came to light.

Opioids aren't being made by trailer-park chemists, or by people like Tommy's patient. Nor are they being trafficked across national borders. Marketing for OxyContin took Purdue Pharma from a small drug maker in the mid-1990s to $3 billion in sales revenue in 2001.[29] By 2017, the Purdue family had a collective net worth of $13 billion. In 2018, the company paid its CEO, Craig Landau, $9 million; board chairman, Steve Miller, nearly $4 million; and five other board members a combined $3.7 million. A year later, Purdue Pharma sought bankruptcy protection from lawsuits seeking to hold it accountable for its role in the opioid epidemic.[30]

In 2016, the Sackler family, with a net worth of $14 billion, made the pages of *Forbes* as the richest newcomer to their list of wealthy families.[31] The Sacklers, like the Purdues, amassed their fortune through the sale of OxyContin. When the companies were finally held accountable, "Purdue Pharma and the Sacklers were permitted to enter into plea agreements that resolve all current federal criminal and civil charges against them."[32] The settlement with the Justice Department required Purdue to "plead guilty to criminal charges for misconduct relating to its opioids" and to pay more than $8 billion in penalties.[33] These will mostly go unpaid – investigative reporters found that in advance of the formal charges, Purdue Pharma created a new company and gradually transferred $10 billion to it in order to shield their assets. Sackler family members agreed to pay $225 million to settle civil claims that they disputed. Despite all this, both Purdue and Sackler are allowed to continue to sell OxyContin.[34]

There was a deliberate plan by corporations to infuse Appalachia with opioids, knowing full well the tremendous suffering this would cause.[35] And lawmakers aided those efforts in order to fill their own pockets. There is a lot of money to be made off the backs of struggling communities. Even if you get caught. Even if it leads to the death of 450,000 people.

In Eastern Kentucky, Jenna Terry's story has a lot in common with millions of other people who live with opioid addiction.[36] You might remember Jenna from earlier chapters. She's a young white woman, enjoying the stability of her new life with her boyfriend and their child. Jenna was adopted at birth by a couple who knew nothing about her birth parents. However, they soon realized they had a baby with serious health problems. Jenna recounts, "My parents had no idea what was wrong with me for the longest time. They tried to go to a bunch of different doctors, and they couldn't figure it out until *finally* one doctor was like, 'She's withdrawing from drugs. That's what's wrong with her.'" Jenna had been born addicted to crack cocaine. Once properly diagnosed, Jenna and her family recovered. In high school Jenna tempted a fate she didn't fully understand by using drugs recreationally with her peers. "I feel like maybe I was kind of like destined to be [an addict], in a way, you know. It's very hard, especially living here." But it wasn't recreational drug use that took Jenna down. It was a prescription for opioids from her doctor.

"I was an opiate abuser," Jenna tells me as she stares me straight in the eye. She pauses. "I broke my back six years ago, fell off a porch, so I got prescribed pain medication for it. In the end, my script ran out, so I started buying them off the street, and then once I was on them for so long, I couldn't get off of them. It's very hard to get off of them." Jenna has an amazing skill of squeezing immense emotions into simple statements of fact. She was addicted before her prescription ran out. Jenna brushes her hair from her face and fidgets in her chair for just a moment. "I went to rehab a couple of times." Jenna pauses and then corrects herself. "I was *sent* to rehab." She prides herself on being open about her struggles. It's an impressive quality that clearly takes focus and effort.

Jenna's addiction to opiates got her arrested several times. Opioid abuse in rural areas has resulted in an enormous increase in arrests, especially among women. The number of women in state and federal prisons jumped 700% between 1980 and 2019.[37] While 13% of men are incarcerated for a drug offense, for women the figure is 26%.[38] For many women, this means sharing a cell for twenty-three hours a day with other addicts who are in withdrawal. In some ways Jenna was lucky. She was jailed for three months and then served a mandated six-month rehab program. Actually, Jenna ended up in rehab several times, but recovery never seemed to stick. It has taken a lot of fierce effort to kick her addiction.

On her fourth stint in rehab, Jenna had some unexpected motivation. "I found out I was pregnant, so that kind of like set the pathway for it. I wanted to definitely not put [my child] through that, you know. I was about to be a mother, so I thought this is the perfect time to stop. Start my family and grow up." Jenna has worked really hard to turn her life around. Even so, she is still dogged by worry when she sees police. "I think once you get into the system here, police don't forget you. They hang on to you for a while. Like you're known now, so any wrong move you make, they're watching, and they see it. And you will pay consequences for it. I've seen it with me and other people who I've known, like once you go to jail the first time. I think all addicts are just worried about police officers, whether they're doing wrong or not." Everything about being an addict is traumatic and it takes a long time to move through it all – even if one never quite gets past it.

Jenna tells me the biggest drug problem in Eastern Kentucky is methamphetamines. "Every time you hear somebody getting arrested here, it's over meth. It's bad here, bad, bad. It's just now getting to the point where it's out of control, but I think it's been around for a very long time – just hadn't really weaseled its way into as many people's lives." Jenna's lost a lot of friends to drug overdoses, including her best friend and a former fiancé. "I think a lot of that is why I used – because I can't deal with emotion very well. I'm not very good with dealing with like really strong emotion, and, of course, drugs kind of just make you not worry. They numb you out, make you kind of forget for the time being."

Where Jenna lives in Eastern Kentucky is about three hours from Athens County, Ohio, where Michael Chase and Rose Taylor live. It's easy to get there on what locals call the heroin highway – a county backroad that nips and tucks along the borders of Ohio, Kentucky, and West Virginia, making it easy to evade police by crossing state lines. Like all locals Michael has long known that heroin and meth are prevalent in Southeast Ohio. He knew about it from growing up a few counties over. But Athens County is an entirely new experience for Michael. While he was used to seeing people strung out at night, here he sees them during the day. And not just on the street. "There's people who come into the store, and they're strung out on heroin. We're not supposed to say anything unless they are stealing or passing out." I'm impressed that this situation is common enough that the store has a policy on it. Michael pauses and shakes his head. "It's a ridiculous policy but it's the policy. This one woman, she almost passed out a couple of times at the register." As he talks, Michael imitates her leaning, nodding off, and falling over. "I had to keep being, 'Ma'am, are you okay?' I had to call my manager, because I was like, I don't know what to do, because I've never had that happen. I was like, do I call like an ambulance? If I do, is she going to leave and not want to go? What do I do?!"

The manager took over and made the appropriate calls, but there was Michael standing in the wreckage that comes with his job. I have scarcely caught my breath when he is on to the next example of things he finds stressful at work. "The worst thing that happens is when we've had people come in, they've been strung out, and they've pooped on our floor. That has happened, like, twice. It's crazy. I was like 'how would you poop on the floor'?! You know what I mean? We have a bathroom. We've had people *pee* on our floor." Michael's distress is clear, and he looks at me as if to ask, "how does any of this make sense?" His story continues at an even faster pace. In so many ways he sounds like a trauma survivor. "There's this one guy who came in, he – I'm pretty sure he was a drug addict – but he was like super drunk, but he peed so much I thought he was pouring a bottle of water from this angle. I thought he was just pouring water. I was like maybe he had the lid off and he's just not thinking or like you're holding a water bottle and not thinking or something. I look over and it's just coming out of his pants. He's just like peeing, and I was like this is crazy. What are you supposed to do? So, I just looked at him and walked away and got my manager. I was like you need to go up there. I don't know what to do." While we all show up to work never really sure of what the day will bring, it should never bring this – to anyone. As we talk, I find myself wishing Michael didn't have so many stories like this. I don't know what to do but listen as his stories carry us well past midnight.

Rose Taylor tells me that drug use has affected everyone's life in Athens County at some point or other. Her brother went into rehab for cocaine and she remembers a student in high school going through opiate withdrawal. "I've seen it with my father. And I've seen it with my friends. And I've seen it affect my life – I've seen people die from it. I don't think that I will ever be a part of that, because I can just see its effects." Rose has been surrounded by people with substance abuse issues her entire life. There's "like a lot of stuff like that, that I'm really lucky about. When I graduated high school, from the time I was eighteen to the time I was twenty-one, I had five friends die in car accidents, and I had one friend who was stabbed, and they all involved alcohol."

In distressed counties where there are few opportunities for entertainment or diversion, drugs and alcohol seem like an obvious go to – and not just for young people. Staying sober in a community where drugs and alcohol are the primary form of socializing is a social problem for Rose. "It's tricky, because it's one thing to be like, 'well, just don't drink,' or to say 'I just don't go to bars.' But all my friends are there. My community is there – you know what I mean?" There's not much to do in Athens apart from hang out in bars.

In low-income communities, drugs can also be primary forms of recreation. "Both of my parents were marijuana users," says Rose. "I knew teachers who were marijuana users. Neighbors – all marijuana users. Like my godmother, who is a doctor, is a marijuana user." If marijuana seems to be the adults' drug of choice in Southeast Ohio, Rose says younger people choose cocaine, opiates, and pills. "A lot of people that work in bars oftentimes will use cocaine to like make sure they can stay up all through their shifts. You know, because they get off work at like 3:30 in the morning, and you have to be like up and serving people and constantly moving; and so sometimes, you know, you don't get automatic sleep, and you're drinking, and so it's like uppers and downers to manage that. Or like people that you know smoke meth, or heroin is really big." Sometimes people walk into the shop where Rose works when they've been using. "It happens frequently, not like every day, but I would say maybe like four or five times a month. We have to kick people out of the shop, because they can't come in here."

In talking with Jenny, Michael, Rose, and others it seems clear that serious levels of substance abuse are common in Southeast Ohio. If that sounds concerning, consider Ohio's gun laws. Ohio is an open-carry state. "Here you go to a bar, and you can see somebody open carry," Rose pauses for a moment. As I take in this information the surprise shows on my face. "It's like a thing," she explains dryly. "I just see a lot, so I feel like I'm almost desensitized to it. Especially being in like Appalachia, there's a lot of people that are like, well, 'I need my guns to hunt so I can provide for food.'" Rose is clearly skeptical about this claim. I know that for some families hunting is a means of patching through. Yet that isn't why people open carry in bars. And it isn't why people own automatic weapons. But these conversations are rarely as complicated as they need to be.

After talking with Rose, I head back toward Glenville, West Virginia. It's a two-hour drive, most of it on WV 47 – a winding, mountainous road. Like many of these roads, the edge is a foot or two from a hillside or a drop off. There are few crossroads, no pullouts, and a 55 mph speed limit. The road is mostly empty, which makes driving less stressful. My cell phone reception drops out in the hills and I am grateful it is a straight shot to Glenville where I have a hotel room. I won't need the map program on my phone. I am tired and carefully navigate the hairpin turns and steep hills. Suddenly the haunch of a large deer is on my hood rolling toward my windshield. I slam on the brake and the deer rolls off of the hood and down the embankment. I see the stunned look on his face. He is a beautiful, big six-point buck with velvet antlers and he rolls four to five feet down the hillside. I stop the car in the road – there is no place to pull over – and watch him struggle to get up. He fails. He struggles, he fails. He looks panicked. I feel my own sense of panic watching him struggle. What should I do?

A new, half-ton pickup truck stops. The truck is so jacked up I think it could drive right over my car. A small woman climbs down from the cab and strides to the front of my car to assess the damage. She shrugs and tells me I'm lucky. Without another word, she climbs back in the cab and is gone. I remain frozen watching the buck struggle and fail. It can't use its hind legs. I have no idea what to do but hope that it dies quickly. In the low light of dusk, another truck stops. It's also jacked-up but older and painted in camouflage. A man steps down from the driver's side and joins me at the edge of the road to assess the buck. A small blond woman climbs down from the passenger side and gives me a quick look. She has the hallmarks of a meth addict: the rotted teeth that locals call meth mouth, the papery skin scraped raw in places, and the nearly skeletal weight. I start to worry. She quickly skitters down the hillside, more interested in the deer than in me. The man stands beside me watching and says with kindness, "I have a gun. I can shoot it."

As I watch this massive and beautiful being struggle and fail to get up, for the first time in my life I think, "Yes, please shoot it." And then I wonder if getting shot might be a more violent death. Before I can answer he reconsiders. "I better not. It's bow season and if I get caught it's a serious problem." I begin to think of what other fates might await the buck and ask about predators in the area that might attack it now. He lists them out for me. I wonder, what should I do? What should I do? The man walks round to inspect the front of my car. He can't believe the lack of damage. I drive a Mini Cooper that now has a small dent across the hood where the buck landed and tufts of hair in the grill. With a touching mix of kindness and wonder, he tells me that my car should be totaled. It's a really big buck. "I raised my truck up high enough to run over them," he explains. "I was tired of having vehicles destroyed by them." I nod appreciatively but I can't stop crying. I haven't stopped crying since the accident, despite my best efforts. He says "Aw, you're like her," nodding his head in the woman's direction. "She cries too. Me I just cuss because of the damage they do."

The moments that pass feel like hours. Finally, the woman shouts, "He's dead!" I am awash in gratitude, relief, and disbelief. She steps closer. The deer is completely still. If he is breathing it is slight; there is no more struggle. I don't know what to do. I stay a while longer – I want to be sure. It's a kind of loyalty to the one who died at my hand. The man and woman stay with me. When we are all sure the buck is dead, I thank the man for his kindness. He stares and says nothing but the look on his face makes me feel as if I'm speaking some other language. We leave at the same time and they follow me down the road. In less than a mile I realize they are no longer behind me. They went back to get the deer. It occurs to me that they're going to eat it. With that thought I am crying again. But a buck of this size could feed a lot of people. It could be a really good thing for them.

Thirty minutes later I arrive at the hotel Glenville and am filled with gratitude for the people who stayed with me. The accident draws a world of possibilities a bit closer. The nearest hospital was more than an hour away. There could have been a world of trouble in any truck that stopped. And if I had gone over the embankment, who knows how long it would have taken to find me. The realization of where I am and the things that can happen becomes a feeling in my body that I can't shake. In the morning, I try every trick I know to get myself started again but I'm a wreck. A storm is coming so I decide to make a stop at Biscuit World and head home a little early.

When Danger Becomes Ordinary

Across the country everyone tells me that regardless of their intentions or their efforts, "things just happen" in life. And that is true no matter where you live or how financially secure you are. Things happen. But some things – meth-lab explosions, shootings, widespread opioid addiction – don't happen everywhere. If these problems seem to affect *individuals* randomly, they do not affect communities randomly. Communities are plagued by shootings, meth labs, and substance abuse when state and local governments fail to protect and care for residents.

Local governments develop policies and practices based on the resources available. This might mean inadequate numbers of police or it might mean inadequate police training and supervision. It might mean inadequate health care or limited public education. Most often it means all of the above. With limited resources and competing priorities, local, state, and national governments often contribute to exceptional levels of stress for families living in struggling communities.

But it would be naïve to think it is just a matter of resources. Too often those who hold public office lack the will to do their job. Sometimes the callous disregard for people's lives is a product of racism. Sometimes of greed. And sometimes of both. Pharmaceutical companies rewarded Republican Congressman Tom Marino and his colleagues with campaign contributions after they made it harder for the DEA to do their job. Marino is not the exception. In 2016, Paul Ryan, then-speaker of the House of Representatives, received $228,670 in donations from the pharmaceutical industry.[39] Overall, pharmaceutical companies poured $4.7 billion – an average of $233 million per year – into lobbying members of Congress between 1999 and 2018.[40] They've invested nearly $1.3 billion in electoral candidates at state and federal levels as well as in national party committees.[41] According to the Center for Responsive Politics, the pharmaceutical industry has about two lobbyists for every member of Congress.[42] Political leaders demonstrate time and again that they are more loyal to their funders than to the electorate. The irony, of course, is that the only people going to jail are those like Jenna.

Living in a struggling community makes people vulnerable to levels of violence, chaos, and disorder that just don't happen in other places. The burdens of belonging to the struggling class are life-encompassing. In severely compromised environments, living without adequate resources for food, rent and health care can create a crucible of potential violence. It also can fuel prejudice. As we will see in the following chapters, these burdens increase dramatically for women generally, and for women and men in communities of color most especially.

6

The Burdens of Prejudice: Class and Race

Brad Pitt's spectacular performance as Dr. Anthony S. Fauci on *Saturday Night Live* earned an Emmy nomination. Even Dr. Fauci was impressed. *The Washington Post* quoted Fauci talking about Pitt's performance: "I think he showed that he is really a classy guy when, at the end, he took off his hair and thanked me and all of the health-care workers. So, not only is he a really great actor, but he is actually a classy person."[1] I suspect most people heard this statement as a compliment, as it was intended. Complaints of classism just don't cut it in a country that still thinks "being classy" is a compliment. Class-based prejudice is justified by construing class as a matter of personal characteristics. In the US class inequalities are seldom talked about as the product of systemic inequalities that include low-wage work and predatory collusions between corporations and government.

Angel, the young Latinx man who lives in Deep East, Oakland, tells me he encounters discrimination regularly, but not in "the way in which the media has portrayed it – having someone scream in your face or get face-to-face with somebody physically." That form of hate does exist, but in Angel's life prejudice is more ordinary and more constant. It is the day-to-day experience of being an unexpected and unwelcome presence at work or school. He hears things like "'Who helped you get this position?' Prejudice is all those little things." The message to Angel was clear and not very subtle. "I was like, okay, a lot of these people are not really in favor of me being here. Maybe they're shocked that someone with my skin tone is here. Or maybe they're shocked that someone here comes from the community in Oakland that I come from." Angel hears the same questions and innuendos in multiple situations and multiple jobs. For many people, encounters with prejudice are an exhausting accumulation of moments like these. In some ways this is much harder to identify and confront because it isn't the big Hollywood scene of someone screaming in your face. Yet they can serve the same purpose: it's impossible to feel safe in environments where it's impossible to feel welcome.

But this chapter is about more than feeling welcome or being judged. It's about the way structural inequalities of race and class become part of everyday interactions. Bigotry is not restricted to communities in struggle; it isn't even more pronounced in those communities. Perhaps the only thing distinctive about the burdens of prejudice in these communities is how visible it is – money and middle-class manners can hide a lot. This chapter explores experiences of class and race prejudice, and as you might imagine it contains a lot of voices. You'll hear from Michael Chase, Jenny Gaines, and Jack Rockwell in Southeast Ohio; Tommy, Peter Walker, and Adelynn Wilkes in Tennessee; Jenna Terry in Kentucky; Two Lance Woman, Erika Brooks, and Ellison Thompson at Standing Rock; Yellow Cloud and Bob Plume at Wind River; and Vanessa Torres, PL, and Tom Sam in Oakland. From their narratives, you will see how daily prejudice is related to structural inequalities in everything from wages and employment to housing and social safety nets. The burdens of prejudice keep struggling people and communities submerged in economic quicksand – much like predatory practices.

Is Classism a Thing?

Expressions of class prejudice occur with regularity, but we are lacking an honest national discourse on the *structural* elements of economic inequality. If poverty was a personal problem, rather than a structural one, we wouldn't have millions of families in the same boat. But without a way to talk about economic struggle in structural terms, not only do we miss potential solutions, struggling people also experience a loss of dignity and a rising sense of shame that compounds the daily economic assaults. The trauma of not having enough isn't just an economic reality; it's also a psychological one that comes with learning to believe that there is something fundamentally wrong with you because you have trouble making ends meet. When families internalize class judgments, it becomes very hard for them to accept the assistance they need and even harder for them to see other families accepting that assistance.

In struggling communities, people know too well that they are looked down upon by wealthier others, particularly by those perceived to be middle class. In Appalachia there is a pervasive awareness of class prejudice. It's a region that has been looked down upon since the founding of the nation.[2] As far back as the 1800s, writers and politicians wondered publicly if it would ever be possible to lift "white trash" into respectability.[3] It's not by accident that there is no racial corollary to "white trash." This is itself a tacit acknowledgment of the role racism plays in economic life.

In Tennessee, Tommy flushes with anger as he tells me, "It's almost like a permissible thing to be kind of looking down your nose at rural, especially southern, people." White people who live in struggling communities are more often viewed by the nation as the source of bigotry rather than the victims of it. In truth they are often both. Tommy continues, "If you think somebody is not educated and you have kind of a superior attitude, that you're smarter than that person, just watch them disassemble a tractor and have all those parts spread out all over the garage, and you stand there and you go, you're putting this back together? 'Yes, I've done it three times. I know what I'm doing.' It's just a whole different level of intelligence." Too often people confuse intelligence with education. The truth is that the talent, intelligence, and skill involved in manual labor is generally unacknowledged. As a nation we too often fail to see that using our hands also requires our minds or that it is worthy, challenging, or interesting work.

You might recall Jenny Gaines in Athens County, Ohio, from previous chapters. In Athens County 59% of children in public school were eligible for free or reduced-cost school lunches in 2016–17.[4] Jenny's children were among them. The National School Lunch Program has long subsidized school lunches for children in families who meet federal poverty line criteria.[5] If Jenny's family earned between $31,980 and $45,510 the government would subsidize the cost of her children's lunches by paying 61 cents on the dollar.[6] If her family earned $31,980 per year *or less* the children would be eligible for entirely free school lunches.

Given how the school lunch program functions, it is clear to all of the kids – and then to their parents – who is and isn't receiving aid from the lunch program. Consequently, even though Jenny's children were *eligible* for free lunches under the program, Jenny and her husband would not enroll them. They also decline other social support programs (including free eye exams and dental care) for which they are qualified. "We don't want to claim those programs, because we don't want someone to feel that we're taking any advantage of anything, but we [do] need that [assistance]," explains Jenny. If it's possible to feel both rich and poor at the same time, then this would be Jenny and her family. It is hard to reconcile being one of the wealthiest families in town with making use of a social safety net. "I always say we want not. We are very blessed. We have everything we need. We have friends and family who are there for us. I worry for some of the people who live down the street from me. I worry about these little children who don't have winter coats or don't have something to eat." Jenny strikes me as very committed to this perspective and it is quite noble. Yet, if Jenny's children received free lunches, they would not be taking resources away from anyone. The other children who come from homes with even less would still be eligible and able to access free lunches. The only difference would be that her own family's economic struggles would be visible. They would become subject to the judgments of others. In Jenny's case it would bring their status in the community into question: either they are not as wealthy as they seem, or they are committing fraud.

Throughout my travels in Appalachia, people typically see government assistance as "getting something for nothing" – and therefore as an egregious form of laziness. Even people who are unable to generate economic security while working multiple jobs would not accept assistance. More often, they express a sense of shame – as if they personally had not done enough. Certainly, wealthier others are more than happy to blame people for the economic instability they face. You might recall a white man named Peter Walker in Tennessee. When we first met, Peter introduced himself to me this way: "My name is Peter Walker. I support myself. I have my own apartment, one vehicle, pay my bills. This is my everyday life." Peter clearly had heard about my research. Yet he also seems to be getting a jump on any class prejudice that I might be bringing to our conversation. Peter is one of the few in the area to still have full-time factory work and a salary that meets the economic self-sufficiency threshold for where he lives. In that sense, his life is good, as might be evident in Peter's sense of personal accomplishment.

Even so, Peter has pushed through some very bleak times in his life, including two divorces and a DUI. His personal troubles blew up his credit and to rebuild it he took out high-interest loans. To Peter's way of thinking, the incredibly high interest rates were just part of a process that he needed to accept. When I ask him about the folks around him who struggle to pay their bills, he tells me very simply: "They don't try hard enough. The food stamp card, that's what a lot of people have, you know. They don't work or nothing. They just use that. Some people, they just want to live off and not do nothing. I've seen a lot of people like that in my time. They've got kids and everything, but like the father figure, he just don't want to work. They draw on insurance money like they're hurting or something like that. I had a brother that way. He didn't really want to work. He has two kids and he's in jail over child support, because he didn't try hard enough."

The view that people who receive some form of assistance are lazy (or worse) is common among white folks in Appalachia, and it emerged as a core belief among those I talked with who follow a literal interpretation of the Bible. Some call to mind a verse in Thessalonians: "The one who is unwilling to work shall not eat." Yet in small towns, you don't have to be particularly religious to have religious beliefs seep into your thinking. Sometimes these beliefs inspire generosity – as was the case with a low-wage worker in Tennessee who saves his tips for the year to help provide a Christmas meal at a local church that he doesn't even attend. At other times, the beliefs manifest in bigoted contradictions.

Adelynn Wilkes is a white woman in Tennessee who works two jobs, one as a part-time hotel clerk and another reselling items on eBay that she buys in bulk from Goodwill; her husband holds a full-time managerial position in a small drug store a county over. They have three teenage children and also support their daughter's boyfriend, who recently moved in with them. With three jobs between them they meet the EPI threshold of a self-sufficiency budget for where they live ($85,839) and, as a result, they have managed to buy a home and put some money into a retirement account. Importantly, Adelynn did not identify as part of the struggling class but as part of the working class. Even so, they have occasional troubles with being overdrawn at the bank, and with four teenagers in the house their food bills create some challenges. "We eat a lot of dollar menu," explains Adelynn, "because a lot of times it's cheaper to feed us going through a drive-through. It's just being frugal with what we're spending, because if I go to the grocery store, a lot of times that will add up to more than what it would if we ate out."

If few people think about nutrition, everyone thinks about food: how long it will last and how much it will cost. Perhaps that's why so many people are quick to notice and to judge families using food stamps at the checkout. "I mean, we work our butts off to get by," says Adelynn. "If I go to the grocery store, I'm pinching pennies, because, whatever I take home those teenagers are going to eat and eat fast. But then, you know, you see people that are on food stamps that are able to go and buy quite a bit of food and eat better than what working-class people eat." In my travels in Appalachia, people commonly disdained anyone receiving food stamps (SNAP). In this respect the region was distinct from other areas I visited. Yet no one really seems to know how food stamps work and most assume that people using them are getting away with something. Eligibility for food stamps or SNAP benefits is tethered to the federal poverty line. Those with incomes that are 130% of the poverty line are eligible. What this looks like is represented in the accompanying table.

Annual Household Income Limit (before tax)[7]

Household Size	Maximum Income Level (per year)
1	$16,588
2	$22,412
3	$28,236
4	$34,060
5	$39,884
6	$45,708
7	$51,532
8	$57,356

In the state of Tennessee, having as little as $2,250 in savings will disqualify families from being eligible for SNAP. In some states, as little as $1,000 in a savings account will disqualify a family, while in thirty-two states, *owning a car valued at more than $4,600* is disqualifying.[8] In addition, in order to receive benefits, all able-bodied persons (broadly interpreted so as to include even those fighting cancer and kidney disease) are required to work or participate in training for twenty hours per week – no childcare is provided.

More than 42 million people received SNAP benefits in 2017.[9] Below is a table of what support you might expect if your family meets the income eligibility requirements. SNAP benefits can't be used for restaurants, even if "eating off the dollar menu" is less expensive than shopping for groceries. Note the difference between the maximum one might receive and the average that is paid out.

SNAP Benefits by Household Size[10]

Household Size	Maximum Monthly Benefit (FY 2019)	Estimated Average Monthly Benefit (FY 2019)
1	$192	$131
2	$353	$239
3	$505	$365
4	$642	$448
5	$762	$506

Despite this reality, many people like Adelynn believe the problem is the assistance and not low-wage work. Adelynn tells me, "I mean, there's poverty because people are lazy. They think that's their only situation. They don't decide to do something about it." Among the religious conservatives I met in Appalachia this is a common view. Adelynn believes that she is financially secure because her parents were financially secure. She sees herself as continuing the "lifestyle" she learned from her parents. "If you're raised in a family that doesn't have any money, then I think most of the time those people continue that lifestyle, because they don't know any different and don't do any different. But I'm a firm believer that work hard, figure it out, and make it happen; you know, if you want more money, then figure out how you're going to get it and go do it." The presence of generational poverty would seem to reinforce Adelynn's perspective on poverty as a "lifestyle." Yet the reality is more complicated.

Economic strain can become a kind of intergenerational trauma in which the relentless effort to make ends meet consumes any space one might have for creating a different future. Economic struggle doesn't just take food off the table, it narrows educational opportunities for children, and it limits a child's future to jobs they might find in the want ads. My siblings and I all expected to find futures in the want ads of the local paper. The idea of a local paper is without doubt a generational phenomenon, yet the concept remains a common one. A colleague once told me that she announced to her family that she wanted to be a physicist, and her sister immediately told her "that's the most stupid thing I've ever heard. I read the want ads regularly and have never seen anyone advertise for a physicist." People of the middle or upper middle classes don't get their jobs through want ads but through networks and associations. The world works differently for middle-class people than it does for people in the struggling class.

It is also possible to understand Adelynn's framing of poverty as a lifestyle as "dog-whistle politics." The phrase refers to statements that might appear to be innocent on the surface, but which carry a coded racist message. In this sense, it is very possible that Adelynn's understanding of poverty "as a lifestyle" is part of a larger racist discourse of dog-whistle politics that associates poverty with people of color. Some scholars argue that in the US, racism, combined with the mistaken belief that most poor people are people of color, prevents white people from supporting the strong economic safety nets found in Canada and Europe.[11] To support this argument, scholars point to the fact that the states that rejected the free expansion of Medicare under the Affordable Care Act were by and large former members of the Confederacy.[12] One thing that is very clear is that the strategy of cutting taxes and removing safety nets hurts larger *numbers* of poor white people, even as the practice falls hard on poor communities of color.

The burdens of prejudice are tethered to structural inequalities. White men, on average, are paid more than women at every level of education; and white workers, on average, are paid more than Black, Latino, and Native American workers, at every level of education.[13] Perhaps this is why, during my time in *struggling* communities, I never heard a person of color characterize struggling folks as lazy. When class prejudice combines with racism people of color face obstacles to employment and equal pay, as well as to personal safety and overall well-being within struggling communities. They know the deck is stacked.

The Faces of Racism

Every person of color I talk with has stories of racism. In some of these stories, racism lingers as part of the environment, like the air. In others it smashes through lives with tremendous violence and loss. In communities where there is already a pervasive presence of racism, the threat of violence is a constant consideration. In Athens County, Ohio, Michael Chase explains that he stays out of areas where his presence as a Black man would cause "unnecessary attention." He tells me, "I don't drive through like Chauncey or other counties at night, because Chauncey had a Ku Klux Klan thing. It was like a couple of years ago. And then there's Gloucester. Gloucester has Confederate flags and stuff, and I just didn't feel comfortable. I only drive through there at daytime. People tell me that they've been through certain parts where people have burned crosses and stuff, things like that." In these circumstances, Michael worries about what would happen if his car broke down at night. In the US, racism is a public health crisis that threatens people's lives and well-being. In struggling communities, racism can undermine the little security that exists in a person's life. It can cost people employment and housing, and sometimes, as we will see, even their children.

In the Oakland community of the Deep East, Vanessa Torres tells me that in elementary school she had a really good Latina teacher but otherwise her teachers were all white. "I think it wasn't until college that I had my first male professor. It was a Latin America/ Latino studies class, and it was a Salvadorian Latino man, and I was like, wow! I was just so shocked when I saw a brown man with black hair walking in. 'That's the professor! I was like, wow, okay!'

If you don't see yourself represented in something, then it sometimes begins to feel hard for you to reach that or even accomplish that, but if you see somebody like you who did it, [you think] I can totally do it too." Vanessa's daily work helps Latinx youth, especially among the undocumented population, to imagine themselves in college and to obtain the skills and knowledge they need to get there. She is an unrelenting optimist in the face of hard realities.

The burdens of prejudice are also evident in unequal wages at work. There are many ways to study wage gaps and each produces slightly different numbers. Some are based on wage differences in the same job, yet these can distort realities since discrimination can prevent people of color and white women from holding the same jobs as white men. On the dollar women still earn about 80% of what white, non-Hispanic men earn.[14] Women of color earn far less: Black women earn 60% of that same dollar, and Latinas only 53%.[15] Men of color also face a wage gap. For every dollar a white, non-Hispanic man earns, on average, Black men earn 87% and Latino men 91% of that same dollar.[16] The government does not even track the wages of Native people.

Vanessa is well aware of the wage gaps and tells me "These are tactics that are used to not pay people for their labor, based on their race. That contributes to low-income communities, and sometimes people don't have the resources or knowledge to advocate for themselves, to ask for a raise or to ask for these types of things. I think a lot of people are taught to just be happy with what they get. A lot of us actually, especially people of color. It definitely hits harder in low-income communities of color." Racism affects how much people are paid, the kinds of work they do, and the kinds of protections they do or do not have at work. It also affects their ability to complain or to change jobs.

A Twisted Logic

In my travels across the country, younger white women often talk with me about racism as a problem in their communities. For example, Jenna Terry in Eastern Kentucky puts it this way: "I've not seen anybody like do anything terrible, but just the way some people talk about certain things or their views on it are just sad really. Like if you're a racist or if you discriminate somebody for something, like I just don't want any part of you." When white people, like Jenna, recognize the presence of racism, they express strong feelings against it on the basis that "we are all people."[17] Yet the experiences of people of color can be so different from that of white people that the sentiment "we are all people" can actually make it harder to see and confront the racism that shapes our lives.

Jenny Gaines, a white woman, tells me that she hasn't seen racism in Athens County. "I mean, I honestly, I would have to say no. When I think discrimination, the little, tiny bits that I've seen, it's because people haven't known something. You know, like kids [wanting to touch] curly hair, maybe because they're African American. It's not discrimination. It's more wanting to know what the other hair is like. I don't really see it." Jenny can't see the costs that this behavior exacts from African American children, or the way it reinforces a sense of entitlement among white children. Racism doesn't always involve a feeling of hate. It is often just about who gets to be included as an ordinary member of a community.

In many ways, Jenny expresses a curious position, but one that I encountered often in my travels. It's not *just* that Jenny is holding her own point of view as being more valid than another. The white people I talk with often feel entitled to define what is and isn't racist – that is to say, they claim the right to limit the kind of behavior that people of color can complain about. This position sometimes leads to my listening to white people declare they are *not* racist, in very racist ways. For example, Adelynn Wilkes tells me "I've never seen racism as far as, you know – I've never felt racist toward anyone. Now I almost think, to a certain degree, that these moves that, you know, the colored people make, going to stand in the road and all of that, I almost think, to a certain degree, they're racist toward us, white Caucasians, just from a standpoint of their actions, especially those of us that don't see color." Adelynn's remarks offer insight into the convoluted thinking that makes white people victims of racism when people of color name or protest racist behavior. Adelynn treats her own perception, and by implication the perceptions of other white people, as having the final word on racism – without realizing that such a view is itself racist.

Adelynn continues talking about racism: "It's not been something I've ever –," she pauses to correct herself. "I did work with a lady at [a local company] and she was a Black lady, and she said that racism did exist. She said, 'I will go out, and I know when people are being racist.' But I think a lot of it's mental. They like that drama. That's what I perceive some of it to be. They want the drama. They want to create the racism. They want to keep it alive, whereas to me I just want to move on, do whatever. You know, I don't care what color your skin is." Here again is an outright denial of racism that is itself very racist. These mental gymnastics are necessary to claiming oneself to be a good person (i.e., not racist) while maintaining beliefs that are racist. Not only is Adelynn unable or unwilling to accept the possibility that Black people experience racism – she claims the right to define the experiences of Black people.

Racism also shows up in how much people are paid and in the cultivation of hostile work environments, which white people often refuse to acknowledge. According to a 2017 poll, 55% of white people across the country say they believe there is discrimination against *white* people today.[18] For example, according to the participants in this survey, white people feel they are systematically overlooked in hiring practices that favor people of color. The experience can also be understood as losing the preferential edge that centuries of racism have provided to white people.

Tommy's family has deep roots in Tennessee, and he delighted talking with his grandmother about how the family grew their own crops and raised their own livestock. One story involved the importance of neighbors. Tommy recounts his grandmother saying "'To the left of us we had the Willaford farm, and across the street we had the Kasen farm, and to the right of us we had the Spivey farm, and up on top of the hill was ni**er Bill. And we all kind of worked together. We all shared things, and if we had a crop that didn't work out, we would share with each other. We were kind of like family.'" Tommy shifts his stance, glances at me for a reaction. He sees none and continues. "I asked her, I said, 'Well, Grandma, why did you call Bill, ni**er Bill up on top of the hill, up on top of the ridge?' She said, 'Well, honey, that's just what we called them back then.' I said, I wouldn't use that nowadays, and she said, 'That's just what we called them in that day.' She goes, 'but do you think I hated Bill in any way?' and I said, I don't know. She goes, 'Bill shared with us, and we shared with Bill. Bill was part of the community,' and she said, 'and there was no one that disliked him or disrespected him. He was part of us.'"

I have to draw a breath in this part of the conversation before I ask: Why didn't your family just call the man Bill? Tommy has a flustered moment and then explains to me with some aggravation that I missed the point of the story. For Tommy, the point of the story is that when white southerners – particularly of that time period – use that word, I shouldn't assume they don't like Black people. He tells me I am an outsider and cautions me to "be careful about what you assume about people and whether or not they were really hateful and racist, because of a word that they used, because that wasn't the case." Tommy grows increasingly agitated in our conversation. Perhaps he thought by invoking my outsider status, I would be more easily persuaded by his view. I am not. He rubs his head as he walks outside. For the moment, the conversation is over.

Of course, we all like to think we see reality exactly as it is – that is part of human nature. But categorically discounting the views of African Americans is itself racist. Minimizing the suffering caused by racism is racist. Yet these are the very strategies I heard some white people use to claim they are not racist – even as they use racial slurs. I heard too often that if racism existed, they would be against it. But since it doesn't exist, they are innocent white people being victimized by people of color who keep claiming there is racism. The reality goes beyond emotionally toxic work environments and unsafe communities. According to the US Census Bureau in 2018, the median Black household earned just 59 cents on every dollar of income earned by the median white household.[19] Racism shapes the experiences of people of color in every economic class.

Combining the belief that racism is a thing of the past with the reality of working ridiculously hard just to keep food on the table means very few white people I talk with can imagine that they benefit from racism.[20] It makes a certain kind of sense. Until you consider Cliven Bundy, a white rancher who grazed his cattle on public land in Nevada. Bundy refused to pay the required grazing fees for twenty years and by 2014 he owed a million dollars in fees and fines. As a result, the Bureau of Land Management sent armed federal agents to confiscate Bundy's cattle. They were met with hundreds of protestors, including an armed militia, in support of Bundy. In the end, the cattle were returned and the white men who held guns on federal agents saw their charges dismissed.[21]

In 2016, Cliven Bundy's sons Ammon and Ryan Bundy, who had participated in the standoff with their father, organized an armed occupation of the Malheur National Wildlife Refuge in Oregon. The occupation claimed that the federal government lacks the constitutional authority to manage public lands. In addition to demanding that the management of public lands be turned over to local governments, the group sought the release of two ranchers who had been arrested for starting fires. At some points, the occupation included an estimated militia of 400 – some of whom *fired* on federal agents. The standoff lasted forty-one days.

More than two dozen people were eventually arrested; those who stood trial were either acquitted or given sentences ranging from probation to one to two years in prison.[22] Dwight and Steven Hammonds were convicted of setting a fire on public land and were given *less* than the legal minimum prison sentence of five years; even so, Dwight Hammond was released after three months and Steven

Hammond after a year.[23] In 2018 President Trump pardoned the Hammonds. Both were Trump supporters.[24] Imagine any scenario in which men of color engage in an armed standoff with federal agents – actually shoot at federal agents – and walk away alive, much less alive with only a slap on the wrist. It just doesn't happen. Look only at what happened to the Native American Water Protectors at Standing Rock.

There are all too many examples of white people being advantaged by our political, legal, and economic systems. Think about the white men armed with automatic and semi-automatic weapons who stormed the Michigan State House in 2020 and threatened Governor Whitmer in an effort to force her to lift the stay-at-home orders.[25] Police did not attack the people who occupied the building; they didn't even arrest anyone in what was deemed an act of "free speech." Or consider the insurrection of January 6, 2021 at the US Capitol, which appeared to have the support of some police. A well-armed group of white domestic terrorists broke into the Capitol and rampaged through the building, stealing and destroying property and threatening legislators. Five people died in the assault, yet the mob was simply escorted out of the building by police. Charges are forthcoming, but it was impossible to watch this moment unfold without recalling that police in full riot gear used tear-gas and concussion grenades to clear peaceful Black Lives Matter protestors from Lafayette Square to make a space for then-president Trump to have his photo taken holding a Bible while standing in front of a church.[26] Racism produces a continual stream of moments that benefit white people.

The participation of Riley June Williams, a twenty-two-year-old white woman, in the attack on the US Capitol was well-documented by video footage and her own social media posts. She was charged with two misdemeanors (trespassing, violent entry to and disorderly conduct on Capitol grounds) and two felonies (aiding or abetting the theft of government property and obstructing, influencing or impeding an official proceeding).[27] The government property was Speaker Nancy Pelosi's laptop. As a result of these charges, Williams is facing potentially decades in prison. Prosecutors did not request that she be held until trial and Williams was released to her family for home confinement. By contrast, in 2010, Kaleif Browder, a sixteen-year-old Black teenager living in New York City, was stopped by police who said they were looking for a thief. They found nothing on him but took him to the 48th Precinct in the Bronx for processing anyway. There, Browder was charged with robbery, grand larceny, and assault for allegedly stealing a backpack. Because he was on probation and pleaded not guilty, he was sent to Rikers Island to await trial. Browder's family could not afford an attorney and he had little contact with the public defender assigned to his case. During his time on Rikers Island, he suffered brutal attacks from guards as well as inmates, and endured long stints in solitary confinement.[28] After *three years* in Rikers, his case was dismissed – no trial, no jury, no verdict. Dismissed. He was free, but he would never be the same. These are just a few examples of how a racist system benefits white people.

Daily Doses of Arsenic

As a Black man living in Oakland, California, PL tells me he faces discrimination in small ways every day: "In the community, you know, you walk by a homeless person, and, you know, they'll say something derogatory to you, or you'll walk on the sidewalk and someone of a different ethnicity will cross the street before they get to you. Sometimes you walk into service stations or you walk into an organization and you don't get service as quick as other people, or you're ignored, so that happens a lot in the Bay Area." These supposedly small incidents are like low doses of arsenic that build up over time.

Tom Sam, a Diné/Comanche man in Oakland, had his first encounter with racist policing as a child. "My younger brother and I were running across the street to return a movie that we had rented. At a crosswalk, we just happened to be running, and as we crossed the street we were pulled over at gunpoint. Had to lay down on our faces, patted down, everything. *Then* (the police officer) asked why we were running." For Tom, racism gives him a constant sense of being a potential target. The college he attended had a Native American mascot and his efforts to end that practice drew hostility. "At school I continually pushed for the eradication of that mascot and got a lot of really negative feedback and hate mail and stuff about why people felt they were appropriate, and even from administration, from the president of the university, from other faculty and staff, alumni, all these different types of characters basically saying that, hey, dehumanizing and demeaning a whole ethnic group of people is okay based on school heritage."

Vanessa Torres, who lives in Deep East Oakland, sums up her experience this way: "You just never truly know once you leave that door what can really happen to you, what you can be exposed to that can put your life at risk." We both pause and draw a breath as we think about this reality. It is a reality. Vanessa continues: "We see tons of examples of racism toward Black people, toward Latinos. It's definitely nasty toward Latinos, because people are assuming that you're an immigrant. They assume you're undocumented, and they'll ask very malicious questions, like if [you] have a Green Card. There's people who are Brown who actually have citizenship and are born here. It's really shady for people to ask do you have a visa? I think especially now in our political climate with this president onboard, that hate speech and hate crimes toward Latinos have definitely gone on the rise. We hear about it all the time."

In Athens County, Ohio, Jack Rockwell, a twenty-something white man, is trying to keep his head above water. He has a full-time job that he enjoys but it pays $8.15 an hour – which gives him an annual *pre-tax* salary of $16,952. This is about $5,000 above the federal poverty line but about half of the EPI self-sufficiency budget.[29] Jack tells me, "I spend about 40% of my income on rent and probably another 25–30% to food. I mean come on, that's not feasible. That's not sustainable. I need to make more money." But Jack hasn't been able to find work that pays any better and on many days he's just glad to have a job. As we talk about work, Jack tells me "I'm half Jewish on my dad's side. I'm non-practicing, and I've noticed that if I bring that up in a work environment, I'm pretty typically teased about it pretty consistently for a while – always in good fun."

I wonder what this good fun might look like and Jack tells me about a job that he had in a fast food restaurant. "Like the fry cook, basically two or three times a week, he would have a new Holocaust joke for me. And there was one guy who was our dishwasher for a while, and he was like pretty openly white nationalist; great guy, liked me, had some great conversations with him. This is an awful thing to say, but it's always, sort of, in good fun. And I hate how that sounds, but that's literally how it came across. He would act like, 'oh, I'm a white nationalist. Oh, you're kind of Jewish. Like this is just how we interact, you know, like ha ha.' There was never any malice about it." If you are having trouble understanding "the good fun" of a white nationalist making Holocaust jokes to a Jew, you aren't alone. Yet this is as common as it is confusing.

Racism as a kind of joke is confusing. It can feel like an invitation to intimacy: "See how close we are, we can joke about these things. We're so close that I can say offensive things to you, and you won't be offended because we're friends, because you trust me." It is nearly impossible to resist this humor without being seen as the one starting a conflict. To resist this kind of "joking" is to be called humorless and to face the possible charge of being racist for naming racism. Jack is compelled to listen – to go along to get along. He had no allies, few safeguards, and fewer alternatives for employment.

Jack continues talking about his work in the fast food restaurant. "We had a Black kid working as a fryer. We sold chicken and, you know, we had a white meal and a dark meal and a mixed meal. His name was Mike and anytime we had a mixed meal, 'give me up a four-piece Mike,' because he had a white dad and a Black mom. I never saw anything withheld from him because he was Black. I never saw like anybody threaten him because he was Black. Never had a server who was like uncomfortable working with him or anything like that, but people were race conscious and not afraid to vocalize that." I have trouble with the idea of this being innocent fun. So, I ask: "How else did that come up?" Jack looks stunned and embarrassed as the words slip out. "People would call him ni**er." Jack looks at me as if this is occurring to him for the first time as we talk, as if he is connecting the dots. I follow up and ask "Coworkers, customers?" "No, never a customer. People who he had a rapport with, and, you know, every time, just like me with the Jewish jokes, he'd laugh it off. It never seemed intended to intimidate or be cruel."

Is there something funny about racism? Is there some way that racism is not cruel? Perhaps to white nationalists. The jokes enable white people to both express racism and to deny its impact. It puts people on notice about the kind of behavior they need to accept to be in a certain environment. This kind of racism can saturate workplaces, making it necessary to talk oneself out of one's feelings. Naming this kind of racism never seems to go well, and too often the person of color is called racist for having brought it up – there is more than one Adelynn Wilkes in the world. It makes parents of color work double-time to protect their children.

In Oakland, Tom Sam worries about sending the girls to a school filled with non-Native teachers. Tom and his wife opted to homeschool their children. At Standing Rock, Erika Brooks doesn't have that option. She tells me "We have a lot of non-Native teachers at the schools and they would show prejudice with the girls in different ways. I would go right away and handle it with them; not in a resentful, confrontational way. But teachers knew that I was going to be there if anything happened with the girls. A friend said when she came to visit that immediately she could feel the prejudice. The level of prejudice that was just in the air, that it was just pervasive."

Erika is smart and responsible. Sitting across from me she is also clearly exhausted. "I don't expect it to come easy, but I shouldn't have to battle for everything that I want just to be at an even level with, you know, respect and consideration in the way that I respect and consider other people." Yet the prejudice she battles feels like a relentless onslaught. Everywhere I traveled, non-Native people openly expressed a strong belief that Native people are receiving huge amounts of undeserved money from the government, which seemed to underscore racist beliefs that Native people are lazy and addicted to drugs and alcohol. Erika tells me "Just because I am Native American people assume that I live off the government. I'm an alcoholic. I do drugs. I don't care about my kids. Everybody likes to think 'oh we *gave* you this reservation.' You didn't give us anything. It's really, like a concentration camp, but not to the far extent of a concentration camp. We're left with the very minimum to get by. There is an inherent sense of mourning that [Native] people have. There's only survival. No one is thriving. What we're seeing now is a result of the historical genocide that's happened."

After generations of US occupation, alcohol and drug use are increasing problems on Standing Rock. "I have to watch my sister and brother destroy themselves and people that I care about," explains Erika. "These social illnesses or social unfunctionings are because of the history. This is what happens if you oppress a people and treat them as prisoners, when you push them down. Non-Native people just think, oh, you're feeling sorry for yourself. If you have a sense of intelligence and you think about the history, then you understand that this is a natural result. It's going to take generations and generations for it to even out, if it ever does – if we don't destroy ourselves in the process. It doesn't happen instantly."

Other women at Standing Rock express similar sentiments. Ellison Thompson explains her experience with non-Native people: "We don't matter to them. They don't even acknowledge us. A lot of people, like when we go to Bismarck, a lot of people look down on us. A lot of people try not to serve us. A lot of people are very rude to us. I've had to deal with racism my whole life." Two Lance Woman worries a lot about her adult children who live in Bismarck "because Indigenous people, especially our men, are always sought out to be in the system. It's the perceptions of us that the men go in prison and the women are murdered and missing. We're dirty Indians, and we're uneducated. Or we're in poverty. I've always told my children, don't become what they say and think you are." Two Lance Woman holds a college degree and a professional job at Standing Rock. She also has anxiety about going to Bismarck because of the pervasive racism there. "There's times where I'm like, oh, going to a store and I'm just like, oh, crap. Am I going to be called a name? Is someone going to come in my face, you know, just this big drama."

Two Lance Woman has known racism her entire life. At eight years old, she was taken from her home by the Mormon Church's Indian Placement Program. Her parents were told she would attend "superior schools." Two Lance Woman spent ten years living with five different white foster families. As a girl and the only Native child around, she faced both racism and sexual assault. Alone. "It's like you're a prisoner of war. There's no childhood." Even now the memories bring her quickly to tears. According to Mormon doctrine, American Indians had hardened their hearts against god – as was evidenced by their dark skin.[30] Consequently, Mormons have believed it is their responsibility to convert Native Americans to Mormonism. To this end, they brought children from over sixty tribes into their placement program with just a signed permission slip from their parents. The program operated from 1954 to 1996, but the post-traumatic stress continues for the people who were raised in that system.[31] Two Lance Woman is part of a lawsuit against the Mormon Church that started in 2004. After having been stalled for years over technicalities, it is finally moving forward again.[32]

"How society thinks of Native Americans is beyond me," sighs Two Lance Woman. Most non-Native people in the US learn about Native Americans from history books – as if Native people exist only in the past. This ignorance is compounded by historical inaccuracies and biases. "We're still in the cowboys and Indians stage, you know." Two Lance Woman pauses. "I don't think the 'wild west' was ever wild." Since her job requires her to interact with a lot of non-Native visitors who come to Standing Rock, Two Lance Woman has a system she relies upon. "I always smudge with sage, you know, and so I always say one of our morning prayers. 'Let us have a good day.' But it kind of gets sickening. Sometimes you can't correct how they think. You just have to let their bad vibes follow them."

The Violence of Hate

In my travels, white people readily assume I will see things from their perspective because I am white. For example, in Riverton, Wyoming, it wasn't unusual to hear white people make a distinction between the things "people do" and the things "Indians do," as if Indians were not people. In a conversation about the troubles Riverton is facing, a white woman remarks to me on the closing of the local Safeway and then adds "we also have Indians." Her words hit hard. I draw a breath and ask: "What's that mean?" Without blinking she says, "Well, their lifestyle is all drugs and alcohol. They get money from the government and spend it all on drugs and alcohol. And now there's a meth problem that's really bad." The presence of racism toward Native Americans here is ever present in casual conversations, in street names (Sq**w Road), in the appropriation of Indian crafts, and in the misuse of traditional Indian symbols.

Racism that pervades an environment is more than background noise and more than a matter of wages or employment. It is a constant threat that can easily be catalyzed into violence. The people living at Wind River Reservation go into Riverton, the largest nearby town, for groceries, gas and other necessities. But Riverton is a kind of living crime scene for Native people. Yellow Cloud is an Arapaho elder in his seventies living at Wind River. His wife and best friend of twenty-three years died just months before we met. Yellow Cloud is now living alone, supported financially by a dividend from the gas and oil lease on the reservation. This is something under $16,000 a year. He tells me that he is "doing all right by myself." When I ask about people who are not "doing all right" he responds quickly and with a pained look: "Oh, I feel so sorry for them. They're homeless, and even if it's 40 below zero they're walking around town." Shelter space is scarce in Riverton.

In his youth, Yellow Cloud did ranch work, drove trucks, and eventually ended up working for a weed and pest control company. He has had COPD for seventeen years and believes he got it from the chemicals used at the weed and pest company. Yellow Cloud's voice is quiet and has a weary edge; arthritis gives him a ragged gait when he walks – some days the arthritis is so bad, he can't walk at all. The weather doesn't help. Snow starts in September and winter temperatures range between zero and 18 degrees Fahrenheit – before you add a wind chill factor.

When he tells me about racism, Yellow Cloud recounts an incident in Riverton when he and his son were unexpectedly jumped by white men. Yellow Cloud wants to be clear they didn't just take the beating. He emphasizes, "We fought back!" Even now his fists clench as he tells the story. Then he sighs. "But we're the ones that had to go to jail, though. White boys got away, but we went to jail. They started the fight. Hit us first and everything. And the police didn't – you try to tell the police *that*. They won't listen to us. We went to jail and they went home." Yellow Cloud lowers his head for a moment and when he lifts his face toward me, I see what I think is a mix of grief and anger. He tells me this is a kind of sport among non-Natives – beating Native men like this. "Even the homeless people, the homeless Indians are always getting beat by them in the town here." Yellow Cloud's voice fills with disgust. I am frozen in my seat for a moment. The pit of racism feels bottomless. A study published by the National Institute of Justice found that 81.6% – more than four out of every five Native men – have experienced violence in their lifetime.[33] More than one-third of American Indian and Alaska Native men have experienced some type of violence in the past year.[34] Yet it never makes the news and, as Yellow Cloud says, the white men are still walking away as the Native men get locked up.

Bob Plume tells me that white people are hateful. "They're very hateful because the Indians still got land and we still got the things that they want. They don't have the culture. They don't have things that they want to have." Bob tells me he can feel that hate every day – when he goes to a store or a bank. Even when he's mowing a lawn. Bob is an Arapaho man in his mid-fifties who also lives on the Wind River Reservation. At first I am surprised as he laments the loss of his friends – he tells me he is the only one left. "All of my friends had head injuries and they all went home. So, I'm the only one that's left. They all died when they're young. They all died in their forties, in their thirties. All due to, all due to head injuries." Head injuries? I don't know how to understand an epidemic of head injuries. Then he explains.

Bob had a home, a job, and a family – until a group of men took him by surprise one night. "I walked out late one night at the truck stop. Walked out of the door and I got boom! This guy says, 'you were with my wife and you were this and that' and I said no you got the wrong person, dude. Then that's how that happened. The doctor was going to have surgery on me that night, but he waited until two or three days, then I went to Casper to have brain surgery." Bob gives me a tour of his head and face starting with his broken eye socket: "I got pins here, pins here, plastic bone here." The injury changed his life.

After the beating, he was unable to recognize his family. "I didn't know who they were. It was like you see on TV. I never thought it would ever happen, but it happened." Even now relationships are hard for him to rebuild and he worries about a future in which he is alone. "I have one boy that I know of. And I have a daughter maybe in Oklahoma that has three kids." Back then, Bob's friends promised him they would make it right. They said they would find the guy who beat him, and this seems to bring a mix of sadness and satisfaction to Bob. "They fixed it. They beat the shit out of him, same thing he had done to me." Bob draws a long sigh.

Of course, nothing is really fixed. Bob's efforts to rebuild his life have been slow. He tried to go back to school but was unable to retain the information. He turned to his uncle and other relatives who drew him in closer to traditional ways where he found renewed meaning for life and some cherished responsibilities. "'Stay focused!' they told me. They say if you mess up by not focusing, you'll wander off and you'll find yourself someplace where you're not supposed to be." Bob tries to live his life by the traditional ways. He credits his life today to tribal elders who used traditional ceremony and healing techniques to help him to stay alive. Elders made him a fire keeper for ceremonies. Healing – for himself and others – remains at the center of his life. While the outcome of Bob's experience is unique, the experience of being beaten by roving groups of white men – often for sport with no pretense of a motive – is not.

Again, racism is structural, not just personal. For example, while the racist laws of *Dred Scott* v. *Sandford* and *Brown* v. *Board of Education* have been repealed,[35] federal laws regarding Native American rights still active today include the Plenary Power Doctrine, which leaves tribes without meaningful judicial recourse against breaches of the federal trust responsibility or intrusions upon tribal interests and sovereignty.[36] The policies and practices that have supported the genocide of Native people remain institutionalized in contemporary law and politics. John Yoo, legal advisor to George W. Bush, famously drew from existing federal law regarding Native Americans to draft policies of indefinite detention and what has become known as "the Torture Memos."[37] Most recently the Trump administration drew from these same laws as the basis of the "Muslim ban" and of migrant family separation and detention.

Lives of Meaning and Consequence

The burdens of class and race prejudice have psychological, physical, and economic consequences that compound the daily struggles to make ends meet. Racism and prejudice are not exclusive to people in the struggling class – nor is structural racism. Yet prejudice, and the violence it generates, always falls hardest on those with the least. Millions of struggling people strive to build lives of meaning and consequence – for themselves and their families – with inadequate resources. They do so in the toxic environments of class bigotry, racism and cultural genocide – environments that continue to be denied, minimized, and distorted. Native people in particular face the continuation of a genocide that is masked when it is conflated with racism. This will become even clearer in the next chapter as Native women talk about what has happened to their lives.

7

The Burdens Women Face

Adelynn Wilkes and I are sitting together in a hotel lobby when she leans forward toward me to tell me about her last job. When she hadn't received a raise that she felt she was due, she went to talk with her boss. Her quiet voice fills with anger. "I reminded this individual of the increase I was supposed to have, and oh he did tell me, 'Oh, if you need a better paying job, you need to tell your husband to get a better paying job.'" We stew for a minute over how this could happen in this day and age. But "this day and age" may not be quite what we think it is. As you might recall, white women on average still earn about 80% of the dollar that white men earn.[1] Women of color earn far less, with Black women earning 60% and Latinas 53% of that same dollar.[2] Women are poorer than men in every state.[3] And Native women have higher rates of poverty in every state than any other group of women in the country.[4] The world is moving so slowly toward equal pay that at this rate it will take 108 years to close the wage gap between women and men and 202 years to bring about equality in the workplace.[5]

Since the majority of low-wage workers in the US are women, and since women are more likely than men to be heads of single-parent households, wage discrimination can literally be life threatening for women and their children. The combination of racism and sexism in education increases the likelihood that women of color will be relegated to low-skilled, low-wage work with little opportunity for advancement.[6] This is another way in which women and their children get trapped in poverty for generations. Consequently, you might think that wage inequality and racism were the most pressing issues raised by the women I talked with, but they were not. Apart from Adelynn, across the country women in struggling communities consistently raised an entirely different set of daily concerns: sexual assault, domestic abuse, and sex trafficking.

Through the narratives of Jenna Terry, Ellison Thompson, Erika Brooks, Two Lance Woman, and Oralia, this chapter provides insight into the level of sexual and physical violence that has become a routine aspect of their daily lives – just like worrying about an unpaid electric bill or how to pay for urgent dental treatment. It's important to say that their stories of domestic abuse, sexual assault, and sex trafficking emerged in conversations about their worries in daily life – not from specific questions about violence.

Challenging Assault

In Athens, Ohio, Rose Taylor tells me "being a college town, sexual assault is prevalent here. I think a lot of it is tied with the drinking culture." Ohio University records show there were ninety-three rapes in 2018. Local news covered police reports of sixteen sexual assaults in the first *month* of the fall semester in 2019.[7] Rose tells me that rape is so common that police didn't even realize there was a serial rapist in town until the same evidence was tied to thirteen different cases. "By the time they caught him and tied him with like his DNA," says Rose, "it was like fifteen or sixteen cases." Keep in mind that these numbers represent only the cases reported to police. Nationally, sexual assault occurs every seventy-three seconds.[8]

All of the women I talked with take measures to protect themselves from men. Think about that for a moment. All of them. Most didn't go out alone at night, some carried weapons, others kept dogs as both pets and guardians. All of these efforts help, but they aren't enough to keep women safe. The implications of high levels of sexual violence for women's lives are huge, and they increase exponentially for low-wage women who face severely limited options in terms of health care, legal support, and workplace protection. Reporting sexual assault is a complicated process fraught with even more troubles. Women in struggling communities lack access to support services when reporting to police and are often discouraged from reporting by the police themselves. I had that very experience when I was sexually assaulted by a physician. With the help of friends, I went to the police to file a complaint but was told that if I filed charges, I should expect to be sued for libel because the doctor was a public figure in the community. As a young woman, I joined the nearly 75% of sexual assault survivors who do *not* file police reports.[9]

Recent studies show that 84.33% of Native women experience violence – including violence from an intimate partner, sexual violence, physical violence, psychological aggression or stalking.[10] In struggling communities of color, women who are sexually assaulted by members of their own community face a complicated and painful choice between protecting themselves or the men in their community. In South Dakota, Native Americans make up 8.5% of the population but 60% of the federal court caseload.[11]

Erika Brooks, like many Native women, found herself caught between the sexual violence of a Native man and what she knows to be a racist justice system. You might recall Erika from earlier chapters. She is a fifty-year-old Lakota woman who has been raising her sibling's children. While two of the youngest color at the table, Erika tells me, "My thirteen-year-old was raped by her uncle, someone she trusted and thought of as a father. He was really close to her dad, too. They talked about her dad a lot, which was why she liked to hang around him, and then this happened. She played with his son a lot; his son is special needs. She went over there, and they were all gone, just this guy was home. She came screaming in one afternoon. 'He raped me! He raped me!' From that time on, it's just been *real* unstable." Erika did her best to assure her niece that nothing was her fault but felt unequipped for dealing with all that comes with the deep betrayal of child rape. Erika quickly became overwhelmed by her niece's rage and fear. Nothing she did helped the child to talk about what happened. With tears in her eyes, Erika tells me that her niece acted out the trauma. "From the time she woke up until the time she would fall asleep, literally she would be attacking me all day verbally, anything but physically, just attacking me and criticizing me for parenting. I understand that. You know, that's a child who's feeling like she wasn't protected."

Erika reached out to law enforcement. Given the US restrictions on tribal law enforcement, the case was immediately handed over to the FBI. The FBI introduced Erika to the Children's Trauma Center for counseling for her niece. Yet the help that looked hopeful at first soon added to her troubles. Erika became worn down by the FBI's need for follow-up and then what felt like a relentless process of being redirected to other agencies who would in turn redirect her somewhere else. "It's a struggle every day," she tells me. But the most distressing troubles that came with reporting have been closer to home.

It's both important and unusual that Erika was able to hold the man accountable for rape. Native women do not want to collude with the federal justice system, but Erika felt compelled to act on behalf of her niece. "Well, I think, you know, the whole community was surprised. He was surprised. His family was surprised that the first thing I did was call the police. Everybody was like, 'Was it serious enough that the police needed to be called? Did you really have to do that?' and I was like, 'excuse me. I just followed through with what I knew was right.' Everyone who has talked to me ... ." Erika pauses to gather herself as her emotions rise. "I've had men say – his name is Walter – they say, 'oh poor Walter.' I'll just turn around and confront them. That is such sick thinking. To even think that is so disgusting. This is a little girl who couldn't defend herself. He literally picked her up, threw her over his shoulder, took her in the bedroom and threw her on the bed. She was powerless. He's a grown man, and he's got no business doing that to a child. No child deserves to be traumatized in that way."

Erika and her niece have been traumatized again by people suggesting the child is lying or that it was her fault. "That's a huge thing to just have random people say things like that. I know her and she didn't lie. That wasn't a child who lied. And this acting out behavior isn't somebody who lied. And then, my sister when she's drunk yelling [at the girl], 'You caused trouble in the family,' you know, blaming her, and it's amazing how in these communities the thinking is so perverted that everybody is feeling sorry for the man that raped her that he had to go to prison." Erika's willingness to protect and defend her niece has come at a high price.

"Everyone has said something to my niece. She can't ride her bike around the community. She can't walk with friends around the streets or anything; somebody says something to her or harasses her, so she comes home upset. She's a tough little girl. She's really resilient, but this has really rocked her to her core. My first thought was, we need to get out of here. The girls asked almost every day, 'When are we leaving? When are we going?' And I'm thinking, 'I'm the adult here. I need to take charge, and I need to find us a home.'" But Erika is stopped by her own unresolved trauma of being tossed into homelessness with four small children when a landlord in Mobridge evicted them. They are a family without the financial resources they need for housing much less trauma counseling. Erika's decision to protect her niece pits her against the very community that she and the children depend upon. It was an unbelievably courageous decision with very high stakes, given the interdependence of people in Native communities and the pervasive racism around her from non-Native communities.

This is a familiar story to many Native women. In Wyoming, Oralia brings up the same topic in a different way at Wind River Reservation. Oralia is an Arapaho woman in her mid-fifties. Her days start early. She is on dialysis and three times a week she drives thirty-five miles to the nearest dialysis center to arrive by 6 a.m. She stays on dialysis for about four hours then drives straight to work at the Wind River Reservation. She's been doing this for three years and has not yet made a transplant list. She is not expecting to make the transplant list. The wear and tear of life seems to have caught up to her – she also has had five heart bypass surgeries. Oralia tells me "It's just like I keep saying, God, now what? God, now what? This friend of mine says, 'Quit asking!'" Oralia lets out a full belly laugh that fills the room. She's a small, frail woman, but in this moment she feels big and powerful. After our conversation, I never think of Oralia as small or frail again.

After thirty-three years of marriage, Oralia divorced. She has three children and seven grandchildren, all of whom live nearby. She holds an associate degree and supports herself on a full-time, professional job that pays a bit more than $45,000. Like all Native people I met, Oralia supports a wide range of family and community members. With six brothers and sisters, three of her own children, and seven grandchildren there is always someone needing a hand. Oralia pays the bills and does grocery shopping for her sister and brother-in-law who also have serious medical problems. She has loaned three family members money to buy cars and bailed her brothers out of jail. "I've got a pretty big family, and everybody's always hitting me up. I'm like, 'What makes you think I have it?' 'Because you work all the time.' 'Well, get yourself a damn job,' you know. But they know Auntie Oralia or sister Oralia will always bail them out." Oralia's willingness to help means that while her own bills are covered and her health insurance is paid, she has no savings and no retirement plan.

Oralia has held steady, full-time, professional work all of her life, which makes her among the wealthier residents at Wind River Reservation. She worked in victim services for twenty years as a victim-witness coordinator: five years with the tribal court and fifteen years for the county courts. As a liaison between the victim and the prosecutor, Oralia says, "I felt like I was the only one that the Native people could talk to. I was the only help out there for them, so I just kept going and kept going. It really took a toll on me. Anytime there was a court date, if they didn't have a ride, I'd go get them. I'd hold their hands and wipe their tears. I fought with the judges and with the prosecutors." She understood how hard it was for Native women to prosecute abusers and tried to provide them with as much support as possible – generally going to their homes, rather than sending letters asking them to report to her office. She had some major accomplishments along the way: she pushed for the Victims' Bill of Rights and was part of a successful effort to persuade the courts to allow video testimony so that victims don't have to face their perpetrators in court.

Oralia worked on any case that came up, and what came up most often was domestic violence. "I'd go through all of the incident reports, and if there was a victim involved, I made contact with them. I went to a lot of homes, saw a lot of bad stuff. After twenty years that was enough." One day she got a report of domestic violence: "he had literally kicked out her two front teeth. I went to the hospital and met her. I helped her get new teeth through victims' compensation. And about a month later she was back with him. Oh, man, I couldn't believe it, you know. But it's amazing how many times they go back. They say usually eight to nine times before they actually really leave. You can't stop them [from going back]. You just have to be there for them each and every time they come back to you, you know." Oralia tells me women keep returning to their battering spouses until the husband turns his violence on the kids. "Usually that's the line for the women."

She was there to protect victims and she took her job seriously. Oralia recounted a few difficult cases in which she had to educate the courts about how to treat Native victims of sexual assault and battery with dignity and cultural sensitivity. The memories of the racism she confronted in those fights quickly brought tears. "One of our judges when I first met him, he was very outspoken about what he felt about Native American people. He would just come down to our office and he'd say stuff. Boy, it didn't take me long to charge out of my office. I would go at it. I would tell him, 'I don't know what gives you the right to think that all people are that way.' I said, 'Look at you. You're a closet drinker. Everybody knows it,' I said, 'but the Native people, they drink theirs out in the public,' I said, 'they're not trying to hide it like you are.' And I walked away from him. Pretty soon my attorney, he says, 'Oralia, you shouldn't talk to the judge like that.' I said, 'Well, he shouldn't talk to me like that.' The thing was, he was real good about certain people, and then he was just hateful toward other people. I'd just ask 'What gives you the right to think you can treat people like that? You're supposed to be the one that's unbiased sitting up there on the bench.'" Without the legal structure to address violence against women in their own communities, Native women are faced with a choice of accepting the violence against them or turning things over to the federal government. If they choose the latter, they must surrender control over the process to the very institutions that have created and implemented genocidal policies toward Native people since first contact.

Sex Trafficking

In Floyd County in Eastern Kentucky, Jenna Terry tells me that she keeps a casual but regular eye on news about sex trafficking. "There's been local cases where like it's getting closer to us. Like I've seen it, you know, in bigger places but it's getting a little bit closer." One of the bigger places that Jenna references is Louisville. The Kentucky Derby, in Louisville, Kentucky, has long been a magnet for sex traffickers.[12] In fact, sex trafficking at the Kentucky Derby may be as established as the Derby itself. Researchers find that around the time of the Derby, local papers experience a spike in coded ads intended to reach the influx of men attending the races who want to have sex with children.

Most cases of child sex trafficking go unreported.[13] Here's what we know in Kentucky. According to the Kentucky Statewide Human Trafficking Task Force's annual report, 697 sex trafficking victims were reported between 2013 and 2017.[14] In 2017 the state received eighty-eight reported incidents of sex trafficking; of these 69% involved girls between the ages of twelve and fourteen.[15] While runaways are especially vulnerable to trafficking, in these reports a majority of the trafficking victims had been exploited by a family member or intimate partner.[16] A study by the University of Louisville found that between 2013 and 2018, 87% of the victims were teenage girls trafficked *by a family member*.[17] This is a hard reality to face. For 43.3% of the children their trafficker was a parent or guardian.[18] This is the confluence of misogyny and poverty in the lives of children.

In Floyd County, every woman I talk with seems to know stories or rumors of attempted abductions. Jenna tells me of a young woman who was shopping at the local Walmart. A man followed her around the store repeatedly asking her to come with him to a prayer group. When she finally asked for details about his church, he left. This isn't a woman Jenna knows personally, still the story stays on her mind. Perhaps the circulation of these stories helps to keep Jenna and others like her more alert and a little safer. In Kentucky, invitations to prayer groups have become known as a strategy used by traffickers. Jenna isn't worried – exactly. But the risk of abduction is on her radar. She and her family keep a gun, a dog, and locked doors.

In struggling communities, and most especially in struggling communities of color, women and their children are tremendously vulnerable to sex trafficking. They face these issues regularly with few resources and often little support. Nowhere in the country is the threat of sex trafficking greater than among Native women and children, who face a risk ten times that of any other population in the United States.[19] Dr. Alexandra (Sandi) Pierce, a leading sex trafficking researcher and Native scholar, writes "the selling of North America's [I]ndigenous women and children for sexual purposes has been an ongoing practice since the colonial era."[20]

At Standing Rock, Ellison Thompson talks easily and often about the joys of children. She is a new mom, with a second child on the way. Yet in one conversation, she pauses to say, "If I have to run in somewhere really quickly or anything like that, if I'm just running to check the mail, I won't leave my son anywhere where I can't see him because I'm scared someone will take him." There's a long pause in the conversation. I wait. Then she takes another deep breath, and the words tumble out. "A few months ago, there was a car in my hometown that actually went around and grabbed kids and were trying to flee town. The cops caught them outside of town and were able to bring the children back to their families." Ellison tells me they were lucky that time. She is sure it will happen again. "It was really calm and quiet in North and South Dakota, and then the oil boom hit," says Ellison. "That brought up a lot of people, a lot of people who aren't from here, and it's just been gradually getting worse from the drugs to sex trafficking, all the way down to just –" Ellison stops abruptly and stares at her hands. As she looks up, she shifts her focus and tells me that the trouble started in the Mandaree area, moved down to Minot, and then to Dickinson, and then to Bismarck. People at Standing Rock have watched with dread as the violence spread from the Bakken fracking fields to their reservation.

The Bakken oil fields extend across 200,000 square miles, from eastern Montana through western North Dakota in the US and across southern Saskatchewan and western Manitoba in Canada. The massive oil production that began in 2008 makes North Dakota second only to Texas in oil production.[21] The oil boom has drawn thousands of men to work in the fields, which in turn has created temporary housing facilities that are known as man camps. In Williston, North Dakota, for example, one man-camp holds 1,850 beds.[22] The man-camp model in the oil business created a robust market for drugs, prostitution, and sex trafficking. It also brought a 121% increase in violent crime, according to a federal report on violent crime in North Dakota's Williston Basin region between 2005 and 2011.[23]

The Bakken fields have also seen a large influx of motorcycle gangs, fighting to claim the territory in the prostitution and drug trades.[24] In 2017, Edith Chavez, a Lakota woman, was abducted from a gas station in Casselton, North Dakota. Chavez was messaging her family when a man came up from behind and knocked her out with a single blow.[25] She was drugged, abducted, beaten, raped, and transported to the Bakken oil fields, likely to be sold into prostitution.[26]

Edith Chavez managed to escape from the backseat of the man's car when he left her alone. After wandering lost for two days in the open country of North Dakota, she was helped by a man who found her.[27] After giving her a meal and a chance to clean up, he then took her to Williston police to file a report. In Williston, however, officers refused to take her statement about the abduction; instead they arrested and jailed her on a bench warrant from 2011 for an unpaid traffic violation.[28] After Chavez spent a night in jail, a woman officer recognized the trauma she was experiencing and intervened; the officer managed to get the charges dismissed and have Chavez transported to a local hospital.[29] Although media picked up her story, there was never a meaningful investigation into her abduction.[30] This is one of many stories local Native women know all too well. And it is the kind of story that can't happen in just any community. But it happens here. A lot.

As Ellison recounts the horrors that have become part of her daily reality, she talks in starts and stops. "Recently, a pregnant woman was kidnapped. Her baby was forcefully removed from her body, and she had been murdered." Ellison pauses and appears to regroup. "There's been a lot of sex trafficking, a lot of kidnapping. It is a lot of Native women." Anger crosses her face as she stops and starts again. "It's a lot of Native people, because we don't get a lot of attention, as much attention as everybody else, because a lot of people still don't even know that we're here, that we're still here. I don't want to say this, but we don't matter as much in the government's eyes. It's a big issue." The deep trauma of the abductions – the onslaught of them – is inescapable. It is embodied in Ellison's anger, grief and fear, in the long pauses and restless hands that seem to have no place to settle.

Also at Standing Rock, Erika Brooks explains: "You know, just a couple of months ago we had strange cars driving around [Standing Rock] and we had incidents of children actually being abducted. People chased down the vehicles to take the babies back." I hear so many stories of abductions and attempted abductions, initially I wonder if they are different versions of the same incident. While that might be the case on occasion, it is clearly not so most of the time. Erika continues with a face full of grief. "There were three girls that were abducted in McLaughlin." The town of McLaughlin has one main street about the length of a short city block.

Then there was the incident near the school in McLaughlin. Both the school and its playground are tucked behind a grassy knoll at the edge of town, away from homes and businesses. Erika tells me "Somebody was parked over there [by the school] watching for kids. Two kids ran home and reported that there was someone strange there asking them questions and wanting to give them candy if they got in their car. When the grandfather went over to confront, the guy took off. Stuff like that is really scary. We have to be extra cautious where we can't let our kids just ride off on bicycles the way that we used to." Native women have reason to worry about their children and each other. In addition to targeting schoolyards, traffickers are known to target girls attending PowWows as well as to use social media to catfish teenage Native girls by pretending to be a peer interested in dating.

The number of missing and murdered Native women, girls, and two-spirit people is a national crisis that few non-Natives are talking about. The crisis has given rise to #MMIW (Missing and Murdered Indigenous Women) and #MMIWG2S (Missing and Murdered

The town of McLaughlin on Standing Rock – still smoky from the Montana fires.

Indigenous Women, Girls and 2-Spirit People). Among the few stories that have made it into national media is that of Marita Growing Thunder, a citizen of the Fort Peck Assiniboine Sioux tribe. Growing Thunder grew up on the Flathead Indian Reservation in Montana and has experienced the deaths of five family members. The police refused to investigate any of these deaths as homicide; even when her aunt's fingernails had been removed and her body clearly beaten, the police declared her death a suicide.[31]

According to the Urban Indian Health Institute, in 2016 nearly 6,000 American Indian and Alaska Native women and girls were reported missing to the National Crime Information Center, but only 116 were officially recorded in the US Department of Justice's federal missing persons database.[32] The Justice Department is well aware that Native women are trafficked at far higher rates than any other racial group, yet federal authorities prosecuted just two trafficking cases in Indian country between 2013 and 2016.[33] Things have not gotten better. Given the US government's inaction, in 2018 Annita Lucchesi, a cartographer and citizen of the Southern Cheyenne, created the first centralized database to track missing and murdered Indigenous women.[34] In that year alone, she added 2,501 cases to her database.[35] In 2019 she created the Sovereign Bodies Institute to provide research and resources for Missing, Murdered Indigenous Women & Girls (MMIWG).[36] Still, US law enforcement has been slow to take her research seriously.

Missing Native women are less likely to be tracked by investigators, less likely to be found, and their abductors and murderers are less likely to be caught. To give this context it helps to know a couple of things. First, it would be hard to argue that US government *ever* had the interests of Native women in mind. There is a pattern of continued hostility. For example, from 1970 to 1976 between 25% and 50% of Native American women underwent forced sterilization when they thought they were having appendectomies.[37] Second, in 1978, the Supreme Court case *Oliphant* v. *Suquamish Indian Tribe* stripped tribes of the right to arrest and prosecute non-Indians who commit crimes on Indian land – the harshest enforcement tool a tribal officer can legally wield over a non-Indian is a traffic ticket.[38] Cases between tribal members are handled in tribal courts, but the maximum sentence the court can impose is three years. Because the US government severely limits the authority of tribal courts, the more serious crimes are taken over by a US attorney. This legal landscape makes it easy for criminals to skate free and makes Native women easy targets for non-Native men. *An overwhelming 96% of sexual violence against Native women is committed by non-Native perpetrators*.[39] Across the country, 88% of the violent crimes against Native women are committed by non-Indians.[40]

Record keeping is also abysmal. Even in urban areas with significant populations of Native people, police report an inability to search their databases for American Indian, Native American, or Alaska Native individuals, despite the common practice of identifying crime victims by race.[41] Without question, there are problems of jurisdiction, funding, and training that complicate the pursuit and prosecution of non-Native people. However, this is an inadequate explanation of a massive law enforcement failure. The US government's lack of urgency and thoroughness when it comes to investigations regarding Native women and children can only be understood as a disregard for their lives and communities. In this sense both the crimes and the federal responses to them look very much like a continuation of the genocide that started with first contact. There have been some changes.

In 2019 the Savanna's Act was advanced to the floor of the Senate by US Senators Lisa Murkowski (R-AK) and Catherine Cortez Masto (D-NV). In 2020 it was signed by President Trump and passed into law. The bill directs the Attorney General to review, revise, and develop the law enforcement and justice protocols needed to respond to missing, murdered, and trafficked Native people.[42] The bill is named after Savanna LaFontaine-Greywind, a twenty-two-year-old woman from the Spirit Lake Nation who was eight months pregnant when she was abducted and brutally murdered by her neighbor in Fargo, North Dakota, in 2017.[43] Savanna's body was found in a river, wrapped in plastic and duct tape. Her unborn child had been cut from her body. The child was found alive and now lives with her father. In 2021 Biden's appointment of Deb Haaland, an enrolled member of the Pueblo of Laguna, to serve as Secretary of the Interior gave many hope. Among her first orders of business was to form a Missing & Murdered Unit (MMU) within the Bureau of Indian Affairs to investigate the crisis.[44]

Daily fears of being trafficked for sex, of having your children, nieces, or sisters stolen or murdered, should never be part of anyone's reality. Yet, as I write in 2020, this is an ordinary part of life for Native women living in the United States. Like women in struggling communities everywhere, Ellison worries about how she will pay her bills each month. But like other Native women at Standing Rock she also faces the very real threats of abduction and murder. Ellison tells me "When I grew up, I used to be able to play out all the way until it got dark and the lights came on. And I would be able just to ride my bike back home and be safe. Now it's not like that. Now if I'm gone longer than an hour and no one knows where I am, you need to panic, because I'm gone, no one knows where I am – anything could happen. Freedom is limited is what I'm trying to say, for our safety. We don't have very much freedom for our safety, because of who's out there." On the reservation, local police are often too underfunded to be of significant help to Native women; one officer might cover seven districts spread over hundreds of miles. Even so, the Government Accountability Office (GAO) reported that 132 tribal law enforcement agencies had responded to human trafficking incidents between 2014 and 2016.[45]

All of the Native women I talked with at Standing Rock spoke about their concern for their safety. Except one. Two Lance Woman. I am curious that she never once mentions the abductions or fears for her safety. So, after the interview and before I leave Standing Rock, I bring up the stories of trafficking that I had heard from other women. Two Lance Woman nods. She is well aware of the local threats and explains: "Sex trafficking has really come to an ultimate high since the Bakken 2. We've had incidents here, on Standing Rock, it's a huge issue. I always say, 'Well, I'm too big. I'm too tall,' 'probably intimidate them,' you know, or 'how are they going to get me in the car?' 'How are they going to get me in the van?' But I carry a weapon. I have a taser. I have my mace and I have a shotgun. I have my pistol. I have a bat. I have my alarm systems. I am okay at home." Standing almost six feet tall and carrying a personal arsenal, Two Lance Woman is the only Native woman I spoke with who feels safe.

Two Lance Woman has thought a lot about safety. "I've always made sure, especially my daughters and my sons, you know, I always tell them, safety is everything. I didn't have to really worry about that. But it seems like once the Bakken started and the pipeline was coming … I was like, common sense, street smart, knowing your surroundings and let everybody know where you're going. It doesn't matter, if you're going to go stop at a gas station to go to the bathroom, just tell them, you know." Two Lance Woman ends her thoughts there. I think of Edith Chavez. The reality is bone deep. And terrifying.

If you're learning about this for the first time, you are not alone. While two of the stories in this section did appear in the media, more than 95% of cases regarding missing and murdered Native women, girls, and two-spirit people have never been covered nationally or internationally.[46] By taking away the right of tribal governments to arrest and prosecute non-Indians who commit crimes on Indian land, and by underfunding tribal police, the federal government has contributed to an environment in which Native women can be, and often are, victimized with impunity – both outside and inside their homes.

A National Crisis

In the US, 2019 might be remembered as the year of the #MeToo movement. Across the nation, record numbers of women – most of them extremely privileged – came forward with charges of sexual assault, sexual battery, and rape. Many women and men were angered by the way charges of sexual violence against Donald Trump, Brett Kavanaugh, and Jeffrey Epstein were handled. Others found reason to hope given the resignations of public figures like Richard Ailes and Matt Lauer, and the conviction of Harvey Weinstein. These are the stories the nation followed to the exclusion of concern for the thousands of Indigenous women who were being murdered or abducted. In 2020, it's hard to overstate the amount of sexual violence that is directed toward women on a daily basis – or the way the systems of poverty, racism, and misogyny entwine. Or the lack of accountability that abusive men face, whether at the Kentucky Derby or the Bakken oil fields. This can only happen in a country that views women and children as disposable.

We have learned to live in a nation where rape, murder, and sex trafficking have become a common part of women's lives. According to the Centers for Disease Control and Prevention, murder is *the third leading cause of death* among American Indian and Alaska Native women.[17] Consider this in light of the law enforcement practices that identify the deaths of Native women as suicide even when their fingernails have been pulled out. If we are honest, the United States government has always treated Native people as an inconvenience, standing in the way of what it wants. As people whose rights are disposable, whose lives are disposable. In this environment, Native women too often stand alone. Deep mourning, fear, anxiety, and anger are healthy responses to the endless assaults on well-being. Yet these feelings exist without resolution.

Sex trafficking, sexual assault, and domestic abuse – most generally crimes committed by men – are crises in the daily lives of women and children, but they have never become crises for the nation. Horrifically, they seem to be a matter of shame only for the girls and women forced into sex – not for the men seeking sex with children, not for the men who assault women, not for men selling the bodies of children, and not for the officials whose inadequate response enables it to happen. Our identities as "good people" call for us to be outraged. But in an era when a president brags of his own sexual assaults against women, that outrage seems to be worth very little. It isn't just that Donald Trump bragged of sexually assaulting women. The problem is the nation that allowed him to do so. The problem is the nation's unwillingness to enforce consequences. In January 2021, Joe Biden became the 46th president of the United States. But Donald Trump and those who support him are still with us. The next chapter takes a look at the relationship between Trump and the struggling class.

8

The Face of a Movement?

The distance from Appalachia to the *Vanity Fair* New Establishment Summit Cocktail Party in Beverly Hills has to be measured in light years, not miles. Every year, cultural titans fill the Wallis Annenberg Center for the Performing Arts for two days and two nights of networking, talks, and cocktail parties. Guests at the event receive "exclusive" rates at the Waldorf Astoria Beverly Hills, where rooms ordinarily *start* at $825 per night. In 2016, one of the featured speakers at the Summit was author Fran Lebowitz, perhaps best known for her sardonic cultural commentary. On the main stage, Lebowitz discussed Donald Trump's recent election with *New York* magazine's Frank Rich. Referring to Trump, she remarked: "He's a poor person's idea of a rich person. They see him. They think, 'If I were rich, I'd have a fabulous tie like that. Why are my ties not made of 400 acres of polyester?' All that stuff he shows you in his house – the gold faucets, marble floors – if you won the lottery, that's what you'd buy."[1] Her well-heeled audience laughed uproariously at the outsiders – both Trump and the poor, white working people said to have voted for him.

To understand Lebowitz's comments as funny, one has to share some class-based assumptions. First that poor people have no idea what rich people are "really" like. To the extent that there is truth in this statement it isn't about the ignorance of poor people, which is a subtle punchline in the story, but rather the consequence of class segregation, which is just not very funny. Second, if poor people see Trump as being "like them" but with more money, rich people clearly do not see Trump as being "like them." Nor do they see poor people as being "like them" but with less money. They are a class unto themselves. Third, polyester is a powerful class marker. In this reference to Trump's ties, Lebowitz takes down both people who can't afford silk ties and those who could afford them but don't wear them. The liberal intelligentsia is doubled over in laughter at what we ought to be able to call "classism." But that word just doesn't carry the power that it should. Even upper-middle-class people laughed long and hard at this characterization – so much so that in 2020, my colleagues still call it to mind. Fewer have asked why the country believes the "white working class" is Trump's fan base. It just seems to be obvious – not only because of polls and pundits, but also because of cultural narratives like the ones that Lebowitz parlayed into a witty quip.

To understand the rise of Trump and his fan base, it is helpful to look back to the 2008 McCain-Palin presidential ticket that made "Joe the Plumber" the face of the white working class for conservatives.[2] Republicans featured "Joe the Plumber" in person and in rhetoric as an authentic voice of working-class Americans. If you were around for the 2008 presidential campaign, you might remember that "Joe the Plumber" attacked then-candidate Obama (as a socialist) and railed against unions (which he called a tool of socialism). Few people will recall that "Joe the Plumber" was in fact Samuel Joseph Wurzelbacher, a conservative commentator and activist from Ohio, who falsely claimed that he was a journeyman plumber.[3] Republicans used "Joe the Plumber" to argue that the white working class was being left behind economically.

With Sarah Palin on board, the Republican platform took a hard-right turn in 2008 and "Joe the Plumber" helped them to do it. In a single ninety-minute debate, McCain raised "Joe the Plumber" twenty-five times.[4] It's telling in itself that politicians and media often talk about a "*white* working class" yet rarely say a word about "the Latinx working class" or "the Black working class," or even just "the working class." Consider as well that when Wurzelbacher took the public stage, his comments were filled with bigotry – not class analysis. Wurzelbacher did not leverage his fifteen minutes of fame in the service of the working class – he leveraged it for a racist and anti-LGBT platform, and to fight efforts to increase taxes on people making over $250,000,[5] all the while claiming he was representative of the (white) working class. Wurzelbacher disappeared from public view after the 2008 election, a failed legislative bid on the Republican ticket (2012), and a wake of scandals. Politicians, pundits, and others regularly and strategically amplify social agendas under the guise of class politics, and over the years the term the "working class" has functioned more as a political tool than as an economic category.

In 2016 conservatives resurrected Wurzelbacher (still not a plumber) in his role as "Joe the Plumber" as the face of the forgotten white working class.[6] In his second appearance on the national stage, Wurzelbacher again leveraged the moment to stump against taxes for those earning more than $250,000, against immigration, and for the NRA (still no class concerns).[7] It was a classic "Joe the plumber" move. Wurzelbacher never once advanced the economic interests of working-class people. Instead, he made them look like small-minded bigots who could think of little else but lowering taxes and arming themselves. I know first-hand that such people do exist in the so-called working class – and I know the reality is more complicated. Appalachia is often touted as Trump country, so I took some time there to talk with people about Trump.

You might recall Tommy from earlier chapters. It's a sunny and breezy day in Tennessee when I meet Tommy in his store. I sip on an iced tea as he leans back against a counter and unwinds a story that starts about twenty years ago and ends with Donald Trump. "We made Oshkosh clothing here. The ladies worked in the factories, and they made children's clothing, some of the best clothing in the country. It was known for quality, and all of those ladies lost their jobs. Those jobs were sent to Mexico. The supervisor says the plant here in our local town was asked to go down and train the new workers in Mexico on how to make these clothes. So where were all of these politicians that were representing the little guy and their health care and their safety standards?" For decades neither political party seems to have cared to keep rural or urban communities from sinking more deeply into poverty – and too often they seem willing to push them right over the edge.

Tommy is a tall lanky man with thick white hair. He wears what looks like a freshly pressed white T-shirt, jeans and sneakers – he feels a little like a local mayor among the young people who congregate in front of his store to smoke. Even as they look away as if disinterested, it's clear from the way they linger at the open door and pause their conversation, that they are paying attention as Tommy talks to me. Tommy slumps just a little and seems both sad and angry. "So, you kind of are in this global economy where poverty is all over the world. So now are we going to take our communities, eventually are we going to bring them down to the standard of living in Mexico and the Sudan and Africa? I mean, is that the end game? Or are we going to bring them down to a level of a Communist Chinese worker? Because that's the only thing I see happening, unless we start bringing some of these industries back. That's what I think you'll see, that's one of the reasons that the rural people fear. They were constantly democratic voters around here. All of them went for Trump. They got the message that we have to do something. Whatever it is, something has to be done to bring back these factories. We cannot sell out our country like we're doing. I don't know where this goes. So, when you've got somebody who says, 'I'll do my best, I'm a businessman. I will do my best to have fair trade agreements, and we'll see if we can start to creep some of these businesses back into rural America.' I think that's why they went for that kind of hope." In that framing it is easy to understand how Trump seemed to promise the expertise of a businessman who understood how politicians had failed US businesses – and hence US workers.

Although liberals like Lebowitz guffawed at Trump, it was in fact his presence as an outsider ill at ease in politics that resonated with folks like Tommy. This is often what makes white men in Appalachia come to Trump's defense. In a passing conversation, a white man in Tennessee tells me, "He's not a perfect guy. No one is, but for what he was saying that he's wanting to do, he's getting kind of the raw end of the deal." Another in Southeast Ohio tells me: "I'm sure Trump has done at least one pretty okay thing that I support since getting into office, and I certainly haven't heard about it." For some it is a sense of patriotism that makes them complain about how Trump is being treated in the media. In Southeast Ohio Jenny Gaines tells me: "I grew up where my mom and dad taught us about politics and that you don't make fun of the president. So *Saturday Night Live* and them making fun of the president … I guess it's because we live in the United States we can do that [but] I think we should not. A president should not be a person that you make fun of. I think that it just makes our society look poorer when we don't respect the people who we are putting into office. But having said that, now there's *reasons*, but again, it's that catch of everything." It is indeed "the catch of everything." Despite the number of white people who tell me Trump is getting a raw deal, in 2018 it is hard to find people in struggling communities who are actually willing to *endorse* him. This squares with polls in 2019 which showed a lukewarm approval rating in Tennessee, Kentucky, and Ohio.[8]

As I spend time in central Appalachia, I happen into a small town that has a square ringed by four or five open businesses. It's a surprising site so I stop to meet folks. This gives me a chance to meet Willadean, who is putting Memorial Day decorations in the window of a second-hand store. Although Willadean declines my invitation for a formal interview, she talks with me at length as she works. The small store is Willadean's second job and she tells me with a big smile that "it doesn't feel like work at all." Willadean is a small woman with a kind face. Her chestnut brown hair forms tight, orderly rows of curls – the kind you get if you don't comb-out a set.

I browse as we talk and before I know it Willadean is telling me about her husband. He had liver troubles from chemicals he used at a local plant where he worked. It's a heartbreaking story of hospitals and home care. Eventually, he was able to get a liver transplant, but died three years later. Willadean has been a widow for about a year. The grief is still fresh in her face as she draws a short breath. She stops her work to look out of the front window, all the while her hands fuss with a small object that she holds. Before I can respond, Willadean quickly names five other women whose husbands died recently – they all had worked at the plant. I start to ask but two other women in the store have been listening and they quickly pick up the conversation and push it on to other topics. This is how conversations about hard times often seem to go. People are impressively open about their hardships, but no one dwells on the pain. It's as if Willadean tells me this story not because it's so awful – although it is – and not because she blames the plant – although she could. She tells me the story because it's just how things are. It's just life. Willadean is fifty-eight.

In many ways, Willadean is the kind of person that gets showcased as a Trump supporter. She is white, blue-collar, and *fervently* patriotic. Willadean gets riled up just thinking of NFL players who might "take a knee" during the national anthem and seems to be against the very idea of protests. America, love it or leave it. So, I was surprised when I asked her about Donald Trump. Willadean took a step back, folded her arms and looked squarely at me. "Obama did what he could – what they would let him. Trump does what he wants. He's got them … ." With a grimace, she balls up her right hand as if grabbing something and squeezing it hard. I'm not sure if she means "he's got them by the throat," or by some other body part, but her point is made. "He's like a boss I had. If you work in a nonunion plant – he's like that kinda boss. You just have to take whatever he decides to do. He can just insult you, and yell at you, and you have to stand there and take it. Trump's like that. He's the president and we've gotta take it." No doubt there are Trump supporters in the area – but Willadean isn't one of them. Nor are any of the women who have gathered to listen to her. A thirty-something white man tells me: "It used to not be bad, but it's got worse since Trump took over." I ask, what's gotten worse? Without hesitation he rattles off: "racism, division, and gun violence." If Fran Lebowitz doesn't see Trump as one of the cultural elite, it's important to say these struggling Tennesseans don't see him as one of them either.

Who are the Trumpsters?

There are scholars who believe the difference between Trump and the Republican establishment is one of style, rhetoric, and temperament, not substance.[9] Studies show that in 2016 Trump won 64% of non-college-educated white voters.[10] This statistic may not be all that remarkable. About 70% of all Republicans don't have a college degree.[11] Trump's appeal to non-college-educated white voters is completely consistent with the base of the Republican Party – not a departure from it. Although Trump's bold rhetoric and volatile temperament are distinctive, in substance he is consistent with long-standing values of the Republican Party. With Trump those values are just much more explicit. To the extent that Trump was successful in his presidency in filling courts with right-wing justices, securing tax breaks, rolling back environmental protections, limiting civil rights, and escaping government accountability, it was because the Republican Party stood with him.

In 2016 Trump did not win the popular vote, but roughly 107,000 votes in three states gave him an Electoral College victory.[12] The 2016 primary data show that across the country, the yearly income of Trump's supporters was well above that of Hillary Clinton and Bernie Sanders supporters. Researchers found that only one-third of Trump voters in 2016 had incomes under $50,000. Clinton defeated Trump by wide margins among voters earning less than $50,000. Two-thirds of Trump's supporters were "country club" Republicans and Libertarians with incomes higher than the national median – often $100,000 or more.[13] Studies show that racism, not class, was what united voters behind Trump in 2016. The American National Election Studies show that on surveys Trump supporters scored 60% higher than other white voters on levels of anti-Black racial resentment or anti-Black animosity.[14] If Trump voters were unhappy about the direction of the economy or the direction of the country, it was not because they belong to the struggling class. The election polls for 2020 tell a similar story. Biden won 57% of the votes among those earning less than $50,000 (Trump 42%), and 56% of the votes of those earning between $50,000 and $99,000 (Trump 43%). Trump prevailed only among people earning $100,000 or more – there he won 54% of the vote (Biden 43%).[15]

Yet the media and politicians have recycled the belief that Trump's fan base is composed of an uneducated, white working class. It is a narrative that fits perfectly within the same class-based bigotry that Lebowitz leveraged for laughs. But it was not the so-called working class showing up at the $100,000 fundraiser dinners or paying $70,000 for a photo with Trump. Despite the economic powerhouses behind the Trump presidency, it seems that for media and political commentators there are no well-heeled white donors. Only "hillbillies."[16] Conservatives made the mythical "white working class" the *face* of Trump's campaign, while behind the scenes wealthy white elites were bankrolling it.

In a 2017 speech on tax reform in St. Charles, Missouri, President Trump told his audience "Our focus is on helping the folks who work in the mail rooms and the machine shops of America – the plumbers, the carpenters, the cops, the teachers, the truck drivers, the pipefitters – the people that like me best. Actually, the rich people don't actually like me, which is sort of interesting."[17] Yet Trump consistently did more to help the wealthy than the struggling. For example, according to the nonpartisan Tax Policy Center, although everyone benefitted to some degree from Trump's Tax Cuts and Jobs Act, the top 1% received about 83% of the benefit. Rich folks have plenty of reason to like Trump's policies. As an additional favor to corporations, Trump stacked the National Labor Relations Board, an independent federal agency supposed to protect employees, with attorneys whose careers have been dedicated to breaking unions for their corporate employers.[18]

Without irony, acknowledgment, or apology, the newly elected Trump nominated Wilbur Ross as his secretary of commerce. Ross's nomination was approved by Congress in February 2017. In Appalachia, Ross is remembered for his ownership of the West Virginia Sago Mine, a company with a long-standing record of shirking state and federal safety regulations. Under Ross's leadership, the Sago Mine had 208 federal safety violations that went unaddressed. These included substantial roof control, ventilation, electrical insulation, and emergency escape violations.[19] On January 2, 2006 an explosion trapped thirteen miners underground in the Sago Mine for two days. Only one person survived. With Trump's appointment of Ross, it was clear that the nation had been "plumbered" again – *working people had been used as the face of a movement that disregards their interests.*

In Southeast Ohio, Rose Taylor, a twenty-something white woman, sounds much like Willadean in Tennessee. They are among the many people in Appalachia who get angry just thinking about Trump. Rose tells me that Trump cares about "money and fame and being able to tell people that he's the president and have people do whatever he wants. I think he likes that part of being the president. I don't think that he likes the actual work of being the president or taking care of the people. I don't think that he truly cares about the working class, no matter what color they are."

On a fall evening in 2017, Michael Chase, a Black man in Southeast Ohio, and I sat in a small backroom talking. Sometime after midnight, Michael caught a second wind and we carried on until 2 in the morning. "I've been walking home by bars and I heard a guy yell 'oh I grab her by the pussy' and think it's funny. That's a legit thing Trump said and possibly, probably, did. That's sexual assault!" Michael worries that Trump is fueling the fires of bigotry and references the Trump administration's ban on transgendered people in the military. "Our society kind of doesn't view transgender people as actual people. [Trump] fans fires and our country is violent enough to carry things out." Michael draws a breath and another example comes to mind: Charlottesville. "I feel like it's very dumb for people to be very pro-military and also pro-neo-Nazi. We went to war with the Nazis! And they're talking about respecting troops and stuff. You really think someone who fought in World War II is going to be like, oh, that's cool, you have a swastika?"

In 2020, when I talk with Michael again, he is somewhat willing to forgive people who voted for Trump in 2016, but not if they vote for him in 2020. "I feel like people who are *still* following Donald Trump now, at *this* point," Michael's voice rises as he rolls his eyes and gives an exasperated shrug. "He is just openly a Nazi. He has shown that he really does not care about people of color, about women for real or none of that. And that's the thing. He's honest about it. Even when he's like, 'oh, no, I'm not racist, I'm not sexist,' [it's clear] he doesn't even care when he's saying that. People want to play dumb. It's just this weird blind allegiance. It's weird, because we're all looking at the same information but they're trying to tell me that an orange isn't an orange – but we're both looking at the same orange!"

Trump's "Make America Great Again" campaign overtly reinforced a fictional image of a homogeneous nation – a white nation – as it churns public resentment toward immigrants, people of color, LGBTQ communities, and feminists. The rhetoric of "Make America Great Again" provokes what Linda Gordon calls a "Klannish spirit – fearful, angry, gullible to sensational falsehoods, in thrall to demagogic leaders and abusive language, hostile to science and intellectuals, committed to the dream that everyone can be a success in business if they only try."[20]

At Standing Rock, Two Lance Woman talks about Trump this way: "You know, the president, I hate to say this, but he just doesn't know what he's doing. His entourage or the entourage of what's under the roof of the White House, senators, the congressmen, how would you say it? The president and everything, they're careless and they're reckless." In Oakland, California, Tom Sam also tells me the Trump administration is racist. "I definitely believe that the current president has definitely polarized the nation. I think they've brought a sense of a very violent attitude into politics, which I think folks had just forgotten about for a really, really long time. Within our Native community, we think of folks like Andrew Jackson, who is known as the Indian killer.[21] We know how violent the government can be." Tom pauses. It's not clear to me if he needs to catch his breath or if he takes a moment to think about the genocidal campaigns of the US government against Native people. When he continues, there is a deep sadness in his voice. "I feel like this president has aggravated a lot of very militant and angry white people to take arms into [public] spaces – that causes everybody else to be at risk in being in those spaces. I think they're very, very detrimental to the process of politics and the process of debating and the process of agreeing to think differently, or the ability to voice a different opinion. I feel that that's the kind of attitude that Donald Trump has promoted since day one. Using folks' gender or body type or skin color to further marginalize via words, to use very hateful and divisive words, whether it be in a campaign or in a speech or in the national address."

Angel Perez also lives in Oakland. Although he doesn't remember "Joe the Plumber," he knows the rhetoric. Referring to Donald Trump, Angel tells me: "This guy represents rich, powerful corporations, CEOs. That's what he represents. Those are the people that he wants to please, or he has to please, because they probably each have their own deal with him. He does not represent who I am or who my family is. I've heard that from different people, Latino Americans, Asian Americans, anybody. I've heard it from every ethnic background. I feel like he's just in it for the money, for himself, for his benefit, and also for the benefit of the CEOs and powerful corporations."

By contrast, Vanessa Torres, who also lives in Oakland, has a different experience. Vanessa shakes her head. "I know Mexicans who are pro-Trump. People think he's a good businessman." Vanessa herself has a few Mexican American relatives who voted for Trump and she argues with them regularly. In 2016 Trump won approximately 28% of the Latinx vote.[22] Vanessa is especially frustrated with Latinx voters who supported Trump because of the way he talks about immigrants and immigration. She wants Mexican Americans to remember their roots, their own journeys. But, she sighs, "within our community too, there's a lot of racism. There's colorism within the Latino community." Vanessa sees colorism as playing into voting patterns among Latinos. There are conservative Mexican Americans who united behind Trump as evangelicals, or as business owners. Yet Mexican Americans did not vote for Trump in large numbers. This was true in 2020 as well. Exit polls in 2020 show 74% of Mexican Americans voted for Biden.[23] By contrast, Cuban Americans tend to be more conservative than other Latinx populations, and in 2016 Trump won 54% of Cuban American votes.[24] In 2020, 54% of Cuban Americans again voted for Trump; Puerto Ricans as well as people from Central and South America tended to vote for Biden.[25] Pundits are only beginning to recognize the diversity among "Latinos" or "Hispanics" and have a long way to go to recognize the diversity among Black and Native American voters.

Under the Trump presidency white nationalist groups thrived and the wealthy prospered – poor white families went deeper into debt. Yet the rhetoric of the campaign masked this by conflating poor white people with racism. I suspect this was possible because much of the country already held such a stereotype. Many educated white people like to believe that they have overcome racism and that it now lingers only in the lives of low-income, uneducated white people. Racism is a part of white, low-income communities; but it also is a part of wealthy white, college-educated communities. Still, the media (and politicians) continue to conflate struggling communities with bigotry and racism and to identify them as Trump supporters. This narrative might be particularly easy to accept because it fits a dominant class stereotype and because levels of class segregation in the US make it very hard to break down such stereotypes. In this sense the struggling class has again been made to stand as a repository of unwanted values. The media do a lot to promote this view of the country. Yet there are some basic problems with crediting poor rural white people with Trump's electoral win.

For example, McDowell County, West Virginia, received a lot media attention in 2016 because Obama had won a majority of votes there in 2008, but in 2016 Trump won it by 74%.[26] What is reported less often is that *Bernie Sanders won twice as many votes as Trump* in the primary election there.[27] When Sanders was not on the ballot, however, 73% of McDowell's registered voters did not vote at all.[28] Yet poor white people, most especially Appalachians, have been made to be the face of Trumpism. Perhaps Ronald Eller had it right when he wrote: "We know Appalachia exists because we need it to define what we are not. It is the 'other America' because the very idea of Appalachia convinces us of the righteousness of our own lives."[29] For outsiders, Appalachia has long been a powerful symbolic force, understood as a place out of time, a monolithic culture that never entered the modern age.[30] As the country increasingly made Appalachia the site of all things backward and uneducated, even Appalachians came to distance themselves from the region in which they live.[31]

Wealthy conservatives have avoided accountability by diligently working to ensure that poor, uneducated white people are the *face* of their movement; they have worked equally hard to politicize science, news, education, and health.[32] With Trump, a more radical conservative movement has emerged characterized by "profound anti-intellectualism, fervent Christian fundamentalism, a visceral suspicion of government, and racial resentment."[33] This radicalization fuels cultural divides to such an extent that many now believe a civil war could happen.

A Looming Civil War

It is a gray and drizzling morning in Southeast Ohio when Jack Rockwell comes into town to meet me at a coffee shop. He is a very lean twenty-something white man, with thick dark hair. Like most everyone here, he wears jeans and a T-shirt. We shake off the drizzle to go inside and find the café has only two tables, one of which is taken by people from the local Appalachian Regional Commission (ARC) who are having a business meeting. We agree to sit at one of the two outside tables, even though the chairs and table are damp. This gives us a little privacy and has the bonus of enabling Jack to smoke. Jack is a noticeably self-conscious smoker who pauses from time to time to wave the cigarette smoke away from me. Our coffees are long gone, and our seats dry, when Jack puts out a cigarette and shifts in his chair. With a soft voice he says "It's difficult not to be anxious. When I woke up this morning and first page on *The Hill* was 'Donald Trump met with his generals, came out and told the reporters: This is the calm before the storm.'" Jack stopped to make eye contact intended to drive home the point. "This is the calm right now," he repeated. Nothing felt very calm. When reporters pressed President Trump to elaborate on what "the storm" might be, Trump heightened the sense of instability, saying only: "You'll find out." Conspiracy theorists had a field day speculating on what was to come.

Jack has learned to adapt to the antisemitism directed at him and the racism directed toward others. He has even managed to scrape by for the time being on $8.15 an hour. But in 2017, the political instability created by Donald Trump was leading him to imagine the unimaginable. Jack explains: "I don't think that anything catastrophic or earthshaking is going to happen. But I am a gun owner, and I have made preparations to be able to survive without a lot of the amenities of civilization. I am concerned about, and somewhat prepared for, the possibility of a second civil war. If things got dire, I would probably just go off into the woods and try to ride things out." He pauses. "It sounds really silly to say out loud." Jack has a very detailed plan, so the possibility of a civil war doesn't feel silly when he says it. It feels scary.

Jack seems caught in a political riptide that makes pragmatic planning indistinguishable from paranoia. He is not alone. Yet Jack is distinctive in that he considers another dimension to the possibilities. "When you have a pervasive sense of unease and uncertainty, people tend to prepare for the worst," he tells me. "And when everyone is prepared for the worst, the worst is more likely to happen." Jack is an avid backpacker and confident about his skills and his preparations. Yet this doesn't bring him much comfort. His interest in reading *The Hill* is unusual in this part of the country, but his concerns about a second civil war are not. "Everything has a breaking point," he tells me. "I've got a lot of cultural anxiety about the next decade or so."

Anxiety about a potential civil war isn't just worrying Jack. In 2019 Joshua Geltzer, a senior Justice Department official under Obama, wrote an op-ed for CNN urging the country to prepare for the possibility that Trump might not "leave the Oval Office peacefully" if he lost in 2020.[34] A year later, senior White House adviser and presidential son-in-law Jared Kushner floated the idea to the media that there was uncertainty about whether or not the upcoming November presidential election would be held, given the pandemic. This possibility was quickly shut down by the media, but it was a worry that Trump nurtured each time he refused to commit to stepping down should he lose the 2020 election. In Trump's world, the only conceivable way he could lose would be if there was fraud – which is exactly what he claimed when he lost. Throughout 2020, he actively created and tested the groundwork for the insurrection at the Capitol on January 6, 2021.

Recall that in February 2020 Trump argued that Covid-19 was a normal flu being hyped by Democrats to undermine his presidency.[35] Trump supporters followed his lead by denying the reality of the pandemic: they refused to wear face masks or to follow social distancing guidelines, as did Republicans in government. The pandemic became completely politicized, while conspiracy theorists circulated misinformation about it that defied both science and logic.[36]

In the spring of 2020 Trump tried to compel all states to open their economies during the pandemic but failed. In this moment of failure, Trump issued a call for insurrection by tweeting that people in Michigan and Virginia needed to "liberate themselves" from the states' stay-at-home orders.[37] Right-wing conspiracy theorists and white supremacists heard the call to insurrection and responded in force. In states with Democratic governors, VDare, Proud Boys, Wolverine Watchmen, and Boogaloo began to show up at state capitols brandishing assault weapons, swastikas, and nooses. Trump praised them for it.[38]

These are the very groups Jack worried about in 2017 when he considered the possibility of a second civil war. Indeed, Boogaloo Boys (or Big Igloo Bois) is a white supremacist group that identifies itself as a citizen militia preparing for civil war. After inciting protests in Michigan, Trump then went further and supported demonstrators, telling media: "These are very good people."[39] "Their life was taken away from them," he told the press. "They want their life back."[40] Trump's wording was nearly the same as that of 2017 when he characterized a deadly white supremacist protest in Charlottesville, Virginia, as having "very fine people on both sides."[41] At Mount Rushmore on July 4, 2020, Trump again unnerved much of the nation when he said: "Our nation is witnessing a merciless campaign to wipe out our history, defame our heroes, erase our values, and indoctrinate our children. Angry mobs are trying to tear down statues of our founders, deface our most sacred memorials, and unleash a wave of violent crime in our cities."[42]

Trump's strategy of parlaying anxiety into a white nationalist agenda has been used throughout US history. In 1990, David Duke supporters claimed he was a working-class champion and that the media was making him look racist. Lyndon B. Johnson in 1964 captured this tactic succinctly in his infamous statement: "I'll tell you what's at the bottom of it. If you can convince the lowest white man he's better than the best colored man, he won't notice you're picking his pocket. Hell, give him somebody to look down on and he'll empty his pockets for you."[43] Certainly, this seems to be the case for the white nationalist movement following Trump.

Trump's commitment to white nationalists was underscored again when his re-election campaign ran ads prominently featuring a Nazi symbol (an inverted red triangle) used to identify political enemies,[44] along with the language: "far left MOBS are running through our streets and causing mayhem."[45] The Republican National Committee paid for eighty-eight such ads to target particular audiences on Facebook during the weeks when Black Lives Matter protests roiled over police violence. After Facebook banned the Nazi symbol, Trump's re-election campaign substituted a variety of other symbols in its place while keeping the same language. Trump's post on Facebook about shooting looters during civil rights protests remained live.[46]

By October 2020 the FBI had exposed a well-prepared plan to kidnap Michigan Governor Gretchen Whitmer and take over the state capitol.[47] As of this writing thirteen people have been charged. According to the FBI, members of the same right-wing, domestic terrorist groups considered kidnapping Virginia Governor Ralph Northam. Trump refused to condemn these plots or the groups that hatched them. Meanwhile, Republicans continued to invoke a battle not of political parties but of "good against evil."

And then Trump lost the election. He and his allies set to work on a multi-pronged approach. They began by filing lawsuits to contest the results. "At least 86 judges – ranging from jurists serving at the lowest levels of state court systems to members of the United States Supreme Court – rejected at least one post-election lawsuit filed by Trump or his supporters."[48] Republicans also demanded and received recounts in Arizona, Georgia, Michigan, Nevada, Pennsylvania, and Wisconsin. No evidence of voter fraud was ever found. At the same time siege strategies began to build.

Right-wing extremists among Trump's supporters began planning and training to break into the Capitol to "stop the steal" and restore Trump to power.[49] Organizers from within the Trump campaign set to work to organize an event on the day Congress was to ratify the Electoral College votes, January 6. Ali Alexander, leader of the "Stop the Steal" movement, created a website called WildProtest.com, on which he posted: "We the People must take to the US Capitol lawn and steps and tell Congress #DoNotCertify on #Jan6!"[50] According to videos, social media posts, and Alexander's own account, he worked with three hardline Trump supporters in Congress to plan the siege: Republican Representatives Andy Biggs (Ariz.), Mo Brooks (Ala.), and Paul A. Gosar (Ariz.).[51] Alexander also worked with Caroline Wren, a Republican fundraiser, to organize and fund the event at the Ellipse. The rally at the Ellipse cost over $500,000, while the concert stage cost an additional $100,000. Julie Jenkins Fancelli, heiress to the Publix Super Market chain, and Alex Jones, a far-right show host, paid for most of the expenses.[52]

Trump publicly encouraged those gathered at the Ellipse to go to the Capitol and was shown on media encouraging the crowd to "fight like hell" to prevent the election from being certified. The Trump supporters who took part in the siege were largely white nationalists, Christian evangelicals, and QAnon members. Consider Jenna Ryan, a real estate broker who took a private plane to DC, filmed herself in the Capitol rotunda and said: "Here we are going to fucking go in here. Life or death, it doesn't matter. Here we go." She then turns to face the camera and adds: "Y'all know who to hire for your realtor. Jenna Ryan for your realtor." Ryan posted this feed on Twitter and it was recirculated in multiple media accounts.[53] Trump supporters at the siege included former police officers, former military, middle-class professionals, and the very rich, like Ryan. Low-wage workers were undoubtedly also in the mix but the event was clearly not driven by "the forgotten working class." This movement has never been about poor, disgruntled white workers. Indeed, it has become clear that far from being a spontaneous expression of public discontent, the January 6 rally and the events that followed were an expensive and orchestrated attempt to subvert the election results.

Evangelicals came to DC for what they saw as a holy war conducted in the name of Jesus to keep Trump in power, proclaiming it was a fight of good against evil.[54] White nationalist groups came because Trump called for them to "stop the steal."[55] They flew into DC and stayed in expensive hotel rooms, and after storming the Capitol flew home to return to work on Monday. Inside the Capitol, they filmed themselves destroying property and searching for politicians to capture and/or to execute, and then posted their photos and videos on social media. Bravado? Stupidity? Or confidence that they had the support of Trump and members of Congress? Trump's support for the event had been clear. He helped to orchestrate it. He spoke half-heartedly against the insurgents only after being warned by White House counsel that he could face legal action for inciting the mob.[56] Trump is an avatar for a movement that has long preceded him.

Nearly two-thirds (126/211) of House Republicans filed a motion with the Supreme Court to prevent swing states from casting Electoral College votes for Biden.[57] And there are credible accusations that at least one Republican Representative, Lauren Boebert (Colorado), gave tours to the extremists just days in advance of the siege.[58] What we know for certain is that after the insurrection, two-thirds of Republican representatives (139/211) and eight Republican senators voted against certifying the electoral college results, thus continuing to assert that the election was stolen.[59] Almost half of Republicans surveyed in a quick poll said they supported the invasion of the Capitol.[60] Five people died in the siege. Even as protestors carried "Support the Blue" flags, about 400 police officers were injured in the siege by direct assaults; their injuries included broken ribs, broken vertebrae, and wounds from being stabbed with a metal fence.[61] Capitol Police Officer Brian Sicknick died from injuries he sustained that day; two other officers committed suicide shortly after the siege. One woman participating in the siege died when she was shot by police; three others died from medical emergencies. The FBI followed up with multiple arrests. As of this writing, 135 arrests have been made and more than 400 suspects identified.[62]

Given the lack of an immediate police response to an assault that was widely anticipated, many within the US have understood these events as an attempted coup by Trump. It is notable that "European intelligence communities are calling this an attempted coup, not a demonstration, not a riot, this was an attempted coup."[63] Intelligence communities who train with American law enforcement argued: "'We're not looking at this from a distance. There is protocol. None of that protocol was followed.' That decision is not made by people on the ground. That decision is made by people fairly high up. And so whether it was explicit or tacit, there was a decision not to defend, not to protect … the halls of our government."[64] The commander of the DC National Guard, Major General William J. Walker, told *The Washington Post* that the Pentagon restricted his authority in advance of the siege, which meant he was not able to roll out troops when he received a phone call from the Capitol Police that the Capitol was about to be breached.[65] Jack Rockwell's concern about a potential civil war, on that drizzling Ohio morning in 2017, appears to have been vindicated; democracy no longer seems to be a secure framework for either liberals or conservatives, although for very different reasons.

The Past Won't Stay Behind Us

Trump has parlayed "Joe the Plumber" rhetoric to advance a white nationalist agenda. The pervasive class bigotry of educated liberals like Lebowitz is a significant factor in explaining why he was able to make struggling, uneducated white people the face of his movement. The ability of Trump to mobilize a following is directedly related to extremist Christian evangelicals, white nationalists, and the normalization of right-wing propaganda.[66] The *Washington Post* identified a total of 30,573 false or misleading statements that Trump made over four years.[67] We have a "propaganda system funded and promoted by billionaires and ultimately beholden to those billionaires."[68] The devastating power of propaganda is not so much that it leads people to believe one thing or the other, but that it destabilizes their ability to tell fact from fiction.[69] This destabilization and disinformation supports the interests of billionaires by facilitating massive tax cuts, deregulation, and the stripping of environmental protections.

Supporters of QAnon, the extremist right-wing conspiracy group among Trump's base, now serve in Congress. Among the dominant QAnon conspiracy theories is that the Democratic Party is a satanic cult of pedophiles in league with Hollywood – and Donald Trump has been sent to save the nation from them.[70] When directly asked to disavow QAnon, by NBC moderator Savannah Guthrie at a townhall, President Trump insisted he had never heard of the group and said "they may be right, I just don't know about QAnon."[71] As of this writing, more than a dozen Republican politicians have endorsed QAnon.[72] To paraphrase Voltaire, those who can make you believe absurdities, can make you commit atrocities. Nowhere is this more evident than in the extremism of QAnon.

We need look only to the armed assault on a pizzeria,[73] armed occupations of state capitols, plots to kidnap a sitting governor, and more recently calls for the assassination of House Speaker Nancy Pelosi. Representative Marjorie Taylor Greene (R-GA) has advocated the assassination of Pelosi; when a reporter asked Greene about her statement, she threatened the reporter with arrest.[74] Disinformation campaigns depend upon the media platforms that both sustain and profit from them. NewsMax, OANN, Facebook, and Fox News have all profited by delivering the nation to this moment. The capitalist drive to maximize profit is unaccountable for the destruction it creates. It is not so much that the nation must reclaim a democracy as it must create one. Too many people have been abandoned by the system we have been told would protect us. Too many people have been taught to believe things that simply are not true. The remaining chapters open the door to these conversations.

9

The Myths We Live By

Talking About Class

In Athens County, Ohio, Jenny Gaines tells me she is always trying to learn new things. Part of that effort includes attending a women's group in her community where she is "coached on how to talk better in mixed groups." Jenny tells me, "I don't know the whole history of everything, so I'm trying to learn things. It's like going to the grocery store, and you forget you're going to see people, so you wear pajamas or something – I do *not* wear pajamas to the store – but a lot of people around here do. For me, it would be not checking to see if you have food in your teeth first, but you walk into the grocery store, and then you run into everybody you know. And then you're like, oh, man, should have checked that first. So, I go to these meetings, and I don't realize, I mean, I'm sitting with some very important people, but I'm absorbing it." When you migrate across class lines it is hard to anticipate what you don't know and too easy to forget to check your teeth, so to speak.

Jenny is learning to cross class boundaries that are as clearly marked as they are unspoken. After each meeting with these "very prestigious men," she reflects back on her behavior and her language to think about how she did. Like many people, Jenny lives in T-shirts and jeans – but perhaps unlike other people, she doesn't have much else in her closet. No doubt this is as much a matter of personal preference as it is of practicality. And yet her preferences reflect an adaptation to a lack of purchasing power. Jenny tells me it's not just that she only has T-shirts and jeans but that she has been wearing the same T-shirts and jeans for the last seven to ten years. As inequality increases, it forces people further from a consumer economy. This is why yard sales have become the department stores of Athens County.

Jenny leans across a table made by high school students in woodshop to tell me about something that happened to her recently at a community development meeting. "I got called out of a meeting, and the man who was in charge of it said, 'I need to talk to you. This is important.' Everybody in the meeting was wearing suits, and when I go to work, I wear jeans and a T-shirt – I make pottery, and now I make food. And I said, 'Is it about my clothes?' and he was like, 'What? No. I was going to ask you if you wanted to be the next president of this group.' I laughed so hard. I said, 'You do not want me to be the president of this group. I don't even know half the words you're using.' He goes, 'You make really good comments. You say really important things.' I said, 'Let me do that. That will be my job. You need a president more like this person or that person. A president needs to see the big picture. I like to be a partner, and I don't mind stepping up if you need me to, but I like to be a partner.'"

I was sorry, but not surprised, that Jenny turned down the position being offered to her. We live in a society that is fundamentally organized by class inequalities and the chasms between classes can be as emotional as they are economic. It's hard to imagine a woman in an old T-shirt and jeans presiding over a meeting filled with "important people" in business attire. And it would be harder still if she were no longer able to listen invisibly when she didn't understand the words being used. Of course, none of this has anything to do with her capacity to actually do the job.

Wealth offers special forms of privilege: better schools, safer neighborhoods, shorter commutes, better health care and easier access to it, and an easier time dealing with the legal system. Sometimes it's hard to imagine all of the forms of privilege that wealthier people can assume. For example, while Jenny feels self-conscious about her T-shirt and jeans, shoppers in an upscale Nordstrom's encounter items like a T-shirt full of holes with a price tag in both dollars ($26) and euros (€14). If Jenny was given it for free, she might well use it for washing windows.

Being able to proudly wear a shirt like the one in the following photo – to actually want to buy a shirt like this – is another expression of class privilege. Just like buying ripped jeans. What makes torn and ripped clothing an embarrassment for the struggling class and a status symbol for wealthier people?

A multimillionaire once told me that he could stand in line at McDonald's and be indistinguishable from everyone else. And in

T-shirt for sale at Nordstrom.

graduate school we used to joke that university professors could easily be mistaken for being homeless. But in fact, I don't recall any such mistake ever being made – despite the disheveled clothing and unkempt hair. Class markers are legible, even though they may not be explicit and often are flat out denied. The multimillionaire and the homeless person both have some idea of what it means to pass as middle class in line at McDonald's. That knowledge is only possible if we recognize class markers. The belief that class is unrecognizable or unimportant is only possible if we agree not to talk about those markers.

To be visible as someone from the struggling class is to be vulnerable to unnamed class judgments that limit opportunity. Decades of research show that people like to hire people like themselves. This is how predominantly white workplaces systematically exclude people of color, even when they don't consciously intend to do so. For many Black, Latino, and Native American people, passing as middle class might not be enough to get a middle-income job. While efforts to counter racism and sexism in the workplace have had some limited and uneven success, the nation has yet to even start the conversation about class bias. In the United States, we still talk as if we believe the old saw that people don't see class. In reality, even if one escapes class judgments from others, everyone in the struggling class learns to internalize them at some point in their lives.

Misinformation about economic inequality comes at us from all corners – this isn't a Democrat versus Republican kind of thing. For example, over the years, Joe Biden has fashioned himself as a champion of the working class. He has launched essentially the same message about the middle class in public talks, town halls, at the Brookings Institute, on Twitter, and at the Century Foundation: "Being middle class isn't a number. It's a value set."[1] According to Biden, people in the middle class value home ownership, safe neighborhoods, good public schools, and the ability to care for an ailing parent. Everyone I talked with shared those values but none of them came close to being part of an economic middle class.

If it strikes you as cruel to say that being middle class is about personal values, consider the Republicans' approach. In 2019, the Trump administration sought to reduce the number of poor people in the country by lowering the poverty line – which we know is already unrealistically low. The Republican proposal would ignore the rate of inflation when calculating poverty. Since inflation has recently been about 0.2% per year this may seem like a small thing – but the impact would be enormous. In 2020, Georgetown University's Center on Poverty and Inequality, a nonpartisan policy research center, estimated that in ten years, under Trump's proposal, 1.6 million people would be eliminated from official poverty counts.[2] This change would force families out of public housing, as well as make them ineligible for Medicaid and food assistance. It's a callous approach to poverty – but not the worst in our nation's history. As a nation, we have come to believe things that are not true. We have also *not learned* a lot of important things about the country that are true. This gives us a very distorted view of inequality. This chapter looks at four broad myths that shape beliefs about class and inequality.

Historical Fictions and Half-Truths

Although children are taught about the original thirteen *colonies*, few people talk about the US as a *colonizer*. We do not talk about the internal colonies that the country created to confine Native people, or the military occupation that paved the way for settlers to gain access to "free" land.[3] Colonial economies are by definition dependent economies. And as is the case around the globe, dependent economies are characterized by systematic underdevelopment and poverty. In the US, enormous segments of the livestock, mining, oil, and fracking industries profit from free (or nearly free) use of public land, all of which was sacred land to the Native people now living under occupation. There is no truthful way to make this sound better – which may be why the nation is so intent on erasing the presence of Native people today. It's impossible to understand the economy of this country without coming to terms with how it is based on the mythical notion "free" land – claimed by deceitful wars, broken treaties, and outright theft.

It's also impossible to understand the economy of this country without coming to terms with how it is based on "free" labor – provided first from slavery, then through the Black Codes established in the mid-1800s to provide prison labor, and then through a modern Prison Industrial Complex that targets people of color. In this context, the willingness of police to target poor communities of color, while protecting wealthy white communities, must be understood as an historical extension of the slave patrols from which policing developed.[4] In 2017, African Americans represented 12% of the US adult population but 33% of the sentenced prison population.[5] We now have the world's largest prison population with more than 2.2 million people incarcerated,[6] and their labor generates about $80 billion in profits each year for 4,100 corporations.[7] Companies using prison labor include McDonald's, Wendy's, Walmart, Kmart, Starbucks, and Victoria's Secret, as well as Sprint, Verizon, American Airlines, and Avis, who use prison labor in their call centers.[8] Prison labor has been used to grow food for Whole Foods and to package products for Microsoft. Prisoners typically earn between 0.23 cents and $1.15 per hour.[9] They worked through the pandemic without hand sanitizer, face masks, or social distancing.[10] Those who risk their lives to fight forest fires – often without adequate training or equipment – earn an extra $1 per hour and sometimes a sentence reduction.[11]

The economy of this country also depends on significant amounts of "free" labor from women: housekeeping, cooking, childcare, and elder care. Attributing this work to "women's nature" has contributed in various ways to women's oppression, including denial of their rights to vote, to own property, to work, to control their own money, and to control their own bodies whether through birth control or abortion.[12] It has contributed as well to limited access to education and employment, and to unfair wages.[13] Today women comprise nearly half of the workforce in the US and on average earn less than men in comparable jobs. As of this writing in 2021 the nation still is unwilling to declare women and men as equals, deserving of equal pay and equal opportunity.

While these histories and others are beyond the scope of this book, many excellent, honest accounts of them have been written.[14] They just are not the histories most commonly taught. Here my goal has been to scratch the surface of the myths on which this country is based. The struggling class reflects the racial and gender diversity of the nation. The path to a better future requires reckoning and repair: reckoning with our past and repairing relationships with those who have paid the steepest price.[15] Reckoning requires in part coming to terms with national mythologies.

Meritocracy and the American Dream

The myth of meritocracy lies at the heart of the American Dream. It is the belief that anyone who tries hard enough can make it in America. If this is a hopeful narrative, it has an ugly shadow that blames people for their inability to "make it." We heard this from Peter and Adelyn in Tennessee, who described struggling people as lazy – and we hear it in the national conversation nearly every day. Pundits suggest that people in poor communities could get out of poverty if they had more determination, or if they moved (don't ask how this would be financially possible), or if they acquired more marketable skills (equally unclear how this would happen). "Americans are more tolerant of income inequality than the citizens of other countries in part because of this faith that in each generation the poor run a fair race against the rich, and the brightest succeed."[16]

The myth of meritocracy encourages us to admire multimillionaires and disparage people who cannot afford housing. It encourages us to believe that the massive shift of wealth into the hands of a few is the result of hard work rather than the result of depressed wages and exploited workers; that the massive rise of tent cities in which millions of people live is about personal problems rather than systemic, economic ones; that racism and sexism do not hold people back and that millions of poor people are just freeloaders. The myth tells us that people are stuck in poverty because they lack moral fiber and drive – not because they are mired in the economic quicksand of low-wage work. In turn, this myth enables many politicians to vote to eliminate or reduce safety nets while slashing taxes on the wealthy.

In the US safety nets are always minimal: they are hard to access, provide less than people need, and are available only for short periods of time. Yet, as we saw in previous chapters, people (even those who struggle) have mistaken ideas about the largesse of safety nets. A person who works full-time and is eligible for unemployment benefits receives 60% of their salary. The national unemployment checks for 2019 averaged around $371.88 per week.[17] However, a person in Kentucky with a minimum-wage job would receive $174 per week in unemployment benefits – that's $696 per month for a family that likely had no savings at the start. Some states, like Florida and Georgia, limit unemployment benefits to twelve weeks; in most it ends at twenty-six weeks. This was the reality millions of Americans faced when they filed for unemployment in the spring of 2020 as the pandemic closed businesses.

Consider that in Scandinavia and much of Europe, countries have a more developed and stronger safety net for workers than the US. This meant that, during the pandemic, nearly all European countries reimbursed workers' incomes directly through their employers at levels between about 60% and 90% of wages.[18] Germany provided business with government subsidies to preserve jobs and help pay workers' salaries until the crisis passed.[19] Not only did Germany invest in workers, the nation maintains a robust health-care system, which also helped to minimize the impact of the pandemic.

Eventually, the US government passed the Coronavirus Aid, Relief, and Economic Security (CARES) Act, which supplemented unemployment benefits with an additional $600 per week for three months.[20] Yet this additional boost caused Senator Mitch McConnell to call the plan "crazy" and to worry along with other Republicans that low-wage workers might earn more on unemployment benefits than they did when employed.[21] (McConnell at the time had a salary of $193,400 and assets over $34 million.[22]) If McConnell or other Republicans ever worried about billion-dollar businesses receiving millions in subsidies from the federal government, no one said so as publicly. Trump donors Archie Bennett and his son Monty Bennett received over $59 million from the Paycheck Protection Plan (PPP) for their luxury hotels without a squeak from Congress.[23] Another billionaire Trump donor, Trevor Milton, received $4.1 million in PPP for his startup company Nikola Motors.[24] Not a word from fiscal conservatives in Congress. The Trump administration also allowed lawmakers, Small Business Administration staff, other federal officials and their families to seek funds for themselves by issuing a blanket approval of applications to bypass long-standing rules on conflicts of interest.[25] The transparency of the loan process was so problematic that eleven news organizations filed a Freedom of Information Act request to learn the names of businesses and the loan amounts for all PPP recipients. In the face of a lawsuit, the Small Business Administration relented and released data on large loans, but not on those of $150,000 or less.[26]

About 80% of the CARES Act changed tax laws to benefit millionaires and billionaires, who, it was estimated, would collectively avoid some $82 billion in tax liability for 2020.[27] Nearly 43,000 of the wealthiest taxpayers will save an average of $1.7 million each.[28] "Congress's official revenue estimators concluded that 82% of the benefits of this provision will go to those with incomes greater than $1 million this year."[29] And this tax cut comes on the heels of tax cuts in 2017,[30] the effects of which are themselves worth a glance.

The controversial Tax Cuts and Jobs Act, signed by President Donald Trump in December 2017, lowered the corporate tax rate from 35% to 21%.[31] That is a big loss in revenue for the federal government, but it doesn't begin to tell the story. Amazon, Netflix, Starbucks, and Aramark were among the ninety-one corporations that paid *no* federal income tax at all while earning billions in profits.[32] Another fifty-six companies paid between 0% and 5% while an additional 379 paid what was effectively a tax rate of 11.3%.[33] Meanwhile, the Tax Cuts and Jobs Act gave the top 1% of households savings of $48,000 on average, while households in the bottom 20% received around $120.[34] Here's the final kicker: the tax cuts for individuals expire in 2025 (when Trump, had he been elected to a second term, would safely be out of office); the tax cuts for businesses are permanent.[35] While the country frets over poor people getting away with something, working people are being fleeced. The tax cuts are taking away funding for public schools, libraries, roadways and infrastructure, as well as safety nets.

There certainly are people who get away with freeloading, but the problem for the nation isn't poor people. In 2014, Eric Garner died in a police choke hold after being suspected of evading taxes by selling cigarettes without tax stamps. Yet the media and politicians drive a US obsession with poor people getting more than they deserve. The result has been policies that reflect both racism and a disdain for poor people. The federal government has been so preoccupied with people playing the system to get something for nothing that it made selling food stamps valued at $100 or more a felony.[36] It's important to look at this because over the years there has been a lot of talk about welfare fraud in the media.

Some families with SNAP benefits and no cash income to speak of do sometimes sell their food stamps in order to buy basic things like socks and shoes that their children need.[37] The Government Accounting Office estimates that 2% of households either use SNAP benefits for nonfood items or trade them for cash.[38] According to the US Department of Agriculture a little over one penny on the dollar is lost to fraud. Selling food stamps is a desperate move – both because you get such a bad return on the dollar and because the punishment can be as high as a fine of up to $250,000 or up to twenty years in jail, or both.[39] To get a sense of just how strongly the government feels about poor people selling food stamps, consider US sentencing guidelines for other crimes. Aggravated assault with a firearm that causes bodily injury to the victim is punishable by up to five years in prison, and voluntary manslaughter can result in up to nine years. Yet a person selling her food stamps will get up to twenty years and a $250,000 fine. I say "her food stamps" because almost 60% of food stamp recipients are low-income women with children.[40]

For the most part, people have been all too willing to find fault with themselves for their economic insecurity and to take pride in themselves for their wealth. Of course, there are always personal aspects that shape opportunity, even in systems of structural inequality. But when economic myths persist – particularly ones as grand as the American Dream and the myth of a meritocracy – it isn't by accident. When we think about class, we have to think about political power. Economist Robert Reich writes: "While there are important differences between parties – Democratic members of Congress are far more socially liberal than Republicans and more concerned about poverty, climate change, guns, and the rights of women and minorities – neither party is committed to challenging the increasing concentration of wealth and power in America. Both have come to depend on that wealth, and therefore defer to that power."[41]

Free Market Capitalism

One of the most dangerous and deceptive myths we cling to is that we live in a free market economy. We learn to believe this imaginary free market exists as a neutral force, outside government and unaffected by how power is allocated in the system.[42] It is this myth of a free market that leads us to believe that inequalities are beyond our control. Indeed, efforts to reduce inequality are often described as constraints on the market's freedom – such efforts are often called "socialism" and are said to produce grave troubles for the country.

Nobel-winning economist Paul Krugman notes that even *asking* questions about income inequality will spur some conservatives to denounce you as un-American.[43] Think about this for a moment. In most industrialized countries, easy access to education and health care, affordable housing, and employment that pays a living wage are a reality. In the United States, to advocate for these opportunities is to be derided as socialist. Socialism has been a scare word in American politics for more than a century. It was used to attack President Franklin D. Roosevelt in 1935 for proposing Social Security, and since then has been hurled at every plan to advance the interests of working people. President Harry Truman observed that socialism "is what they call public power … anything that helps all the people."[44]

There are many forms of socialism, yet US school systems tend not to teach about a variety of economic systems. So, it's important to be clear what people are talking about when they use the term "socialism." People on the left point to Scandinavia, where two-thirds of workers are covered by unions, college education is free, and everyone enjoys a robust standard of living supported by long vacations.[45] Nordic countries enjoy social democracy – a democratic political system with robust social programs that enhance daily life. This is exactly what Bernie Sanders advocated in the presidential primaries of 2016 and 2019. By contrast, when people on the right invoke the word socialism, they point to Venezuela and the Soviet Union, where low-wage work, poverty, and repression have dominated.

Rose Taylor is among the young white Appalachians who tell me why Sanders' program appealed to them: "I think the reason why he resonated so much with me is just because he was saying we have all of these people, and they all need to be taken care of, and we have this money. We're spending so much money on military and not enough on education and not enough on the arts and not enough on making sure that working-class people can pay their rent and their bills and their food. I really understood that, because I've struggled obviously with that, and I know so many of my friends have, and so many of the people that are in my age group have, and it's really hard, and so I think that really resonated with me." Rose is very clear on the details of what is needed for what she sees as a better life.

The same can be said of Michael Chase, a young Black Appalachian who is all for free education: "My feeling is even if I get taxed more, even if I don't choose to go to college, I'm helping another person that wouldn't have these opportunities. Even now, I have more privilege than people who are my age. Even if I'm paying into something that might not directly affect me, if it helps a bunch of other people, why not? We cannot handle paying for college. It's too expensive. Make it free. With all the debt from medication and medical bills, we've shown that as a country we need to have free medical care. Everyone is in debt. Everyone has debt. I have debt from hospital bills, and they're not getting that money for a while."

If young people are very clear about their needs and what they want to see for the country, the labels are more confusing. Rose summed it up this way: "I think that it's also a little different socialism or democratic socialism. What those exact systems are has never been explained to the general public. Exactly what the differences are, especially with health care and stuff like that? I know so many people that don't go to the doctor and don't go to the dentist because they simply can't afford it. There's just no way they could pay it off, or there's no way they can save for it, and then that just leaves them...." Rose drifts off for a moment. "I had a tooth that died, what would have happened to that infection if I hadn't caught it in time? You know what I mean? A lot of those things, especially with your teeth, can result in heart issues if you don't catch them in time. Something that you think is little could become life threatening."

Yet for many people in the United States, there isn't even an open door to the conversation that younger people are having. For these folks, it's impossible to imagine democracy without capitalism. But the connection between the two is actually the result of concerted efforts by business. Corporations paid Edward Bernays (Freud's nephew) a great deal of money to ensure that in the mind of the public the political system of democracy would become synonymous with the economic system of free market capitalism.[46] To understand how this happened it helps to know that Bernays used Freud's theories of the unconscious to develop propaganda for the Wilson administration when it sought to reverse standing policy and take the country into World War I.

After the war, Bernays again put Freud's theories to work to build a consumer culture in the United States. Corporations paid him large sums to help them create markets for their products, without regard for the intrinsic value of those products. By then, however, the term propaganda had acquired a bad name, so Bernays rebranded his work as "public relations."[47] Bernays cemented the connection between capitalism and democracy through his work shaping the 1939 New York World's Fair.[48] At Bernays' insistence, the Fair was designed to model capitalist democracy as the future of the United States. The term "capitalist democracy" renders democracy not as a political framework that could work with various economic systems (including socialism) but as a system in and of itself. Over time, this ideology became ingrained in the United States – so much so that we now mistakenly call it "democracy."

Even if we make the distinction between the political system of democracy and the economic system of capitalism, the truth is that no country in the world – not even the US – has free market capitalism. The US government intervenes in the market all the time – it just does so to the benefit of business with subsidies, tax breaks, and bailouts. For example, taxpayers gave GM a $50 billion bailout in 2017. As part of the rescue deal, GM workers allowed the company to make new hires at about half its prevailing hourly wage and with skimpier retirement benefits, to bring on temporary workers at even lower rates, and to outsource more jobs abroad.[49] Yet once GM was back to making big profits, it didn't raise wages, restore retirement benefits, eliminate temporary workers, or stop outsourcing. This led almost 50,000 workers to go on strike in September 2019.[50] In the US, unlike what we are led to believe, the economic success of businesses rarely translates into economic success for workers.

The so-called free market is used to justify the fact that full-time Walmart workers earn an annual wage ($25,149) that is less than what the Walton family earns in dividends in *a single minute*.[51] Interestingly enough, no one is complaining about the moral fiber or work ethic of a company that pays workers so poorly, deprives them of health care and other benefits, while making a bundle at their expense. The government practically *gives away* public land to corporations that strip out and sell its natural resources – without being accountable to the land or to the people their extractions affect. Yet when struggling people are in need, we are told that it isn't the job of government to look after them – because we have a free market. When the narratives of the economic elite become the dominant narratives in the country, the structures that enable radical inequality are erased from view. We might see economic disparities, but we have no accurate way to understand systemic inequalities if we don't see the structures that create them.

Taking Care of Business

When the 115th Congress convened for the first time in 2017, the total wealth of its members was at least $2.43 billion; as a group they were 20% more wealthy than the previous Congress. The median net income for Congress members was $511,000, while the wealthiest members had incomes ranging from $28 million to $283 million.[52] By 2020, when the 116th Congress convened, the median net worth (of those who filed) was just over $1 million.[53]

These politicians have been elected to serve the entire electorate, but they know best how to care for the interests of their own class.[54] If we think about class locations as shaping knowledge about the world and our place in it, we shouldn't be too surprised that typically legislation benefits the wealthy people who write it and their friends who put them into office. When it comes to everyday worries, risks, and opportunities, we really do inhabit different worlds.

Almost half of retiring members of Congress now move on to become lobbyists; up from about 3% in 1970.[55] With forty-five of its fifty-one lobbyists coming from government, JP Morgan made good use of the $5,960,000 it spent on lobbying in 2018.[56] When JP Morgan and other big corporations donated to the Republican Party in 2016, their investments were paid off with tax cuts. "As a result of that tax cut, JP Morgan would receive about $20 billion in tax savings over five years. Pfizer, whose donations to the GOP in 2016 totaled $16 million, would reap $39 billion in tax savings. GE contributed $20 million and will get back $16 billion in tax savings. Chevron donated $13 million and received $9 billion."[57] Here again corporate gains failed to support workers. Massive tax cuts for corporations just don't "trickle down" into the lives of their employees – in fact, corporations often act against the interests of workers. We saw one example of that in Chapter 3 when banking lobbyists fought *against* efforts to constrain predatory lending. We saw other examples in Chapter 4 when industries and state governments fought *against* measures that would protect people and communities from toxic heavy metals. And we saw more examples in Chapter 5 when lobbyists for pharmaceutical companies supported legislators who derailed DEA investigations of the opioid crisis. While Congress does pass some legislation that benefits people in lower economic brackets, it rarely does so at the expense of the wealthy.

As long as politicians are beholden to corporations, we can forget about adequately addressing the rising levels of poverty, racism, and climate change, or the soaring costs of health insurance, pharmaceuticals, college, and housing. There will be no antitrust enforcement to restrain the power of giant corporations. Instead, they will grow larger.[58] When you've got a government with an economy doing well for people with money but not for everyone else, the government is no longer serving the people. It's serving the special interests of banks and corporations. Government is failing to address issues of equity because big corporations have become so effective at preventing the government from addressing them.[59] Economist Robert Reich tells us that *if corporate power seems to be beyond the control of government, it is because corporate power controls the government.*[60]

In the election cycle of 2016, the richest one-hundredth of 1% of Americans – 24,949 extraordinarily wealthy people – accounted for a record-breaking 40% of all campaign contributions.[61] In that same election cycle, corporations flooded the presidential, Senate, and House elections with $3.4 billion of donations; by contrast, labor unions contributed $213 million.[62] By October 2020, the richest one-hundredth of 1% of Americans had contributed nearly $2.3 billion to the presidential race.[63] In this legislative environment attention is directed to corporate bailouts and tax cuts, rather than to meaningful responses to the nation's crises in employment (it is a crisis when more than half the country can't afford an unexpected $400 expense), accessible health care, affordable housing, and environmental protection.

Similarly, rather than confront wealthy donors, most legislators have buried their heads in the sand regarding the global climate crisis, others work actively to support the economic and political interests of lobbyists and donors. Although the crisis affects the entire world, the poorest people in every country (including the US) carry the heaviest burden because they are the least resilient. Hurricanes may take down expensive summer beach homes costing owners and insurance companies millions, but when tornadoes flatten trailer parks there is no second home to which families can retreat and often little support to help them through. Some of the first studies on the climate crisis were done by oil companies in the 1970s; they buried those studies when they saw what it would mean for their business.[64] The same is true today. The science is clear but rather than radically reorder our economic and political systems, as the crisis requires, government and corporations are doubling down on the sacrosanct notion of a so-called free market system.

We have not done what is needed to combat the climate crisis because the actions required fundamentally conflict with deregulated capitalism. You would be hard pressed to find experts denying the reality of the climate crisis other than those who are paid by fossil fuel companies. They are following the same strategies used by the Lead Industries Association for nearly sixty years to prevent lead from being banned (see Chapter 4), and by the tobacco industry for more than fifty years.[65] "We are stuck because the actions that would give us the best chance of averting catastrophe, and that would benefit the vast majority, are extremely threatening to an elite minority that has a stranglehold over our economy, our political process, and most of our major media outlets."[66]

Typically, politicians arrive at Congress supported by campaigns funded by corporations, lobbyists, political action committees, and wealthy donors. This is not altruistic funding. Donors of this magnitude expect something in return. Pharmaceutical companies, for example, expect "their" politician to vote against any measure that would threaten their interests. It's common sense when you think about it. Despite the rhetoric about democracy, we seem to know this. "The reason the American oil industry gets $2.5 billion a year from the government in special benefits, including the rights to drill for oil on public lands and take private lands for oil pipelines, has nothing to do with the public's interest in obtaining more oil. It is because Big Oil spends some $150 million a year backing pliant politicians. That $2.5 billion worth of government benefits is a remarkably good return on investment."[67] According to a study published in 2014 by Princeton professor Martin Gilens and Northwestern professor Benjamin Page, the preferences of the typical American have no influence at all on the legislation emerging from Congress.[68] The majority of voters are not able to counter the economic power of the corporations that bankroll campaigns. In 2017, 60% of workers earned less than $40,000, according to the Social Security administration.[69]

Big money matters. But big money funders make up a very small proportion of voters. A politician who wants to win a democratic election needs to be able to vote in favor of the wealthy without losing the votes of the ordinary people who make up their electoral base. One way of doing this is to shift the conversation away from economic issues and toward "cultural issues," as we saw in Chapter 9 with "Joe the Plumber." To be clear, no cultural issue – not gun control, not racism, not abortion rights, and not the right to marry – is purely a cultural issue. They are related to, but stand apart from, issues of employment, wages, affordable housing, and so on and yet they are issues that cut across class in that they affect people in every economic class. Big money plays a substantial part in these issues as well.

What Next?

The struggles of working people are not just about factories closing down. They are about an economic system that pushes workers into precarious lives without adequate wages, health care, housing, or stability – and then blames them for their circumstances. The struggles of working people are the result of a perilous and unsustainable betrayal that threatens the entire economy. Without a language for talking about class exploitation, it is all too easy for people to blame themselves for being stuck in economic quicksand. Even knowing that government and business are working against you, there is little sense among ordinary people that they can do anything about it. In these contexts, racism and sexism in struggling white communities come to the surface, while in wealthy white communities they remain hidden in boardroom handshakes.

In the midst of a global pandemic and facing the specter of a civil war, millions of people try simply to survive day to day. If we are to turn things around, we need to start talking about economic struggles in a language that accurately characterizes those experiences. As politicians and media stay focused on an unrealistically low poverty line and simplistic analyses of unemployment, they mask the realities that people live with every day because low-wage work dominates the economy. The daily struggles of working people are not represented by Joe-the-so-called-plumber. And they are not represented by the economic elites that fill the halls of government.

In the spring of 2020, as I was writing this book, the Covid-19 pandemic hit. The ensuing battle between epidemiologists and politicians made me wonder even more deeply if anyone had the interests of low-wage workers in mind. In May and June 2020, I circled back to as many people as I could to ask about how they had been affected by the pandemic. You'll hear from them in the next chapter.

10

And Then, the Pandemic…

The pandemic, and the government response to it, exposed and exacerbated long-standing inequalities. It also exposed a long-standing system of collusion between business and government that enables a small number of people to thrive at the expense of workers. In February 2020, Secretary of State Michael Pompeo announced that the federal government would ship almost 17.8 *tons* of Personal Protective Equipment (PPE) to China.[1] In March, PPE was in short supply in the US and the federal government began seizing PPE from states. For example, at the port of New York, federal agents seized 3 million N95 masks purchased by the state of Massachusetts for its health-care workers and first responders.[2] The seizure of medical supplies from states was so consistent that when Republican Governor Larry Hogan acquired 500,000 Covid-19 testing kits from South Korea for his state of Maryland, he ensured the cargo was guarded in transit and hidden in an undisclosed location when it arrived.[3] Further, as PPE became critical to health-care workers and first responders, the federal government *escalated* the cost of PPE by forcing individual states to bid against each other – and sometimes against the federal government itself – for medical supplies.[4]

While the nation worried over PPE and unemployment, the Environmental Protection Agency, headed by Andrew Wheeler, a former coal lobbyist, stepped in to weaken critical environmental laws. The Trump administration rolled back thirty-four environmental rules and regulations – this was in addition to the sixty they had already rolled back in the previous three years.[5] Wheeler gave reporters a familiar line that we heard earlier from Justice Scalia when he said: "'One would not say it is even rational, never mind appropriate, to impose billions in economic cost in return for a few dollars in health benefits.'"[6] This roll back wasn't even *sought* by power companies since they had already invested billions to meet the EPA restrictions under the Obama administration. And it came on the heels of a 2019 study that found that unsubsidized renewable energy is often the cheapest source of energy.[7] Even as oil companies faced record low oil prices and difficulties storing the oil they already had, the Trump administration fast-tracked efforts to drill for oil and gas on public land. One of Trump's last acts in office fulfilled a long-standing goal of Republicans when he auctioned off drilling leases in Alaska's Arctic National Wildlife Refuge to oil and gas companies.[8] "Federal scientists estimate that a third of [polar] bear's maternal dens lie within the area the administration opened up for energy development."[9]

For many of the nation's corporations the pandemic brought an economic windfall. In just ten months, the wealth of just fifteen US billionaires grew by $1.14 trillion.[10] Meanwhile workers, many without health insurance or sick time, were risking their lives in low-wage jobs because they couldn't afford to stay home. Even in this context, billionaires overwhelmingly favored cuts to their own taxes and a reduction of social safety nets, as they continued to make political contributions to protect their interests.[11]

Seeing once again how government supports the interests of corporations at the expense of the nation and its people, I wondered again about those who had been burdened by the corruption of democracy long before the pandemic. Across the country millions of workers came into the crisis holding multiple low-wage jobs. I wanted to know how the people I had interviewed for this book were doing. In May and June of 2020, I circled back. It didn't surprise me that I was unable to reach most folks by phone or internet. What did surprise me was that I was able to talk with eight people on Zoom: Ellison and Two Lance Woman at Standing Rock Reservation; Michael Chase, Rose Taylor, and Jenny Gaines in Southeast Ohio; and Tom Sam, Angel Perez, and Vanessa Torres in Oakland. I didn't know what to expect. The global pandemic has been hardest on people who have the least. Yet their stories in this chapter surprised me and may surprise you. People who had been living on the edge for so long were resourceful and tenacious in the face of the health crisis.

When Challenges Turn to Crises

When Oakland schools closed down, Vanessa Torres was able to move her work online. You might recall from Chapter 2 that she works for an educational nonprofit that serves Latinx high school students. The ability to work online is a privilege that many people just don't have. "In my community, there's a lot of folks who do labor jobs. There's a lot of food vendors, so now they really can't be out. A lot of folks were left without jobs and not being able to provide for their family." Before the pandemic, Vanessa's mom sold tamales once a week, and her dad worked as a laborer. Her parents are not able to work in the pandemic and don't qualify for unemployment. She also has three younger siblings – one of whom is old enough to work and has a job. In the best of times, Vanessa would describe herself as "the rock" that everyone relies on – and things are a long way from the best of times. Vanessa carries the financial burden for the family. "Latinos, especially in East Oakland," she explains, "have been the ones hit hardest during the pandemic, because they are all essential workers. It's ridiculous. I think it shows that they don't care about your life. They care about making money. That's not all right, because someone's health, someone's life can never be returned. If you're sick and you're not able to come in one day, you're just disposable and replaceable."

Before the pandemic, Angel Perez worked as a teaching assistant in Oakland public schools. He didn't have *enough* work, but he did have work. Now, Angel's job has gone online, which requires that he stakes out space at the dining-room table to work. In a family accustomed to physical labor, twenty-something Angel has to explain over (and over) again to his dad that he *really* is working. "So that's the difficult part, my dad thinks I'm just sitting at the computer all day, because I want to be lazy." While Angel is trying to get his dad to recognize that what he is doing *is* work, farmworkers are constantly on his mind. "They still continue to work. They still continue to provide all the groceries that we eat. Just thinking about all of that affects me." Life in East Oakland might be 100 miles from agricultural communities, but their closeness is palpable in my conversations with Angel.

California grows over a third of the country's vegetables and two-thirds of the fruits and nuts. The vast fields are harvested by over 850,000 farmworkers – nearly half of whom are undocumented.[12] Agricultural work pays about $17,500 a year. Some workers earn the hourly minimum wage ($10.50 in 2017), while others are on a piece rate dependent upon how much they pick or prune.[13] It's seasonal, back-breaking work that leaves workers exposed to dangerous chemical fertilizers and pesticides. Farmworkers have been declared "essential" in the pandemic and so they return to the fields, day after day, hoping they don't bring the virus home to their children at night.[14]

During the pandemic the majority of government aid has been directed toward the 9% of farms run by agribusiness, including the $28 billion in bailout money provided to counteract recent trade policies, the $19 billion from the CARES Act that went to large agribusiness, and the $48.4 billion in CARES Act relief that went to the USDA.[15] Farmworkers and small farmers are not seeing this money.[16] Government subsidies are propping up big agribusinesses. But it isn't only farmworkers who continue to labor in unsafe working conditions.

Latino and Black workers are disproportionately employed as low-wage, "essential" workers. Almost half of workers in the meatpacking industry are Latino and one-quarter are Black.[17] According to the Bureau of Labor Statistics, the average pay for slaughterers and meatpackers was about $13.68 an hour in 2018.[18] This amounts roughly to a pre-tax, annual income of $26,000 per year. Yet many workers in the meat processing industry are contractors who earn about one-third of employees.[19]

Just four companies – Tyson Foods, Cargill, Smithfield Foods, and JBS – control 80% of beef production, about 70% of pork production, and around 60% of poultry production in the nation.[20] In early April 2020, Covid-19 testing at the JBS plant in Colorado revealed that half of the 200 managers had the virus. In response, the company *abandoned* plans to test the entire 3,200-plus workforce.[21] By mid-April, slaughterhouse workers had begun to die from Covid-19 in Colorado, South Dakota, Iowa, Pennsylvania, and Georgia. In a single week, Covid-19 cases surged from sixty to 800 at a JBS Packerland meatpacking plant in Wisconsin.[22] Throughout April, the CDC documented nearly 5,000 Covid-19 cases in meat and poultry processing plants.[23] Yet on April 28 Trump signed an executive order requiring meatpacking plants to remain open, affecting nearly 500,000 meatpacking workers.[24] As it turns out, the meat processing industry not only pressed Trump to keep the plants open, ProPublica found that just weeks before his order, the "meat industry's trade group drafted an executive order that bears striking similarities to the one the president signed."[25] They essentially drafted the policy for him. In the coming months thousands more workers tested positive in meat processing plants, and companies pushed back on testing.[26]

Trump promised to shield meat plants from legal liability if employees sued them for placing their health at risk. Senate Majority Leader Mitch McConnell (R-Ky) made limiting corporate liability his top priority and threatened to block relief packages that did not protect corporations. Health and Human Services Secretary Alex Azar went a step further and blamed the spike in coronavirus cases on workers who live in overcrowded conditions, rather than the fact that they had been working shoulder-to-shoulder without protective equipment. Azar suggested that one solution would be to send more law enforcement officers to those communities to enforce social distancing.[27] In an industry where the majority of workers are not citizens, the threat was clear.[28] Even after 200 meatpacking plant workers had died, the Smithfield Foods plant in South Dakota and a JBS plant in Colorado faced meager fines of $29,000 for safety violations. In 2019, Smithfield had revenue of nearly $14 billion and JBS $51.7 billion.[29]

While Trump's executive order was framed as being needed to keep food on the table for American families, less than two months later the US *exported a record 129,000 tons of pork to China*.[30] Clearly, the demand that workers risk their lives by going to work were not motivated solely by a need to keep food on US tables. For corporations, the money kept rolling in. By August 2020 the Bureau of Economic Analysis was reporting that the price of beef had risen 20.2% and eggs more than 10% since February, and food banks that the wholesale cost of rice had tripled.[31]

Before the pandemic, Tom Sam in Oakland experienced more than his share of thin months where he would patch through by taking on work as a singer at graduations, birthday parties, and powwows. That's no longer an option. When I first interviewed Tom, he was supporting a family of five – his wife, two young daughters (now six and eight) and a niece (now twenty-three). Since then, his niece has moved to San Diego. You might recall that Tom is a Diné/Comanche man who works for a nonprofit that supports Native children in public schools. When the pandemic shut down schools, Tom's work didn't enable an easy transition online. "We were completely out of work [for several weeks] and trying to figure out how we were going to proceed. We've really tried to focus on online resources, online tutoring, online gatherings. But several of the grants that I'm paid by are based on one-on-one services, tutoring services, face-to-face time. That was impossible to do in March and April. We're now in May and still our hours are definitely rolled back quite significantly."

What began as a challenge quickly turned into a financial crisis. "Within my household, we're scraping by. We still have a roof over our heads, and we have food in our refrigerator. It definitely has been hard to make payments. We've had to call and set up several stop payments on different things, different credit card bills." Tom is still paying off debt he and his wife accrued as college students, well before their children were born. Recently their car broke down adding more financial pressure. "It's been really hard just getting stuff paid for, making sure that we have what we need. I'm the type of person that I'll figure all that stuff out. If I need the money, I'll figure it out. I'll go recycle cans or do what I need to do to make sure that ends meet."

To keep food on the table, Tom and his family have relied on food banks. He has begun to volunteer at the places where he receives food. "When I take a box, I feel okay because I gave some time. I feel like I earned it at least. But that's just, again, my style of thinking. Nothing comes exactly for free. You've got to kind of work for it." He has also started a garden. Tom has a very deep seat of core values that are community-based and chafes at what he sees around him. "This is a very social status and financial status, elitist type of society – the elites have what they have, and they're still growing their wealth, even in this time of pandemic. The folks who have less financial status in this country are being treated as if their lives are expendable." In the pandemic, inequalities come into sharp focus. "I see impoverished communities being hit harder than affluent communities. I see certain groups of color being hit the hardest. Our indigenous communities ... what the Navajo Nation is going through is extremely, extremely sad."

The Navajo (Dine'é) Nation is about the size of West Virginia; it's 27,000 square miles of high mountain desert across the borders of Arizona, Utah, and New Mexico. It is home to about 175,000 people, 44% of whom lived *below* the federal poverty line before the pandemic; nearly one-third of homes do not have electricity or running water.[32] The Indian Health Service, established by the federal government, is drastically underfunded; it receives one-third the amount of money, per person, allocated to Medicare and the Veterans Administration.[33] Among the many consequences of this federal policy is that the reservation has a severe shortage of doctors and hospital infrastructure. By July 2020, the Covid-19 infection rate on the reservation was 3.4% and the Navajo Nation faced 177 deaths per 100,000 people – a higher mortality rate than any single state in the US.[34] Although Congress passed the CARES Act in March, it took more than four months and a court battle for the Navajo Nation to receive just 60% of the funding to which they were entitled.[35]

Tom describes the situation this way, "We're part of this nation within a nation that's not going to always have our best interest in mind. The only people who are going to look out for our own best interest is ourselves. This pandemic has just encouraged me to see how I could best get involved to support folks that are really in need at this time." From a worldview that sees all life as connected, Tom thinks of the dominant US culture as ill in fundamental ways. "I think that the old guard or folks on the right, folks that believe in racism and racial inequality, are really reaching to hold on to things. They know they're outnumbered and they're getting desperate. Their desperate attempts sometimes get physically violent. That's part of what's going on out in South Dakota right now where the COVID checkpoints that the tribes have put up are being threatened."

When South Dakota reached 6,353 cases and eighty-three deaths, the Cheyenne River Sioux and the Oglala Sioux Tribes declared a state of emergency and established Health & Safety Checkpoints on roads entering their reservations.[36] The checkpoints require residents and nonresidents to fill out a health questionnaire each time they enter or leave tribal lands. Those planning to drive straight through the reservation are allowed to pass once they clear the checkpoints. Nonresidents are allowed in on essential business if they have a travel permit issued by the tribal government. Governor Noem objected to the restrictions and threatened legal action.[37]

At Standing Rock Reservation Ellison Thompson tells me "I definitely have issues with our current governor, Kristi Noem, demanding that the reservations take down their checkpoints. She has no jurisdiction over what the tribal government does. She's claiming that they're stopping essential businesses from going in the reservation, but they're not. It's an *inconvenience*, because people have to go to a different route instead of going through the reservation. That's what her whole issue is. There's so many other things going wrong in the state that she should focus on instead of trying to pick a fight with the tribal leaders about a checkpoint. There are two reservations that have checkpoints right now. It's Cheyenne River and the Oglala Sioux Tribes at the bottom of the state, and she's demanding that they take their checkpoints down or there'll be legal action. It's just a mess."

Cheyenne River Sioux Chairman Harold Frazier refused Governor Noem's demands to take down the checkpoints and responded: "We will not apologize for being an island of safety in a sea of uncertainty and death."[38] Native American reservations have vulnerable populations, few medical resources, and a history of facing deadly epidemics. Contact with Europeans introduced epidemics of smallpox, tuberculosis, scarlet fever, and measles throughout the Americas. For the tribal leaders, refusing to protect their people in a global pandemic would have been beyond reckless. But Governor Noem didn't see it that way and asked President Trump to intervene. When the federal government pressed forward, the Cheyenne River Sioux Tribe sued President Donald J. Trump and ten other members of his administration over what they deemed to be an unlawful invasion of tribal lands.[39]

Ellison is frustrated. "I know there's been a lot of protests going on about people being stressed about the lockdown being so long. I don't have a whole lot of faith that the government has the people's best interests when they're making choices and decisions. We as Native Americans fall even lower on their level of concern. People are protesting for salons and restaurants to open up. Someone needs to tell these people they need to calm down. Getting a haircut, it's not something you need, and they're acting like they're being robbed of their rights, because they can't go get a haircut." In August, Governor Noem supported a biker rally that drew 460,000 people from across the country to Sturgis, South Dakota. It is an event that brings in about $2 million in revenue.[40] Subsequently, an estimated 266,796 cases of Covid were linked to the rally, according to San Diego State University's Center for Health Economics & Policy Studies.[41] As of this writing, the reservations remained protected by checkpoints.

Just before the pandemic hit, Ellison's life was in high gear. She and her husband had celebrated the arrival of their second child. "I have a two-year-old and a three-year-old now," she says with a broad smile. "They raise cane all day long. They're double-trouble!" Ellison rolls her eyes and shakes her head at the thought. She and her family also have mourned the loss of her grandfather. He left Ellison his home, and for the first time she and her family have a place of their own. "We live in a trailer house now," she says with excitement. "It's a nice place. It's a three-bedroom, so the kids have their own rooms."

Despite her grandfather's death and the birth of a second child, there is stability in Ellison's life. She has the same service industry job as when we last talked. Her husband still does childcare. And, although he still doesn't cook, Ellison has grown accustomed to stretching to make meals happen every day. In addition to working full-time, Ellison has been attending Sitting Bull College. "When the pandemic hit, my schedule was crazy," she explains. "I worked full-time, and I was at school full-time." The pandemic brought work to a stop and Ellison's classes went online. She is now one class away from completing an associate degree in business administration. When we talk, it has been a month and a half since she worked – but she has not lost wages or health care. The Standing Rock tribal government secured a federal Paycheck Protection Program (PPP) loan that ensured that everyone getting laid off would receive full pay and health insurance through May.[42] "We were supposed to open up last Friday, but there was a protest at the travel council building about opening up – that they should care about the people instead of making money. The council ended up voting to keep the things closed for one more week."

The PPP loans were used at Standing Rock exactly as intended, to prevent financial crises for workers and their families. It was a tremendous success for Ellison and her family. Yet it appears that Standing Rock may be more the exception than the rule. In principle, PPP loans were intended for small businesses with fewer than 500 employees. However, a significant portion of the loans went to well-financed businesses with private equity investors.[43] According to data released by the Small Business Administration, nearly 90,000 companies in the program took the aid without promising on their applications to rehire workers or to create jobs.[44] And some companies with few employees received millions of dollars. For example, CCU Coal and Construction received over $5 million for 148 workers.[45]

In the face of unprecedented job losses, many US corporations chose to protect the interests of their shareholders over the needs of their workers.[46] Caterpillar closed down operations in three facilities in late March, and two weeks later gave shareholders $500 million in cash dividends; Levi Strauss announced on April 7, 2020 that it would stop paying 4,000 workers and on the same day announced it was paying shareholders $32 million; Stanley Black & Decker furloughed all of its workers and two weeks later issued shareholder dividends of $106 million.[47] All of these workers lost their jobs and, if they had it, their health insurance. Unlike the workers in these companies, about 70% of all shareholders have incomes in excess of $200,000, according to the Internal Revenue Service.[48]

Standing Rock not only ensured their workers had full pay and health care, they also put other protections in place as well. Ellison describes life at Standing Rock during the pandemic. "The stores all have plexiglass up in front of all the cashiers. Kids aren't allowed in any of the stores. No one under sixteen can be in the store. You have to go in stores with a mask. There's only ten people allowed in each store at a time, but, other than that, it's been rather normal here. I guess because people are used to living paycheck-to-paycheck, so the pandemic hasn't really affected us so much. We haven't really had any cases either. I think the whole reservation has seen four cases at most.

Thankfully, though, while things were shut down, the employees were still being paid our normal wages, so I'm really thankful that we still got paid, even though things were closed down."

By Ellison's account, Standing Rock has done a terrific job of caring for people in the face of the pandemic. Ellison seems to be flourishing. But life is complicated. Almost as an afterthought, she mentions that her husband almost died – twice, in one week. Everyone thought he was having some health trouble caused by high blood pressure. It turned out that he had undiagnosed diabetes. "It got to the point where he started to lose kind of a little bit of his sight, and he was really weak. He went into the ER and found out that his blood sugar was at 1,200, which could have put him into a coma.[49] He went from the emergency room into the ICU. Then he finally got better, and he got discharged on Sunday on our anniversary. Then a couple of days after that, he wasn't feeling well, and his leg hurt." Ellison convinced him to go back to the hospital in Mobridge and they found blood clots in his legs. Then they discovered that his kidneys were failing too and transferred him from Mobridge to Bismarck (about two hours away). He spent several more days in ICU and had been released just days before we spoke. Ellison's experience drives home both the vulnerability of Native people and the limited access they have to health-care resources on or near the reservation.

Two Lance Woman tells me, "Standing Rock is closed. We're not allowing visitors. Here at Standing Rock, we only got seven ventilators. If we get a breakout, we're screwed. We're screwed. We still have our treaty rights, and we're going to act on them. I'm really proud of Standing Rock. They're supporting Rosebud, Oglala, and Cheyenne River [who have put up checkpoints]. Here, the tribal chairmen have been pretty honorable, just trying to get resources to the communities, especially elders. We're all worried about our elders. We're all worried about the children. We've been surviving for so long that this is nothing new. People are going to help each other, which has been happening. I guess being in a poor reservation, that we are supposed to be devastated or something. No. We're helping each other."

Two Lance Woman is involved in supporting the Standing Rock community – both on and off work. "I helped to get masks for the elders. We did for the EMTs. We did for the hospital. I'm collaborating with some other ladies. We're trying to get all of the people on the reservation, which is 8,000, face masks. I don't know if that's going to be possible. We've been helping a lot with Navajo Nation, helping out with Cheyenne River, Oglala, Rosebud, some of the Oceti Sakowin tribes. The tribe here has been getting donations for food, some masks, different medicines. People are just showing support, trying to help." Through her efforts to address the pandemic, Two Lance Woman is growing closer to Native communities and to her traditions.

She tells me, "Before colonialism, before any Europeans came, we had millions of people here. We knew our place [in the world]. Now, half the time, people [non-Natives] don't know what they're doing here. When they were saying, 'we're having a toilet paper issue,' I was just like, wow, this is crazy. Now we're having issues with meat. It kind of proves the point that money is everything. Hoarding is acceptable."

The pandemic has highlighted or exacerbated inequalities because it amplifies our values. Nowhere is this more evident than in the contrast between the federal government response and the Standing Rock tribal government response. The federal government emphasized corporate subsidies and individual freedom. It not only abandoned the most vulnerable people but showed its willingness to sacrifice low-wage workers. By contrast, the Standing Rock government emphasized a sense of connection to and responsibility for others. Too familiar with the impact of pandemics, the Native people I talked with prioritized caring for each other, especially protecting children and elders. They are guided by an ethics of care that has enabled them to endure in the harshest of times.

Connecting the Dots

When I first met Michael Chase he was working two jobs, had no health insurance, and shared an apartment with several roommates. It was exhausting. Shortly before the 2020 pandemic hit, Michael strategized on how to get ahead. He moved in with his parents, earned three state certifications, and took a full-time job as a direct support professional. In his new job, Michael works with, and administers medication to, people with developmental disabilities. He provides some direct care in their homes across Athens County and also provides services in a center the company operates. Michael likes the job and the feeling that he's making a difference.

He started his new job as a medication aide at $10.50 an hour and soon made a raise to $11.25 an hour. Because of the pandemic, he was given hazard pay of $0.75 per hour bringing him to $12 an hour. He decided to forgo the company-sponsored health insurance. "The insurance, it's like $200-something a month. It's very expensive. They're like, 'look, this is what we can offer, but we understand, don't take it. This is a bad offer.' It would be nice to have insurance, but I can't afford that. I also asked my management, and they're like, 'yeah, the insurance, no one here has the insurance.'" His new employer offers health insurance and hazard pay that meet bureaucratic guidelines but do nothing to actually address workers' needs.

Being a direct support professional, Michael faces a number of employer restrictions on his activities outside of work. He is not allowed to leave the county, and is not allowed to participate in outdoor gatherings, even if everyone is wearing a mask and maintaining social distancing. The new job also requires a lot of driving. Although his 2002 Toyota has 359,000 miles on it, he loves the car. Thanks to his stepdad, his car runs well, which is a big relief given that he works both day and night shifts. "Since the pandemic happened, people quit. So now everyone's working overtime. A lot of times I'm working 14-hour shifts." Michael is twenty-something and looks permanently tired. He is a tall man with a baby face and dark rings under his eyes that never seem to leave. As a Black man, Michael's sense of being unsafe in much of Athens and surrounding counties has not changed. He carries a constant awareness that he is at risk of being violently attacked, and this sense of risk is compounded by a job that requires so much travel, some of it at night.

With the rising number of Black men and women being murdered by police, Michael is extremely worried about doing anything that would draw attention to himself in a store or that would get him pulled over by police. The callous killing of George Floyd by Minneapolis police officers brought a long-standing epidemic of police brutality to the national forefront. Protests erupted across the country to denounce the state-sanctioned violence that has terrorized Black communities for centuries and inspired #BlackLivesMatter protests around the globe. Even in the context of massive protests, police murders of unarmed Black men and women continued in the United States. Less than three weeks after the killing of George Floyd, Rayshard Brooks was killed by officer Garrett Rolfe in a Wendy's parking lot; an inebriated Brooks was running away when Rolfe fired three shots at his back from 18 feet away.[50]

Michael thought long and hard about the consequences of wearing a mask in this environment of police violence. Would some colors be confused with gang affiliations? His mother worried as well and stepped in to make masks for him. Michael wears a yellow mask with smiley face emojis. "In Athens County, there is a lack of trust in science and so most people either don't wear a mask or they wear a bandana. It's really weird. They're all wearing bandanas, which is like a gang affiliation. I'm not about to wear that. I'm wearing smiley faces." The smiley face emoji solved part of the problem. Michael continues to work at night.

"When they had the stay-at-home order [in Ohio], police were out at night in town, but not on the highways. I'd be fine on the highway, but driving through town, you're passing four or five police." Michael tries to anticipate and plan for what might happen if he is stopped by police. He runs scenarios through his mind. For a while he worried enough about being stopped by police that he would call someone to say where he was and where he was going – especially when he was assigned to a community with high rates of poverty and drug addiction. "It's a poor area," he explains. "There a lot of people are on drugs. A lot of people don't have teeth. The police are always there. I don't want them to think, 'well, I don't know of any Black people that live here. What are you doing here at 10?' You know everything is closed and this is a meth area. That's going to look suspicious. I would say for a good two weeks, I'd be getting bad anxiety and sweating and stuff if I had to work nights or even if I got off at 10 p.m. to go home." As the visible police presence in towns has diminished Michael has begun to feel safer. He isn't having anxiety attacks – but he is a long way from being able to move through the world without worrying about police.

In Southeast Ohio, the public response to the pandemic frustrates Michael. "You have scientists and doctors who have spent their whole life dedicated to understanding this type of stuff, and they're saying, 'hey, this is a pandemic.' And all these people are dead and people getting infected. And [the government is] just like, 'just wash your hands and go to work.' I'm like NO! This is stopping the whole world. Then we found out that Donald Trump had known about it beforehand and didn't say anything. I'm not a conspiracy person, but I'm looking at facts of how this is really affecting Black and Brown communities." Michael counts off issues with overcrowded housing and the predominance of Black and Brown people in service industries. "We are holding the country up. But the government is going like, 'all right, this is the chance to kill all the Black and Brown and poor people.' Because that's who is getting affected the most if we're going to be real. It's not going to affect the 1% because they are able to isolate and go to places. They own their houses meanwhile all these [other] people are getting evicted."

Michael's voice rises as he talks. He is passionate, frustrated, and scared when he looks at what is happening around him. He isn't alone. The #cancelrent movement was born in April 2020, when 30% of renters were unable to pay their monthly rent. The movement became the largest coordinated rent strike since 1930. Renters argue that the large real estate corporations and powerful landlords are in a better position to suffer the loss than they are. Their ability to pay rent has fluctuated with states opening and closing businesses as they try to balance the risks to the economy against the risks to public health. Yet missing from this balancing act is the reality that *before* the pandemic, millions of families were already struggling to pay their bills because they held low-wage jobs.

Before the pandemic, according to Feeding America, 37,227,000 people were struggling with hunger, of which 11,174,000 were children.[51] Feeding America reported that the pandemic brought a 98% increase in demand at member food banks,[52] and estimated that more than 50 million people (including 17 million children) were experiencing food insecurity.[53] In cities across the country, the pandemic meant that many families were no longer able to pay their electricity or water bills. It exacerbated an existing crisis that millions of families were facing because of low-wage work, the high cost of housing, and unaffordable health care.

The unemployment rate in April 2020 was 14.7%.[54] By May 2020, according to the US Department of Labor, over 33 million jobs had been lost and one in five workers had filed for unemployment.[55] If this isn't grim enough, we know that people who are underemployed are not counted in the unemployment rate. If we consider people who are unemployed but have not filed for unemployment (perhaps they were unemployed before the pandemic) and include part-time workers (who nearly doubled in number between March and April 2020 – from 5.8 million to 10.7 million) the number of people without work or adequate work hours rises to about 26.4%.[56] This is an important reality to keep in mind as the official unemployment rate drops.[57]

The stress of living in a struggling community is more acute now. "It's the biggest mind fuck sitting here," says Michael. "People are dying. But at the same time, we still have to continue to work, because if not, the economy is going to fall. If we're going to be real, if it means saving a whole bunch of people's lives or letting the economy fall – well, we've bounced back before from stuff like that. Either we go through a depression or we send all these people to work and let them die. It doesn't make sense."

As we talk, Michael's thoughts drift to Minneapolis. The murder of George Floyd and the response to the pandemic are part of a long history of government-sanctioned racism that has included medical experiments and murder. This knowledge is deeply rooted in histories and families. It is embodied among Black people in ways that white people might (at best) understand only intellectually. The expression on Derek Chauvin's face as he slowly murders George Floyd is not separate from Donald Trump's response to the pandemic. They are both part of a cultural history of cruelty toward Black and Brown people. Michael follows the Minneapolis protests through social media, and wonders if the government will find a way to punish Black people for the destruction caused by protests. He says in jest, "I feel after what happened in Minneapolis, we're definitely not getting those stimulus checks." It would be a funnier joke if the second stimulus package had arrived.[58]

Before we wrap up, Michael has one more thing to add to our conversation. He worries for farmworkers. "I'm scared for the illegal immigrants, the ones who work the fields picking fruit and vegetables. They are the backbone to our nation. They're the ones out there putting foods on our tables, putting vegetables in the grocery store and slaughtering the animals. I feel like after this, there should be no excuse for them not to get full citizenship."

Despite Michael's best efforts to get ahead he remains in a precarious position. For Michael, the writing is on the wall: he can't stay here. "I know it sounds kind of rash, but I've been thinking about this for years, about just leaving Ohio." He worries that if he doesn't leave soon, he'll be trapped, like many others he knows. Low-wage work and increasing debt commonly trap people in places they don't want to be. He has a friend in Indiana and thinks that might be a good move. So, for now he works and saves. And he worries.

In the midst of a global pandemic, the experiences of white people stand in juxtaposition to those of people of color. You might remember Rose Taylor from previous chapters. Rose had been working two jobs in Athens County when we first met in 2017. Even with more than sixty hours a week of low-wage work, Rose's ability to get ahead was continually challenged by expenses like medical care and car repairs. When you met her in Chapter 2, she was about to take out a medical loan to pay for dental treatment. When I catch up with Rose in 2020, she is sporting several new tattoos, new facial piercings, and what she calls "a very gay haircut." (It's clipped short on the sides and the very long hair on the top of her head is pulled back into a knot.) She seems really happy.

Rose changed jobs and, along with her dog, moved to Columbus, Ohio to live with her girlfriend. "I wasn't making enough money to do more than just survive, basically. I met my girlfriend, and we started dating, and she lives in Columbus, so we dated long-distance, an hour drive back and forth, and then after a year of doing that, I started looking for work up here."

When I ask Rose how the dental problem was resolved, she winces. "Yeah, I took out a loan. I ended up borrowing $2,000. What ended up happening was that I had a dead tooth, and they had to go in and fix my tooth, and then I had a little bit of an infection in my gum, because of the dead tooth. They had to take out some of my upper jaw up here and give me really strong antibiotics to kill it, and then they refilled my tooth. It's something I'll have to obviously keep an eye on, just to keep on top of it." The bad news is that all of this could have been avoided if she had been able to receive dental care promptly. The good news is that three years later, the loan is paid off.

In Columbus, Rose is making better money in her new job, doing body piercing in a shop that employs about a dozen piercers. "I feel really good about that, and there's more people that work there that have more experience. A lot of my coworkers have eight- or nine-years piercing experience, and some of them have twenty-five years. It's really nice. I've learned on an apprentice scale, it's learning as you're doing. It's all a really good thing and I'm down to one job!" There's no more worry about having to work double-shifts three or four days a week.

An increased ease is apparent in her body. The dark circles under her eyes are gone and she smiles through most of the interview. I suspect this is as much about her new love as her new job. Rose makes $10 for every piercing that she does plus tips. There are no benefits, no health insurance, sick time, holidays, etc. She doesn't even earn a base salary like wait staff do. Her income is entirely dependent on how many people walk through the door and choose her. Despite all of this, Rose is heartened by that fact that she is at the low end of the company's pay scale. There is room to earn more. "I'm guaranteed a certain number of shifts or hours a week, and then it just depends on how many people walk in the door to get a piercing that day." Things were going great, and then on March 13 her studio closed down for the pandemic.

"I knew I wasn't going to get unemployment. I'm a 1099, which means I'm an independent contractor, so I did not get unemployment. I didn't have a paycheck for two months, and I didn't get a stimulus check. It's *really* hard. And it's sad to see just how many people, especially in my industry, the artists that just are getting no help at all." Fortunately, her girlfriend who she lives with continued to work full-time for a school system. Between her salary and what Rose could contribute using her credit card they managed. "I'm pretty proud of the fact that I was able to really stretch the dollar and make it all work. It was really tricky."

As proud as Rose is of her own efforts, she is angry at Donald Trump. "If he was really concerned about the working class, he would make sure that we're safe. With all of his messages, he's like, 'oh, it's not that bad. We're going to open back up, or we're going to make sure our economy is strong again.' Everybody in the White House has to be tested every single day, but there's no tests for all [of us]. In fact, if you want to get tested – my friend just sent me a link – you can go and get tested, but it's $120 out of your own pocket. Well, that's not feasible. If he really cared," continues Rose, "he would make sure that people are getting unemployment, getting that stimulus check for more than a few months."

Rose tells me that her boss in Columbus understood the problems she faced. "My boss at this new studio owns three tattoo shops in Columbus. He took us all grocery shopping four different times during the pandemic. He would email everybody, telling us to meet him at the grocery store. We would meet him at the grocery store, and he would just pay for all of our groceries. He did it four times. The first time he spent $3,000. The second time he spent $7,000. The third time he spent another $6,000, and the last time he spent $4,000 or $3,000. He took us grocery shopping!" The sense of loyalty this helped to instill in Rose is as clear as the hard times themselves.

"He would email all of us and ask about our financial health and our mental health – just kind of make sure that we're all doing okay. But he's also trying to run a business too, so as soon as the studios opened up, my boss was emailing us. He was like, 'you know, we're trying to get staff to come back, but only when you feel comfortable and safe.' So, when he asked for help, there was a lot of us that were like, yeah, of course, we'll come back as soon as we can to try and help out. Financially I didn't really have a choice. I think that if I had gotten unemployment, I would have waited a little bit longer to come back." It isn't clear if the $20,000 that Rose's boss spent on his employees' grocery shopping was his own money or part of a PPP allocation, but I can't help thinking about how different things are for Ellison at Standing Rock. The support Ellison received reinforced a sense of community that enabled her to resist going back to work before she felt safe. The charity Rose received didn't alleviate her financial problems and reinforced a sense of indebtedness that motivated her to go back to work even though she didn't feel safe.

"Right now, we're doing by appointment only, because of everything that's going on in our crazy world, but all of our appointments have been booked up. We opened the doors on Friday, and it was a *madhouse*. I worked four shifts, and I made $1,500 this week. We're not doing any oral or nostril piercings whatsoever, so our clients are always wearing masks, and the appointments are spaced out. I'm not with another person for longer than twenty minutes at a time. And obviously I clean between every single client. Honestly, my mental health, not having something to do during the day, I didn't realize how crazy I was until I went back to work and I was like, oh, my God, I'm so thankful I get to talk to other people now." Rose tells me with sadness, "I think [the pandemic] will leave a lasting impact on how close we get to people and who we let in our inner circle, who we hug, who we spend time with, who we allow in our houses. I think that that'll be a lasting impact." It's a lonely thought.

Back in Athens County, Jenny Gaines was finally able to take her two kids for a long-overdue visit to see her mom in Florida. It had been about four years since they had seen each other, and the kids had grown a lot. Jenny remembers that at the time the coronavirus felt like a rumor in Ohio, but Florida was already panic shopping. Jenny and the kids arrived in Florida on March 12, 2020, "with a suitcase full of hand sanitizer and toilet paper, all of that for my mom, because she said already people were hoarding it down there. By the time we got there, it seemed like everything had just changed. My friends at home were calling me saying, you know, there's no toilet paper. There's no hand sanitizer." The political and emotional landscape of the country was changing quickly amid conflicting threat assessments of Covid-19. Health officials announced that it was a potentially devastating global pandemic that needed a swift response; the White House announced that it was a hoax and compared it to a cold or flu.

When we talk, Jenny is still caught in this swirl of information. "I don't know, I'm not all-knowing. You have the people who believe wearing a mask is important and the people who feel that you don't need a mask. Nobody's right or wrong on these things – until you're right or wrong. We were able to go to the beach, and then the next day the beaches were closed." Jenny was visiting Naples when the state closed restaurants. "We saw those folks cry. People said, 'well, we can't eat here. It's not safe.' It wasn't that it was *not* safe. They *felt* safe, [but] they had to close down for precautionary reasons. After that, you just didn't feel safe going places." The next day, on March 13, Jenny got a call from staff at her shop who wanted to close the store. They'd only had four customers in two days and were worried about getting sick. "I talked with them on the phone throughout the day. We went ahead and donated all the food to the local food pantry and to the churches, and then I told them they could take whatever they wanted home as a bonus, since we didn't know how long we'd be closed." Jenny canceled their return flight.

Two weeks later, she and her children "ended up driving home in a very small four-door car and not using any public bathrooms and eating the sandwiches that we brought. Actually, none of us seemed very hungry on the forty-hour trip, because there were rainstorms, and we slept [parked] in a gas station. It was a whole adventure the whole way home." When they got home, everything in Southeast Ohio was closed down. Jenny was able to take phone orders. "I probably got three calls a day of local people who needed things, so we were able to do some deliveries. People would call me or text me and ask if I had certain wines. I would leave them in a little brown bag out front, and they could put a little cash or a check in my mailbox, and so we were doing some commerce that way. I sold honey, maple syrup, a couple of T-shirts. People wanted some gifts for wedding gifts or baby showers." With the store closed, Jenny averaged about twelve or fifteen sales a week.

When I ask what this meant to her in terms of her expenses, Jenny tells me she doesn't want to have a "small business chat." She would rather talk about community service, so the conversation shifts. Before the pandemic, Athens County had one of the highest rates of food insecurity – 18.9% of residents did not have reliable access to adequate food and 65% qualified for SNAP benefits.[59] In the best of times, the town library was inundated with kids who didn't have a place to go or anything to eat. Integrated Services Behavioral Health (ISBH) stepped in and created the HIVE – a safe place for kids to hang out, get help with homework, get something to eat, and perhaps pick up free clothing. To meet community needs, eventually the HIVE added a shower, as well as a washer and a dryer for kids. "What they found," Jenny tells me, is that "these kids worried about their families, so when we did a winter coat drive, the kids didn't want just a coat for themselves. They wanted a coat for their uncle, or they wanted a coat for their neighbor, so they were able to send these kids home with things for other people. Well, then they started this community dinner."

During the pandemic ISBH approached Jenny about creating a community meal and offered her $300 for 270 meals. "We did cookies. We did sandwiches, and we did a side salad or a pasta salad. We did it for two weeks in a row. It took almost fifty hours for each of the meals and the prep. The first week was very hard, because you're learning to make 270 meals by a certain time. The second week was much easier to be prepared and do it. I would love to do it more often, but they also have other people in the community who are participating with that as well. For me it was trying to figure out how we were going to use up some of the cheeses and the lunch-meats." The community meal program had been successful before the pandemic. Once everything went into shut down, it became even more important. Even the local schools began delivering food to students every other day; for some, that was their only meal.

Since I last saw Jenny in 2017, she and her family have moved into a larger house and she's enjoyed the extra space. Yet as Jenny talks, it's clear to me that she and her family are struggling more than before. You might recall that even though Jenny's family qualified for public assistance, they would not apply for it. "About six months ago, maybe eight months ago, I convinced my husband to put our [two] kids on the Buckeye Health Care Program, because as a combined family, we only make $41,000. We don't qualify for health care, but [our kids] do qualify for free-and-reduced lunch, and we qualify for the kids to have assistance. His family is quite proud and didn't want us to take that road, but now our kids are able to get their eyes checked, their teeth cleaned. I had to convince him that we do a lot for the community, so maybe this is something that the community can do for us." For many struggling families, accepting is much harder than giving. The pandemic has pushed pride to the side for families across the country.

In the last moments of our conversation, Jenny loops back to my question about how her business is doing. "We're hoping that it will be absorbed by a nonprofit. There's where I'm currently at. I'm working with several different local nonprofits on the needs that our community is going to have, and one of them is a kitchen that can provide community meals. They need a place where people can pick stuff up. The free meals are covered by grants and community members want a place where you can teach people work skills. So, it's going to be a learn-to-earn facility. We've come up with a manual. We have people who are already knowledgeable in each of these areas – retail, social media, marketing, food, kitchen prep, cleaning. They will know how to do it, but they can train the other people how to be better at it, and then those folks will be filtered out to other positions in Athens County that need good workers." The vision seems like a perfect expression of Appalachian pride and innovation.

Bearing the Weight

Across the nation, an individual's risk of Covid-19 infection depends in large part on the work they do – hence on their economic class. Economic class determines whether or not you can afford Covid testing, whether or not you can afford health care, and whether or not you are in good health. Economic class determines whether you can "socially distance," at work or at home, and whether or not you are at risk of becoming homeless. It also determines whether or not collecting and recycling cans seems like a good way to supplement your income.

The pandemic has not been easy for anyone, but the weight of it has fallen heaviest on those most marginalized. If some have been inconvenienced by working online and staying indoors, millions of low-wage workers have had to choose (once again) between two bad options: risking their lives and perhaps those of their loved ones, or fending for themselves without a job or unemployment benefits. People who are not even paid a living wage have suddenly been declared "essential" to the economy. They often work without health insurance, hazard pay, adequate protection, or the ability to properly distance themselves from others. They risk their lives and those of their families because they can't afford to stop working.

Those who have been able to work from home – protecting both their income and their health – openly express their appreciation of so-called essential workers. But the nation has not increased its efforts to protect workers. In fact, it has done just the opposite, protecting corporations at the expense of workers. What does it mean to appreciate workers as essential when you treat them as disposable? In this environment, Standing Rock is remarkable for its ability to care for workers as well as for tribal members more generally. Native nations are holding a line against the federal government to protect their people, even though this means having to sue the federal government.

This crisis has been made worse by the willingness of politicians to collude with business at the expense of workers. Congress left for their break as the support that government had provided to workers expired. They eventually passed a second package in late December. And then Trump delayed signing the package. As a consequence, people who had been receiving unemployment pandemic support fell out of the program and lost one week of benefits.[60] This second package gave workers a one-time payment of $600 and boosted unemployment checks by $300. Much like the first relief package, tucked into the 5,593-page bill were tax breaks worth more than $110 billion.[61] No wonder tax experts have called these bills "gravy trains for lobbyists."[62] The national crisis is not static. It is also not just a crisis brought on by Covid-19. The country has faced a series of deep, long-term crises that can only be understood as the result of a profound unwillingness to care for all of the nation's people.

There is no way for me to know what happened to two thirds of the people I talked with in 2017–18 but couldn't reach in 2020. Those I did reach illustrate the resourcefulness and the survival skills of people who were already patching through in their day-to-day lives before the pandemic. They know how to live with the ebb and flow of resources. Their courage, resourcefulness, and tenacity emerges in all that they have been willing to do to get by – whether pressing through anxiety attacks, collecting cans to take to recycling to pay an electric bill, networking with other tribes, or accepting federal assistance in the face of family shame and pushback. The people interviewed in this chapter are very aware of and connected to community – geographic and cultural. The class struggle isn't over. It's just getting started anew.

11

The Future We Want

As of this writing in early 2021, the richest 1% of American households now own almost as much wealth as the bottom 90% of households *combined*. The entire bottom half of America now owns just 1.3% of the wealth.[1] Advances in technology and productivity have failed to translate into benefits for working people or for the country as a whole. Instead, generations of people across the country have been relegated to lives of economic struggle – they are the collateral damage of corporations seeking to maximize profit. Sometimes valuing profits over people is the blatant intention of government policies. Sometimes regions and communities struggle because it just isn't profitable to anyone that they not struggle.

Many factors contribute to economic struggle. As we have seen throughout this book, a lack of jobs that pay a self-sufficiency wage, high rents, a lack of affordable health care, underfunded school systems, and an absence of social and economic safety nets relegate communities to poverty. This is bad enough, but it isn't even the full picture. It is not just that the country has high levels of poverty, but that small numbers of powerful people in business and government have gotten incredibly rich by *creating* systemic poverty. This is precisely why it is critical to focus on inequality rather than poverty. We need only think about Walmart to appreciate just how rich people can become while driving their workers so far into poverty that they need public assistance to keep food on the table. We've also seen the predatory business practices that keep families in debt by charging them more for less – whether a bottle of milk at a dollar store, or a high-interest loan. In communities with limited access to quality health care, people continue to watch friends and family members struggle with addiction because pharmaceutical companies flood their communities with highly addictive painkillers. A relatively small group of people – with the help of government – are making enormous amounts of money off of the suffering of others. Hard times have become a way of life for millions because government prioritizes the interests of business.

Across the country, environmental degradation deprives communities of safe drinking water and has produced life-threatening health problems for residents that will last generations – even if they could afford the health care needed to address those problems. The pandemic is not the beginning of a health crisis in struggling communities – it is an extension of one. Struggling communities face severe, sustained, and interconnected sets of crises. All of which are an expression of a single and profound failure of the nation to adequately care for the health and well-being of its citizens. Ruthless economic competition that places profit over people has left the United States with truly extreme levels of inequality.

The problem is not just capitalism – it is what the corporate takeover of government has done to the ability of a democracy to function; it is also what colonialism, racism, sexism, and greed have done to the ideals of democracy. We have a nation founded not only on high principles but also on deceitful wars, broken treaties, land theft, slavery, racism, misogyny, and the economic exploitation of workers. We learn as children to repeat a daily pledge to "freedom and justice for all," yet we are also taught to ignore the systemic injustices. In this time of extraordinary inequality exacerbated by police violence, a global pandemic, and a climate crisis, we have a chance to learn from experience and step forward into the storm to build the kind of society that we want for our children. This requires learning to think and to behave as a nation that cares for all of its people – even in the midst of deep cultural divides.

The route to renewal runs through reckoning and repair: reckoning with our past and repairing relationships with the communities who have paid the steepest price.[2] We need to value the future in ways that we have been taught to dismiss. Most especially, as a nation, we must be guided by an ethics of care that prioritizes the health and well-being of all people – including the generations that we hope will come after us. While this view is foundational to most indigenous cultures, to non-Native people it can seem incredibly idealistic. In the twenty-first century, this kind of idealism is also a pragmatic path. We need solutions as big and bold as the problems we face. History shows us that crises of this magnitude have the potential to change dominant views about economies, society, and inequality.[3] In this chapter we'll hear from ordinary people whose ideas for a better world come from their lived experiences. But first, to understand how to effectively create a pathway forward, it helps to glance back in time.

Power Surrenders Nothing[4]

If we want to understand both the existence of tremendous income inequality and how we might end it, we need to understand the lengths that government and corporations have gone to in order to *maintain* inequalities. History shows us that when workers fight to improve their communities, they find themselves up against some of the most powerful people on the planet. Oppressive working conditions are never an accident or the result of an oversight. Efforts to gain basic protections, such as child labor laws and an eight-hour workday, were met with violent repression from businesses and government. Government and corporate repression of justice movements in the workplace has gone far beyond "labor disputes." For example, the 1892 Homestead steel strike in Pittsburgh – also known as the Homestead massacre – was one of the most violent labor conflicts in history. Workers went on strike to prevent Carnegie Steel from shrinking their wages and inserting a nonunion clause in their contracts. The mill hired armed Pinkerton agents to end the strike. When this was insufficient, the plant manager Henry Clay Frick appealed to Governor William Stone for help. Stone sent 8,000 militia to Homestead to break the strike. After an armed battle with workers, the strike was crushed, wages were cut, the length of workdays was extended, and 500 people lost their jobs.[5] Two years later, in the Pullman Strike of 1894, the US Army was used against workers protesting wage cuts. Thirty workers were killed. In 1914, coal miners along with their spouses and children faced deadly machine gun fire from the National Guard when they went on strike in Colorado coalfields for better pay and safer working conditions. The strike became known as the Ludlow Massacre.[6]

By 1918, a mineworker in West Virginia was more likely to die on the job than a US soldier fighting overseas in the First World War.[7] Yet in West Virginia, striking miners suffered vicious assaults from federal troops in battles remembered as the Matewan Massacre and Bloody Mingo. The 1921 Battle of Blair Mountain in West Virginia, led by Mary Harris "Mother" Jones, was perhaps the largest organized labor uprising in history. Federal troops brought in to suppress the strike not only shot workers, they also bombed the miners' homes. Many of the workers who survived the battle faced trial for murder and treason. Strikes for better working conditions continued for decades in nearly every industry from textiles to railroads, from coal to steel. When Representative Alexandria Ocasio-Cortez asks today if voters are prepared to choose people over money, in Appalachia this resonates with a long-standing Appalachian question: which side are you on?[8]

The US government has allied with business to suppress organizing outside of workplaces as well. Civil rights and anti-poverty movements, by their nature, critique existing systems of inequality. In the 1950s, the FBI harassed anti-poverty workers in the coal fields of Pike County, Kentucky, accusing them of being communists.[9] This attack on progressive anti-poverty movements has been sustained. For example, in 1967 Louie B. Nunn, governor of Kentucky, used his power to end the anti-poverty programs that he claimed were detrimental to the soul of the nation. At the federal level, then-president Nixon appointed Donald Rumsfeld in 1969 *to weaken* the very organizations and legislation that Lyndon Johnson's War on Poverty had tried to strengthen, including the Economic Opportunity Act.[10]

History shows us that the US government has targeted civil rights movements as if they were enemies of the state. The FBI created COINTELPRO (1956–71) as a surveillance and infiltration program aimed at "disruptive" social groups – its primary targets were African American, Native American, and feminist civil rights movements. COINTELPRO was an intensely corrupt operation known for planting evidence, leaking false stories to the press, wrongful imprisonment, illegal violence, and assassination. The government collusion with business to repress dissent continues. Following Trump's inauguration in 2016, at least seventeen states introduced legislation to criminalize pipeline protests.[11] The FBI has gone so far as to identify environmental groups as possible domestic terrorists, while the Trump administration sought to have Black Lives Matter protestors declared "domestic terrorists" for peacefully seeking an end to racism.[12]

In the summer of 2020, massive protests over the death of George Floyd spread across the US, as did efforts to remove monuments honoring the Confederacy. The federal government used an executive order to protect monuments by sending federal law enforcement teams to cities across the country run by "liberal mayors." Perhaps none of these occupations was more notable for federal assaults on protestors than that in Portland, Oregon, where law enforcement officers specifically targeted *medics* with tear-gas and projectiles, causing head injuries, severe lacerations, and chemical burns, according to a report by Physicians for Human Rights.[13]

As was also evident in Portland, the police, the FBI, and the CIA are now using an artificial intelligence startup, Dataminr, for social media surveillance related to protests.[14] Police have been using facial recognition software to identify people in social media posts of the protests and then arrest them. They are also using Digital Receiver Technology (aka Drtboxes) to intercept data and to track mobile phones, as well as Stingray technology designed to gather information from phones. Both technologies can also install malware.

Much of the brutal physical and economic violence at the heart of this country's history is ignored in state-sanctioned textbooks. And, at times, it has been displaced by later philanthropic efforts. For example, Andrew Carnegie is more often remembered for founding libraries, for the Carnegie Endowment for Peace, and for the Carnegie Institution for Science than for the conditions in his mills, the low wages he paid his workers, or for the Homestead Massacre. Even today, we want to believe that it is possible to amass extraordinary wealth while treating workers and the environment with responsibility and fairness.

Despite a long history of very brutal repression, people have continued to unite in the service of social justice. In 1968, people from across Appalachia joined the Poor People's Campaign, organized by Dr. Martin Luther King Jr. and the Southern Christian Leadership Conference. One press release from an Appalachian group announced that they were participating "to let our Congressmen and Senators, our President, our people and the people of the world know that the poor people of Appalachia, white and black, are standing together with the poor people of the Mississippi delta, the poor people of the Indian reservations, the Mexican Americans, the Puerto Ricans, the grape pickers of California, the potato harvesters of Maine – we all stand together."[15] More recently, people in Appalachia also offered support and solidarity to communities in Flint Michigan and Standing Rock – they understand that the struggles for clean water are local, national, and global.[16] A Poor People's Campaign has also united people across the country in a movement lead by Rev. Dr. William Barber II.

As we face the consequences of a pandemic, unemployment that rivals the Great Depression, and a climate crisis unprecedented in human history, several visions for the future are circulating. A few come to mind immediately: The New Green Deal spearheaded by Representative Ocasio-Cortez; a labor movement called Bargaining for the Common Good; a proposal by the economist Robert Reich; and Naomi Klein's The Leap – a movement "to advance a radically hopeful vision for how we can address climate change by building a more just world, while building movement power and popular support to transform it into a lived reality."[17] In reading about these plans and listening to political speeches, I have consistently stumbled upon a frustrating tension: the plans that seem to be "doable" also seem too limited to take on the crises as they exist, while the plans that would seem capable of creating effective change seem far too idealistic. More than once I found myself saying, "well, that will never happen." I had to ask myself some tough questions: What does it mean when the only hopeful plans we have seem to be impossible? Am I really willing to give up, rather than to pursue idealism?

For much of my life I have had to fight against a sense of resignation – a belief that things can't *really* change. I know from experience that it takes a ridiculous amount of unfounded hope to create a future that is radically different from the present. I have had to forge ahead even when I couldn't always (or often) see how change was possible. In the process, I learned that the world is more than what happens outside of us. It is also what happens inside of us. For me, hope was based in one reality: I knew I couldn't survive in the life that others had laid out before me. But before I could make my life different, I had to be able to *imagine* something other than what I had. I had to imagine something I had actually never seen – or perhaps had only seen in bits and pieces. It was a messy process.

Imagination doesn't take up the details, it's a wash of broad strokes. If we allow the *how* to drive the *what* we will always reproduce what we have. Once we imagine where we want to go, we can decide how best to get there. Imagination expands our minds and our possibilities. We need to begin by valuing the future in ways that we have been taught to dismiss. Most especially, we need to imagine how our actions might affect future generations. It's incredibly idealistic – but in this moment it is also a pragmatic path if we want to turn these crises around. So, it is with that same sense of impossible hope that I share some thoughts about moving forward from conversations with Rose Taylor, Tom Sam, Jack Rockwell, Vanessa Torres, Angel Perez, Michael Chase, and Jenny Gaines. As Naomi Klein so aptly said: If it seems impossible to move forward from capitalism, remember that it once seemed impossible to move beyond the Divine Right of Kings.[18]

Talking About Leadership

Millions of Americans have experienced four decades of economic flat-lining as the rich have grown richer. For communities of color, this is a continuation of practices that are centuries old. The US political and economic system has locked generations out of the ability to attain economic self-sufficiency. Given this failure of democracy, it shouldn't be surprising that many of the people I talked with no longer see the ballot box as capable of bringing meaningful change. By 2017, even those who believed the rhetoric of the Trump campaign soon found his words to be as empty as those of the career politicians they distrusted. It just doesn't pay for politicians who are backed by big money to look out for working people.

So, it's little wonder that when I ask people if they see anyone in political leadership who has a vision that aligns with their own, the answer is a resounding "no." My question causes many people to reflect on the promise of Bernie Sanders, which I'll turn to in the next section, but in the current political landscape of 2020 there is no one. Jenny Gaines doesn't take much time to say "At this time, I don't [see anyone]." She's quick to add she has needed more personal time lately and just hasn't been paying attention. "It's not because there isn't somebody out there." I suspect Jenny is the kind of person who is always going to be more focused on the people and community around her than on the politics of Washington.

By contrast, Michael Chase has been paying attention – and he doesn't trust any politician. "I think that when they first start running, they have all these strong views. They might agree with everything you agree with and have the same views as you do for how you think things should run. But when people are challenging them, I've never seen one politician be like, this is exactly what I'm standing for, and I will fight for this 110%." Michael's frustration is both with how the media package politicians and how corporate power shapes them. Ultimately, he doesn't trust them to be good for their word.

When Michael thinks about the upcoming 2020 presidential election, he makes a sour face. "I am going to vote, but I honestly do not know who I'm going to vote for. I'm definitely not going to vote for Donald Trump. I'm obviously going to vote. I'm going to do that, but at the same time, a part of me just feels like – it doesn't matter." Michael pauses and corrects himself. "I'm not saying *voting* doesn't matter. I'm saying how we keep seeing all these states, like Georgia with Stacey Abrams, have all these rigged elections and all this voter suppression."

We talk about the United States as a democracy, yet it is no secret that the government actively and successfully prevents citizens from voting. Political representation is fundamentally skewed in anti-democratic ways. First consider that all states have two senators. California, with a population of roughly 40 million, is able to elect only two senators; the same number as Iowa, which has just over 3 million residents. Second, consider that more than half the population lives in just nine states, which means the majority of the population is represented by just eighteen of seventy-six senators; less than half of the population controls 82% of the Senate.[19] By 2040, just 30% of the population will elect over seventy senators.[20] Voting is also skewed in other ways. Black and Native citizens have been systematically disenfranchised. Not until the Voting Rights Act of 1965 did the government even attempt to protect the right of all citizens to vote.

Throughout history, the ways in which voting has been manipulated are transparent: gerrymandering, heightened ID requirements, closing polls, understaffing polls in key districts, and misinformation campaigns that direct voters to the wrong places and times to cast their ballots. In 2020 Republicans set up illegal ballot boxes in California and shut down numerous voting places.[21] In some communities in Georgia, lines to vote had a ten-hour wait.[22] We also saw the state government in Wisconsin refuse to allow mail-in ballots to be counted if they were postmarked before the deadline but arrived after it – a decision that was challenged in but upheld by their state Supreme Court.[23] Texas limited mail-in ballots for the presidential election to voters over the age of sixty-five – those most likely to vote conservatively.[24] The decision was challenged but the US Supreme Court refused to fast-track it, allowing the decision to stand for the 2020 election.[25]

Meanwhile, President Trump sought to close the US Post Office in advance of the November election and appointed Louis DeJoy as the US Postmaster General. Although DeJoy had no relevant experience for the post, he is a long-time Trump supporter who has donated $1.2 million to the Trump Victory Fund as well as millions to the Republican Party. DeJoy and his wife Aldona Wos own between $30 million and $75 million worth of assets in businesses that *compete* with the US postal service.[26] Almost immediately DeJoy began to undermine the Post Office by cutting workers' hours and substantially delaying mail delivery.[27] The government physically removed the mailboxes that people would use to post their mail-in ballots. DeJoy joins Wilbur Ross as another Trump appointee who has undermined workers and the welfare of the country.

And then, of course, there is the Electoral College system, which enabled Donald Trump to win the 2016 election even though Hillary Clinton won the popular vote by nearly 3 million ballots. (This was the fifth time the Electoral College overturned the popular vote. The last time, in 2000, gave George W. Bush the presidency despite Al Gore having won the popular vote.) The Electoral College was created by the "Founding Fathers" to offset the popular vote. This fear of the popular vote is notable since, at the time of the framing of the Constitution, only about 6% of the US population was eligible to vote. In this sense, the US has never been the democracy it claims to be. The Electoral College continues to stand in direct opposition to a representative democracy in which every person has an equal vote.

Even in the midst of all of these concerns about voter suppression, Trump's rhetoric changed the landscape in relation to voter fraud. "At this point," reflects Michael, "with all the stuff about Donald Trump, how he's been complicit with voter suppression, I wouldn't be surprised if he has enough power to make the votes add up to him." There was no end to the speculation about how voters would be discounted, and Michael was not alone in his worries about systemic fraud. Although Michael went "all in" for the 2016 election, he has lost faith both in the candidates and in the process of voting. "I probably will end up voting for Joe Biden," he says with resignation. Michael's lack of enthusiasm calls to mind the number of voters in Appalachia who voted for Sanders in the 2016 primaries but didn't show up at the polls when faced with a choice between Clinton and Trump in the election.

In Oakland, Tom Sam has even less confidence in the government. "I'm a firm believer that the two-party system is a faulted system. Until you have some other parties that can run on different platforms and have the same [amount of] financial backing and same type of just influence across the nation – you have a Republican/Democrat bottleneck. In reality [they] have the same interests and end goal, which is to make the rich richer, to keep the poor working. In that sense, I feel like any candidate who can win the presidency is going to uphold this systemic structure. I believe this systemic structure needs a big overhaul. A lot of folks are saying, 'We need health care for all. Health care should be a basic human right here in this country.' So we'll just kind of see how this plays out."

By now, it shouldn't be surprising that people in the bottom 50% of income tend not to vote.[28] Parties on both the right (Libertarians) and the left (Justice Democrats, Greens) have been seeking change. Of course, the political machines of the Republicans and the

Democrats want two things: power and predictable elections. It's hard to think about increasing the number of political parties when we do not truly have a democracy in which people could vote for them. The system we have now is driven by corporate influence that has infiltrated the cornerstones of our democracy: the presidency, the Congress, the courts, and voting. One thing seems crystal clear when I talk about politics with struggling people: the fight to address inequalities means a fight to create a true democracy as well as a new economy.

As we have seen in previous chapters, corporate and political leaders – the beneficiaries of the current system – are not going to initiate political and economic change that threatens their own well-being. Nor will they allow others to do so. Most typically, those in power advance proposals that address the *symptoms* of inequality rather than the roots of it – which actually works to stabilize and maintain the system as it is. There are many ways to address the symptoms of inequality that stop short of meaningful change – like increasing employment but failing to pay a sustainable wage, or focusing on poverty rather than on inequality and the system that creates poverty. As the theologian Reinhold Niebuhr observed, "The powerful are more inclined to be generous than to grant social justice."[29] But generosity is never a substitute for justice.

Feeling a moral duty to *help* others is quite different from having a moral obligation to ensure a self-sufficient life is possible for all. To fight inequality means fighting to change the system. Poverty is a material reality; inequality is a nexus of power. It isn't enough to have some idea of what life looks like for people who live in struggling communities. We need to understand how those struggles are produced and exacerbated by government policies and the predatory business practices that make others wealthy. It is not *just* that wages are insufficient, housing is unaffordable, and health care is out of reach – it is that we have a system that cares more for wealth accumulation than for the welfare of people, the environment, or the country itself.

The problems of inequality, affordable housing, accessible health care, environmental devastation, civil rights, and the climate crisis are so broad and so interconnected that we are not going to "reform" our way out of them in an election cycle. If we want a democracy, we need a government that supports publicly financed campaigns, enables multiple parties, removes corporate influence over elections, and ensures easy, accessible, and fair voting for all. Yet even this basic assertion remains problematic to many in power because it threatens the system that works for them.

Imagining the Future We Want

When Jack Rockwell in Southeast Ohio stops to think about the things the nation needs, he begins with better access to quality grocery stores and free access to mental health care. So, I am especially surprised by where he goes next. "Honestly, a universal basic income [UBI] for everybody making under $100K, just like $10,000 a year, I think would be amazing. I really think something that radically socialist could really be a huge force for good, especially in a lower-income community like this one. I'm not sure you could make NYC much better by giving everybody a little bit of financial breathing room, but around here I think it would lead to huge reinvestment in the community. I would love to see that. When people have more economic freedom, they have more freedom in every other aspect of their lives." Having disposable income goes a long way toward increasing the mental health of individuals and the economic success of communities. One of the most intransigent and least considered problems of poverty is the mind-numbing boredom and depression it creates. Take away all disposable income and you weaken people's sense of community, their ability to be creative, and their desire to be engaged. A UBI could be exactly what is needed to motivate grocery stores – perhaps even a clothing store – to open in low-income communities.

Yet Jack's pragmatic streak wrestles with his idealism. "It's really difficult for me to reconcile my more socialist tendencies with my increasing realization that this is likely the way things are going to continue for the rest of my life." His tone becomes more somber. "If I want to provide well for myself and my eventual family, I've got to buy into the system. I can continue to be an advocate for change, but it's tough to be the change you want to see in the world when you're facing such powerful economic pressures to just keep your nose to the grindstone and get going. I certainly don't deny that harder-working people tend to do better than lazy people, but I think success is largely attributable to your previous success and people who have a vested interest in seeing you succeed. A lot of people express a lot of hopelessness to me about the possibility of moving forward from where they are, and all of them seem to have the sense that the system is, in some way, rigged against them, but nobody really seems to agree on which aspects of the system require fundamental change." Others I talk with don't make the distinction between pragmatism and idealism. For many, the need for change is so clear that to be idealistic is to be pragmatic.

"I'm all about having people become more educated," says Angel. He tells me that everyone should have more opportunities for education, employment, and housing. Angel continues, "I started following Bernie because I would have loved it if that [plan] would have become a reality. I feel like he's really for the people, like he says. Other people say that they're for the people but are really for corporations. I feel like he really knows what everybody needs, at least those of us who work day-to-day or paycheck-after-paycheck or that have been working paycheck-to-paycheck."

Angel pauses. He looks both sad and introspective as we talk. "If we're going to talk about the nation, [then we have to talk about] police brutality and targeting people of color, specifically immigrants, and the whole thing where ICE was putting Central American kids in cages. Now with this whole pandemic, a lot of people inside of detention centers are fearing for their lives. They've been dying, because of the virus. The media never talks about the inhumane treatment, especially females and kids, are receiving from ICE agents. There's always sexual abuse and rape and all those things going on that we don't really hear in the actual news. We end up finding out when we do our own investigation or [from] articles that we read here and there." In the best of times, the US is dependent on immigrant labor – in particular undocumented immigrant labor. As we saw in Chapter 10, low-wage immigrant workers in manufacturing, agriculture, and meat production were declared "essential" workers during the pandemic, and yet continued to be treated as disposable workers as they faced mandates to work in unsafe conditions without PPE or health insurance.

Living just a few miles from Angel in Oakland, Vanessa Torres also saw the promise of Bernie Sanders. "Bernie has *not* just been talk. He has a track record of actually fighting and doing the work for the people, the actual people; not the 1% of the people out there who a lot of these politicians work for. He's actually a man for the people. I don't think these socialist ideas are super radical. They're just basic-ass human needs that need to be met – like health care."

As Vanessa thinks about a vision for the future, she talks with a strong sense of purpose and quickly moves through a list that is similar to Angel's. "I think that we should defund ICE. We should release people from cages. Immigration is not a bad thing. People come here to change their lives. They have to flee different things in their home countries – poverty, violence – we can't just shunt them away." Without pausing Vanessa moves on to health care and education. "We should be providing health care to all people, not just people who don't have preexisting conditions. That's bullshit.

They're the ones that need it the most. There is no equity. There is no equity at all. Also making sure that education is free. When you talk about education, it's not just college. People need to have access to pre-K or kindergarten. There's research about how that's the most important part of a child's learning and really sets them up in the future. When we talk about free education, again, we talk about getting people out of poverty. For the folks that are thousands and thousands in debt in student loans, they're still not able to climb up the social ladder. They're still being tied down again, and if we erase all of that, people are able when they actually work to save up that money, and, hey, build a home, buy a car, and better themselves in their lives and their current situation. Education should be free for all. This shouldn't just be for the folks who can afford it."

What else is on her vision board for the country? "Wages. Paying people what they deserve! Because, like I mentioned, there's wage inequality on race, gender, age as well too.

If America were to shift closer toward a socialist society, because obviously capitalism is not working, we would be at a very good place, at a better place." When a nation provides free quality education and health care to its residents, it can actually strengthen families, workers, and the economy, just as Vanessa describes. And she is correct that for an economy to run well, people need to have a fair wage that puts money in their pockets – the ability to purchase what they need, to have a bit of disposable income, and to save for the future. Ironically the system that we have now, the system so many want to protect, actively prevents a strong economy for the majority of workers.

In Southeast Ohio, Michael Chase is also a strong advocate for free education and socialized health care. "If you look at other countries, like Sweden or whatever, all these other countries in Europe, they're fine. Even countries with higher rates of happiness and lower rates of depression overall and stuff like that, and they have low rates of crime. When everyone has the same opportunities for education and jobs, no one's going to be out here committing crimes, and if they are, it's going to be like bank fraud or something, not robbery or murder, things like that."

When Rose Taylor thinks about the future, she thinks about luck. She tells me, "If I was just born just like a few counties away, being gay, my whole experience would be totally different. You know what I mean?" Rose also credits her mother's ability to leave her father with creating more stability for her. She wonders what would have happened if her mother hadn't been able to get away from an abusive relationship. "I just think that there are a lot of things in my life that

I have by luck or chance, that like without a few of those things I would be like *so* struggling – you know what I mean?" I do know what she means. I've encountered a lot of domestic abuse as well as a lot of heterosexism/homophobia in my travels. Luck and chance play a part in everyone's life, but in the lives of struggling folks they too often play a part in survival.

Rose was and remains a Sanders supporter. When we talk about the world Rose would like to live in, it's clear to me from the speed of the list she reels off that she's thought a great deal about this. "My vision of the future would be socialized medicine, definitely more environmentally friendly companies, and heavier taxes on larger companies to make sure that they're more environmentally friendly. We as Americans create so much waste and so much pollution compared to other countries and other people. I think that really needs to change drastically for us to be able to survive as a planet."

Rose is learning as well from her girlfriend, who once taught in a wealthy west coast neighborhood whose schools had a lot of resources, and now works in a very low-income neighborhood where students don't have access to lunches or computers. Rose sighs. "We're in the same country, but it's so vastly different. If you were born into this poor neighborhood, then your education opportunities are so vastly different from if you're born in just another zip code. I really wasn't quite aware of how much different it was until I was seeing it kind of firsthand." Thinking about educational experiences by zip codes offers some insight into class segregation in the US and how the system perpetuates itself. When schools are funded by property taxes, the class divide is both secured and entrenched.

As you might imagine by now, Tom Sam thinks about the big picture of inequality. "When I think about other forms of government, whether it be socialist or capitalist or communist or any other type of regime, those structures are kind of set up in the same way. These are oligarchical types of ideologies, where you have a head, and then you have a bunch of people who are accountable to that head person, and then you have other people who are accountable to those folks." As Tom talks about the problems of *any* form of government run by a small number of elites, it's easy for me to hear threads of Robert Reich's critique that "Americans cannot thrive within a system run largely by big American corporations, which are not organized to promote the well-being of Americans. Oligarchy is good only for oligarchs."[30]

Yet Tom is not referencing Robert Reich – he is thinking from within an indigenous framework in which governing is about caring for people. He continues: "The policies [of the country] should reflect the things that folks are asking for. There's a large majority in this country who say that health care should be provided for all people. If the government can go and seize someone's assets for owing a delayed parking ticket – maybe it's an abuse of power [but maybe they could do] something like say, 'We're going to freeze your bank account, because you don't need any more money, and we're going to distribute anything over this amount to everybody else across the nation.' Maybe I was just raised differently, but I have this idea that, if you have an abundance, you share it." In some Native cultures, wealth is evidenced by what one shares, not by what one hoards. It might sound strange to think of wealth as hoarding but what else would you call amassing an amount of wealth that is impossible to spend in one's own lifetime? Especially when it comes at the expense of others and in the face of so much need.

In the US we are taught to hoard not just money but also opportunity. Tom continues: "When that old style of thinking that my skin makes me more important than you, or my hair makes me more important than you, or the color of my eyes, or the religion that I practice, or the amount of money I have in my savings account makes me more important than you – when that thinking is gone, we're going to be in a way better place. If we think about how long it has taken us, say from 1492 to where we're at now, who knows how long it's going to take for us to get to a place that is my utopia? I hope that in some generation my descendants will know that they had an ancestor who was advocating for that type of lifestyle for them." Tom's orientation toward future generations is exactly the kind of thinking we need to begin to address the deep crises we face as a nation.

A deep sense of connection to spouses, children, grandchildren, nieces and nephews, siblings, and parents – and, for some, to future generations – threaded through everyone's hopes for the future. Parents found joy in seeing their children learn new skills, and many laughed about the long hours on little league benches and time spent at school recitals. Everyone drew hope from seeing kindness extended to the poorest members of their communities through sponsored holiday meals, from the support given to developmentally disabled adults, and from the courage of those who fought to overcome addiction. Everyone wants a world in which education, housing, and health care are easily accessible and affordable for all. Everyone wants a world free from hate in which children thrive, a world in which caring for the earth and all of its inhabitants is a priority. Those with power might call this vision naïve. Those without it might call it delusional. But when millions of families struggle to keep food on the table, there is nothing naïve or delusional about the need for broad-based, systemic change. There is nothing un-American about people who want to change a system they know is untenable. Rather it is what many hail as the American spirit.

The Last Two Cents

Where do we go from here? The only thing certain is that it must be somewhere other than where this system has taken us. The need for change is clear both from the experiences of everyday families and from their own analyses of the kind of help they need in their communities: a fair wage, accessible and affordable housing, free health care, free education, and potentially a universal basic income. The important work of Jenny Gaines, Tom Sam, Two Lance Woman, and others who are striving to care for their communities may well mean the difference between hunger and a full belly for some, it may mean access to a winter coat or a much-needed pair of shoes, or it may mean the ability to wear a mask in a pandemic. It's essential and compassionate work that can have a big impact in their communities. And it is also carrying water in a bucket with a hole in it.

Pundits have been fond of saying that if we have learned anything from Covid-19 it is that health-care insurance cannot be linked to work. For people in the struggling class, it is *not* linked to work. Health care insurance simply does not exist for low-wage workers. In some cases, companies will offer an expensive health-care policy that they know their employees cannot afford. This practice meets the letter of the law and allows them to escape accountability while placing their own workers at risk. Again, it's profits over people – the people companies depend on for their business. It's clear that low-wage workers are nothing in this economy if not expendable.

The only people I talked with who had health care were Native people – some because they worked for tribes that provided Blue Cross/Blue Shield and others because they lumbered through the broken system of Indian Health Services. Universal health care is on everyone's mind. The cruelty of the corporate/political one-two punch is that uninsured, low-wage workers were declared "essential" and sent back to work in a global pandemic, while those with better paying jobs (and health insurance) worked from home. What more do we need to see in order to understand the failure of government to care for its people?

In our current system, the pharmaceutical companies have insisted on a provision in Medicare law that renders the US government – the largest purchaser of medications in the world – unable to negotiate pricing. As a result, they charge Medicare 73% more than other insurers for brand-name drugs, and taxpayers like those in this book foot the bill.[31] Taxpayers fund pharmaceutical research and then pay extraordinary prices for medications that are treated as the private property of the industry. It's a long-standing practice of publicly funding drug development and allowing corporations to treat the results as private property. Those very medications are unaffordable to the uninsured people who need them. The institutions and systems that are supposed to protect and care for people have been twisted toward other ends.

In the midst of the pandemic, government was unable to respond quickly or efficiently to the health and economic needs of the people. It did however respond quickly and efficiently to the needs of corporations. The pandemic invited what Naomi Klein calls disaster capitalism: leveraging a crisis to push through agendas that would seem impossible to pursue in other circumstances. For example, the fossil fuel industry was declared critical work and it then pushed to speed up production on public land. Companies are rushing to make multibillion-dollar investments in new infrastructure to extract oil, natural gas, and coal from some of the dirtiest and highest-risk sources on the continent.[32] These efforts follow the Heritage Foundation's playbook that literally urged the White House to use the pandemic to justify curtailing or eliminating environmental rules and oversight.[33] It might be clear by now just how little environmental oversight there is to start with when entire communities have been left with toxic water, polluted air, devastated landscapes, and unimaginable amounts of toxic sludge.

A narrow elite has overtaken government and limited democracy – and not just within the last four years, although the consequences may be arriving on the doorsteps of some for the first time. The problem is the system itself that prioritizes profits over people. Businesses profit from systemic poverty just as they profit from undocumented migrants, immigrant detentions, and prison labor. Company towns – in which one dominant industry owned the housing and the stores that workers were forced to use – may be a thing of the past, but the logic that created that system is not. As low-wage, unreliable work drives people into poverty, corporations profit not only from their own labor practices but also from the businesses that spring up in struggling communities, including dollar stores, medical lenders, payday lenders, and other forms of high-risk (and high-profit) lending.

The system prioritizes profits over all life – not just human life – as we see with the decimation of mountains, rivers, and lakes. It's impossible to understand the climate crisis or the economic crisis without understanding that we have an economy based on unlimited and unaccountable growth that places the desires of a few over the needs of the many. As a nation, we have to begin to think about the way forward through connections, relationships, and sustainability. We need to think about the purpose of government and what it means to create a democracy because the US has never been a democracy that served the interests of everyone, much less the interests of the majority.

If we want a representative democracy in which every person has an equal vote, we need to revise the way Congressional seats are apportioned and eliminate the Electoral College, voter disenfranchisement, gerrymandering, and corporate-funded elections. This would include vacating the Supreme Court ruling known as Citizens United which recognized corporations as people and removed limits on their election spending. It would mean limiting campaign finance to equal public funding in all races. And it would mean making it easier to vote: simple voter registration, a national election holiday, perhaps a federal subsidy (or fine) to encourage voting, and allowing people who have served prison time to vote. Reducing democracy to voting is both naïve and woefully inadequate, but there is no democracy without free and fair elections. By reorienting government from serving corporations, lobbyists, and the wealthy and toward supporting citizens we have the possibility of creating social and economic justice.

The Broad Strokes of Hope

Economies run best when people have purchasing power. Two ways of getting purchasing power into the hands of all families have been suggested: paying a self-sufficiency wage, and providing a universal basic income. These are not mutually exclusive ideas. History shows us how hard corporations have worked to *avoid* paying fair wages. These corporations also gut local governments by requiring hefty tax breaks and infrastructure support for creating jobs. To ensure self-sufficiency incomes businesses would need both to raise workers' wages and to cap the compensation of high-level executives. In the US, CEO compensation has grown 1007.5% since 1978 – that's right, over one thousand percent – while wages for the typical worker have increased 11.9%.[34] The issue is inequality, not poverty. The system is clearly working for some people, at the expense of others.

Jobs that underpay workers and a real estate market that gouges them for housing have created a sustained housing crisis across the country. For most people, affordable housing is a misnomer and fair market rents are neither fair prices nor market prices. The way we talk about housing actually obscures what is happening. We currently subsidize homeowners with deductions for mortgages, real estate tax, and tax exclusions on capital gains from housing. Taking these together, the government spends twice as much on subsidizing homeowners as it does on helping low-income renters through Section 8 housing vouchers, low-income housing tax credits, public housing, and tax credits for people who own low-income housing.[35] Here again the government protects landowners at the expense of renters, forcing poorer people to shoulder the economic burdens. There are other options. One of them is to create a social housing sector that is both subsidized and permanently price-restricted. Low- and medium-cost social housing would be treated as a utility in that it would remove the cost of land and construction, as well as finance and management, from the speculative market.[36]

Jobs that underpay workers also drive up demand for SNAP resources to help feed families. Our current food assistance program is woefully outdated. It is predicated on a time when women were largely full-time homemakers and food comprised 30% of the family budget. The cultural assumptions on which the budget for supplementary food assistance is based need to be overhauled as badly as the budget for the poverty line. In 2018, 71.5% of mothers were in the workforce.[37] Many of these women are low-wage workers with children. Chef José Andrés is one of the nation's visionaries in thinking about the experiences and needs of those who have the least. "Imagine one mother with three or four children. Wouldn't it be smart, especially if she lives in a low-income part of the city, that she can go to a diner and order three, four meals that will be part of a special menu? Then she can take them home and feed her children and herself."[38] A people-first orientation can create humane solutions to the chronic social and economic troubles created by profit-first thinking.

Reckoning and Repair

This chapter closes as it opened, recognizing that the route to renewal runs through reckoning and repair. There is no mythic white working class. There are millions of low-wage workers across diverse communities that have been driven into deep economic struggle and held there. Certainly, it is not the same experience in every community. And too often struggling people who share economic interests have been divided by hate, as we have seen in previous chapters. For people to recognize their shared economic exploitation, it will be necessary to overcome attempts to scramble to higher ground by stepping on or over others. Hate is strategically exacerbated and leveraged by those attempting to hold the system in place. We must not allow ourselves to be "plumbered" any longer.

As idealistic as this chapter might seem, we are only truly being unrealistic if we fail to reckon with our past and repair our relationships with the communities who have paid the steepest price. Some readers who have had no trouble accepting the economic arguments of this book might find themselves challenged by notions of reckoning and repair. We all will find ourselves challenged in the process of envisioning and creating substantial change. Too often we have learned to move forward by ignoring the suffering of others – even as we promise "liberty and justice for all." In order to succeed, we will all need to think of the needs of others as being as important as our own. That may be the biggest challenge of all. But our fates are tied together, not only by economic struggle but also by the pandemic and the climate crisis. The system cannot sustain itself. How it will change is up to us.

While recognizing that reparations will never correct the wrongs of the past, they can nevertheless mitigate the impact of those wrongs as we move forward. A reckoning surely must include addressing the fact that much of our corporate production of food and clothing relies on the poorly paid labor of undocumented workers. The pandemic left millions of immigrant workers either unemployed or forced to work in dangerous conditions, with most of them unable to access adequate health care. Young people like Angel and Vanessa – the so-called Dreamers – live in a virtual nightmare, their fates tossed about by political winds in Congress. In the course of writing this book, decisions affecting their future have changed their lives twice (once by a Supreme Court decision upholding DACA and another by an executive order requiring they report every year rather than every other year).

If planning a future is challenging for most youth, the US seems to be doing all it can to undermine both the productivity and the hope of DACA recipients. While Angel languishes without a career path going forward, Vanessa saves relentlessly for the day when she learns her family has been swept up in an ICE raid. Today, government practices and policies both severely limit legal immigration and collude with US businesses that rely on a substantial pool of undocumented immigrant workers. More than one ICE raid has been conducted on the day before payday. Clearly, the country needs to provide citizenship for workers and address the practices of corporations in order to develop a fair and just immigration policy. Yet there is even more that must be faced.

The US has a long history of fashioning the nation as a refuge for immigrants. In truth, immigration was a tool to help the colonizers occupy the lands of Native nations. And even then immigration policy was decided on racial terms, with the US accepting higher numbers of immigrants from Europe than elsewhere. It can be a hard reality to face for those unaffected by these practices. I think of Willadean's attitude of "my country love it or leave it." That might be a reasonable attitude toward those with power, but it is harder to defend when we look at how the US treats those with the least. The country once protected asylum seekers and provided them with a fair hearing. Now we have a system that separates children from their families at the border and warehouses both in overcrowded cages. We have become a country that sends thousands of *toddlers* to immigration courts for hearings in which they are expected to defend themselves.[39] The fight for transformation is as moral as it is idealistic and pragmatic.

Reckoning and repair must also address reparations for the descendants of slaves. Before the financial crash of 2007–8, lower-income white families had ten times as much median wealth as lower-income Black families; after it they had four times as much.[40] Think about what that might mean in struggling communities. Just as it's impossible to work one's way out of poverty with low-wage jobs, it's impossible to close this wealth gap by individual effort. Reparation might involve a system of payments to families descended from slaves. It might involve substantial investment in Black communities, in infrastructure, in education to build and strengthen those communities, and/or in grants for housing down-payments. Reparations are needed to make communities like Ghost Town in Oakland thriving centers of education and opportunity.

Reckoning and repair must also go beyond economic reparations for Black families and communities. It is impossible to separate the development of the current policing system from the system created to capture runaway slaves, or the Prison Industrial Complex from the Black Codes of the 1850s.[41] Much as in the 1850s, prisons in 2020 supply the unpaid labor for a vast number of major corporations (Microsoft, Whole Foods, Walmart, Victoria's Secret, Starbucks,

Target, etc.). Today men of color – predominantly Black men – are over-policed and disproportionately incarcerated. We cannot think of reparations without also thinking about reforming the criminal justice system, from policing to sentencing to the nature of prisons themselves. As the Black Lives Matter activists remind the nation, this country was not only founded on the exploitation of Black labor, it continues that exploitation in myriad ways today. The systematic exploitation of Black people is based on a nexus of intersecting systems that wastes valuable talents by confining entire communities to dead-end futures.

A reckoning and repair must also address the treaties the US government made with Native peoples – and then broke. As all Native people in this book have noted, they are nations within a nation, yet they are treated as wards of the state and lack fundamental sovereignty. Changing this system would include replacing the Bureau of Indian Affairs with a system created by Native nations and ensuring that Native people are in charge of their own resources. While it is impossible to return all stolen lands to the Native nations from which they were taken, it would be possible to return *public* lands to Native nations. And, just as the Supreme Court overturned the *Dred Scott* v. *Sandford* ruling which denied citizenship to African Americans, the Court must also invalidate existing laws that diminish Native people, including but not limited to the Plenary Power Doctrine, used to restrict Native sovereignty.

It's important to recognize that capitalism, colonialism, white nationalism, and the climate crisis are all connected. Naomi Klein writes: "We know that our reliance on dirty energy over the past couple hundred years has taken its highest toll on the poorest and most vulnerable people, overwhelmingly people of color, many Indigenous. That's whose lands have been stolen and poisoned by mining. And it's poor urban communities who get the most polluting refineries and power plants in their neighborhoods. So, we can and must insist that Indigenous and other front-line communities be first in line to receive public funds to own and control their own green energy projects – with the jobs, profits, and skills staying in those communities. This has been a central demand of the climate justice movement, led by communities of color."[42] Of course, part of this effort must include laws that ensure that all corporations pay their fair share of taxes, pay the full price of the resources they use, protect the environment in which they operate, and pay for the past damage they have inflicted on workers, communities, and environments. As we saw in Chapter 4, corporations have been allowed – indeed enabled – by government to destroy entire towns as well as vital resources like water tables that will be polluted for generations. And they have done so largely without consequence. The words of Indigenous activist Winona LaDuke are apt: "Let us be the ancestors our descendants will thank."[43]

Moments of crisis are ripe for progressive transformation because they lay bare existing inequalities. It is possible to create a coherent movement that brings together the struggling members of society – if we actually pay attention to their lives and act on what we learn. We know the federal government has been willing to support corporations with trillions of dollars in subsidies. What corporations and politicians have opposed is spending money on people: on health care, public education, housing, labor and environmental protections, and social safety nets.

Regaining a democracy will mean ending the exploitation of the many by the few. With vision, effort, and some luck, it will be a win for the people of the country. It is past time that "liberty and justice for all" actually meant something.

Appendix A: Methods, Methodology, and Theory

Methods

From 2017 to 2018, I travelled the country to talk with people who live in communities where hard times have become a way of life. My research design was based on regions of the country characterized by deep and sustained levels of poverty – even as they have been fundamental to producing national wealth. I first located regions that had sustained significant levels of economic distress – in some cases for decades, in other cases for more than a hundred years. This took me to economically distressed counties in Appalachia, to the Standing Rock and Wind River Reservations in the Midwest, and to poor neighborhoods in Oakland, California. Within these regions I sought as much diversity in race, age, gender, ability, and sexual orientation as I could find. I struck up conversations whenever possible, with whomever they were possible.

Living in an economically depressed community isn't a single experience; not everyone I interviewed had the same level of economic struggle, nor did people think about their experiences in the same ways. My goal was never to write about groups of people but to examine the systems and practices that create the conditions of hardship. Yet I didn't want to produce a collection of statistics. I wanted to have a sense of what it means to live in these communities today and I wanted to understand the conditions that shape people's lives.

Most often, I met people in grocery stores, laundromats, farmers' markets, casinos, parks, gas stations, flea markets, small shops, community centers, pawn shops, and nonprofits. After an initial conversation, I invited people to do formal interviews. In the initial round of fieldwork, I conducted twenty-four in-depth interviews. I asked every person the same set of questions and collected the same demographic information from each. Over the course of my research I drew on previous field experience to inform my approach. For example, I never took people's time without offering something in return. I have no illusion that it was commensurate, but to me, it was important. And my fieldwork many years ago with people unable to afford housing also taught me the importance of placing people at ease when I enter their environment by doing what I could to both blend into the landscape and be true to the reality of being an outsider.

When I found people on this journey treating me with some distance, I wondered if I carried class markers – were the jeans and jackets I wore at home closing conversations before they started? I bought a few things at a Walmart to see if it might make a difference. My experience with Walmart clothing is that it never quite fits. I learned to stop worrying about whether or not my buttons pulled across my chest, or if I needed to yank up the stretched-out jeans that would not stay put. My hope was to be less immediately recognizable as out of place, which I believe gave me a chance to start conversations. Once those conversations started, if my own experience with poverty served as a bridge it was only because others chose to meet me part way. Many refused. Hearing the important stories that people want to tell is never as simple as just sitting down together. It was really the trust and kindness of strangers that made this book possible.

I am grateful to all of the people I met and most especially to the people who were willing to take a gamble on recording interviews. The interviews sometimes surprised me – moving both of us to tears over losses, into stunned silence as a new clarity rose for the person speaking, and sometimes into fits of laughter. We talked a lot about family, and I told a few stories about my mom and my desire to write a book she could read. I answered honestly every question that people wanted to ask about me and this project. I was surprised (and somewhat relieved) that no one ever asked me if I was married or if I had children. In many places, it would have been no problem to identify as queer; in others it would have closed doors.

My travels also brought forward parts of myself that I have protected from my life in academia. I was surprised by the sense of ease and relief that came over me as the language and grammar of my childhood flooded back into my speech. In conversations over cold coffee and worn tables, I often felt at home. Yet I also heard the whiteness of my language and my way of thinking land with a thud at times. I have actively engaged as an anti-racist for more than forty years, but my conversations with Native, Black, and Latinx people reflected back to me the limits of my experience and of my knowledge. When this came up, I did my best to respectfully name it – to own it.

Throughout I kept detailed ethnographic field and interview records, which included written notes, recorded notes, and photographs. I asked everyone who was willing to sit for a formal interview to speak only for themselves and offered each of them a prepaid Visa Card worth $25–40.[1] I also offered everyone the opportunity to keep the card and erase the tape completely at any time they were dissatisfied with the interview in any way. No one asked for the tape to be erased; rather, people remarked on the interview being a really good experience because they felt heard. Each interview was professionally transcribed and for the most part the excerpts in this book are literal transcriptions. In a few places, the excerpts have been edited to reduce colloquial features of speech (e.g., you know, like, um) and some recursive elements common to spoken language. A few excerpts were placed into standard English for clarity. I made this choice for the benefit of readers who might otherwise find the insights and ideas harder to parse in the original. However, I have to acknowledge this as an act of class-based violence. I tried to keep the original phrasing whenever possible.

After the pandemic struck in the spring of 2020, I followed up with every interviewee that I was able to contact by phone or email. This enabled me to reach six of the original people. I also took this opportunity to reach out again to the Latinx community in Oakland. As you might imagine, working people who lack both disposable income and leisure time have a limited presence in public space. Given the hyper-segregation of poor Latinx communities, and the lack of public space in those communities, my first round of interviews in Oakland had missed people from the Latinx community. In the second round of interviews, I networked online to find people who fitted the criteria and would be able to talk with me. I conducted three first-time interviews during the pandemic: with Santiago Ramirez, Angel Perez, and Vanessa Torres. As before, I asked them the same set of interview questions and also added the second round of interview questions. By the end of my research, I had talked with over a hundred people and conducted twenty-seven in-depth interviews.

Since *Living on the Edge* is based on the lived experiences of the people I met, some very important aspects of how poverty is lived are not addressed. For example, in some states, people who cannot make bail – on any charge, including an unpaid traffic violation – will be held over in jail until the end of their hearing which could be months or years. They soon lose their job, their home, and often their family from the stress of the crisis. No one that I talked with had this experience and so I do not cover the justice system. But the book is not intended as a comprehensive examination of poverty. It is an illustration of lived experience and a strategic consideration of how the conditions of economic struggle are created and maintained by broader social structures.

Methodology

Our lives are shaped by immensely complex social, economic, and political processes. In that sense, the everyday world is rooted in language and social relations that go well beyond it. Consequently, I set out to conduct an institutional ethnography rather than a classical one. Dorothy Smith, a Canadian sociologist at the University of Toronto, developed and pioneered institutional ethnography (IE) as a critical qualitative methodology that examines how people's everyday lives are organized by institutional forces.[2] This means that in order to examine the social organization of knowledge and power my analyses situate the experiences of my interviewees within the social structures that shape their lives. For example, as I noted at the start of this book, when someone took out a medical loan, I researched medical loans in their area.

The objectives of IE are quite different from classic ethnographic research, which has the primary goal of explaining the behavior and attitudes of groups of people, to offer a thick description of their communities and lives. IE researchers treat local experience as a window into how broader power relations operate. This involves examining how people's daily lives are shaped by what Smith called "relations of ruling," referring to culturally and historically specific apparatuses of management and control that have arisen with corporate capitalism.[3] Consequently, this book does not offer thick descriptions of specific places but examines how the struggling class is embedded in relations of power that go far beyond the immediate context of people's daily lives. In the process, I examine how the struggling class is continually recruited into social and economic relations that produce their own economic oppression and marginalization.

One of the strengths of this book is the diversity among the interviewees – in terms of both region and demographics. This is consistent with the premise of IE, which approaches the contingencies of experience by taking up a variety of standpoints, since each person in this broad field of inquiry has a different vantage point. Each standpoint is different yet interrelated. However, standpoints should be understood as positionalities (not identities) that can be used to investigate power relations by revealing processes of exclusion and oppression.[4]

The *institutional* aspect of IE does not refer to specific organizations (although IE can be conducted in that way). Smith's understanding of institutions is as "a complex of relations forming part of the ruling apparatus ... We might imagine institutions as nodes or knots in the relations of the ruling apparatus to class, coordinating multiple strands of action into a functional complex."[5] IE begins with a set of procedures (in this case fieldwork and interviews) to make the institutional organization of daily experience visible in its functioning. The analytic focus is on how the everyday world is both organized by, and sustains, institutional processes. The results of an institutional ethnography are not intended to offer specific solutions but to support the efforts of those working politically to see where and how they might affect transformations.[6] Each interview provides avenues for investigation into the policies, practices, and organizations that shape local experience and knowledge.

The Precariat

Class has always been a complicated topic for sociologists. If some have been comfortable basing class categories on income, many have insisted that class is also about the kind of work being done, not just the wages being paid. Others have argued that purchasing power must be considered and still others focus on the importance of class as a system of knowledge. Changes in the economy have forced some sociologists (and economists) to rethink the nature of socio-economic classes. The long-familiar categories of lower, working, middle and upper classes (with all of their variations) no longer seem to hold.

Guy Standing, a British economist and professor of Development Studies at the University of London, asserts that the working class no longer exists because workers no longer share a common situation, as was once the case when manufacturing dominated the economy. He goes on to argue that a new class is evolving, which he calls the precariat. The precariat class is characterized by temporary jobs, part-time hours, intermittent work, and very flexible labor contracts.[7]

It is a familiar concept previously explored by scholars including but not limited to Michel Foucault, Jürgen Habermas, and Pierre Bourdieu. Workers also have taken up this concept in a plainer language. By the mid-1980s, "McJobs" was being used to refer to poorly paid, dead-end work. By 2011, the word had made it into dictionaries, despite protestations from McDonald's.

Within the context of globalization, Standing's best-known book, *The Precariat: The New Dangerous Class*, dominates contemporary discussions of inequality. According to Standing, the precariat does not have occupational identity – precarious workers do not hold careers. Rather, they hold jobs that provide low wages and no benefits (health insurance, sick leave, vacation, retirement plans) and often do not have access to a public safety net (unemployment benefits, school lunch programs, and food stamps among them). Yet Standing's precariat includes all people whose work life is filled with insecure employment, from top-level professionals to unskilled, low-wage migrant workers. According to Standing, the struggles of daily life among the precariat create anxiety, frustration, and anger, which often leads them to reject mainstream politics. This rejection of mainstream politics, he argues, is precisely what makes them dangerous. Standing urges the implementation of a universal basic income to stimulate economic growth and to prevent the rise of far-right groups and widespread social upheaval. He also argues that in order for the precariat to gain economic security they need recognition, representation in all agencies and institutions, and the redistribution of key resources; they also need high-quality, liberating education, including financial knowledge and other forms of social and cultural capital.

Standing's conceptualization of the precariat is challenged by scholars who argue that precarity must be understood as an economic condition induced by economic transformations and not as a distinct socio-economic class. Some assert that there is no *permanent* distinction between precarious and non-precarious workers; workers move into and out of states of precarity.[8] From this perspective, more and more workers, at all class levels, recognize the increasing precarity of their own economic well-being, and this is a normal development under a neoliberal economy in which organizations demand increasing flexibility from workers as their rights and safety nets disappear. Still others contend that the notion of the precariat is part of a nostalgic European discourse that does not speak to countries in the Global South.[9]

It seems inevitable that Standing's theory of the precariat must fail to the extent that all grand narratives must fail. Even within the North Atlantic context, the broad strokes of the theory seem to miss the dramatic difference between the economic insecurity among top-level professionals and the survival-level insecurity lived by low-wage workers. The experiences of risk also deepen as we consider race, gender, and coloniality.[10] With that said, the people with whom I talked in the self-named struggling class seem to be the embodiment of the precariat Standing describes. They struggle not because they are unemployed but because they are stretched between multiple low-wage jobs. Their precarious economic situations are not entirely new and are not going to end soon – indeed, without systemic change, they likely will never go away. In these ways Standing's theory of the precariat maps very closely onto the experiences and views of people in the struggling class. His work also finds relevance with regard to a universal basic income and concerns about a civil war in the United States. Yet the conditions faced by the struggling class are not just a matter of economics; they are also the consequence of power relations. And here, Standing's argument for *government* intervention seems to be asking the fox to repair the hen house.

French sociologist Pierre Bourdieu (1930–2002) was less concerned with class categories than with power relations when he theorized economic precarity. Notably, Bourdieu described not "the precariat" but *precarity*, which he described as a new form of dominance that forces workers into submission.[11] While the claim of the newness of precarity warrants scrutiny, Bourdieu's focus on relations of power provides an important context for understanding the structural changes and increasing uncertainty among workers who are forced to assume more responsibility and greater risks.

Bourdieu's notion of precarity as a relation of power is evident in several ways among the struggling class. First, people without regular hours need to be available for work whenever it is offered because there is little certainty of when it will be offered again. Second, precarity narrows the range of possible options that people encounter in life. Third, precarity produces so much instability for workers that they are constantly trying to adapt to changing hours and increasing expenses, which leaves little energy for planning futures, much less subverting a system. And yet people do protest – for example the unemployed miners who camped out on Kentucky railroad tracks refusing to allow coal to leave until they were paid for their work. There is in fact a long history of worker protests, many of which have forced business to acquiesce to extremely important changes, often at a huge personal price. However, the fundamental system of exploitation remains unchanged.

My concern with Standing's theory of the precariat is that it would at best stabilize a system predicated on the exploitation of workers. In this sense, Bourdieu may more effectively help scholars to think through the relations of power that shape economic exploitation. Yet even this is a top-down solution. It is my hope that *Living on the Edge: When Hard Times Become a Way of Life* will contribute to a vision of transformation based on the needs of the people who live under the boot heel of the system.

Appendix B: Table of Interviewees

Northern Appalachia (Southeast Ohio and West Virginia)

Name	*Age*	*Race*
Michael Chase	18–24	Black/White
Jenny Gaines	40–49	Caucasian
Rose Taylor	25–30	White
Jim Smith	50–59	White
Jack Rockwell	18–24	White

Central Appalachia (Tennessee and Kentucky)

Name	*Age*	*Race*
Tommy	60–69	White
Peter Walker	31–39	White
John Bravo	31–39	White
Carries Jade	25–30	White
Adelynn Wilkes	40–49	White
Jenna Terry	25–30	White

Standing Rock Reservation (South Dakota and North Dakota)

Name	*Age*	*Race*
Two Lance Woman	40–49	Native American/American Indian
Ellison Thompson	18–24	Standing Rock Sioux
Erika Brooks	50–59	Standing Rock Sioux
Kinajin	70–79	Sioux

Wind River Reservation (Wyoming)

Name	*Age*	*Race*
Bob Plume	50–59	Arapaho
Oralia	50–59	Arapaho
Yellow Cloud	70–79	Arapaho

Oakland, California

Name	*Age*	*Race*
Puppy Love (PL)	50–59	African American
Tom Sam	31–39	Diné/Comanche
Honest	18–24	Black
NDCX	31–39	White/Italian
Marvin X	70–79	Black
Klema Rose	50–59	Caucasian
Santiago Ramirez	25–30	Latino
Vanessa Torres	18–24	Mexicana
Angel Perez	25–30	Mexican/Latino

Notes

Preface

1 See, for example, https://www.epi.org/productivity-pay-gap.

2 Polls done by Nielsen and Harris for the American Payroll Association and CareerBuilder, respectively, were widely reported in news media. See, for example, http://press.careerbuilder.com/2017-08-24-Living-Paycheck-to-Paycheck-is-a-Way-of-Life-for-Majority-of-U-S-Workers-According-to-New-CareerBuilder-Survey.

3 FOTTRELL, Q. 2018. 50 Million American Households Can't Even Afford Basic Living Expenses. *Market Watch*, June 9.

4 See https://www.ers.usda.gov/topics/rural-economy-population/rural-poverty-well-being.

5 LOWREY, A. 2020. The Great Affordability Crisis Breaking America. *The Atlantic*, Feb 7; BOARD OF GOVERNORS OF THE FEDERAL RESERVE SYSTEM. 2019. Report on the Economic Well-Being of U.S. Households in 2018.

6 WILE, R. 2017. The Richest 10% of Americans Now Own 84% of All Stocks. *Money*, Dec 19.

7 Details of the interview process and interviewees are in the appendices.

8 Scholars refer to this as economic precarity. In this book, I write about precarity as people describe it: a state of perpetual vulnerability, high risk, and bad choices. See Appendix A for theories of precarity.

9 REICH, R. B. 2020. *The System: Who Rigged it, How We Fix It*, New York, Alfred Knopf, p. 15. Incorrectly rendered as "1%" in the first printing.

10 HART-LANDSBERG, M. 2018. Class, Race, and US Wealth Inequality. *Reports from the Economic Front*. At https://economicfront.wordpress.com/2018/01/03/class-race-and-us-wealth-inequality.

11 In the US, the response to, and impact of, the pandemic has been

politicized by systemic disinformation campaigns that continue to declare the Covid-19 virus a hoax and claim that mask mandates are an infringement on personal freedom.

12 AMERICANS FOR TAX FAIRNESS. 2020. Net Worth of Billionaires Has Soared by $1 Trillion – to the total of $4 Trillion – Since the Pandemic Began. At https://americansfortaxfairness.org/issue/net-worth-u-s-billionaires-soared-1-trillion-total-4-trillion-since-pandemic-began; see also COLLINS, C. 2020. Updates: Billionaire Wealth, U.S. Job Losses and Pandemic Profiteers. At https://inequality.org/great-divide/updates-billionaire-pandemic.

13 Harlan County earned the nickname "Bloody Harlan" after a series of labor strikes in the 1930s were met with violent attacks initiated by coal corporations and law enforcement agencies.

1 The Lay of the Land

1 TEMIN, P. 2017. *The Vanishing Middle Class: Prejudice and Power in a Dual Economy*, Cambridge, MA, The MIT Press.

2 This program is now called the Supplemental Nutrition Assistance Program (SNAP). Benefits are received in the form of debit cards rather than as coupon books.

3 TEMIN, P. 2017. *The Vanishing Middle Class: Prejudice and Power in a Dual Economy*, Cambridge, MA, The MIT Press.

4 TICKAMYER, A. R. & WORNELL, E. 2017. How to Explain Poverty? In: TICKAMYER, A. R., SHERMAN, J. & WARLICK, J. (eds.) *Rural Poverty in the United States*, New York, Columbia University Press.

5 NATIONAL CONFERENCE OF STATE LEGISLATURES. 2019. National Employment Monthly Update. At http://www.ncsl.org/research/labor-and-employment/national-employment-monthly-update.aspx.

6 FOTTRELL, Q. 2018. 50 Million American Households Can't Even Afford Basic Living Expenses. *Market Watch*, June 9. Also, according to research by PayScale, 46% of workers identified themselves as underemployed before the pandemic. *The Atlantic* (August 2020) reported that before the pandemic, one in ten workers wanted more hours than they had and 42% of recent college graduates held jobs that did not require a college degree.

7 AMADEO, K. 2019. Unemployment Rate, Effect, and Trends. At https://www.thebalance.com/unemployment-rate-3305744.

8 ALSTON, P. 2018. Report of the Special Rapporteur on Extreme Poverty and Human Rights on His Mission to the United States of America. At https://digitallibrary.un.org/record/1629536?ln=en.

9 ALEXANDER, S. 2019. Walton Family Fortune Increases $3.3 Billion on Walmart Earnings. *Bloomberg*. At https://www.bloomberg.com/news/articles/2019–02–19/walton-family-fortune-increases-3–3-billion-on-

walmart-earnings; KESSLER, G. 2019. Does the Walton Family Earn More in a Minute Than Walmart Workers Do in a Year? *The Washington Post*, Feb 19.

10 METCALF, T., et al. 2019. The World's Wealthiest Family Gets $4 Million Richer Every Hour. *Bloomberg*. At https://www.bloombergquint.com/labs/richest-families-in-the-world.

11 O'CONNOR, C. 2014. Report: Walmart Workers Cost Taxpayers $6.2 Billion in Public Assistance. *Forbes*, April 15.

12 FITZ, N. 2015. Economic Inequality: It's Far Worse Than You Think. *Scientific American*, March 31. At https://www.scientificamerican.com/article/economic-inequality-it-s-far-worse-than-you-think.

13 WATKINS, S. 2018. Kroger Ranks Among Top Employers of Workers on Food Stamps. *Cincinnati Business Courier*, Sept 12.

14 REICH, R. B. 2020. *The System: Who Rigged it, How We Fix It*, New York, Alfred Knopf, p. 35.

15 Ibid., p. 113.

16 PLATOFF, E. 2018. How Might Texas Win Amazon's Second Headquarters? Not Because of Flashy Financial Incentives. *The Texas Tribune*, Jan 25.

17 EVANS, W. 2019. Ruthless Quotas at Amazon are Maiming Employees. *The Atlantic*, Nov 25.

18 Ibid.

19 FOTTRELL, Q. 2018. 50 Million American Households Can't Even Afford Basic Living Expenses. *Market Watch*, June 9. Importantly, the Census Data tracks household income, which by their definition includes the sum income of all people fifteen years or older living in a household. So, some of these median household incomes may be based on a single wage earner while others represent the combined contribution of multiple people. There is also no distinction for the numbers of jobs a wage earner holds.

20 According to HUD, in the 1940s, the maximum affordable rent for federally subsidized housing was set at 20% of income, which rose to 25% in 1969 and 30% in 1981.

21 LEE, C. & RANDALL, C. 2018. Surviving the Waiting Game for Housing Aid. At https://www.citylab.com/equity/2018/03/how-section-8-vouchers-work-in-st-louis/554927.

22 FMR is based on surveys of rentals that include utilities across the US to determine the average rents for each of about two thousand regions. In 2016, to increase their accuracy, HUD finalized a rule that enabled them to calculate FMR based on small geographic areas defined by zip code. Known as Small Area FMR (SAFMR), this new calculation captures changes across neighborhoods within the area. In 2017, HUD suspended mandatory SAFMRs and made it discretionary. This has led to lawsuits and delayed implementation.

23 See https://reports.nlihc.org/oor.

24 THRUSH, G. 2018. As Affordable Housing Crisis Grows, HUD Sits on the Sidelines. *The New York Times*, Sept 19.

25 California, New York, New Jersey, Maryland and the District of Columbia.
26 See https://www.nlc.org/article/2019/05/09/does-your-city-have-access-to-inclusionary-housing.
27 CALLIES, D. 2020. Mandatory Set-Asides as Land Development Conditions. *The Urban Lawyer*, 42/43, 307–29.
28 Ibid.
29 METCALF, G. 2018. Sand Castles Before the Tide? Affordable Housing in Expensive Cities. *American Economic Association*, 32, 59–80.
30 By contrast, Western European countries have a mix of publicly and privately owned housing. The publicly owned, known as social housing, is cost regulated to meet the needs of both working-class and middle-class families.
31 DUTTA-GUPTA, I. 2020. Measuring Poverty: Why It Matters, & What Should & Should Not Be Done About It. *Economic Security and Opportunity Initiative*. Center on Poverty and Inequality: Georgetown Law. At https://www.georgetownpoverty.org/issues/measuring-poverty-why-it-matters-what-should-should-not-be-done-about-it.
32 ALSTON, P. 2018. Report of the Special Rapporteur on Extreme Poverty and Human Rights on His Mission to the United States of America. United Nations. At https://digitallibrary.un.org/record/1629536?ln=en.
33 See https://aspe.hhs.gov/history-poverty-thresholds.
34 DUTTA-GUPTA, I. 2020. Measuring Poverty: Why It Matters, & What Should & Should Not Be Done About It. *Economic Security and Opportunity Initiative*. Center on Poverty and Inequality: Georgetown Law.
35 The calculations for childcare are drawn from *Parents and the High Cost of Child Care*, a publication of Child Care Aware of America (CCAoA). Calculations for transportation are based on data provided by the Center for Neighborhood Technology (CNT) and derived from CNT's Housing and Transportation Affordability Index. Health care is calculated based on the Affordable Care Act (ACA) health insurance exchange premiums and out-of-pocket expenditures. Premiums are obtained through the Henry J. Kaiser Family Foundation's 2017 Health Insurance Marketplace Calculator and supplemented with data from the US Department of Health and Human Services. The EPI calculation of "other necessities" is derived from Bureau of Labor Statistics (BLS) Consumer Expenditure Survey (CEX) data. It includes apparel, personal care, household supplies (including furnishings and equipment, household operations, housekeeping supplies, and telephone services), reading materials, and school supplies. For tax estimates, EPI uses the National Bureau of Economic Research's TAXSIM, a microsimulation model of the US federal and state income tax systems, which uses twenty-two variables. For more information, go to the EPI website at https://www.epi.org/publication/family-budget-calculator-documentation.
36 See https://datacommons.org/place/country/USA.

37 JOUET, M. 2017. *Exceptional America: What Divides Americans from the World and Each Other*, Oakland, University of California Press.

38 PIKETTY, T. 2014. *Capital in the Twenty-First Century*, Cambridge, MA, The Belknap Press of Harvard University Press.

39 Ibid., pp. 329–30.

40 Ibid., p. 265.

41 SOCIAL SECURITY ADMINISTRATION. 2017. Wage Statistics. At https://www.ssa.gov/cgi-bin/netcomp.cgi?year=2017.

42 TEMIN, P. 2017. *The Vanishing Middle Class: Prejudice and Power in a Dual Economy*, Cambridge, MA, The MIT Press.

43 See https://www.epi.org/blog/top-1-0-percent-reaches-highest-wages-ever-up-157-percent-since-1979. See also SOCIAL SECURITY ADMINISTRATION. 2017. Wage Statistics. At https://www.ssa.gov/cgi-bin/netcomp.cgi?year=2017.

44 In 2018, this group of workers paid an income tax rate of 24.2% – a rate that has been relatively steady. Meanwhile, the 400 wealthiest families faced an income tax rate of 23%. If this might seem fair, given that a larger sum of money is being taxed, consider that the income tax rate for the wealthiest 400 families was 47% in 1980 and 56% in 1960. See SAEZ, E. & ZUCMAN, G. 2019. *The Triumph of Injustice: How the Rich Dodge Taxes and How to Make Them Pay*, New York, W. W. Norton & Company.

2 The Struggling Class

1 In the 1890s Berea College president William Goodell Frost made the first attempt to create "Appalachia" by consolidating 194 counties in eight states. In 1921, John Campbell expanded the area to include 254 counties in nine states. The Appalachian Regional Commission redrew the boundaries of Appalachia to include regions beyond the Appalachian Mountains that share nothing with the region but entrenched poverty. Today, Appalachia stretches across 700,000 square miles and includes counties in thirteen states: Alabama, Mississippi, Georgia, South Carolina, North Carolina, Tennessee, Virginia, Kentucky, West Virginia, Ohio, Maryland, Pennsylvania, and New York. West Virginia is the only state entirely within Appalachia.

2 Even so, the US Census located a significant Shawnee community on the Little Kanawha River in 1902.

3 MARTIN, R. 2014. For $20 Million, a Coal Utility Bought an Ohio Town and a Clear Conscience. *The Atlantic*, Oct 16.

4 In 1965 the Johnson administration redefined "Appalachia" to include 420 counties and created the Appalachian Regional Commission as part of the "War on Poverty." ARC ranked the counties on a scale of economic distress. The intent was to target strategies that would support economic development. ARC's economic ranking of counties

continues today and has helped to make Appalachia visible to the rest of the country as a place of poverty.

5 Five of these villages have populations that hover around 500; two have populations of close to 1,000 and a third has about 1,700 people.

6 To qualify for SNAP benefits (food stamps) family eligibility is capped at 130% of the federal poverty line. In Athens County 70% of the population earns less than this. MORRIS, C. 2017. Going Hungry in Athens County. *Athens News*, May 21.

7 INGRAHAM, C. 2014. 1.6 Million Americans Don't Have Indoor Plumbing. Here's Where They Live. *The Washington Post*, April 23.

8 The firefighters who battle those blazes include massive numbers of prisoners who, without adequate protection or equipment, work for $2 a day. They earn an extra $1 for every hour they are actively battling a fire.

9 WILKINS, D. & LOMAWAIMA, K. T. 2001. *Uneven Ground: American Indian Sovereignty and Federal Law*, Norman, OK, University of Oklahoma Press.

10 The Laramie Treaty of 1851 created the Great Sioux Reservation which crossed the boundaries of North Dakota, South Dakota, Nebraska, Wyoming and Montana. In 1874, when settlers discovered gold in the Sioux's Black Hills, the Sioux were removed from their sacred sites and moved into a smaller area. In 1980, the Supreme Court ruled that the sacred lands of the Black Hills were illegally taken and that tribes were due nearly $106 million in compensation. The tribes refused the money offered for their sacred sites and continue to demand return of the land.

11 The Lakota and Dakota had been known by their neighbors the Ojibwa as the Nadouwesou. French traders later shortened and corrupted this name to Sioux.

12 STANDING ROCK SIOUX TRIBE. 2018. 2018–2022 Comprehensive Economic Development Strategy.

13 There are several Sioux divisions, each with a distinctive language and culture. The Dakota people of Standing Rock include the Upper and Lower Yanktonai. The Lakota people of Standing Rock include the Hunkpapa and Sihasapa.

14 Since no other racial/ethnic group in the United States has signed treaties with the federal government, American Indians have a unique standing that distinguishes them from other "minority" groups. See WILKINS, D. & LOMAWAIMA, K. T. 2001. *Uneven Ground: American Indian Sovereignty and Federal Law*, Norman, OK, University of Oklahoma Press.

15 The ability to determine who is and isn't part of a tribe is an essential element of what makes tribes sovereign entities. While individual tribes are able to set their own membership qualifications, the federal government's requirement of a 25% "blood quantum" is the basis for all federal recognition including all census data and entitlement programs. As of this writing, only 566 tribal nations are federally recognized.

16 STANDING ROCK SIOUX TRIBE. 2018. 2018–2022 Comprehensive Economic Development Strategy.
17 LEE, T. 2014. No Man's Land: The Last Tribes of the Plains. *MSNBC*, Sept 21.
18 STANDING ROCK SIOUX TRIBE. 2018. 2018–2022 Comprehensive Economic Development Strategy.
19 Ibid.
20 REGAN, S. 2014. 5 Ways the Government Keeps Native Americans in Poverty. *Forbes*, March 13.
21 TICKAMYER, A. R. & WORNELL, E. 2017. How to Explain Poverty? In: TICKAMYER, A. R., SHERMAN, J. & WARLICK, J. (eds.) *Rural Poverty in the United States*, New York, Columbia University Press.
22 The Districts are: Fort Yates, ND (pop 1961); Cannon Ball, ND (pop 847); Bear Soldier, SD (pop 758); Wakpala, SD (pop 707); Running Antelope, SD (pop 695); Bullhead, SD (pop 692); Kenel, SD (pop 259); Porcupine, ND (pop 210). STANDING ROCK SIOUX TRIBE. 2018. 2018–2022 Comprehensive Economic Development Strategy.
23 The surrounding community has a population density of about nine people per square mile.
24 See https://www.unitedstateszipcodes.org/58528/#stats.
25 LEE, T. 2014. No Man's Land: The Last Tribes of the Plains. *MSNBC*, Sept 21.
26 Ibid.
27 HARRIS, D. 2019. The Cost of Raising a Baby. At https://www.parenting.com/pregnancy/planning/the-cost-of-raising-a-baby.
28 The national benchmark (90% percentile nationwide) for low birthweight is 6%. Both Sioux County and Corson County are above this level, at 7.1% and 6.9% respectively, indicating that a wide range of environmental factors, health-care access, and health behaviors are affecting maternal and infant health on the reservation. STANDING ROCK SIOUX TRIBE. 2018. 2018–2022 Comprehensive Economic Development Strategy.
29 The motor vehicle crash death rate is highly significant on the reservation as compared to North and South Dakota more generally. Sioux County has a crash death rate of 109 per 100,000 people, 5.7 times higher than North Dakota; Corson County (where Ellison lives) has 137 crash deaths per 100,000 people, six times higher than South Dakota. Ibid.
30 HALPERN, S. 2019. The One-Traffic-Light Town with Some of the Fastest Internet in the U.S. *The New Yorker*, Dec 3.
31 Racist stereotypes about Native people and alcohol abuse abound. The science is contradictory. Surveys by the National Institute of Health (1991–2 and 2001–2) found that Native Americans were twice as likely as other racial groups to be alcohol dependent. However, a more recent study conducted between 2009 and 2013 by the University of Arizona found no elevated rate of alcoholism among Native American populations. See CUNNINGHAM, J.,

SOLOMON, T. & MURAMOTO, M. 2016. Alcohol Use Among Native Americans Compared to Whites: Examining the Veracity of the "Native American Elevated Alcohol Consumption" Belief. *Drug and Alcohol Dependence*, 160, 65–75.

32 See https://datausa.io/profile/geo/oakland-ca/#:~:text=The%205%20largest%20ethnic%20groups,and%2087.5%25%20are%20U.S.%20citizens.

33 LEVIN, S. 2018. "We're Being Pushed Out": The Displacement of Black Oakland. *The Guardian*, June 1.

34 LEVIN, S. 2019. "There's No Way to Stop This": Oakland Braces For the Arrival of Tech Firm Square. *The Guardian*, July 2.

35 Vanessa refers to having a good social security number through her DACA status. Consequently, she is able to work legally.

36 PRESTON, J. 2020. The True Costs of Deportation. *The Marshall Project*, June 18.

37 BUDIMAN, A. 2020. Key Findings About U.S. Immigrants. Pew Research Center, Aug 20.

38 Ibid.

39 Ibid.

40 FERGUSON, C., TADAYON, A. & BARON, E. 2019. ICE Used Oakland Airport to Deport and Transfer Tens of Thousands of Immigration Detainees. *The Mercury News*, July 22.

41 Ibid.

42 BRINKLOW, A. 2019. 4,000 People Applied for 28 Affordable Homes in Oakland. *CURBED*, May 22.

43 KENDALL, M. 2019. Oakland's Homeless Population Grows 47 Percent in Two Years. *East Bay Times*, July 23.

44 SALVIATI, C. 2017. Rental Insecurity: The Threat of Evictions to America's Renters. At https://www.apartmentlist.com/rentonomics/rental-insecurity-the-threat-of-evictions-to-americas-renters.

45 See https://www.hudexchange.info/homelessness-assistance/ahar/#reports.

3 A Hazardous Life: The High Price of Being Poor

1 MIN, S. 2019. Dollar General is No. 1 Retailer For Opening Stores This Year. *CBS*, June 5.

2 See https://www.statista.com/statistics/253398/number-of-dollar-stores-in-the-united-states.

3 HANBURY, M. 2018. Dollar General Has Suddenly Become One of the Biggest Retailers in the US by Store Count. *Business Insider*, Dec 16.

4 FRAZIER, M. 2017. Dollar General Hits a Gold Mine in Rural America. *Bloomberg Businessweek*, Oct 11.

5 CENTER FOR SCIENCE IN THE PUBLIC INTEREST. 2020. The Rise of Dollar Stores: How the Proliferation of Discount Stores May Limit Healthy Food Access. Washington, DC: Center for Science in the Public Interest.

6 Ibid.

7 MITCHELL, S. & DONAHUE, M. 2018. Report: Dollar Stores Are Targeting Struggling Urban Neighborhoods and Small Towns. One Community Is Showing How to Fight Back. Institute for Local Self-Reliance, Dec 6.

8 BENNETT, J. N. 2019. Fast Cash and Payday Loans. *Economic Research*. Federal Reserve Bank of St Louis. At https://research.stlouisfed.org/publications/page1-econ/2019/04/10/fast-cash-and-payday-loans.

9 Colorado is unusual in specifying a minimum repayment period of six months. According to a study by the Pew Charitable Trust in 2014, most people who take out a payday loan earn about $30,000 a year and use the loan to cover recurring expenses such as rent, utilities, and groceries.

10 BARTH, J. R., HILLARD, J. & JAHERA, J. S. 2015. Banks and Payday Lenders: Friends or Foes? *International Advances in Economic Research*, 21(2), 139–53, BENNETT, J. N. 2019. Fast Cash and Payday Loans. *Economic Research*. Federal Reserve Bank of St Louis.

11 RIVLIN, G. 2016. Money For Nothing. *The Intercept*, June 23.

12 TEMPKIN, A. & MALONEY, C. 2019. Expensive Loans to Desperate People Built This $90 Billion Industry. *Bloomberg*, Feb 14.

13 BENNETT, J. N. 2019. Fast Cash and Payday Loans. *Economic Research*. Federal Reserve Bank of St Louis.

14 Ibid.

15 TEMPKIN, A. & MALONEY, C. 2019. Expensive Loans to Desperate People Built This $90 Billion Industry. *Bloomberg*, Feb 14.

16 Ibid. See also https://www.pewtrusts.org/en/research-and-analysis/articles/2020/12/23/states-of-innovation-small-loans-large cost.

17 Thirteen states prohibit payday lenders: Arizona, Arkansas, Connecticut, Georgia, Maine, Maryland, Massachusetts, New Jersey, New York, North Carolina, Pennsylvania, Vermont, and West Virginia and the District of Columbia.

18 See https://www.ustatesloans.org/law/ca. See also LAZARUS, D. 2017. Payday Lenders, Charging 460%, Aren't Subject to California's Usury Law. *Los Angeles Times*, June 2.

19 TEMPKIN, A. & MALONEY, C. 2019. Expensive Loans to Desperate People Built This $90 Billion Industry. *Bloomberg*, Feb 14.

20 HANCOCK, L. 2019. Ohio's New Payday Loan Law Goes Into Effect Saturday. What Will Change? At https://www.cleveland.com/news/g66l-2019/04/b172cdced12409/ohios-new-payday-loan-law-goes-into-effect-saturday-what-will-change-.html.

21 Since 1956 highway spending has accounted for four-fifths of all government investment in transportation. CROSS, R. J., DUTZIK, T., MIERZWINSKI, E. & CASALE, M. 2019. Driving Into Debt: The Hidden Costs of Risky Auto Loans to Consumers and Our Communities. At https://uspirg.org/sites/pirg/files/reports/WEB_USP_Driving-into-debt_Report_021219.pdf.

22 Ibid.

23 Ibid.
24 Ibid.
25 ROCHESTER, S. 2018. *The Black Tax: The Cost of Being Black in America*, New Jersey, Good Steward Publishing.
26 See https://www.arc.gov/map/county-economic-status-in-appalachia-fy-2019.
27 This website offers a quick glance at these counties: https://www.onlyinyourstate.com/kentucky/poor-counties-ky.
28 See https://wfpl.org/census-data-show-some-ky-counties-among-nations-poorest.
29 See https://data.pnj.com/unemployment/floyd-county-ky/CN2107100000000/2018-june.
30 See https://www.onemainfinancial.com.
31 CROSS, R. J., DUTZIK, T., MIERZWINSKI, E. & CASALE, M. 2019. Driving Into Debt: The Hidden Costs of Risky Auto Loans to Consumers and Our Communities.
32 Ibid.
33 SHAPIRO, H. 1978. *Appalachia on Our Mind*, Chapel Hill, University of North Carolina Press.
34 The ARC designations are based on poverty rate, per capita market income, and three-year average unemployment rate.
35 According to Feeding America, 71% of residents in Overton County have incomes *less than* 130% of the federal poverty line.
36 See https://www.arc.gov/distressed-designation-and-county-economic-status-classification-system.
37 While rural areas have been hit hardest by hospital closures, even in the urban centers of California residents have faced waves of hospital closings – particularly those that serve struggling communities. In the East Bay, Alta Bates Hospital fights to stay open. While some argue that urgent care facilities in the Bay Area are good alternatives, they don't have the capacity to address gunshot wounds, heart attacks, or to perform surgeries. Since 1998, fifty California hospitals have closed. According to the American College of Emergency Care, California has *6.7 emergency departments per 1 million people* – the lowest ratio in the nation. See IOFFEE, K. 2017. A New Plan to Save Bay Area Hospitals from Closure. *East Bay Times*, March 6.
38 ELLISON, A. 2019. State-by-state Breakdown of 102 Rural Hospital Closures. Becker's Healthcare: Hospital CFO Report.
39 Ibid.
40 THE CHARTIS GROUP. 2020. The Rural Health Safety Net Under Pressure: Rural Hospital Vulnerability. At https://www.chartis.com/forum/insight/the-rural-health-safety-net-under-pressure-rural-hospital-vulnerability.
41 There are some details that are hard to calculate accurately since Tommy's dependants are his daughter and grandchildren.
42 CENTER ON POVERTY AND INEQUALITY. 2018. Will You Count? American Indians and Alaska Natives in the 2020 Census. Economic

Security and Opportunity Initiative. Georgetown Law. At https://www.urban.org/sites/default/files/publication/49116/2000178-How-are-Income-and-Wealth-Linked-to-Health-and-Longevity.pdf.

43 Only Oregon, Nevada, Nebraska, Indiana, Pennsylvania, Connecticut, West Virginia, Virginia, Louisiana, and Washington, DC still consider EMS services to be essential. EDWARDS, E. 2019. What If You Call 911 and No One Comes? Inside the Collapse of America's Emergency Medical Services. *NBC*, Oct 22.

44 Hospitals are suing their patients to recoup their losses when bills go unpaid. In Tennessee, Methodist University Hospital filed more than 8,300 debt lawsuits in 2018 against people who could not pay their medical bills. This means that court fees and interest charges are added on to an already unpayable medical debt. Typically the lawsuits result in a court order to deduct payments from paychecks, which can leave low-wage workers unable to pay for basic living expenses.

45 GLENZA, J. 2019. Family Swamped by Avalanche of Bills After Son's Death: "It's Continuous." *The Guardian*, June 4.

46 CENTERS FOR DISEASE CONTROL AND PREVENTION. 2019. Reproductive and Birth Outcomes. At https://ephtracking.cdc.gov/showRbPrematureBirthEnv.action.

47 Ibid.

48 See https://odh.ohio.gov/wps/portal/gov/odh/know-our-programs/infant-vitality/infant-vitality.

49 HIMMELSTEIN, D. U., LAWLESS, R. M., THORNE, D., FOOHEY, P. & WOOLHANDLER, S. 2019. Medical Bankruptcy: Still Common Despite the Affordable Care Act. *American Journal of Public Health*, 109(3), 431–3.

50 LI, S. 2020. Using the Pandemic as an Excuse to Limit Abortion. *The Hastings Center*, July 6.

51 TEPPER, T. 2018. Most Americans Don't have Enough Savings to Cover a $1K Emergency. *Bankrate*, Jan 18.

52 See https://www.federalreserve.gov/publications/financial-stability-report.htm.

53 CareCredit has removed its standing promises of approval on loan applications "within seconds" and a chance to reapply with a co-borrower if your credit is declined from their website.

54 CONSUMER FINANCIAL PROTECTION BUREAU. 2013. CFPB Orders GE CareCredit to Refund $34.1 Million for Deceptive Health-Care Credit Card Enrollment. *CFPB*, Dec 10.

55 IBISWORLD. 2018. Medical Patient Financing Industry in the US – Market Research Report. *IBIS World*, updated Feb 29, 2020.

4 Sacrifice Zones: The Places We Call Home

1 CLARK, A. 2018. *The Poisoned City*, New York, Metropolitan Books, Henry Holt and Company.

2 HWANG, K. 2019. Oakland's Lead Paint Problem Persists. *East Bay Express*, Jan 25.
3 See https://www.cdc.gov/nceh/lead/prevention/blood-lead-levels.htm.
4 PELL, M. B. & SCHNEYER, J. 2016. The Thousands of U.S. Locales Where Lead Poisoning is Worse Than in Flint. *Reuters Investigates*, Dec 19.
5 ENVIRONMENTAL PROTECTION AGENCY. 2018. West Oakland Lead Sampling (Scribe) Data Points, West Oakland CA, 2018, U.S. EPA Region 9. See also PELL, M. B. & SCHNEYER, J. 2016. The Thousands of U.S. Locales Where Lead Poisoning is Worse Than in Flint. *Reuters Investigates*, Dec 19; and BONDGRAHAM, D. 2016. Oakland's Toxic Lead Contamination Isn't in the Water. It's in the Buildings and Dirt, and It's Bad. *East Bay Express*, Dec 29.
6 RABIN, R. 2008. The Lead Industry and Lead Water Pipes "A MODEST CAMPAIGN." *American Journal of Public Health*, 98, 1584–92.
7 GUENTHER, R. 1904. *Dangers of White Lead*. HathiTrust: Sherwin Williams Company.
8 ESCHNER, K. 2016. Leaded Gas Was a Known Poison the Day It Was Invented. *Smart News*. At https://www.smithsonianmag.com/smart-news/leaded-gas-poison-invented-180961368.
9 RABIN, R. 2008. The Lead Industry and Lead Water Pipes "A MODEST CAMPAIGN." *American Journal of Public Health*, 98, 1584–92.
10 Ibid.
11 See, for example, the considerable research on environmental racism, including ZIMRING, C. 2016. *Clean and White: A History of Environmental Racism in the United States*, New York, New York University Press.
12 Seven schools in Oakland were found to have lead levels exceeding the federal recommendation of fifteen parts per billion: Glenview Elementary (at the Santa Fe campus): 60 ppb; Burckhalter Elementary: 30.8 ppb; Joaquin Miller Elementary: 21.2 ppb; Brookfield Elementary: 20.4 ppb; American Indian Charter High (Lakeview Elementary campus): 17.3 ppb; Fruitvale Elementary: 16.3 ppb; Thornhill Elementary: 15.9 ppb. See TUCKER, J. 2017. Lead Contamination Found in Water at 7 Oakland Schools. *SFGate*, Oct 26. According to the California Office of Environment Health, significant portions of Oakland have lead levels in excess of 256 parts per million.
13 TADAYON, A. 2018. It Could Cost Oakland Schools $38 Million to Fix Lead Contamination. *East Bay Times*, Feb 8.
14 PEW CHARITABLE RESEARCH CENTER. 2017. 10 Policies to Prevent and Respond to Childhood Lead Exposure. At https://www.pewtrusts.org/en/research-and-analysis/reports/2017/08/10-policies-to-prevent-and-respond-to-childhood-lead-exposure. Research also shows a high correlation between children's levels of exposure to

lead and juvenile delinquency. See https://www.brookings.edu/blog/up-front/2017/06/01/new-evidence-that-lead-exposure-increases-crime.

15 CLARK, A. 2018. *The Poisoned City*, New York, Metropolitan Books, Henry Holt and Company. Some cities, including Philadelphia and Baltimore, have newly minted policies that require all private and public housing rentals to obtain lead-safe certificates. This is an important step in the right direction but clearly not sufficient in scope.

16 ELLER, R. D. 2008. *Uneven Ground: Appalachia since 1945*, Lexington, University Press of Kentucky.

17 Ibid.

18 See BUDIG, J. 2019. The Co-Tenancy Act and the Modernization of West Virginia's Oil and Gas Law. *West Virginia University Research Repository*, 122, 631–64.

19 Ibid. In 2018 the West Virginia House of Delegates passed House Bill 4268 that set forth these requirements.

20 BROWN, A. 2020. Trump's Pick to Manage Public Lands Has a Four-decade History of "Overt Racism" Toward Native People. *The Intercept*, Aug 1.

21 COUTIN, S. B., RICHLAND, J. & FORTIN, V. 2015. Routine Exceptionality: The Plenary Power Doctrine, Immigrants, and the Indigenous Under U.S. Law. *UC Irvine Law Review*, 4, 97–120.

22 Ibid.

23 See https://www.smithsonianmag.com/history/horrific-sand-creek-massacre-will-be-forgotten-no-more-180953403.

24 WYOMING STATE HISTORICAL SOCIETY. 2018. Coming to Wind River: The Eastern Shoshone Treaties of 1863 and 1868. At https://www.wyohistory.org/encyclopedia/coming-wind-river-eastern-shoshone-treaties-1863-and-1868.

25 SHOSHONE TRIBE OF INDIANS v. UNITED STATES. 1937. *George M. Tunison and Albert W. Jefferies for the Shoshone; Homer S. Cummings, Atty. Gen. and H. W. Blair, Asst. Atty. Gen., for the United States*. Case Law.

26 Ibid.

27 In 1887, the US Congress passed the General Allotment Act, often referred to as the Dawes Act for its chief sponsor, Senator Henry Dawes (1816–1903) of Massachusetts. The Act required Native American heads of household to take up individual land allotments on their respective reservations.

28 JACKSON HOLE HISTORICAL SOCIETY & MUSEUM. 2020. An Introduction to the Wind River Indian Reservation of Wyoming. At https://jacksonholehistory.org/an-introduction-to-the-wind-river-indian-reservation-of-wyoming.

29 RUSINEK, W. 1990. A Preview of Coming Attractions? *Wyoming* v. *United States and the Reserved Rights Doctrine*. *Ecology Law Quarterly*, 17, 355–412.

30 *Northern Arapaho Tribe, et al.* v. *Wyoming et al.* and *Eastern Shoshone Tribe, et al.* v. *Wyoming, et al.*

31 RUSINEK, W. 1990. A Preview of Coming Attractions? *Wyoming* v. *United States and the Reserved Rights Doctrine. Ecology Law Quarterly*, 17, 355–412.

32 See https://www.city-data.com/city/Ethete-Wyoming.html. The US Census does not report on population but notes 378 housing units. See https://www.census.gov/search-results.html?q=Ethete+WY&page=1&stateGeo=none&searchtype=web&cssp=SERP&_charset_=UTF-8.

33 See https://datausa.io/profile/geo/ethete-wy. The US 2010 Census, which does not have a population count for Ethete, records the poverty level as being 16.3%. Since the Census cannot provide a population count, I find this number to be unreliable.

34 See https://www.census.gov/library/publications/2020/demo/p60–270.html#:~:text=The%20official%20poverty%20rate%20in,consecutive%20annual%20decline%20in%20poverty.

35 See https://datausa.io/profile/geo/fort-washakie-wy. The US Census provides population and poverty rates for the county only (7,805 pop; 11.1% living in poverty). At https://www.census.gov/search-results.html?q=FT+Washakie+WY&page=1&stateGeo=none&searchtype=web&cssp=SERP&_charset_=UTF-8.

36 While census data is available that relies on blood quantum, I prefer to use data provided by the tribal nations themselves. See https://datausa.io/profile/geo/fort-washakie-wy.

37 POUND, E. 1981. Trouble from Wind River: Indians, Oil Leases and the U.S. Geological Survey. *The New York Times*, April 4.

38 Ibid.

39 SHOSHONE INDIAN TRIBE OF THE WIND RIVER RESERVATION 2012. *Plaintiff–Appellant, The Arapaho Indian Tribe of the Wind River Reservation, Wyoming, Plaintiff–Appellant,* v. *United States.*

40 Ibid.

41 ZHOROV, I. 2014. Wind River Tribes Plan Ahead For Settlement Checks. *Wyoming Public Media*, April 21.

42 GUERIN, E. 2014. Huge Payout for Wind River Reservation. *High Country News*, May 6.

43 CROUSE, A. 2018. Idle Oil, Gas Wells Threaten Indian Tribes While Energy Companies, Regulators Do Little. *InvestigateWest*, Sept 5.

44 See https://www.census.gov/search-results.html?q=pavillion+WY&page=1&stateGeo=none&searchtype=web&cssp=SERP&_charset_=UTF-8.

45 MEEKS, L. 2010. Gas Drilling Has Blighted My Life. *High Country News*, Oct 12.

46 BANERJEE, N. 2019. Fracking Study Finds Toxins in Wyoming Town's Groundwater and Raises Broader Concerns. *Inside Climate News*, March 29.

47 STAFF. 2013. Tribes, Residents Say EPA Deserted Them in Pavillion. *WyoFile: People Places & Policy*, June 25.

48 STAFF. 2013. Tribes, Residents Say EPA Deserted Them in Pavillion. *WyoFile: People Places & Policy*, June 25.

49 Ibid.
50 DIGIULIO, D. C. & JACKSON, R. B. 2016. Impact to Underground Sources of Drinking Water and Domestic Wells from Production Well Stimulation and Completion Practices in the Pavillion, Wyoming, Field. *Environmental Science & Technology*, 50, 4524–36.
51 SMITH, S. 2014. Coal Slurry Catastrophes Continue: West Virginia Hit With Another Environmental Emergency. *EHS Today*, Feb 19.
52 GABRIEL, T. 2014. Thousands Without Water After Spill in West Virginia. *The New York Times*, Jan 10.
53 The spill affected Boone, Lincoln, Kanawha, Jackson, and Putnam counties. GHABRA, O. 2015. After the Spill: Life in West Virginia's Coal Country. *The Atlantic*, Jan 9.
54 See https://ohvec.org/oops-industry-accidents.
55 HENDRYX, M. & LUO, J. 2015. An Examination of the Effects of Mountaintop Removal Coal Mining on Respiratory Symptoms and COPD Using Propensity Scores. *International Journal of Environmental Health Research*, 25, 265–76; HENDRYX, M., YONTS, S., YUEYAO, L. & JUHUA, L. 2019. Mountaintop Removal Mining and Multiple Illness Symptoms: A Latent Class Analysis. *Science of the Total Environment*, 657, 764–9.
56 See https://development.ohio.gov/files/research/plchist.pdf.
57 LANE, M. B. 2012. Bought-out Cheshire Village Lives On. *The Columbus Dispatch*, June 24.
58 MARTIN, R. 2014. For $20 Million, a Coal Utility Bought an Ohio Town and a Clear Conscience. *The Atlantic*, Oct 16.
59 LANE, M. B. 2012. Bought-out Cheshire Village Lives On. *The Columbus Dispatch*, June 24.
60 MARTIN, R. 2014. For $20 Million, a Coal Utility Bought an Ohio Town and a Clear Conscience. *The Atlantic*, Oct 16.
61 Ibid.
62 BUCKLEY, G., BAIN, N. & SWAN, D. 2005. When the Lights Go Out in Cheshire. *Geographical Review*, 95, 537–55.
63 American Studies Professor Peter Ling counts twenty-six towns, while *The Post Athens* counts more than seventy mining towns. See https://www.geotab.com/ghost-towns; and http://projects.thepostathens.com/SpecialProjects/ohios-hidden-history-ghost-towns-mining.
64 The towns include Alum Springs, Big Right Hand, Fire Creek, Indian Creek, Kay Moor, Lindytown, Mercers Saltworks, Mill Run (Tucker County), Mill Run (Pocahontas County), Nuttallburg, Sewell, Smoke Hole, Thurmond, Twilight, Walker Hill and Winona.
65 BOARD, G. 2015. W.Va. Officials Applaud Supreme Court Ruling Against EPA's Mercury/Air Toxics Standards. West Virginia Public Broadcasting. At http://wvpublic.org/post/wva-officials-applaud-supreme-court-ruling-against-epas-mercuryair-toxics-standards#stream/0.
66 In a 5–4 vote the Supreme Court said that the Environmental Protection Agency failed to take the costs into account when it first decided to regulate the toxic emissions from coal- and oil-fired plants. Ibid.

67 *Michigan* v. *E.P.A.*, 135 S. Ct. 2699, 2707 (2015)
68 *Michigan* v. *E.P.A.*, 135 S. Ct. 2699, 2714 (2015) (dissent by Kagan, J.).
69 TRUMP, D. J. 2016. Remarks at Seven Flags Event Center in Des Moines, Iowa. At https://www.presidency.ucsb.edu/documents/remarks-seven-flags-event-center-des-moines-iowa.
70 Before resigning in 2018 from the Environmental Protection Agency amid scandals of corruption, Scott Pruitt revoked the 2015 Clean Water Rule which secured drinking water for more than 117 million people and safeguarded 2 million miles of streams and 20 million acres of wetlands.
71 CBS. 2011. The South's Top 10 Eco-Dangers. *CBS News*. At https://www.cbsnews.com/pictures/the-souths-top-10-eco-dangers/9.
72 SOHN, P. 2011. Cumberland Plateau Placed on Top 10 Endangered List. *Times Free Press*, Jan 20.
73 LEARY, C. 2011. Cumberland Plateau. At https://www.mnn.com/earth-matters/wilderness-resources/photos/10-most-endangered-places-in-the-south/cumberland-plateau.
74 SOUTHWINGS. 2019. Coal Slurry and Coal Ash. At http://www.southwings.org/our-work/coal-slurry-ash.
75 U.S. ENVIRONMENTAL PROTECTION AGENCY. 2009. U.S. Environmental Protection Agency and Tennessee Valley Authority Kingston Coal Ash Release Site. At https://www.epa.gov/sites/production/files/2016–02/documents/projectcloseout_dec2014_factsheet.pdf.
76 For the original data see https://www.ewg.org/tapwater/state.php?stab=TN. For distillation of localities, see BELT, D. 2017. 30 Tennessee Water Systems Have Harmful Pollutants In Drinking Water, New Study Says. *Patch*, July 26.
77 See https://www.census.gov/search-results.html?q=kentucky+child+poverty&page=1&stateGeo=none&searchtype=web&cssp=SERP&_charset_=UTF-8.
78 They are the best paid jobs, if you get paid. Recall that in 2019, Blackjewel shut down their mining operations without the required notice. Two paychecks to miners bounced and the corporation didn't even cut a check for their last week of work. More than a month without income led miners to sit on the train tracks to prevent coal from leaving the region until they were paid. Eventually, they won their case and back wages.
79 See https://eec.ky.gov/Energy/News-Publications/Quarterly%20Coal%20Reports/2019-Q1.pdf.
80 ELLER, R. D. 2008. *Uneven Ground: Appalachia since 1945*, Lexington, University Press of Kentucky.
81 UNION OF CONCERNED SCIENTISTS. 2009. Coal Slurry Spill Investigation Suppressed. At https://www.ucsusa.org/resources/coal-slurry-spill-investigation-suppressed.
82 Ibid.

83 Ibid.
84 See https://www.ucsusa.org/resources/coal-slurry-spill-investigation-suppressed.
85 SCOTT, S., MCSPIRIT, S., HARDESTY, S. & WELCH, R. 2005. Post Disaster Interviews with Martin County Citizens: "Gray Clouds" of Blame and Distrust. *Journal of Appalachian Studies*, 11, 7–29. See also MCSPIRIT, S., SCOTT, S. L., HARDESTY, S. & WELCH, R. 2005. EPA Actions in Post Disaster Martin County, Kentucky: An Analysis of Bureaucratic Slippage and Agency Recreancy. *Journal of Appalachian Studies*, 11, 30–59.
86 Ibid.
87 BRUGGERS, J. 2017. Kentucky Ranks Poorly in New Water Quality Study. *Courier Journal*, May 2.
88 DWYER-LINDGREN, L., BERTOZZI-VILLA, A. & STUBBS, R. W. 2017. Inequalities in Life Expectancy Among US Counties, 1980 to 2014. *Health Care Policy and Law*, 177, 1003–11.
89 RYERSON, S. & SCHEPT, J. 2018. Building Prisons in Appalachia: The Region Deserves Better. *Boston Review*, April 28.
90 AP. 2002. South Kentucky: Hard Time on Soft Ground. *The New York Times*, July 26.
91 THE SENTENCING PROJECT. 2012. Parents in Prison. At https://www.sentencingproject.org/publications/parents-in-prison.
92 In 2021, the Office of Budget Management of the US government again proposed defunding the prison project because of lack of progress. THE OFFICE OF BUDGET MANAGEMENT OF THE U.S. GOVERNMENT 2021. A Budget for America's Future: Major Savings and Reforms. In: GOVERNMENT, T. O. O. B. M. O. T. U. S. (ed.).
93 RUGER, T. 2020. Powerful Appropriator Battles Justice Over Prison in Kentucky. *Roll Call*, March 11.
94 STEBBINS, S. & SAUTER, M. 2019. Kentucky Counties Make Up 10 of the 25 Worst Places to Live in the US. *Courier Journal*, March 13.
95 VANCE, J. D. 2016. *Hillbilly Elegy*, New York, HarperCollins.
96 KLINE, M. 2018. J. D. Vance Dissed at Appalachian Studies Association. *Accuracy in Academia*, April 25.
97 PERRY, M. 2013. 6 Facts About North Dakota Oil. American Enterprise Institute. At https://www.aei.org/carpe-diem/6-facts-about-north-dakota-oil.
98 LEE, T. 2014. No Man's Land: The Last Tribes of the Plains. *MSNBC*, Sept 21.
99 NOBEL, J. 2020. America's Radioactive Secret. *Rolling Stone*, Jan 21.
100 Ibid.
101 ENVIRONMENTAL PROTECTION AGENCY. 2002. Exemption of Oil and Gas Exploration and Production Wastes from Federal Hazardous Waste Regulations. Environmental Protection Agency, Office of Solid Waste. At https://yosemite.epa.gov/oa/eab_web_docket.nsf/Attachments%20By%20ParentFilingId/945EF425FA4A9B4F85257E

2800480C65/$FILE/28%20-%20RCRA%20E%26P%20Exemption.pdf.

102 NOBEL, J. 2020. America's Radioactive Secret. *Rolling Stone*, Jan 21. In Ohio, Senate Bill 165 would slash environmental safeguards and make it easier to sell fracking brine as a de-icer.

103 REICH, R. B. 2020. *The System: Who Rigged it, How We Fix It*, New York, Alfred Knopf, p. 30.

104 VOLCOVICI, V. & VALDMANIS, R. 2017. Keystone's Existing Pipeline Spills Far More Than Predicted to Regulators. *Reuters*, Nov 27.

105 The NRDC writes: "In 2014, the U.S. Environmental Protection Agency stated that tar sands oil emits 17% more carbon than other types of crude, but ironically, the State Department revised this number upward three years later, stating that the emissions could be '5 percent to 20 percent higher than previously indicated.' That means burdening the planet with an extra 177 million metric tons of greenhouse gas emissions annually, the same impact as adding 37 million passenger vehicles to the road." DENCHAK, M. 2017. What is the Keystone Pipeline? *NRDC*. At https://www.nrdc.org/stories/what-keystone-pipeline.

106 CORNELL UNIVERSITY GLOBAL LABOR INSTITUTE. 2011. Pipe Dreams? Jobs Gained, Jobs Lost by the Construction of the Keystone XL. At https://archive.ilr.cornell.edu/sites/default/files/GLI_keystoneXL_Reportpdf.pdf.

107 VOLCOVICI, V. & VALDMANIS, R. 2017. Keystone's Existing Pipeline Spills Far More Than Predicted to Regulators. *Reuters*, Nov 27.

108 RUEB, E. & CHOKSHI, N. 2019. Keystone Pipeline Leaks 383,000 Gallons of Oil in North Dakota. *The New York Times*, Oct 31.

109 THORBECKE, C. 2016. Why a Previously Proposed Route for the Dakota Access Pipeline Was Rejected. *ABC News*, Nov 3.

110 HERSHER, R. 2017. Key Moments in the Dakota Access Pipeline Fight. *NPR*, Feb 22.

111 See https://www.nwd-mr.usace.army.mil.

112 See https://www.state.gov/keystone-pipeline-xl.

113 See https://web.sas.upenn.edu/quechua/2019/03/24/ladonna-brave-bull-allard-at-penn.

114 These pipelines are recognized as a tremendous threat to land and water by Native people in North America. In 2019, Wet'suwet'en land defenders in Canada led a protest of the TransCanada Pipeline. A Haudenosaunee solidarity protest shut down the Canadian National Railway for days, while other nations have occupied Prime Minister Justin Trudeau's office.

115 LEVIN, S. 2017. Revealed: FBI Terrorism Task Force Investigating Standing Rock Activists. *The Guardian*, Feb 10.

116 See https://www.aclu.org/issues/free-speech/rights-protesters/stand-standing-rock.

117 BROWN, A., PARRISH, W. & SPERI, A. 2017b. Counterterrorism Tactics Used at Standing Rock to "Defeat Pipeline Insurgencies." *The Intercept*, May 27.
118 Ibid.
119 "For water protectors, the fight against the pipeline was only the latest episode in two centuries of native resistance to U.S. government incursion into the northern Great Plains, part of a lineage that includes the 1876 Battle of Greasy Grass, where indigenous people defeated the U.S. 7th Cavalry in defense of their treaty rights to South Dakota's Black Hills; the 1890 massacre at Wounded Knee, where as many as 300 Lakota people were killed by U.S. soldiers; and the 1973 occupation of Wounded Knee, where armed members of the American Indian Movement faced off with federal agents in protest of a corrupt local government and the U.S. government's legacy of broken treaties." BROWN, A., PARRISH, W. & SPERI, A. 2017. The Battle of Treaty Camp. *The Intercept*, Oct 27.
120 LEVIN, S. 2017. Revealed: FBI Terrorism Task Force Investigating Standing Rock Activists. *The Guardian*, Feb 10.
121 MILMAN, O. 2016. Scientists Find Fracking Contaminated Wyoming Water After EPA Halted Study. *The Guardian*, April 7.
122 HAUSS, B. 2017. Standing Rock Protest Groups Sued by Dakota Access Pipeline Company. *Speak Freely*. At https://www.aclu.org/blog/free-speech/rights-protesters/standing-rock-protest-groups-sued-dakota-access-pipeline-company.
123 LEFEBVRE, B. & ADRAGNA, A. 2019. Trump Administration Seeks Criminal Crackdown on Pipeline Protests. *Politico*, June 3.
124 LENNARD, N. 2017. Still Fighting at Standing Rock. *Esquire*, Sept 19.
125 CAGLE, S. 2019. "Protesters as Terrorists": Growing Number of States Turn Anti-Pipeline Activism into a Crime. *The Guardian*, July 19.
126 Ibid.
127 KACZKE, L. 2019. Gov. Kristi Noem Signs Bills Aimed at Keystone XL Pipeline Protests. *Argus Leader*, March 27.
128 Ibid.
129 THEBAULT, R. 2019. Oglala Sioux Tribe Tells the South Dakota Governor She is "Not Welcome" on Their Reservation. *The Washington Post*, May 3.
130 BUBACZ, K. 2018. What Happened After Standing Rock? *BuzzFeed*, Feb 28.
131 VOLCOVICI, V. 2020. Trump Revamps Key Environmental Law in Bid to Fast Track Pipelines, Roads. *Reuters*, July 15.
132 WAMSLEY, L. 2020. Court Rules Dakota Access Pipeline Must Be Emptied For Now. *NPR*, July 6.
133 See https://www.law360.com/articles/1334007/the-biggest-energy-rulings-of-2020-part-2.
134 JUNKINS, C. 2021. "Climate Emergency": President Joe Biden Quickly Stops Keystone XL. *Capital Journal*, Jan 21.

135 CATTE, E. 2018. Passive, Poor and White? What People Keep Getting Wrong About Appalachia. *The Guardian*, Feb 6.

5 Ordinary Things That Can Only Happen Here

1 THE CHIEF JUSTICE EARL WARREN INSTITUTE ON LAW AND SOCIAL POLICY. 2014. When and Where Does Crime Occur in Oakland? A Temporal and Spatial Analysis (January 2008–July 2013). At https://www.law.berkeley.edu/files/When_and_Where_Does_Crime_Occur_in_Oakland.pdf.

2 Of these, twenty-three were abductions witnessed by others, 471 were suspected but not witnessed abductions, and 2,901 people disappeared in unknown circumstances. See California Department of Justice statistics at https://oag.ca.gov/missing/stats.

3 DEBOLT, D. 2019. After a Year of Lower Crime, Oakland Looks to Hire More Officers. *The Mercury News*, Jan 4.

4 Ibid.

5 Ibid.

6 Ibid.

7 Sixty-nine people were identified as Black or Hispanic; thirty-three as "other" or "unknown." See https://www.washingtonpost.com/graphics/2019/national/police-shootings-2019.

8 According to a National Survey on Drug Use and Health (NSDUH) published in 2017, the average age of new methamphetamine users in 2016 was 23.3 years old. According to Centers for Disease Control and Prevention, deaths involving psychostimulants (methamphetamines MDMA and Ritalin) increased by 21% to 10,749 in 2017. That's more than 14% of all overdose deaths.

9 WINKELMAN, T., ADMON, L. & JENNINGS, L. 2018. Evaluation of Amphetamine-Related Hospitalizations and Associated Clinical Outcomes and Costs in the United States. *JAMA Network Open*, Oct 19.

10 The states where meth-related seizures were most prevalent in 2018 were Michigan, New York, Indiana, Illinois, North Carolina, California, Pennsylvania, Tennessee, Ohio, and Florida. See the rankings here: https://www.mshp.dps.missouri.gov/MSHPWeb/DevelopersPages/DDCC/methLabDisclaimer.html.

11 NATIONAL INSTITUTE ON DRUG ABUSE. 2019. Overdose Death Rates. At https://www.drugabuse.gov/drug-topics/trends-statistics/overdose-death-rates.

12 See https://www.justice.gov/archive/ndic/pubs11/18862/transport.htm.

13 ALLEN, G. 2011. The "Oxy Express": Florida's Drug Abuse Epidemic. At https://www.npr.org/2011/03/02/134143813/the-oxy-express-floridas-drug-abuse-epidemic.

14 CENTERS FOR DISEASE CONTROL AND PREVENTION. 2017. U.S. State Prescribing Rates 2017. At https://www.cdc.gov/drugoverdose/maps/rxstate2017.html.

15 SULLIVAN, A. 2018. The Poison We Pick. At https://nymag.com/intelligencer/2018/02/americas-opioid-epidemic.html.
16 MALONEY, M. 2019. The Hillbilly Miracle and The Fall. In: HARKINS, A. (ed.) *Appalachian Reckoning: A Region Responds to Hillbilly Elegy*, West Virginia: West Virginia University Press.
17 MCGREAL, C. 2019. Why Were Millions of Opioid Pills Sent to a West Virginia Town of 3,000? *The Guardian*, Oct 2.
18 LURIE, J. 2018. "I Was Directed to Market OxyContin": A Purdue Pharma Rep Tells How He Was Paid to Push Opioids. *Mother Jones*, May 4.
19 WARREN, K. & ROGERS, T. N. 2020. The Family Behind OxyContin Pocketed $10.7 Billion from Purdue Pharma. *Business Insider*, March 23.
20 BERNSTEIN, L. 2019. West Virginia Reaches $37 Million Opioid Settlement with Drug Shipper McKesson. *The Washington Post*, May 2.
21 In 2007, federal courts fined OxyContin's manufacturer, Purdue Pharma, $634 million for misrepresenting the drug's addictive effects to doctors and patients. After being charged with a second offense, McKenzie Corp. paid a $150 million fine for distributing opioids without proper controls; Cardinal Health agreed to pay $44 million to settle federal lawsuits. In 2019 an Oklahoma judge ordered Johnson & Johnson to pay $572 million to remedy the devastation it caused in Oklahoma.
22 See https://www.cdc.gov/drugoverdose/epidemic/index.html.
23 See https://www.archives.gov/research/military/vietnam-war/casualty-statistics.
24 See https://www.cdc.gov/drugoverdose/data/prescribing/overdose-death-maps.html.
25 HIGHAM, S. & BERNSTEIN, L. 2017. The Drug Industry's Triumph over the DEA. *The Washington Post*, Oct 15.
26 Ibid.
27 Ibid.
28 Ibid.
29 GIRIDHARADAS, A. 2018. *Winners Take All*, New York, Knopf Doubleday Publishing Group.
30 REICH, R. B. 2020. *The System: Who Rigged it, How We Fix It*, New York, Alfred Knopf, pp. 48–9.
31 WARREN, K. & ROGERS, T. N. 2020. The Family Behind OxyContin Pocketed $10.7 Billion from Purdue Pharma. *Business Insider*, March 23.
32 DAVIS, C. 2021. The Purdue Pharma Opioid Settlement – Accountability, or Just the Cost of Doing Business? *The New England Journal of Medicine*, 384, 97–9.
33 Ibid.
34 SPECTOR, M., TERHUNE, C. & GIRION, L. 2020. Sacklers Cited Fear of OxyContin Lawsuits Before Transferring $10 billion from Their Company, Documents Show. *Reuters*, Dec 21.

35 MACY, B. 2018. *Dopesick: Dealers, Doctors, and the Drug Company that Addicted America*, New York, Little, Brown and Company.
36 There are roughly 14,000 licensed addiction-treatment facilities in the country and on average they serve fewer than 100 people at a time. See https://www.hhs.gov/opioids/about-the-epidemic/opioid-crisis-statistics/index.html.
37 THE SENTENCING PROJECT 2020. Incarcerated Women and Girls. At https://www.sentencingproject.org/publications/incarcerated-women-and-girls.
38 Ibid.
39 MCGREAL, C. 2017. How Big Pharma's Money – and its Politicians – Feed the US Opioid Crisis. *The Guardian*, Oct 19.
40 WOUTERS, O. 2020. Lobbying Expenditures and Campaign Contributions by the Pharmaceutical and Health Product Industry in the United States, 1999-2018. JAMA Internal Medicine, 180(5):1-10. At https://jamanetwork.com/journals/jamainternalmedicine/fullarticle/2762509.
41 Ibid.
42 CENTER FOR RESPONSIVE POLITICS. 2020. Industry Profile: Pharmaceutical Manufacturing. At https://www.opensecrets.org/industries/lobbying.php?ind=H4300.

6 The Burdens of Prejudice: Class and Race

1 ZAFAR, N. 2020. Anthony Fauci Praises "Classy"' Brad Pitt After SNL Impersonation. *The Washington Post*, April 28.
2 CATTE, E. 2018. *What You Are Getting Wrong About Appalachia*, Cleveland, OH, Belt Publishing.
3 ELLER, R. D. 2008. *Uneven Ground: Appalachia since 1945*, Lexington, University Press of Kentucky.
4 See https://www.countyhealthrankings.org/app/ohio/2019/measure/factors/65/data.
5 When I met Jenny and her family in 2017 the federal poverty line for a family of four was $24,600.
6 Reduced-price lunches are available to children in households between 130% and 185% of the federal poverty line; free lunches are available to children in households with incomes at or below 130% of the federal poverty line. See https://www.ers.usda.gov/topics/food-nutrition-assistance/child-nutrition-programs/national-school-lunch-program.
7 Source: www.benefits.gov/benefit/1344.
8 The maximum allowable savings in any state is $2250. See https://www.clasp.org/sites/default/files/publications/2018/04/2018_eliminatingassetlimits.pdf.
9 ECONOMIC RESEARCH SERVICE. 2020. Percent of Residents Participating in SNAP Varies Across States. United States Department

of Agriculture. At https://www.ers.usda.gov/data-products/ag-and-food-statistics-charting-the-essentials/food-security-and-nutrition-assistance.

10 Estimated average benefits are calculated using fiscal year (FY) 2019 income eligibility standards and deductions and FY 2017 SNAP Quality Control Household Characteristics income and expense data, inflation-adjusted to FY 2019. Source: www.cbpp.org/research/food-assistance/policy-basics-the-supplemental-nutrition-assistance-program-snap.

11 METZL, J. 2019. *Dying of Whiteness: How the Politics of Racial Resentment is Killing America's Heartland*, New York, Basic Books.

12 TEMIN, P. 2017. *The Vanishing Middle Class: Prejudice and Power in a Dual Economy*, Cambridge, MA, The MIT Press.

13 GOULD, E. 2019. *State of Working America: Wages 2018*. Washington, DC: Economic Policy Institute.

14 However, the Institute for Women's Policy Research found that when they accounted for pay cuts that come from taking time out of the labor force women earn 49 cents to the dollar that men typically earn. See CLARK, J. 2018. Women Earn Just Half of What Men Earn Over 15 Years. Institute for Women's Policy Research press release. At https://iwpr.org/media/press-releases/women-earn-just-half-of-what-men-earn-over-15-years.

15 HEGEWISCH, A. 2018. The Gender Wage Gap: 2017 Earnings Differences by Gender, Race, Ethnicity. Institute for Women's Policy Research. See also the Department of Labor Statistics at https://www.dol.gov/agencies/wb/data/earnings.

16 Department of Labor Statistics at https://www.dol.gov/agencies/wb/data/earnings.

17 This is known in sociology as "color-blind racism." See, for example, Eduardo Bonilla-Silva's *Racism without Racists: Color-Blind Racism and the Persistence of Racial Inequality in the United States* (2003).

18 See https://www.hsph.harvard.edu/horp/discrimination-in-america. The RWJ Foundation and Harvard T. H. Chan School of Public Health survey was based on a sample of 3,453 adults across the country.

19 See https://www.census.gov/data/tables/time-series/demo/income-poverty/cps-hinc/hinc-03.html.

20 See, for example, *White Fragility* by Robin DiAngelo and *Racism without Racists* by Eduardo Bonilla-Silva.

21 SIEGLER, K. 2020. Federal Appeals Court Upholds Dismissal of Cliven Bundy Case. *NPR*, Aug 6.

22 Ibid.

23 ALLEN, J. 2018. Trump Pardons Oregon Ranchers Who Inspired Refuge Standoff. *Reuters*, July 10.

24 Ibid.

25 GREGORIAN, D. 2020. "Calls to Violence": Michigan Gov. Whitmer Says Armed Protests Could Lengthen Stay-at-home Order. *NBC News*, May 13. Notably, the FBI later uncovered a right-wing plot to kidnap the Michigan governor. See also DAVIS, A., BENNETT, D., CAHLAN,

S. & KELLY, M. 2020. Alleged Michigan Plotters Attended Multiple Anti-lockdown Protests, Photos and Videos Show. *The Washington Post*, Nov 1.

26 BENNETT, D., CAHLAN, S., DAVIS, A. & LEE, J. S. The Crackdown Before Trump's Photo Op. *The Washington Post*, June 8.

27 WORDEN, A. & LATI, M. 2021. Judge Chides Suspected Pelosi Laptop Thief: "The Constitution Prevails Here Today." *The Washington Post*, Jan 21.

28 GONNERMAN, J. 2014. Before the Law. *New Yorker*, Sept 29.

29 In 2017, when we talked, the federal poverty line for an individual was $12,060; a self-sufficiency budget for a single person in Athens County, Ohio was $34,545.

30 DUFFY, J.-C. 2008. The Use of "Laminite" in Official LDS Discourse. *Journal of Mormon History*, 34, 118–67.

31 FOWLER, L. 2016. Why Several Native Americans Are Suing the Mormon Church. *The Atlantic*, Oct 23.

32 Ibid.

33 ROSAY, A. B. 2016. Violence Against American Indian and Alaska Native Women and Men. *National Institute of Justice Journal*, 277, June 1.

34 Ibid.

35 Dred Scott had been enslaved in Missouri. He lived in Illinois (a free state) from 1833 to 1843 and in the Louisiana Territory, where slavery was also forbidden. He sued for his freedom in 1856 on the grounds that he lived in a free territory as a free man. The case decided that people with African ancestry (free or enslaved) were not entitled to US citizenship and therefore could not sue in federal court. *Brown* v. *the Board of Education* consolidated law suits in four states and the District of Columbia to challenge segregated education. The Supreme Court upheld segregated facilities as long as they were "separate but equal."

36 The Supreme Court's 1873 decision on Modoc Indian prisoners allowed that anyone identified as "Indian" could be killed legally and also held legally responsible for any crimes committed against US soldiers. This decision has been used by at least three administrations to justify actions taken in the so-called war on terrorism.

37 ALEXANDER, J. C. 2012. John Yoo's "War Powers": The Law Review and the World. *California Law Review*, 100, 331–64.

7 The Burdens Women Face

1 CLARK, J. 2018. Women Earn Just Half of What Men Earn Over 15 Years. Institute for Women's Policy Research press release. However, when the Institute for Women's Policy Research accounted for pay cuts that come from taking time out of the labor force, they found that women earn 49 cents to the dollar that men typically earn.

2 HEGEWISCH, A. 2018. The Gender Wage Gap: 2017 Earnings Differences by Gender, Race, Ethnicity. Institute for Women's Policy Research.
3 CLARK, J. 2018. Women Earn Just Half of What Men Earn Over 15 Years. Institute for Women's Policy Research press release.
4 NWLC. 2016. Poverty Rates by State 2015. *Current Population Survey, Annual Social and Economic Supplement*. U.S. Census.
5 CANN, O. 2018. World Economic Forum. At https://www.weforum.org/press/2018/12/108-years-wait-for-gender-equality-gets-longer-as-women-s-share-of-workforce-politics drops.
6 TICKAMYER, A. R. & WORNELL, E. 2017. How to Explain Poverty? In: TICKAMYER, A. R., SHERMAN, J. & WARLICK, J. (eds.) *Rural Poverty in the United States*. New York, Columbia University Press.
7 HLAVATY, K. 2018. 16 Sexual Assault Reports Made Since Beginning of Ohio University's Fall Semester. *News 5 Cleveland*, Oct 4.
8 RAINN. 2019. The Criminal Justice System: Statistics. At https://www.rainn.org/statistics/criminal-justice-system.
9 Ibid.
10 NATIONAL CONGRESS OF AMERICAN INDIANS. 2018. Violence Against American Indian and Alaska Native Women. Policy Research Center. ROSAY, A. B. 2016. Violence Against American Indian and Alaska Native Women and Men. *National Institute of Justice Journal*, 277, June 1.
11 UNITED STATES SENTENCING COMMISSION. 2013. Native Americans in the Federal Offender Population.
12 WHITCOMB, D. 2019. Kentucky Derby a Magnet for Human Trafficking, Officials Warn. *Reuters*, April 22.
13 See https://polarisproject.org/myths-facts-and-statistics.
14 KENTUCKY OFFICE OF THE ATTORNEY GENERAL AND CATHOLIC CHARITIES OF LOUISVILLE. 2017. Kentucky Statewide Human Trafficking Report. At https://ag.ky.gov/AG%20Publications/HT_2017-Annual-Report.pdf.
15 Ibid.
16 CHRISTIAN, A. 2019. Sold at Derby: Sex Trafficking in Louisville. *Louisville Magazine*, May 1.
17 COLE, J. & ANDERSON, E. 2013. Sex Trafficking of Minors in Kentucky. Center on Trauma and Children Reports. University of Kentucky.
18 Ibid.
19 NCAI POLICY RESEARCH CENTER. 2016. Human and Sex Trafficking: Trends and Responses across Indian Country. At https://www.ncai.org/policy-research-center/research-data/prc-publications/TraffickingBrief.pdf.
20 PIERCE, A. & KOEPPLINGER, S. 2011. New Language, Old Problem: Sex Trafficking of American Indian Women and Children. VAWnet: A project of the National Resource Center on Domestic Violence.

21 See https://www.eia.gov/state/analysis.php?sid=ND.
22 OGDEN, E. 2018. Man Camps in Western ND Filling Up. *Pioneer*, June 8.
23 HORWITZ, S. 2014. Dark Side of the Boom. *The Washington Post*, Sept 28.
24 Ibid.
25 CORNELIUS, B. 2018. Little Justice for Native American Women Victimized by Non-Native Attackers. *Michigan Journal of Race & Law*, 23.
26 Ibid.
27 Ibid.
28 Ibid.
29 Ibid.
30 See SULLIVAN, Z. 2016. Crimes Against Native American Women Raise Questions About Police Response. *The Guardian*, Jan 19.
31 GRAY, L. A. 2018. Forgotten Women: The Conversation of Murdered and Missing Native Women is Not One North America Wants to Have – But It Must. *Independent*, Aug 14.
32 URBAN INDIAN HEALTH INSTITUTE. 2019. A Nationwide Data Crisis: Missing and Murdered Indigenous Women and Girls. Seattle Indian Health Board. See also GAMBINO, L. 2019. "Essential First Step": Congress Moves to Act on Crisis of Violence Against Native Women. *The Guardian*, May 1.
33 CORNELIUS, B. 2018. Little Justice for Native American Women Victimized by Non-Native Attackers. *Michigan Journal of Race & Law*, 23.
34 GRAY, L. A. 2018. Forgotten Women: The Conversation of Murdered and Missing Native Women is Not One North America Wants to Have – But It Must. *Independent*, Aug 14.
35 SCHILLING, V. 2018. Efforts To Increase #MMIW Awareness Include a Film, Website, Law and Daily Tweet. *Indian Country Today*, April 20.
36 The database runs from 1900 to the present day, and is compiled using general missing people lists, social media, limited news coverage, archives and police databases. See https://www.sovereign-bodies.org.
37 KO, L. 2016. Unwanted Sterilization and Eugenics Programs in the United States. PBS. At https://www.pbs.org/independentlens/blog/unwanted-sterilization-and-eugenics-programs-in-the-united-states.
38 US SUPREME COURT. 1978. *Oliphant* v. *Suquamish Indian Tribe*.
39 NATIONAL CONGRESS OF AMERICAN INDIANS. 2018. Violence Against American Indian and Alaska Native Women. Policy Research Center.
40 NCAI POLICY RESEARCH CENTER. 2016. Human and Sex Trafficking: Trends and Responses across Indian Country.
41 URBAN INDIAN HEALTH INSTITUTE. 2019. A Nationwide Data Crisis: Missing and Murdered Indigenous Women and Girls. Seattle Indian Health Board.

42 MURKOWSKI, L. 2020. Murkowski's Legislation Addressing Crisis of Missing, Murdered, and Trafficked Indigenous People Passes Senate. Senator Murkowski's Office.
43 OLSON, D. 2018. Savanna Greywind Wasn't Dead When Baby Cut from Womb, Prosecutors Say at Abductor's Sentencing. *Twin Cities Pioneer*, Feb 3.
44 GOLDEN, H. 2021. "Suddenly I'm Breathing": Hope as Haaland Takes On Crisis of Missing and Murdered Native Americans. *The Guardian,* April 11.
45 See https://www.gao.gov/products/GAO-17-624.
46 URBAN INDIAN HEALTH INSTITUTE. 2019. A Nationwide Data Crisis: Missing and Murdered Indigenous Women and Girls. Seattle Indian Health Board.
47 Ibid.

8 The Face of a Movement?

1 See https://www.vanityfair.com/news/2016/10/fran-lebowitz-trump-clinton-election.
2 A fuller context would require going back to Ronald Reagan; I will leave that to another book.
3 When he was first video-taped in a conversation about taxes with then-candidate Obama, Wurzelbacher had claimed that he was interested in *buying* a plumbing company.
4 MACASKILL, E. & GOLDENBERG, S. 2008. US Election: Who is "Joe the Plumber" – aka Joe Wurzelbacher? *The Guardian*, Oct 16.
5 ROHTER, L. & ROBBINS, L. 2008. Joe in the Spotlight. *The New York Times*, Oct 16.
6 REID, T. 2016. "Joe the Plumber" Praises Trump, Cites his "Beautiful Women." *Reuters*, March 4.
7 Ibid.
8 TEIXEIRA, R. & HALPIN, J. 2019. The Path to 270 in 2020. Center for American Progress.
9 JOUET, M. 2017. *Exceptional America: What Divides Americans from the World and Each Other*, Oakland, University of California Press.
10 PEW RESEARCH CENTER. 2018. An Examination of the 2016 Electorate, Based on Validated Voters. The Pew Charitable Trusts.
11 Ibid.
12 HRUBAN, E. 2017. (In)divisible: Voices from a Polarized America. Berelsman Foundation.
13 ROPER CENTER FOR PUBLIC OPINION. 2016. How Groups Voted in 2016. Cornell University. See also OSNOS, E. 2020. How Greenwich Republicans Learned to Love Trump. *The New Yorker*, May 3.
14 AMERICAN NATIONAL ELECTION STUDIES. 2016. 2016 Time Series Study. At https://electionstudies.org/data-center/2016-time-series-study.

MCELWEE, S. & MCDANIEL, J. 2017. Economic Anxiety Didn't Make People Vote Trump, Racism Did. *The Nation*, May 8.

15 See https://www.statista.com/statistics/1184428/presidential-election-exit-polls-share-votes-income-us.

16 CATTE, E. 2018. *What You Are Getting Wrong About Appalachia*, Cleveland, OH, Belt Publishing.

17 See https://www.whitehouse.gov/briefings-statements/remarks-president-trump-tax-reform-2.

18 See, for example, LIEBMAN, W. 2020. Workers Play Against a Stacked Deck at Trump's NLRB. At https://morningconsult.com/opinions/workers-play-against-a-stacked-deck-at-trumps-nlrb. And PRESCOD, P. 2020. Trump Claims He's Pro-Worker. But His Labor Board is Trying to Destroy Worker Organizing. *Jacobin*, Sept 22.

19 CLAYTON, M. & PAULSON, A. 2006. Sago Raises Red Flags for Mine Oversight. *Christian Science Monitor*, Jan 6.

20 GORDON, L. 2017. *The Second Coming of the KKK: The Ku Klux Klan of the 1920s and the American Political Tradition*, New York, Liveright Publishing Corporation, pp. 208–9.

21 For more information, see http://www.nativepartnership.org/site/PageServer?pagename=airc_hist_indianremovalact; and https://www.history.com/topics/native-american-history/trail-of-tears.

22 ROPER CENTER FOR PUBLIC OPINION. 2016. How Groups Voted in 2016. Cornell University.

23 See https://electioneve2020.com/poll/#/en/demographics/latino.

24 KROGSTAD, J. M. 2020. Most Cuban American Voters Identify as Republican in 2020. Pew Research Center. At https://www.pewresearch.org/fact-tank/2020/10/02/most-cuban-american-voters-identify-as-republican-in-2020.

25 See https://electioneve2020.com/poll/#/en/demographics/latino.

26 REICH, R. B. 2020. *The System: Who Rigged it, How We Fix It*, New York, Alfred Knopf.

27 In 2016, Bernie Sanders' popularity was the result of his attacks on trade agreements, Wall Street greed, income inequality, and big money in politics. See, for example, ibid., p. 161.

28 See https://www.civisanalytics.com. See also, BILLINGS, D. 2019. Once Upon a Time in "Trumpalachia": *Hillbilly Elegy*, Personal Choice, and the Blame Game. In: HARKINS, A. & MCCARROLL, M. (eds.) *Appalachian Reckoning: A Region Responds to Hillbilly Elegy*. Morgantown, West Virginia University Press.

29 ELLER, R. D. 2008. *Uneven Ground: Appalachia since 1945*, Lexington, University Press of Kentucky, p. 67.

30 Ibid.

31 Ibid.

32 This isn't an entirely new strategy. American big business has long sacrificed people to profits. And both Republican and Democratic administrations have politicized and suppressed scientific evidence. The evidence that smoking caused cancer was rebutted for sixty years

by industry-sponsored studies, before truth won out over profit. See ORESKES, N. & CONWAY, E. 2010. Defeating the Merchants of Doubt. *Nature*, 465(7299), 686–7. The Centers for Disease Control and Prevention have been prevented from doing research on firearm injuries and deaths since 1996.

33 JOUET, M. 2017. *Exceptional America: What Divides Americans from the World and Each Other*, Oakland, University of California Press, p. ix.

34 See https://www.cnn.com/2019/02/23/opinions/trump-contest-2020-election-loss-geltzer/index.html.

35 EGAN, L. 2020. Trump Calls Coronavirus Democrats' "New Hoax." *NBC News*, Feb 28.

36 Some said Covid-19 was manufactured in China to take down the US economy. Others reinforced Trump's message that Covid is a normal flu being hyped by Democrats to hurt Trump. Still others asserted that Anthony Fauci along with other scientists engineered Covid-19 for billions of dollars in profit.

37 MCCORD, M. 2020. Trump's "LIBERATE MICHIGAN!" Tweets Incite Insurrection. That's Illegal. *The Washington Post*, April 17.

38 SMITH, D. 2020. Trump Calls Protesters Against Stay-at-home Orders "Very Responsible," *The Guardian*, April 17.

39 GRAHAM, B. A. 2020. "Swastikas and Nooses": Governor Slams "Racism" of Michigan Lockdown Protest. *The Guardian*, May 3.

40 SARGENT, G. 2020. Trump's Support for Right-wing Protests Just Got More Ugly and Dangerous. *The Washington Post*, April 20.

41 In 1989 Trump took out four full-page ads in New York City newspapers calling for the execution of five Black teenagers accused of battering and raping a Central Park jogger. The men were eventually exonerated by DNA evidence. Aaron Rupar reported for *Vox* that Trump was asked on June 8, 2019, if he would apologize for the ads. Trump refused to do so and once again told reporters, "You have people on both sides of that." See https://www.vox.com/policy-and-politics/2019/6/18/18684217/trump-central-park-5-netflix.

42 COSTA, R. & RUCKER, P. 2020. Trump's Campaign of Resentment. *The Washington Post*, July 4.

43 MOYERS, B. 1988. What a Real President Was Like. *The Washington Post*, Nov 13.

44 STANLEY-BECKER, I. 2020. Trump Campaign Runs Ads with Marking Once Used by Nazis; Facebook Deactivates Them. *The Washington Post*, June 18; BRENNAN, D. 2020. Trump Appears to Threaten CNN Over Network's July 4th Speech Coverage. *Newsweek*, July 5.

45 Wong, J.C. 2020. Facebook Removes Trump Re-election Ads That Feature a Nazi Symbol. *The Guardian*, June 18.

46 In response to hate-based content and voter suppression tactics on Facebook, a growing list of more than 500 advertisers including Unilever, North Face, REI, Patagonia, Coca-Cola, and Hershey's

stopped advertising on the platform as part of a "Stop Hate for Profit" campaign. As of this writing Facebook knowingly hosts over 100 active white supremacist accounts.

47 GABBIT, A. 2020. How the Domestic Terror Plot to Kidnap Michigan's Governor Unravelled. *The Guardian*, Oct 22.

48 HELDERMAN, R. & VIEBECK, E. 2020. "The Last Wall": How Dozens of Judges Across the Political Spectrum Rejected Trump's Efforts to Overturn the Election. *The Washington Post*, Dec 12.

49 HSU, S., WEINER, R. & JACKMAN, T. 2021. Self-styled Militia Members in Three States Began Planning in November for Recruits, Weapons Ahead of Capitol Breach, U.S. Alleges. *The Washington Post*, Jan 27.

50 RAMACHANDRAN, S., BERZON, A. & BALLHAUS, R. 2021. Jan. 6 Rally Funded by Top Trump Donor, Helped by Alex Jones, Organizers Say. *Wall Street Journal*, Jan 30.

51 ARMUS, T. 2021. A "Stop the Steal" Organizer, Now Banned by Twitter, Said Three GOP Lawmakers Helped Plan his D.C. Rally. *The Washington Post*, Jan 13.

52 RAMACHANDRAN, S., BERZON, A. & BALLHAUS, R. 2021. Jan. 6 Rally Funded by Top Trump Donor, Helped by Alex Jones, Organizers Say. *Wall Street Journal*, Jan 30.

53 See, for example, MILMAN, O. 2021. "I'm Facing a Prison Sentence": US Capitol Rioters Plead with Trump for Pardons. *The Guardian*, Jan 16.

54 SUTTON, M. A. 2021. The Capitol Riot Revealed the Darkest Nightmares of White Evangelical America. *The New Republic*, Jan 14.

55 HELDERMAN, R., HSU, S. & WEINER, R. 2021. "Trump Said To Do So": Accounts of Rioters Who Say the President Spurred Them to Rush the Capitol Could Be Pivotal Testimony. *The Washington Post*, Jan 16.

56 BAKER, P. & HABERMAN, M. 2020. Capitol Attack Leads Democrats to Demand that Trump Leave Office. *The New York Times*, Jan 7.

57 LEVINE, S. & GAMBINO, L. 2020. Nearly Two-thirds of House Republicans Join Baseless Effort to Overturn Election. *The Guardian*, Dec 11.

58 SALCEDO, A. 2021. GOP Rep. Lauren Boebert Gave Capitol Tour to "Large" Group Before the Riots, Democratic Lawmaker Says. *The Washington Post*, Jan 19.

59 STEVENS, H., SANTAMARINA, D., RABINOWITZ, K., UHRMACHER, K. & MUYSKENS, J. How Members of Congress Voted on Counting the Electoral College Vote. *The Washington Post*, Jan 7.

60 POWELL, J. 2020. In: Storming the Capitol: Trumpism's Last Stand? *Othering & Belonging Institute*. At https://belonging.berkeley.edu/video-storming-capitol-trumpisms-last-stand-askobi.

61 JACKMAN, T. 2021. Police Union says 140 Officers Injured in Capitol Riot. *The Washington Post*, Jan 28.

62 See https://www.bbc.com/news/world-us-canada-55626148.

63 POWELL, J. 2020. In: Storming the Capitol: Trumpism's Last Stand? *Othering & Belonging Institute*. See also PROTHERO, M. 2021. Some Among America's Military Allies Believe Trump Deliberately Attempted a Coup and May Have Had Help from Federal Law-Enforcement Officials. *Business Insider*, Jan 7.
64 POWELL, J. 2020. In: Storming the Capitol: Trumpism's Last Stand? *Othering & Belonging Institute*.
65 SONNE, P. 2021. Pentagon Restricted Commander of D.C. Guard Ahead of Capitol Riot. *The Washington Post*, Jan 26.
66 See for example, PASCALE, C.-M. 2019. The Weaponization of Language: Discourses of Rising Right-wing Authoritarianism. *Current Sociology Review*, 67, 898–917.
67 KESSLER, G., RIZZO, S. and KELLY, M. 2021. Trump's False or Misleading Claims Total 30,573 Over 4 Years. *The Washington Post,* Jan 24. At https://www.washingtonpost.com/politics/2021/01/24/trumps-false-or-misleading-claims-total-30573-over-four-years.
68 POWELL, J. 2020. In: Storming the Capitol: Trumpism's Last Stand? Othering & Belonging Institute.
69 PASCALE, C.-M. 2019. The Weaponization of Language: Discourses of Rising Right-wing Authoritarianism. *Current Sociology Review*, 67, 898–917.
70 LEVIN, B. 2020. Donald Trump Insists It's Entirely Possible Democrats Are Running a Satanic Pedophile Cult. *Vanity Fair*, Oct 16.
71 Ibid.
72 Republicans who won their primaries by openly endorsing QAnon include Angela Stanton-King, Marjorie Taylor Greene, Jo Rae Perkins, Alison Hayden, Lauren Boebert, Mike Cargile, Theresa Raborn, Johnny Teague, Rob Weber, Philanise White, Billy Prempeh, and Erin Cruz.
73 In 2016 QAnon circulated a rumor that the Comet Ping Pong pizzeria in Northwest Washington, DC, was the center of a pedophile ring being run by Hillary Clinton. Edgar Welch drove from North Carolina to DC to liberate the children. With an assault rifle, he searched every room of the pizzeria and ultimately surrendered to police.
74 SHEPHERD, K. 2021. A Reporter Tried to Ask Rep. Marjorie Taylor Green About Her False Claims. The Journalist Was Threatened With Arrest. *The Washington Post*, Jan 28.

9 The Myths We Live By

1 BIDEN, J. 2019. Vice-President Joe Biden's 5 Ideas for Helping America's Middle Class. *Brookings Institute*, April 19.
2 DUTTA-GUPTA, I. 2020. Measuring Poverty: Why It Matters, & What Should & Should Not Be Done About It. *Economic Security and Opportunity Initiative*. Center on Poverty and Inequality: Georgetown Law.

3 Nor do we talk about the fact that the US continues to administer sixteen territories including Puerto Rico, American Samoa, Guam, Northern Mariana Islands, US Virgin Islands and eleven smaller territories.
4 SPRUILL, L. 2016. Slave Patrols, "Packs of Negro Dogs" and Policing Black Communities. *Phylon*, 53, 42–66.
5 GRAMLICH, J. 2019. The Gap Between the Number of Blacks and Whites in Prison is Shrinking. Pew Research Center. At https://www.pewresearch.org/fact-tank/2019/04/30/shrinking-gap-between-number-of-blacks-and-whites-in-prison.
6 See https://www.prisonstudies.org/news/more-1035-million-people-are-prison-around-world-new-report-shows.
7 CORPORATE ACCOUNTABILITY LAB. 2020. Private Companies Producing with U.S. Prison Labor in 2020: Prison Labor Part II. At https://corpaccountabilitylab.org/calblog/2020/8/5/private-companies-producing-with-us-prison-labor-in-2020-prison-labor-in-the-us-part-ii.
8 GARCIA, C. & RAFIEYAN, D. 2020. The Uncounted Workforce. *NPR*, June 29.
9 See https://www.bop.gov/inmates/custody_and_care/unicor_about.jsp.
10 MCDOWAL, R. & MASON, M. 2020. Cheap Labor Means Prisons Still Turn a Profit, Even During a Pandemic. *PBS*, May 8.
11 When they are injured or killed fighting fires, official records list them as firefighters, not inmates. For more detailed accounts see https://www.themarshallproject.org/records/764-prison-labor.
12 PASCALE, C.-M. 2001. All in a Day's Work: A Feminist Analysis of Class Formation and Social Identity. *Race, Gender, and Class*, 8, 34–59.
13 Ibid.
14 See, for example, FONER, E. 1988. *Reconstruction: America's Unfinished Revolution: 1863–1877*, New York, Harper & Row; ZINN, H. 1980. *A People's History of the United States*, New York, Harper & Row; WILKERSON, J. 2019. *To Live Here, You Have to Fight: How Women Led Appalachian Movements for Social Justice*, Urbana, University of Illinois Press; WILKINS, D. & LOMAWAIMA, K. T. 2001. *Uneven Ground: American Indian Sovereignty and Federal Law*, Norman, OK, University of Oklahoma Press; DAVIS, A. Y. 1983. *Women, Race & Class*, New York, Vintage Books.
15 For more see KLEIN, N. 2020. *On Fire: The (Burning) Case for a Green New Deal*, New York, Simon & Schuster.
16 REEVES, R. 2017. *Dream Hoarders*, Washington, DC, Brookings Institution Press.
17 KOEZE, E. 2020. The $600 Unemployment Booster Shot, State by State. *The New York Times*, April 23.
18 HIRSH, M. & JOHNSON, K. 2020. A Tale of Two Rescue Plans. *Foreign Policy*, April 24.
19 BEVINS, V. 2020. How Germany is Saving Jobs During the Pandemic. *New York Magazine*, May 18.

20 The government hoped to replace 100% of workers' income during the pandemic but was unable to quickly provide an unemployment supplement scaled to each person's income, so they did the next best thing by creating a flat payment. See Coronavirus Aid, Relief, and Economic Security Act. 116th Congress of the United States of America.
21 ROMM, T., STEIN, J. & WERNER, E. 2020. 2.4 Million Americans Filed Jobless Claims Last Week, Bringing Nine-week Total to 38.6 Million. *The Washington Post*, May 21.
22 KESSLER, G. 2020. Mitch McConnell Got "Rich" the Old-fashioned Way. *The Washington Post*, June 2.
23 FANG, L. 2020. Small Business Rescue Money Flowing to Major Trump Donors. *The Intercept*, April 24.
24 Ibid.
25 O'CONNELL, J. & GREGG, A. 2020. SBA Exempted Lawmakers, Federal Officials from Ethics Rules in $660 Billion Loan Program. *The Washington Post*, June 26.
26 O'CONNELL, J., GREGG, A., RICH, S., NARAYANSWAMY, A. & WHORISKEY, P. 2020. Treasury, SBA Data Show Small-business Loans Went to Private-equity Backed Chains, Members of Congress. *The Washington Post*, July 6.
27 HOLPUCH, A. 2020. Millionaires to Reap 80% of Benefit from Tax Change in US Coronavirus Stimulus. *The Guardian*, April 15.
28 ZIV, S. 2020. How Some Rich Americans Are Getting Stimulus "Checks" Averaging $1.7 Million. *Forbes*, April 14.
29 WAMHOFF, S. 2020. The CARES Act Provision for High-Income Business Owners Looks Worse and Worse. Institute on Taxation and Economic Policy.
30 HOLPUCH, A. 2020. Millionaires to Reap 80% of Benefit from Tax Change in US Coronavirus Stimulus. *The Guardian*, April 15.
31 KRANHOLD, K. 2019. You Paid Taxes. These Corporations Didn't. Center for Public Integrity.
32 INSTITUTE ON TAXATION AND ECONOMIC POLICY. 2019. Corporate Tax Avoidance in the First Year of the Trump Tax Law. At https://itep.org/corporate-tax-avoidance-in-the-first-year-of-the-trump-tax-law.
33 Ibid.
34 WAMHOFF, S. & WIEHE, M. 2020. Why the GOP Senate Bill Fails to Address the Crisis, and Why a Democratic Bill Looks More Promising. Institute on Taxation and Economic Policy.
35 TAX POLICY CENTER. Briefing Book. Urban Institute & Brookings Institution. At https://www.taxpolicycenter.org/briefing-book.
36 EDIN, K. J. & SHAEFER, H. L. 2015. *$2.00 a Day: Living on Almost Nothing in America*, Boston, Mariner Books.
37 Ibid.
38 GOVERNMENT ACCOUNTING OFFICE. 2018. Supplemental Nutrition Assistance Program: Disseminating Information on Successful Use of Data Analytics Could Help States Manage Fraud Risks. Report to Congressional Requestors. Government Accounting Office.

39 EDIN, K. J. & SHAEFER, H. L. 2015. *$2.00 a Day: Living on Almost Nothing in America*, Boston, Mariner Books.
40 Ibid.
41 REICH, R. B. 2020. *The System: Who Rigged it, How We Fix It*, New York, Alfred Knopf, p. 69.
42 Ibid., pp. 91–2.
43 KRUGMAN, P. 2020. *Arguing with Zombies: Economics, Politics, and the Fight for a Better Future*, New York, W. W. Norton & Company.
44 REICH, R. B. 2020. *The System: Who Rigged it, How We Fix It*, New York, Alfred Knopf, p. 42.
45 KRUGMAN, P. 2020. *Arguing with Zombies: Economics, Politics, and the Fight for a Better Future*, New York, W. W. Norton & Company, p. 290.
46 To learn more about Edward Bernays and the founding of public relations in the US, see the British documentary, *The Century of the Self*, available online at https://www.youtube.com/watch?v=eJ3RzGoQC4s.
47 MILLER, M. C. 2004. *Propaganda: Edward Bernays*, New York, IG Publishing. It's worth noting that Joseph Goebbels admired Bernays' understanding of mass psychology and when he became minister of propaganda for the Third Reich, he used Bernays' work to promote the Reich and the cult of the Führer.
48 See *The Century of the Self*, available online at https://www.youtube.com/watch?v=eJ3RzGoQC4s.
49 VLASIK, B. & BOUDETTE, N. 2017. Shell of Old G.M. Surfaces in Court Fight Over Ignition Flaw. *The New York Times*, Aug 17.
50 REICH, R. B. 2020. *The System: Who Rigged it, How We Fix It*, New York, Alfred Knopf, p. 48.
51 See KESSLER, G. 2019. Does the Walton Family Earn More in a Minute Than Walmart Workers Do in a Year? *The Washington Post*, Feb 19.
52 HAWKINGS, D. 2018. Wealth of Congress: Richer Than Ever, But Mostly at the Very Top. *Roll Call*, Feb 27.
53 EVERS-HILLSTROM, K. 2020. Majority of Lawmakers in 116th Congress Are Millionaires. Center for Responsive Politics.
54 For example, Rep. Collin Peterson (D-Minn.) was worth an estimated $123,500 in 2008; by 2020 as chairman of the House Agricultural Committee he had assets of about $4.2 million, according to his recent disclosure.
55 BERMAN, R. 2018. An Exodus from Congress Tests the Lure of Lobbying. *The Atlantic*, May 1.
56 REICH, R. B. 2020. *The System: Who Rigged it, How We Fix It*, New York, Alfred Knopf, p. 61.
57 Ibid., p. 57.
58 Ibid., p. 17.
59 Ibid., p. 28.
60 Ibid., p. 7.
61 Ibid. By contrast, in 1980, the top 1% accounted for only 15% of all contributions.

62 Ibid., p. 16.
63 BRIFFAULT, R. 2020. Election 2020 Sees Record $11 Billion in Campaign Spending, Mostly from a Handful of Super-rich Donors. *The Conversation*, Oct 13.
64 HALL, S. 2015. Exxon Knew About Climate Change Almost 40 Years Ago. *Scientific American*, Oct 26.
65 See *Merchants of Doubt* by Noami Oreskes and Erik Conway for an excellent analysis of how corporations manufacture studies to support their own interests, despite the facts.
66 KLEIN, N. 2020. *On Fire: The (Burning) Case for a Green New Deal*, New York, Simon & Schuster, p. 249.
67 REICH, R. B. 2020. *The System: Who Rigged it, How We Fix It*, New York, Alfred Knopf, p. 56.
68 Ibid., p. 54.
69 SOCIAL SECURITY ADMINISTRATION. 2017. Wage Statistics. At https://www.ssa.gov/cgi-bin/netcomp.cgi?year=2017.

10 And Then, the Pandemic…

1 POMPEO, M., SECRETARY OF STATE. 2020. The United States Announces Assistance to the COVID-19. US Department of State.
2 ASIAMAH, N. 2020. 3 Million Masks Ordered by Massachusetts Were Seized at Port of NY in March. *22NEWS*, April 3. See also ROSE, J. 2020. A "War" For Medical Supplies: States Say FEMA Wins By Poaching Orders. *NPR*, April 15.
3 SIU, B. 2020. Maryland Hiding Testing Kits, Purchased from South Korea, from US Government: Hogan. *ABC News*, April 30. See also NIRAPPLI, F., COX, E. & SCHNEIDER, G. 2020. With Focus on Testing, Maryland Buys 500,000 Coronavirus Test Kits from South Korea. *The Washington Post*, April 20.
4 ROSE, J. 2020. A "War" For Medical Supplies: States Say FEMA Wins By Poaching Orders. *NPR*, April 15.
5 ENVIRONMENTAL & ENERGY LAW PROGRAM. 2020. Regulatory Rollback Tracker. Harvard School of Law.
6 DENNIS, B. & EILPERIN, J. 2020. EPA Overhauls Mercury Pollution Rule, Despite Opposition from Industry and Activists Alike. *The Washington Post*, April 16.
7 INTERNATIONAL RENEWABLE ENERGY AGENCY. 2020. Renewables Increasingly Beat Even Cheapest Coal Competitors on Cost. IRENA, June 2. See also ELLSMOOR, J. 2019. Renewable Energy is Now the Cheapest Option – Even Without Subsidies. *Forbes*, June 15.
8 EILPERIN, J. & MUFSON, S. 2021. Trump Auctions Drilling Rights to Arctic National Wildlife Refuge. *The Washington Post*, Jan 6.
9 Ibid.
10 COLLINS, C., OCAMPO, O. & PASLASKI, S. 2020. Billionaire Bonanza 2020. Institute for Policy Studies.

11 Ibid.
12 HAJEK, D. 2020. Farmworkers, Deemed Essential, Don't Feel Protected From Pandemic. *NPR*, March 31.
13 MARTIN, R. & COSTA, D. 2017. Farmworker Wages in California. Economic Policy Institute.
14 HAJEK, D. 2020. Farmworkers, Deemed Essential, Don't Feel Protected From Pandemic. *NPR*, March 31.
15 SUBRAMANIAN, C. & FRITZE, J. 2020. Trump's $19 Billion Relief Package For Farms Hurt By Coronavirus Includes Payments For Farmers. *USA Today*, April 17.
16 Nationally, 91% of farms are classified as small farms – they sell less than $250,000 per year.
17 FREMSTAD, S., RHO, H. J. & BROWN, H. 2020. Meatpacking Workers Are a Diverse Group Who Need Better Protections. Center for Economic and Policy Research, April 29.
18 See https://www.bls.gov/oes/2018/may/oes513023.htm#nat. The top 10% of slaughterers and meatpackers made $18 per hour and the bottom 10% earned $10 per hour.
19 WALDMAN, P. & MEHROTRA, K. 2017. America's Worst Graveyard Shift is Grinding Up Workers. *Bloomberg Business Week*, Dec 29.
20 KINDY, K. 2019. This Foreign Meat Company Got U.S. Tax Money. Now it Wants to Conquer America. *The Washington Post*, Nov 7.
21 KLEMKO, R. & KINDY, K. 2020. He Fled Congo to Work in a U.S. Meat Plant. Then He – and Hundreds of his Co-workers – Got the Coronavirus. *The Washington Post*, Aug 6.
22 FLYNN, M. 2020. Wisconsin Chief Justice Sparks Backlash by Saying Covid-19 Outbreak is Among Meatpacking Workers, Not "the Regular Folks." *The Washington Post*, May 7.
23 See https://www.cdc.gov/mmwr/volumes/69/wr/mm6918e3.htm?s_cid=mm6918e3_e&deliveryName=USCDC_921-DM27224.
24 FREMSTAD, S., RHO, H. J. & BROWN, H. 2020. Meatpacking Workers Are a Diverse Group Who Need Better Protections. Center for Economic and Policy Research, April 29.
25 GRABELL, M. & YEUNG, B. 2020. Emails Show the Meatpacking Industry Drafted an Executive Order to Keep Plants Open. *ProPublica*, Sept 14.
26 Ibid.
27 CANCRYN, A. & BARRON-LOPEZ, L. 2020. Azar Faulted Workers' "home and social" Conditions For Meatpacking Outbreaks. *Politico*, May 7.
28 See https://www.epi.org/blog/meat-and-poultry-worker-demographics.
29 KINDY, K. 2020. More Than 200 Meat Plant Workers in the U.S. Have Died of Covid-19. Federal Regulators Just Issued Two Modest Fines. *The Washington Post*, Sept 13.
30 CORKERY, M. & YAFFE-BELLANY, D. 2020. As Meat Plants Stayed Open to Feed Americans, Exports to China Surged. *The New York Times*, June 16.

31 SIEGEL, R. 2020. For the Unemployed, Rising Grocery Prices Strain Budgets Even More. *The Washington Post*, Aug 4.
32 See https://gotr.azgovernor.gov/sites/default/files/navajo_nation_0.pdf.
33 MOZES, A. 2020. COVID-19 Ravages the Navajo Nation. *WebMD*, June 9.
34 SILVERMAN, H., TOROPIN, K., SIDNER, S. & PERROT, L. 2020. Navajo Nation Surpasses New York State For the Highest Covid-19 Infection Rate in the US. *CNN*, May 18.
35 NAVAJO NATION OFFICE OF THE PRESIDENT AND VICE PRESIDENT. 2020. U.S. Department of the Treasury Announces the Release of a Portion of CARES Act Funding for Tribes Weeks After the Approval of Congress. Window Rock, Az: Navajo Nation.
36 LAKHANI, N. 2020. South Dakota Governor Threatens to Sue Over Sioux's Coronavirus Roadblocks. *The Guardian*, May 14.
37 Ibid.
38 *Cheyenne River Sioux* v. *Trump, et al.*, Case No.: 1:2020-cv-01709. United States District Court for the District of Columbia, p. 18. At https://www.indianz.com/covid19/wp-content/uploads/2020/06/crstvtrump.pdf.
39 Ibid.
40 SHAMMAS, B. & SUN, L. H. 2020. How the Sturgis Motorcycle Rally May Have Spread Coronavirus Across the Upper Midwest. *The Washington Post*, Oct 17.
41 DHAVAL, D., FRIEDSON, A., MCNICHOLS, D. & SABIA, J. 2020. The Contagion Externality of a Superspreading Event: The Sturgis Motorcycle Rally and Covid-19. At https://www.iza.org/en/publications/dp/13670/the-contagion-externality-of-a-superspreading-event-the-sturgis-motorcycle-rally-and-covid-19.
42 Although she has access to Indian Health Services established by the federal government, its reputation is terrible. As a consequence, Standing Rock provides Blue Cross/Blue Shield to its employees.
43 O'CONNELL, J., GREGG, A., RICH, S., NARAYANSWAMY, A. & WHORISKEY, P. 2020. Treasury, SBA Data Show Small-business Loans Went to Private-equity Backed Chains, Members of Congress. *The Washington Post*, July 6.
44 Ibid.
45 HOLDEN, E. 2020. Over 5,600 Fossil Fuel Companies Have Taken at Least $3bn in US Covid-19 Aid. *The Guardian*, July 7.
46 By January 2021 workers across the country were claiming that companies were using the pandemic to break unions. See SAINATO, M. 2021. US Companies Using Pandemic as a Tool to Break Unions, Workers Claim. *The Guardian*, Jan 26.
47 WHORISKEY, P. 2020. U.S. Companies Cut Thousands of Workers While Continuing to Reward Shareholders During Pandemic. *The Washington Post*, May 5.
48 Ibid.
49 Normal blood sugar is about 140mg/dL.

50 SONMEZ, F., DREIER, H., SHAMMAS, B. & WILLIS, H. 2020. Killing of Black Man in Atlanta Puts Spotlight Anew on Police, as Prosecutors Contemplate Charges Against Officer. *The Washington Post*, June 14.

51 FEEDING AMERICA. 2018. Understanding Hunger and Food Insecurity. At http://www.feedingamerica.org/hunger-in-america/food-insecurity.html.

52 FEEDING AMERICA. 2020. Feeding America Network Faces Soaring Demand, Plummeting Supply Due to COVID-19 Crisis. At https://www.feedingamerica.org/about-us/press-room/feeding-america-network-stays-resilient-during-covid-19-crisis#:~:text=According%20to%20the%20survey%20conducted,average%20increase%20of%2059%20percent.

53 FEEDING AMERICA. 2020. The Impact of Coronavirus on Food Insecurity. At https://www.feedingamerica.org/sites/default/files/2020-10/Brief_Local%20Impact_10.2020_0.pdf.

54 See https://www.bls.gov/opub/ted/2020/unemployment-rate-rises-to-record-high-14-point-7-percent-in-april-2020.htm?view_full.

55 RUGABER, C. 2020. 33 Million Have Sought US Unemployment Aid Since Virus Hit. *Associated Press*, May 7. See also https://www.bls.gov/news.release/archives/empsit_05082020.htm.

56 See https://www.bls.gov/news.release/archives/empsit_05082020.htm. Note that by December 2020, the number of people who were jobless for less than five weeks had increased to 2.9 million, while the number of people who had been unemployed between fifteen and twenty-six weeks declined to 1.6 million. The number of long-term unemployed (people unemployed for more than twenty-seven weeks) remained at 4 million.

57 By December 2020, 25.7 million workers were officially unemployed. SHIERHOLZ, H. 2020. One Million People Applied For Unemployment Insurance Last Week. At https://www.epi.org/blog/one-million-people-applied-for-unemployment-insurance-last-week-unless-congress-acts-millions-of-people-will-soon-be-left-without-a-safety-net.

58 A second stimulus check for $600/person arrived in December 2020.

59 FEEDING AMERICA. 2019. Food Insecurity in Athens County Before Covid-19. At https://map.feedingamerica.org/county/2019/overall/ohio/county/athens.

60 LIPTAK, K., BENNETT, K., LUHBY, T., COLLINS, K., HOFFMAN, J., MATTINGLY, P. & DIAMOND, J. 2020. Trump Signs Coronavirus Relief and Government Funding Bill Into Law After Lengthy Delay. *CNN Politics*, Dec 28.

61 TORBATI, Y. 2020. Tucked Into Congress's Massive Stimulus Bill: Tens of Billions in Special-interest Tax Giveaways. *The Washington Post*, Dec 22.

62 Ibid.

11 The Future We Want

1 REICH, R. B. 2020. *The System: Who Rigged it, How We Fix It*, New York, Alfred Knopf, p. 15. When people talk about wealth, they are talking about what people own: homes, investments, savings, and so forth.

2 KLEIN, N. 2020. *On Fire: The (Burning) Case for a Green New Deal*, New York, Simon & Schuster.

3 PICKETTY, T. 2020. *Capital and Ideology*, Cambridge, MA, Harvard University Press.

4 In 1857 Frederick Douglass delivered a West India Emancipation speech in which he astutely argued: "Power conceded nothing without a demand. It never did and it never will."

5 For more information see https://www.pbs.org/wgbh/americanexperience/features/carnegie-strike-homestead-mill.

6 For more information see https://www.zinnedproject.org/news/tdih/ludlow-massacre.

7 CORBIN, D. 1981. *Life, Work and Rebellion in the Coal Fields: The Southern West Virginia Miners, 1880–1922*, Urbana, University of Illinois Press.

8 During the 1931 Black Mountain Coal strike an infamously corrupt sheriff in Harlan County terrorized workers. When the sheriff and deputized coal company operatives ransacked Florence Reece's home, looking for her husband, the strike organizer, Florence wrote one of labor's most famous anthems: "Which Side Are You On?"

9 SHAPIRO, H. 1978. *Appalachia on Our Mind*, Chapel Hill, NC, University of North Carolina Press.

10 Ibid.

11 INGRAHAM, C. 2017. Republican Lawmakers Introduce Bills to Curb Protesting in at Least 18 States. *The Washington Post*, Feb 24.

12 MATTHEWS, S. & CYRIL, M. 2017. We Say Black Lives Matter. The FBI Says That Makes Us a Security Threat. *The Washington Post*, Oct 19. See also https://www.foxnews.com/us/giuliani-trump-black-lives-matter-domestic-terrorism and https://foreignpolicy.com/2017/10/06/the-fbi-has-identified-a-new-domestic-terrorist-threat-and-its-black-identity-extremists.

13 HAMPTON, K., HEISLER, M. & MCKAY, D. 2020. "Now They Seem to Just Want to Hurt Us": Dangerous Use of Crowd-control Weapons against Protestors and Medics in Portland, Oregon. *Physicians for Human Rights*, Oct 8.

14 BIDDLE, S. 2020. Police Surveilled George Floyd Protests with Help from Twitter-Affiliated Startup Dataminr. *The Intercept*, July 9.

15 WILKERSON, J. 2019. *To Live Here, You Have to Fight: How Women Led Appalachian Movements for Social Justice*, Urbana, University of Illinois Press, Loc 1465.

16 CATTE, E. 2018. *What You Are Getting Wrong About Appalachia*, Cleveland, OH, Belt Publishing.

17 KLEIN, N. & LEWIS, A. 2020. From Pandemic to Prosperity. At https://theleap.org/peoples-bailout.
18 KLEIN, N. 2020. *On Fire: The (Burning) Case for a Green New Deal*, New York, Simon & Schuster.
19 See https://www.census.gov/data/datasets/time-series/demo/popest/2010s-state-total.html.
20 See https://demographics.coopercenter.org/national-population-projections.
21 RAY, S. 2020. California Election Officials Order GOP to Remove Unofficial Ballot Boxes Set Up in Parts of the State. *Forbes*, Oct 12.
22 LEVINE, S. 2020. More Than 10-Hour Wait and Long Lines as Early Voting Starts in Georgia. *The Guardian*, Oct 12.
23 BARNES, R. 2020. Supreme Court Rejects Request to Extend Wisconsin's Deadline for Counting Mail-in Ballots. *The Washington Post*, Oct 26.
24 JONES, A. & SPARBER, S. 2020. How Texas Has Made It Easier and Harder For People to Vote in the Pandemic. *The Texas Tribune*, Oct 8.
25 KRUZEL, J. 2020. Supreme Court Declines to Fast-track Texas Democrats' Bid to Expand Mail-in Voting Before July Primary. *The Hill*, July 2.
26 BOGAGE, J. 2020. Postal Service Overhauls Leadership as Democrats Press for Investigation of Mail Delays. *The Washington Post*, Aug 7.
27 Ibid.
28 See https://econofact.org/voting-and-income.
29 REICH, R. B. 2020. *The System: Who Rigged it, How We Fix It*, New York, Alfred Knopf, p. 28.
30 Ibid.
31 STIGLITZ, J. 2013. *The Price of Inequality*, New York, W. W. Norton & Company; STIGLITZ, J. 2019. *People, Power, and Profits*, New York, W. W. Norton & Company, p. 168.
32 KLEIN, N. 2020. *On Fire: The (Burning) Case for a Green New Deal*, New York, Simon & Schuster.
33 HERITAGE FOUNDATION. 2020. Saving Lives and Livelihoods: Recommendations for Recovery. At https://thf_media.s3.amazonaws.com/2020/NCRC_FINAL.pdf.
34 MISHEL, L. & WOLFE, J. 2019. CEO Compensation Has Grown 940% Since 1978. Economic Policy Institute. At https://www.epi.org/publication/ceo-compensation-2018. Note: From 1978 to 2018 CEO compensation grew by 1007.5% (940.3% under the options-realized measure).
35 METCALF, G. 2018. Sand Castles Before the Tide? Affordable Housing in Expensive Cities. *American Economic Association*, 32, 59–80.
36 Ibid.
37 See https://www.dol.gov/agencies/wb/data/mothers-and-families.
38 CARMAN, T. 2021. José Andrés Talks About Feeding the National Guard, Tipping and Whether He'd Work in the Biden Administration. *The Washington Post*, Jan 23.

39 JEWETT, C. & LUTHRA. 2018. Defendants In Diapers? Immigrant Toddlers Ordered To Appear In Court Alone. *The Washington Post*, June 27. See also EGKOLFOPOULOU, M. 2018. The Thousands of Children Who Go to Immigration Court Alone. *The Atlantic*, Aug 21.
40 PEW CHARITABLE RESEARCH CENTER. 2017. How Wealth Inequality Has Changed in the US Since the Great Recession, by Race, Ethnicity and Income. At https://www.pewresearch.org/fact-tank/2017/11/01/how-wealth-inequality-has-changed-in-the-u-s-since-the-great-recession-by-race-ethnicity-and-income.
41 At the end of slavery, Black Codes were enacted throughout the South to limit the freedom and rights of people descended from slaves. For example, in Mississippi, if African Americans left a work contract before it was over, they would be forced to forfeit earlier wages and were subject to arrest. The Black Codes enabled the local governments to arrest Black people on petty charges and hearsay and sentence them to prison and a lifetime of hard labor. The Black Codes essentially provided free labor for building the infrastructure of the South. Without rights as citizens or as property, Black men and women were now literally worked to death.
42 KLEIN, N. 2020. *On Fire: The (Burning) Case for a Green New Deal*, New York, Simon & Schuster, pp. 199–200.
43 See http://www.honorearth.org/global_women_s_climate_justice_day_of_action.

Appendix A: Methods, Methodology, and Theory

1 I was unable to pay everyone $40 and unwilling to ask for people's time without offering something in return. I decided who received which gift card based on my own circumstances as well as those of my interviewee. I also provided gift cards for all follow-up interviews.
2 SMITH, D. Institutional Ethnography: A Feminist Method. *Resources for Feminist Research/Documentation sur la Recherche Féministe*, 15, 6–13.
3 SMITH, D. 1990. *Texts, Facts, and Femininity: Exploring the Relations of Ruling*, New York, Routledge.
4 SLADE, B. 2012. Institutional Ethnography. In: MILLS, A., DUREPOS, G. & WIEBE, E. (eds.) *Encyclopedia of Case Study Research*, Los Angeles, Sage.
5 SMITH, D. Institutional Ethnography: A Feminist Method. *Resources for Feminist Research/Documentation sur la Recherche Féministe*, 15, 6–13 (p. 8).
6 DEVAULT, M. 2006. Introduction: What is Institutional Ethnography? *Social Problems*, 53, 294–8.
7 STANDING, G. 2011. *The Precariat: The New Dangerous Class*, London, Bloomsbury Academic.

8 CHOONARA, E. 2011. Is There a Precariat? *Socialist Review*, Oct.
9 MUNCK, R. 2013. The Precariat: A View from the South. *Third World Quarterly*, 34, 757–62.
10 CHOONARA, E. 2011. Is There a Precariat? *Socialist Review*, Oct.
11 BOURDIEU, P. 1977. *Outline of a Theory of Practice*, Cambridge, Cambridge University Press.

Index